D1105238

Farm Bureau In Illinois

FARM BUREAU IN ILLINOIS

History of Illinois Farm Bureau

By John J. Lacey

Illinois Agricultural Association
Bloomington, Illinois

Copyright 1965 By Illinois Agricultural Association
Library of Congress Catalog Card Number: 64-66194

Foreword

Farm Bureau in Illinois. Progress has been made which would extend the creative imagination of those minds who first dreamed of a general farm organization called Farm Bureau.

The story is told in the lives of the men and women who have been dedicated to the Farm Bureau principles and who have given much to achieve these principles; in the programs and activities of Farm Bureau and in the advancements made through the affiliated companies with the successes or the failures of the many ventures undertaken in these fifty years.

This book was written by one of the few men who could do it expertly. John J. Lacey has worked with farmers all his life—much of it as a Farm Bureau staff member. He has lived through the years in which Farm Bureau was born and grew, known its great leaders, and was with such men as Earl Smith and Ed O'Neal during many of the early battles. This book is the capstone of Mr. Lacey's career of service and challenges the memory and makes use of much. He has written in a very interesting narrative manner the unprecedented story of Farm Bureau in Illinois from its birth through the move of the Illinois Agricultural Association offices to Bloomington, Illinois.

Many wise talents of people with long experience in Farm Bureau were used in counseling before this book finally had the stamp of approval by Mr. Lacey. O. D. Brissenden was chairman of the staff committee and his wide understanding and knowledge of Farm Bureau were unselfishly blended with his great constructive ability in working with Mr. Lacey in the arduous task of checking the thousands of details in this book.

The answer to the question, "Why has Farm Bureau been so phenomenally successful in Illinois?" is portrayed in this book. I would recommend it to you for a very interesting and rewarding story.

Wm J. Kuhfuss
President
Illinois Agricultural Association

Contents

Preface

I consider it a very great honor to have been invited to write this book. The task, one of the most rewarding ever assigned to me during twenty-six years with Farm Bureau, has been greatly simplified by the generous counsel and cooperation of many IAA staff people, county Farm Bureau officials, University people, farm paper editors, and many others.

I am deeply indebted to: Dave O. Thompson, IAA secretary from 1919 to 1922; Guy Carlyle "Lyle" Johnstone, vice president of the IAA in the beginning; Herman Steen of Wheaton, who wrote many Farm Bureau stories for *Prairie Farmer* in the early IAA days; Ed B. Heaton, first farm adviser in Du Page county; Paul Johnson and James C. Thomson of *Prairie Farmer*; Dean Louis B. Howard of the College of Agriculture of the University of Illinois; John C. Spitler, H. C. M. Case, and Martin L. Mosher, retired staff members at the College; the late Frank W. Bill, long-time farm editor of the *Daily Pantagraph* of Bloomington; and W. Floyd Keepers, one-time managing editor of *Prairie Farmer* and the following IAA staff members: Oscar D. Brissenden, Wilfred Shaw, Paul E. Mathias, Charles S. Mayfield, Walter B. Peterson, and William W. Allen.

The manuscript has been read with meticulous care by at least seven people. My associates join me in the hope that no errors of fact have escaped this scrutiny, and that the material herein set down will serve as a perpetual reminder (to this generation and to all who are to come) of the origin of Farm Bureau and the sound principles upon which it was founded. We should be forever conscious of and grateful for the combination of circumstances which caused Farm Bureau to be jointly sponsored by farmers *and* the University of Illinois. Farm Bureau simply could not have grown and developed as it did without the strong right arm of the Extension Service; and conversely, Extension could not have attained its rugged stature in Illinois without the solid backing of organized farmers. Farmers looked to the University for factual information, not only for use in their own business, but also to use in formulating policies for the Farm Bureau and its business affiliates. The fruitful results of half a century of teamwork by these great institutions are apparent everywhere in Illinois.

November 14, 1963

John J. Lacey

Farm Bureau In Illinois

Chapter 1

Golden Years

The times were the best farmers had ever known. The period, 1909 to 1914, later came to be known as the "parity period," or as some would have it, the Golden Age of agriculture in America.

We now say that farm prices and farm costs were in balance. In buying power, the farmer's dollar was equal to anybody else's dollar. Farmers were prosperous. They could trade on even terms.

If you drive almost anywhere in the Midwest today, you will notice many old homes, most of them big and many of them rather pretentious, which date back to that time. Farm families, through long years of toil and sweat, had finally paid off or substantially reduced their mortgages, and they were beginning to live better. Bathrooms and electric light plants were put in many of the new homes. Farm boys and to a lesser extent farm girls, were going to college in increasing numbers.

The age was also an age in which hundreds of thousands of farm couples, having reared their families and attained "comfortable" circumstances, moved to town, leaving the farm in the hands of one of the sons who had helped his parents through the hard years, and who was now rewarded with modest help in starting farming for himself.

All of this is not to say that farmers were in the affluent class. They were considered modestly well-to-do. Nearly everyone would admit that they had earned all they had. As a matter of fact, the bulk of the wealth they possessed had come from rising land values. They had been fortunate investors. Any "profits" from their farm operations were small indeed when measured in terms of accounting. In fact, it would not be far from the truth to say that the bulk of farm income in those days was the result of the unpaid labor of the farm family. All pitched in to help get the work done, generally with no wages except clothing and "spending money." Several boys in a family might remain at home until they were well into manhood, knowing, or at least hoping that when the mortgage was paid off, their parents would set them up in farming. This happened in countless cases.

When Pa and Ma moved to town to make way for the next generation on the farm, the outcome for the older folks was not always what they had hoped for. They had known grinding toil all their lives. Now they looked forward to years of ease in their retirement. When they built a home in town, there was always a big front porch. They planned to do a lot of resting there. What followed in most cases was bitter disillusion. Pa, particularly, soon found that resting from hard labor was not as rewarding as he had hoped. In a short time he got restless. He missed the companionship of his livestock. He didn't know what to do with his time. If he kept a horse in town, he could drive out to the farm occasionally, but there were long periods when bad weather and poor roads were barriers; and anyway it was daily activity that he needed to make life interesting.

The lot of the average retired farm couple was not always a happy one. Some made the transition successfully, but many did not. The situation was aired in the farm press. In their editorials, farm paper editors urged farmers of retirement age to consider "retiring on the farm," even if it meant building a cottage beside the old home. That probably was good advice, but few followed it.

On the farm, everything seemed to go better than ever. Farmers had the money to buy new machinery, electric light plants, water systems, and other improvements. And farmers generally were avidly seeking better methods of farming. They were buying 8-foot-cut binders and 4-section drags, manure spreaders, and cars. The tractor was coming in. Through the farm papers and the Farmers' Institute, a new gospel of soil building, proclaimed by Dr. Cyril G. Hopkins of the University of Illinois, was attracting a lot of attention. His gospel of "lime, legumes, and phosphate" was coming to be well-known, and it wasn't long until it received wide acceptance.

If Dr. Hopkins was the prophet of the new age in agriculture, Frank I. Mann of Gilman was certainly its St. Paul. Mann had adopted the Hopkins program of soil building and maintenance in its entirety, and over the years it had proved a spectacular success. Yields of 50 bushels of wheat and 80 bushels of corn were common on the Mann farm. That was astonishing, particularly because Mann was a grain farmer. He kept no livestock beyond minimum needs, hence manure had no place in his plans for soil building.

The best-known man in the University of Illinois College of Agriculture was probably Dean Davenport, a hard-headed scholar (a geneticist by training), who had farmed in Michigan for eleven years before being called to Illinois as dean. It was characteristic of him that he always signed his name, "E. Davenport." When he undertook his duties at Illinois, he was appalled by the number of times his heavy correspondence and official documents required his signature. To conserve his time, he used the initial rather than his name, which was Eugene.

Dean Davenport gave Dr. Hopkins every encouragement. The oldest experimental plots in the country were the Morrow Plots at the University, and the lessons they taught were there for all to see. Where corn was grown on the same plot year after year, the yield steadily declined. Where corn and oats were alternated on a plot, yields were noticeably better. And where corn, oats and clover made a rotation, yields rose amazingly. And

Dean Eugene Davenport

when lime and phosphorus were added to the soil, the yields were little short of stunning.

And so it was that the "Illinois System of Soil Fertility" began to attract nation-wide attention. Dr. Hopkins was in great demand as a speaker at farm gatherings, particularly at the Farmers' Institutes, which were short courses in better farming, usually held at the county seat for several days during the winter. Here farmers gathered to learn of the latest developments in better farming. Better seed selection, better feeding practices, better care of the soil, better sanitation in handling livestock—all were featured subjects of Institute lecturers.

It was a time of ferment in farm circles in Illinois. Farmers were enjoying what was for them a new experience—a period when crop yields were good and prices stable. They were getting some return for their labor, and they were not plagued with money "panics" or difficulties in obtaining loans. Farm mortgages became a favorite form of investment for many townspeople.

Life was good on the farm. It is true that most farm homes still lacked running water and electricity, that roads were often poor, that the children had to walk long distances to school, and that many farms were isolated. But improvements were on the way. Rural Free Delivery and the telephone, as well as better roads in many areas, were helping out tremendously. Poor roads had cost farmers plenty. Often when prices were high they couldn't get their hogs or grain to market. Their demands for better roads were insistent.

But country living had its compensations. The real farmer wouldn't care to trade places with most people he knew in town. To begin with, he was his own boss. He was the proprietor of a business. Sometimes he thought it was a mighty poor business, what with prices fluctuating in wide swings over the marketing season, and the buyer, not the seller, setting the price. But he was a proprietor, and he gloried in his independence.

Farm families lacked conveniences in the home, but they had real advantages over townspeople in many respects. What other group could or did eat as well as farmers did in those days? Fresh meat was not available at all times, but think of the foods that were available in abundance! Hams and bacon and chicken at all times, and often beef in winter. It was common practice to buy "a quarter of beef," generally from some fellow farmer for use in winter. And in some areas, town butchers brought fresh meat to farms once a week during the summer months.

For anyone who grew up on a farm in those days to recall the meals served is still a mouth-watering experience. The food was fresh from henhouse, milk house, smokehouse, or garden, and if Mother was a good cook, its flavor was something that city people often simply didn't know about. One who has missed a farm dinner consisting of new potatoes, fried chicken, new peas, sliced tomatoes and sweet corn fresh from the field, and dripping with butter, along with wilted lettuce, pickles, jams and jellies, home-made bread, and luscious cherry pie, has not experienced the true joys of eating. Practically nobody in a big city can know the taste of sweet corn as we knew it on the farm in those days. To enjoy the best flavor, you must have it cooked and on the table within two hours of picking. The same thing is true to some extent in the case of garden peas. Farm people, blessed with lusty appetites, knew the delights of good eating as few people in the city could possibly know them.

Breakfasts of fried cornmeal mush with maple sirup, or better still, sorghum molasses and country butter, together with home-cured ham or bacon are something to remember. Or buckwheat cakes and sausage. Or a dinner of pork and beans, or corned beef with vegetables to make up a boiled dinner, topped off with pumpkin pie and coffee! Those were the days! If someone will object that all farm families didn't eat well, I can only say that it was their own fault if they didn't. They could produce at home nearly all the ingredients at trifling cost.

A boyhood on the farm in those days was a rich and rewarding experience. For a boy who liked animals and growing things, the farm was truly a place of perpetual wonder and enchantment. There was hard work but there was endless fun. Hunting and trapping and skating in the winter, and limited fishing, plus base-

8

ball and swimming in the summer, provided the finest recreation. Daily papers and other reading materials were brought to our doors, and the telephone was a great boon, especially to the womenfolk.

We had fun at school. The late Frank Loucks, who became a successful farmer in Will county and a good Farm Bureau worker, was a schoolmate of mine. One day during the noon recess we were playing "pump-pump-pull-away" or some such game. Frank had some arrowheads and some kitchen matches in the back pocket of his overalls. He was knocked down to a sitting position, but quickly got up and resumed playing. Suddenly he started jumping up and down, grabbed his rear end and yelled: "Pin's jabbin' me; pin's jabbin' me." Just then we noticed smoke coming from his back pocket. The emergency didn't require such drastic action, but four boys grabbed him by hands and feet and rushed him to the school pump, where we held him while two strong boys on the pump handle sluiced a veritable Niagara of water over him. When Frank got over his scare, and began to protest that we were carrying this thing too far, somebody said: "But Frank, we had to make sure the fire was out. You wouldn't want to burn up, would you?"

That was an example of the good, *clean* fun we had. Frank never held it against any of us that we had had a little fun in "saving his life." He and I had a good laugh about it one time at an IAA annual meeting. He told me then that when he got home from school that night his mother had given him a good lecture about carrying matches.

We learned things at school too. Few teachers had ever attended teachers' colleges, but they seemed to know the subjects they taught. We probably did about as well as the town kids. George McIntyre, one of the boys who participated in the above escapade, later practiced medicine for many years in Chicago. Frank himself didn't do so badly. Some of the boys moved away, and I lost track of them. But years later I heard that Rodney Speece had done exceptionally well in business.

The fact that country schools had only one room was an advantage in some respects. All recitations could be heard by every-body, and some prepared themselves pretty well for the next grade by listening.

All of my friends seemed to find country life quite rewarding. In our neighborhood, people were too unfamiliar with the ways of the world (or maybe just too plain decent) to have religious prejudices. They were of all persuasions, from agnostics to Catholics, but they were all alike in neighborliness and generosity. "Live and let live" seemed to be our motto.

I don't recall any boy in our community who had what is today known as an inferiority complex. And I don't believe any of them considered themselves "underprivileged." Some were sons of farm owners, others of renters, and still others were sons of hired men. But your standing with other boys depended on what you could do. The fastest runner, the best swimmer, the best ball player, the best hunter or trapper, the one who could load a bundle-wagon best,—and even the best student—attained status with the other boys. Some were poor, but everybody was working to get ahead, and many of the poorer boys went further in life than the others.

Farmers generally were living better than ever. They were getting around more and keeping track of political and economic developments. They had money in their pockets, which gave them more assurance as they faced the world as a group. Farmers were "feeling their oats."

Such, briefly, was life on the farm in Illinois when, in 1912, a vague movement which had been in ferment for some years crystallized into action that was to have far-reaching significance for farm people, for agriculture, and for the entire farm economy. Farmers were ready to move into a new era.

Chapter 2

De Kalb

It was entirely fitting that De Kalb county farmers should be in the vanguard of a new movement. They had always had progressive instincts, apparently. We find that the second annual fair was held in Sycamore on September 29 and 30, 1858, only 26 years after the Black Hawk War, and only 40 years after Illinois had attained statehood! Livestock, fruits, vegetables, needlework, and millinery were shown, along with many other items. "The town literally swarmed with people on Thursday," reported D. M. Kelsey, for the County Committee for the State Agricultural Society, in his report dated November 1. "The State gave $100," continued the report, "citizen subscriptions, $105; tickets, $439.49. Overplus funds from 1857, $12.00." There follows an enthusiastic comment on progress in the county. The population was 7,540 in 1850; 13,636 in 1855; and by 1858 it had reached 21,000. Also, not less than 100 miles of Osage orange hedge had been set out in the last four years, but a large part of it had been killed by winter and other causes. "Farmers are abandoning this method of enclosing their fields," reported Mr. Kelsey.

It was just as well that they slowed up on setting out Osage orange, because in 20 years or so Isaac Leonard Ellwood, at first in association with Joseph F. Glidden, the inventor, was to bring lasting fame to De Kalb by starting in to manufacture barbed wire on a commercial scale. Barbed wire gave the final knockout punch to Osage orange.

It seemed that De Kalb was always getting into the limelight. In 1890, during the Paris Exposition, U.S. dairy interests created a sensation by shipping fresh milk and cream, by rail and steamship, to Paris to be consumed by the 47,000,000 people who visited the Exposition. Three farms supplied the milk and cream, one from New York, one from New Jersey, and—naturally—one from De Kalb. The dairyman was Henry B. Gurler, who owned a big dairy farm a few miles south of De Kalb. U.S. representatives in Paris had a hard time convincing the French that the milk and cream were indeed fresh on arrival 15 to 20 days after leaving the farms in the United States. Surely, the French thought, some preservative must have been added. But none had been added. It was a remarkable demonstration of the value of cleanliness, and of maintaining low temperatures by the use of ice during shipment. World-wide notice was given the achievement, and De Kalb had another jewel in its crown.

And then there was Henry H. Parke of Sycamore, a college professor and research worker with an advanced degree, who came home from a college job to till the ancestral acres. He took a deep interest in the Farmers' Institute, and he helped every movement that came along which seemed to be dedicated to the advancement of agriculture. He was one of the first alfalfa growers in the county, and he preached its virtues everywhere he went. He organized the Sycamore Farmers' Club in 1909, and aided in organizing others.

There were other outstanding men, including bankers and newspapermen, in De Kalb county who were dedicated to agriculture. All were backers of the Farmers' Institute, and all, it seemed, were convinced that the Institute alone wasn't enough. It worked too slowly. The idea gradually developed that the only effective way to speed the spread of new knowledge was to have a farm expert in the county at all times to test soils, suggest rotations and other soil-building practices, fight livestock diseases and pests—in short, to bring all available knowledge about agriculture direct to farmers.

The precedent for such action had already been set. As *The Aurora Beacon* said editorially a year or so later, it was the boll weevil that started the movement for the "crop doctor" business and crop demonstration work by the U.S. Department of Agriculture. The ravages of the pest caused the USDA to send experts into the counties to teach farmers how to combat the boll weevil. "The number of crop doctors has increased in 7 years to more than 600 in 13 states," said the *Beacon,* and went on to say: "The agricultural South has been given a new lease on life. In the North, where conditions are much more favorable for crop production, the 'crop doctor' will justify the cost of his maintenance beyond any question."

The *Beacon* expressed the opinion of thousands and the idea gathered increasing support. In De Kalb county, sentiment was crystallized, according to the *De Kalb Chronicle,* in a meeting called at the Elk's Club in De Kalb on January 5, 1912, by George Gurler, brother of H. B., the dairyman who had shipped sweet milk to Paris some 22 years before. From then on, things moved fast. On January 20, the group met again and, according to the minutes kept: "Moved by D. S. Brown, seconded by C. E. Bradt that the combined associations of the De Kalb County Farmers' Institute, the De Kalb County Newspapermen's Association and the De Kalb County Bankers' Association be incorporated as the De Kalb County Soil Improvement Association." The committee appointed to "perfect the association" consisted of Samuel Bradt, Henry H. Parke, and F. B. Townsend, and was authorized to "contract with W. G. Eckhardt." Eckhardt was a soils man, protege of Dr. Cyril G. Hopkins, who was in charge of the University of Illinois experimental fields in northern Illinois. He was well known in De Kalb county.

The committee moved fast. It met on March 23 in the office of W. W. Coultas, county superintendent of schools, and decided that headquarters would be in the courthouse, but that the "De Kalb County Soil Expert" would be in De Kalb. Henry H. Parke kept the minutes of the meeting.

Apparently, the committee had had a successful interview with Eckhardt, because the County Board of Supervisors hired him at a salary of $2,000 a year. In return, he was to manage the County Farm (sometimes called the "Poor Farm"), in addition to his duties with the De Kalb County Soil Improvement Association.

On May 11, the committee met to approve the constitution and bylaws, and to elect the following officers: Dillon S. Brown of Genoa, president; Charles E. Bradt, De Kalb banker, vice president; and Henry H. Parke of Sycamore, secretary-treasurer. Article II of the constitution read as follows:

"The object of the Association shall be:

1) To promote a more profitable and more permanent system of agriculture in De Kalb County;
2) To encourage dissemination of agricultural information in every feasible manner;
3) To supervise, direct and assist the activities of the De Kalb County Agricultural Demonstrator."

Directors of the new Association were to be named as follows: Three each from the Farmers' Institute, the Bankers' Association, and the Newspapermen's Association, and one from each of the nineteen townships.

Note well that the bankers and newspapermen had a big part in organizing the association. Invariably in those days, whenever farmers started organization activities, they sought the support of business interests, and got it. In fact, the drives for membership were similar to drives for funds for a hospital, or the Red Cross. The new organizations were universally backed because they were considered as a step forward in agriculture. Those who backed them considered it more or less a public duty to support them because they would lead agriculture to better things. The bankers and newspapermen of De Kalb county had the quaint idea that anything that was good for agriculture would also be good for their business. Most of the bankers involved had farms of their own, hence had a personal interest in improving agricultural conditions. It might be said, too, that bankers who held mortgages on farms were interested in improving farm incomes so that the mortgagors could more easily pay off their debts.

Years later, after Farm Bureau had developed sensationally, groups of detractors appeared, proclaiming the idea that business interests had aided in forming the early organizations so that they could control them, thus preventing them from performing useful services to farmers. All businessmen who helped were tagged as nefarious characters, interested only in protecting their own vested interests from cooperative activities by farmers.

If such business ever achieved any control at all over the young organizations which were the forerunners of Farm Bureau, diligent search has failed to reveal it. In fact, the De Kalb County Soil Improvement Association, heavily backed by bankers, was hardly housed in an office before the board of directors authorized Eckhardt to buy limestone on a cooperative basis for members. And on July 23, less than two months after starting operations, the board authorized the purchase of clover seed, up to $20,000, and at not more than $12 a bushel. Farmers wanted to buy their own seed and clean it themselves so that they could be sure of clean seed.

In November, Eckhardt was authorized to buy a moisture tester to use on corn, and on March 12 of the following year he was authorized to purchase rock phosphate in carload lots for members.

The time was to come when the Association developed such a huge business in seeds, grain, sugar and other commodities that a subsidiary had to be set up to handle it. (The outcome of that venture is a story well worth a book by itself. Briefly, that business association, the De Kalb County Agricultural Association, was to become the biggest producer of hybrid seed corn in the world. Stock in the Association, sold originally for $100 a share, is now worth thousands.)

As a matter of fact, in nearly all Farm Bureau counties, the organization has set up business affiliates which have competed successfully with other businesses, including insurance, the distribution of petroleum products, feeds and fertilizers—in direct competition with old-line business interests. And yet the canard has persisted to this day that Farm Bureau was and is controlled by business interests rather than by farmers. It persists when Farm Bureau has more members than all other general farm organizations combined.

It should not be inferred that De Kalb county farmers went into the seed business to make money, or to hurt anyone else's business. They started to buy seed because it was almost impossible to get reliable seed from dealers. Illinois was the dumping ground for worthless seed, due to the lack of any state standards and effective regulation of the business. Farmers made up their minds that they had to buy their own seed from reliable producers and then clean it themselves to avoid disappointment and often disaster. (They soon found that there was mighty little profit in handling clover and grass seed. The dead and dirty seed was so cheap that it was like pulling teeth to get farmers to pay prices high enough to assure themselves of good seed.)

Naturally, the farm press was unanimously enthusiastic about the new venture in farm organization. *The Prairie Farmer,* edited by Clifford V. Gregory, lost no time in giving generous space to reporting developments. In the August 1 issue, the pioneering efforts of the De Kalb people were recounted in words and pictures. "A few far-sighted men behind the scheme," said *Prairie Farmer,* "had a dream of doubled crop production—of prosperity resulting from these bountiful yields that should make De Kalb county the best place in the world to live." The idea caught the imagination of the people of De Kalb county. Meetings were held, committees appointed, and the work was started with an unselfish enthusiasm that cannot help but carry it to a successful conclusion. More than 700 of the county's farmers contributed their cash to the fund—the amounts varying from $1 to $25. The county supervisors voted $2,000. The farmers' clubs—and by the way, De Kalb county has the finest lot of farmers' clubs that can

C. V. Gregory

be found in any one county in the country—got behind the movement with their organized strength. The bankers' association put a subtantial shoulder to the wheel. The eighteen editors in the county organized a press association and gave liberally of their space to boosting the movement.

"The best part of it was that no one had an axe to grind. It was unselfish, patriotic work, which accounts for much of its success. County demonstration work that is backed by men whose chief thought is to sell the farmer something can never attain the fullest measure of success.

"Prof. W. G. Eckhardt, of the University of Illinois, was hired as the county expert. He has been on the job since the first of June. Already the soil expert in his little runabout has become a familiar sight to the De Kalb county farmers. They flag him as he is coming down the road, or head him off by telephone. . . .

"One of the things that Prof. Eckhardt discovered was that about 75 per cent of the soil in the county is acid. A soil auger and a package of litmus paper accompany the soil expert wherever he goes. 'You'll have to have limestone,' he tells the farmer after he has sampled the soil. The farmer lies awake that night wondering how much money he can raise to put into limestone. One man has ordered seven carloads. In another community ten cars have been ordered as a result of a little neighborhood meeting on one of the farms. . . .

"Usually the soil expert spends the larger part of a half day on each farm, going over each field and giving advice as to its management. Then there are emergency calls to be attended to. One day it is a man whose soybeans have succumbed to a combination of sour soil, poor inoculation and weeds. The next day it is a man who wants to know if it will be necessary to disc his alfalfa ground again, and when the seed should be sown.

"The editor spent a day with Prof. Eckhardt not long ago, being anxious to find out just what De Kalb county's 'crop doctor' was doing. One of the first stops was at the farm of George Klein, a farmer whose hog-tight fences, thrifty oats and clean corn made the services of a crop doctor seem superfluous.

" 'The corn in this field isn't doing as well as it should,' said Mr. Klein, after we had been over a good part of the farm. 'I guess the seed must have been pretty weak.'

"The crop doctor pulled up a hill of corn and shook the soil from the roots. 'It isn't the seed altogether,' he said 'Look at the roots.' They were alive with corn root lice, which had been sapping the strength of the plant. 'These lice live on the roots of almost everything but clover,' he went on. 'If you raise clover once every four years you won't have any trouble with them. In the meantime, if you will keep your corn ground well-stirred from the time spring opens until planting time, to keep down the weeds and break up the ants' nests, you can pretty nearly do away with the lice.'

" 'By gol, you won't see any of those things on my place next year,' Klein exclaimed, after we had found the lice working in half a dozen other places in the field. 'I'll stir things up so they won't have a chance at all.'

"Before the soil expert left he gave Klein a prescription which read something like this: 'Limestone 2 tons per acre any time this fall or winter. Follow in the spring with 14 pounds of clover seed per acre. That will start you on the right track,' he remarked. 'When you get this soil sweetened, and clover to supply the nitrogen, you won't be satisfied with anything less than 75 or 80 bushels of corn per acre every year. By that time you will be ready to put on some rock phosphate, and after that a hundred bushels won't be too much to expect.' "

On another farm, reported the editor, the sickly clover plants were the result of a sour soil, revealed by the litmus-paper test. On another farm, corn, grown for the third consecutive year in the same field, showed promise of no more than a 40-bushel yield. The villain—corn rootworms. An "alkali spot" on the same farm was tested for potassium, and found wanting in this necessary element. The remedy prescribed was potash.

On another field, the corn in one area was much better than in the rest of the field. Questions by the soil expert revealed the fact that clover was grown on the entire field three years before, but did not do well except in this one patch. The litmus-paper test showed an abundance of limestone in that part of the field, while the land all around it was strongly acid. On the patch of sweet soil, the good stand of clover has added enough nitrogen to the soil to make the present corn crop look twice as good as on the rest of the field.

Word of such discoveries got around fast in De Kalb county. A great light was beginning to dawn. Hundreds of farmers began to grow clover regularly to build up the soil for better crops of corn and to checkmate pests such as the corn root lice.

Editor Gregory went on to relate: "So far the greater part of Eckhardt's campaigning has been for limestone and clover, because they are needed most badly. He finds time to speak many good words for alfalfa also, and a good deal of it will be sown in the county this fall. Soybeans is another crop that the soil expert is pushing. He has a fine field on the county farm and will have more next year. The county farm is under his direct supervision, and he plans to use it for demonstration purposes."

Gregory ends his story with the following tribute: "It is epochal, this work that De Kalb county is doing. With unselfish courage and high ideals the people are blazing a new trail—a trail that will lead to undreamed of prosperity, a trail that will be eagerly followed by other counties as their eyes are opened to the way of agricultural salvation."

To fully appreciate the background of the above events, we do well to note the following, appearing in the first 1912 issue of *Prairie Farmer,* Editor Gregory, upon learning that the cost of maintaining Congress was getting out of hand, commented: "Some day people will learn to demand what they pay for. They will insist that a Congress that is costing $30,000 a day is too expensive to use as a political machine." *Prairie Farmer* was fighting for parcel post legislation. Subjects of editorials in the same issue: "Prejudice Against Mules Disappearing;" "How to Keep from Being Beaten in a Horse Trade;" "A County Library for Farmers;" "Don't Let the Bees Down;" "Profit in Cooperative Marketing;" "Repairing Harness;" "What Farmers Think About Autos."

Automobile advertisements in that issue included Chalmers and Willys Overland. . . . A mechanical contrivance, the "Easydun Dish Washer" was also advertised.

Typical of the popular support accorded the new venture in building a "new agriculture," was the editorial comment in *The Breeder's Gazette* for January 22, 1913, as follows:

"There is something new in the land. A man, clad with no authority to compel, but armed with a knowledge of good farm practices, goes about his county, counselling this man and that to reform his ways, to forsake his slipshod or erroneous farm practices, feel change of heart and help in the great movement for farm uplift. This man is the county demonstrator."

In the meantime, exciting events were transpiring in Kankakee county, where John S. Collier began work as the "Farm Expert" on the same day, June 1, as Eckhardt started in De Kalb. Since the De Kalb county association had been organized some months ahead of the one in Kankakee, De Kalb has been generally accorded the honor of being "first" in Illinois, even though work in both counties began on the same day. Detailed discussion of the work in Kankakee will appear later on.

It is necessary to describe the early work of the new county farm organizations rather exhaustively, because only in this way can we get a clear idea of the basic objectives of the organizations, or full appreciation of the contributions of the farm advisers to the development of the Farm Bureau, the name to be used by all the county organizations after its first adoption in Tazewell county. Without any question, farm advisers were the line sergeants of this new agrarian army which was destined to mount so many offensives within a few years against the forces that farmers believed barred them from attaining economic equality with other groups. The relationship between the farm adviser (county agent) and farm organization in Illinois was unique. The County Farm Bureau selected the farm adviser from a list of eligible men supplied by the University of Illinois, and the Farm Bureau paid part of the farm adviser's salary, supplied him with a car, an office, and office help. For the farm adviser, it was a most attractive arrangement, not only on account of the high salaries which pre-vailed, but also because he had an organization back of him to help out in the 4-H club work, soil-improvement work, and in fact all of his activities. This setup gave him a tremendous lever-age in his efforts to pry out the obstacles that stood in the way of improved technology on the farm. This leverage was reflected in results attained. The time was to come when Illinois farmers were to use more than 25 per cent of all the agricultural lime-stone used in the entire country. Without any question, this ar-rangement was the key to the truly sensational progress that was made in improving farm practices—a degree of progress that, under existing conditions, could have been made in no other way. This relationship with Extension was to be savagely attacked, and successfully, later; but for many years it worked wonderfully well. The sequel will be discussed in later chapters.

Chapter 3

Chain Reaction

The De Kalb county developments received wide notice, and farmers in other counties hastened to follow suit in organizing to hire a "farm expert." In the summer of 1912, the *Woodstock Sentinel* reprinted the *Prairie Farmer* story about what Eckhardt was accomplishing in De Kalb county. Apparently, it stirred the McHenry county folks to get busy.

On September 14, M. J. Wright, president of the Farmers' Institute in the county, called a meeting at the courthouse in Woodstock at which bankers, farmers, and educators voted to go ahead with plans for a soil improvement association, and they discussed the matter of hiring a "farm adviser." As far as is known, this was the first time that this term was applied to the farm expert in Illinois. The bankers present agreed to put up $2,000 to cover initial expenses.

On November 28, the *Sentinel* ran a story headlined "Organize Soil Improvement Association," with the subhead, "Prominent Farmers Lend Aid in Venture." Fremont Hoy, of the Farmers Exchange Bank at Woodstock, helped get things started, along with C. B. Wright of the Citizens State Bank of Crystal Lake, and R. M. Patrick of Marengo, "one of the patriarchs in county banking."

The constitution adopted that day carried the following preamble: "The object of this association is to improve the agricultural interests of McHenry county along economic, scientific and institutional lines. It aims not only at the conservation and correction of our soils, but seeks also the elimination, so far as possible, of waste in the selling of farm produce and the purchasing of farm equipment, seed, fertilizer, etc. It will encourage cooperation among farmers and strive to enrich the institutional life of county communities." Dues were set at $5.00 a year.

Homer Whipple was named president; C. W. Colton, vice president; A. M. Shelton, county superintendent of schools, secretary; and Fremont Hoy (banker), treasurer. The executive committee was to consist of two from the bankers association, two supervisors, and three farmers. (Evidently the bankers did not object to farmers going into cooperative buying and selling ventures.)

The *Sentinel* on December 12, 1912, carried the news of the Farmers' Institute meeting at Huntley, where M. J. Wright reported that in Boone county, the Grange and the Farmers' Institute were working hard to get farmers organized. The Belvidere Commercial Club was lending a hand. It was evident that the leaven was working. The movement was taking on the proportions of a crusade for better farming. In the same issue it was noted that 37 silos had been built in one township that year. Progress!

The *Sentinel* on December 26 reported that the United States Department of Agriculture had telegraphed M. J. Wright to inquire if the McHenry county association was ready to qualify for federal aid amounting to $1,200 a year. Wright answered, "yes."

George W. Conn, Jr., writing in the *Sentinel* in the same issue, discussed the job of the "farm agent": "The farm agent is the general hired man of the farmers. He will be kept busy testing soils and prescribing treatment and cultivation, fighting farm pests and diseases, noxious weeds, handling problems in livestock feeding and breeding, and cooperative buying and selling by farmers. It would be wonderful to have him find out the cost of producing milk, as well as the just share of the consumer price for the farmer. Armed with this information, farmers can deal to better advantage with the buyers of milk. Working with the boys and girls through clubs (4-H) should take a lot of time. Seed selection and drainage problems deserve study. A good "agent," he contended, "can earn $10 for each dollar that he costs the farmers." He admitted that the agent could not be a specialist in all things agricultural, but that he would know where to get any information that he needed.

Conn of the *Sentinel* was a real crusader for the new organization. His story on January 13 was headlined, "Bumper Crops Do Not Guarantee Bumper Values." He pointed out that the 1912 corn crop was bigger than the previous year by 638 million bushels, but that its market value was $100 million less than the value of the 1911 crop. To correct this seemingly unjust situation, he urged farmers: "Get busy with your farm organizations and don't forget that the McHenry County Soil Improvement Association has one additional distinctive feature about it and that is that the farm agent shall be expected to look at the business end of farming as well as to the conservation of the soil and the increase of fertility."

Also, announcing a "whirlwind campaign" for membership to be staged the following week, he wrote: "There is no rest in sight for anyone who is in the least interested in this movement for better farming and for better living until the farm agent is on the ground in McHenry county."

On January 30 it was noted that the newspapermen of the county had met twice and enthusiastically voted to back the new organization to the limit because, "whatever adds to the prosperity of the farmers will increase ours." (It is apparent that they were not worried that their businessmen advertisers might look dimly on a movement which was interested in farmers going into cooperative business, maybe in competition with some of them.)

On February 6, the *Sentinel* announced that Delos James, who had grown up near Grafton and had been president of the first boys' corn club in the county, had been hired as "Consulting Agriculturist." His office was to be in the courthouse for a time.

James promptly started writing pieces for the *Sentinel*. In the February 13 issue, he discussed rations for dairy cows. In the same issue, Conn wrote that farmers were organizing to cut distribution costs. "When it costs $7 billion to market about $6 billion worth of farm produce, it is high time that somebody woke up." Further, he said that farmers don't expect "wholly to eliminate the middleman, but reduce their number and lessen somewhat the abnormal percentage of profit."

Apparently, the bankers were proving themselves strong allies of the farmers, because on March 6 a *Sentinel* headline announced "Bankers Join To Aid Dairymen in Fight for Better Prices."

On August 14, it was reported that James had started an experimental alfalfa plot, and on November 30, it was announced that the Association would buy seeds for farmers on a cooperative basis. It was reported that some counties were saving as much as $5,000 a year by cooperative buying.

James, by this time, was using "county adviser" as his title. On February 12, 1914, he reported that in 1913 he had visited 202 farms, wrote 3,000 letters, had gotten 300 farmers to treat their seed oats for smut, 150 to test their seed corn, 600 to use balanced rations. He reported 3,500 acres of alfalfa seeded, 66 carloads of limestone and 10 cars of phosphate purchased. He had also planned 150 crop rotations, and addressed 30 meetings. The "county adviser" was a busy man.

In Will county, which was organized in 1913, the genesis of the first organization followed much the same pattern as in De Kalb county. A meeting was called by Fred M. Mulig, assistant superintendent of schools for the county, was attended by Dr. Cyril G. Hopkins of the University of Illinois, Frank I. Mann of Gilman, Healy Alexander of Lockport, Frank Sprague and son, George, of Joliet. Ed L. Wilson of Manhattan was chairman of the Farmers' Institute, and he named the above local people as a committee to form a soil improvement association.

This committee laid the groundwork for the Will County Soil and Crop Improvement Association. According to Leonard Braham, who later served as farm adviser in the county, those helpful in organizing the association included Ed L. Wilson, John Keniston, Frank Stauffenberg, Mark and Wayne McClure, W. F. Smith, George Boardman, Mungo J. and James W. Patterson, Ray Goist, Clayton and Victor Smith, Ferris Gaines, George Hinze, George Baker, Parry Wallace, Evan Lewis, Vic Beutein, Morgan Lewis, John Polley, Frank Rowley, Nick Welter, James Bentley, George L. Francis, Fred Dirst, C. S. Lewis, Ralph Davis, W. M. Herlitz, James W. Owen, John Snider, Howard Klett, and Harry L. Eaton, as well as others.

In the constitution adopted, we find the purpose of the organization set forth as follows:

"The object of this organization shall be to promote the development of the most profitable and permanent system of agriculture possible in this county, and the educational, social and financial welfare of its inhabitants in every legitimate and practical manner."

Leonard Braham, writing a short history of the early days, stated: "The fundamental purpose . . . was to secure for the farmers of Will county the advantages that would accrue from having trained men, full time, here in Will county, helping to develop a better and more profitable agriculture."

Ed L. Wilson was elected the first president and Frank C. Grannis, a graduate of the University of Illinois who had been working in Iowa, was hired as the first "farm expert." Frank Grannis was a soils man, and it is a fair assumption that his familiarity with the Hopkins doctrine on soil building was a factor in his favor. He preached "lime, legumes, and phosphate," and staged field days and farm tours to demonstrate good practices. That sort of program grew with the years, and resulted in the application of hundreds of thousands of tons of limestone and phosphate to Will county soils.

An "annual farm tour" was staged on August 27, 1914, only a year or so after the Association was organized. A newspaper report stated: "Conservation of the soil and increasing production

27

were dominant features of the day's trip." Nearly 50 cars carried the observers from farm to farm. On Mark McClure's farm of 240 acres, the good results of rotation and good management were observed. He had 35 acres of alfalfa. Attention was centered, however, on 40 acres of alsike clover grown for seed. It yielded eight bushels to the acre, and, according to the report, "cleared $100 per acre." That was sensational. Ira S. Brooks and Roy C. Bishop, lately appointed as "farm experts" in LaSalle and Livingston counties, were the principal speakers. On other farms, good livestock and dairy practices were demonstrated.

Grannis held seed corn meetings in each township. He urged farmers to tag early-maturing ears in August, and later pick them for seed. There was too much soft corn produced, and he tried to get everybody to plant early-maturing seed. He also urged all farmers in a community to grow one variety.

The new soil practices caught on quickly. In a short time, farmers in the Wheatland community pooled their resources to buy a portable rock crusher to grind the limestone rock that was present in numerous areas. Later, it was found more feasible, and really cheaper, to buy a truck and haul the ground limestone from the big quarries which sold it at low prices as a by-product.

A soil survey had been completed in the county in 1912 by the USDA, and released in 1914. That survey reinforced the conviction that many soils in the county were short of limestone. In spite of the tonnage of this material spread in the county in the early years, Braham reported that he, as farm adviser, in 1928 tested the soil of 156 farms and found only 13 on which no lime was needed.

The work of the Association went on with vigor, but it was soon in trouble because of lack of members. The money paid and pledged soon ran out, and within two years there was a debt of more than $7,000. No really comprehensive system of building membership had been adopted. But there was a hard core of determined men in the Association. Seventeen men signed notes for a total of $1,300, and one man, Ed L. Wilson, contributed some thousands of his own funds to see the organization through the crisis. After the finances had been straightened out, the executive committee suggested repayment, and Wilson settled for 50 cents on the dollar. That was the kind of support that carried the organization through the crisis and later built it into one of the largest county Farm Bureaus in the state.

Some attempts had been made to sign up new members, but it simply was not pushed hard enough. I know from experience how the membership work was carried on. After supper one summer evening, Frank Grannis and a farmer from some other part of the county called at our home near Elwood. I had been reading in the farm papers and the local press about the new organization, and I was all ears as the men talked to Dad. In fact, I distinctly remember some of the reasons given for joining the Association. Dad asked what it could do for the farmers. I remember that the farmer with Grannis said that an organization was needed to work on school and road and tax problems that a farmer by himself could do nothing about. I remember that he said it wouldn't be many years before nearly everybody would be driving cars and would demand hard roads everywhere. He suggested that it would break farmers up to pay for the taxes for roads along their farms, therefore, some new method of paying for the roads would have to be found. That was indicative of how far ahead some of the farm leaders were thinking at the time.

I remember too that this man told Dad that farmers should organize to do something to stabilize farm prices. When Dad asked how that could be done, he replied that he didn't know, but that possibly it could be done by legislation. He said that tariff legislation had apparently done a lot for industry, and maybe we could find something that would work as well for agriculture. Dad joined the organization, all right, but the point I am making is that membership work was done casually at odd times, and didn't begin to reach any great number of farmers. At the beginning it was hoped that the organization was so obviously necessary and so helpful that thousands would join up without solicitation, but that was a vain hope.

Years would pass before the Association was put on a solid

footing and properly incorporated as a nonprofit corporation, under "An Act Concerning Corporations, approved April 18, 1872." The incorporators were John L. Keniston, Robert A. Baker, Arthur States, Fred Francis, C. J. Luther, Mark McClure, and E. L. Wilson.

The year 1913 was a big year for the farm adviser movement. Before the year was out, Roy Bishop was working in Livingston county; Ernest T. Robbins in Tazewell county; Ed B. Heaton in Du Page county; Henry Truitt in Peoria county; Charles H. Oathout in Champaign county; and Jerome E. Readhimer in Kane county. In 1914, Albert M. TenEyck went to work in Winnebago county, followed by Lewis W. Wise in Iroquois; A. M. Wilson in Hancock; Charles J. Mann in Bureau; Ira S. Brooks in La Salle, and Frank H. Demaree in Grundy. A pattern had been established, and farmers found it good.

Many people helped the new movement along. For example, Ed Heaton, first farm adviser in Du Page county, recalls that a gift he appreciated greatly was a Graflex camera (new then) and slide projector costing $150. It came from John Lamson, who was in charge of agricultural activities for the Burlington Railroad. With it, he could take pictures of oats infected with smut, and then show the slides at local meetings. A good camera was a necessity to the farm advisers.

Herman Bandemer, a farmer near Glen Ellyn, but also president of a bank, was the main advocate and organizer of the Du Page County Agricultural Improvement Association, which was organized in 1912, but it was May 1, 1913, before a qualified farm adviser could be found. Ed Heaton started work on that day. William Hammerschmidt lived on a farm near Lombard, but his main interest was the Elmhurst-Chicago Stone Company. He was a rugged supporter of the new organization, and he went with Heaton to the Peoria meeting in 1919.

In every county there was a small group of farmers who backed the farm adviser to the limit, and who carried the burden of making policies. In Du Page county, in addition to those already mentioned, there were George Keller, John J. Case, Frank

Fraley, Peter Hoy, Harold C. Vial, D. O. Sayre, and William Patrick.

A word should be recorded here too of the importance of the Farmers' Institute in the various counties. Most Institute leaders regarded the new movement as a needed extension and enhancement of the work that had been carried on for so long by their efforts, and they backed it enthusiastically. In one case, at least, and probably in others, the farm adviser managed the county Farmers' Institute program. Eventually, the Farm Bureau superseded the Institutes. The Institute really kept the spirit of inquiry and of farm progress alive during a very critical period, and it should receive generous recognition.

Chapter 4

The Farm Adviser's Job

The "farm expert" or "county agent" movement was moving with tornado-like speed. By August 15, 1914, the 30th county agent had been hired in Indiana (Wells county), and the Will County Soil and Crop Improvement Association (Illinois) had been approved for federal aid of $1,200 a year.

On February 15, it had been announced that the salary of Ernest T. Robbins, adviser in Tazewell county, had been raised from $3,500 to $4,000. You could live affluently on a salary like that in those days. Boards of supervisors were getting generous. Under state law, they could appropriate as much as $5,000 a year to help soil and crop improvement associations. Kane county supervisors, by a vote of 37 to 4, gave $4,000 to the county association.

In the fall of 1914, Farm Adviser Eckhardt of De Kalb county had stored 3,200 bushels of Western Plowman seed corn, a variety that had yielded 4 to 19 bushels more to the acre than other varieties. It was pointed out that if all the corn land in the county had been planted to Western Plowman and had yielded only four bushels more, it would have meant $250,000 more farm income.

The farm adviser movement was getting much favorable notice. The *Burlington* (Iowa) *Hawkeye* commented editorially on the news that Dave Thompson had been hired by the McLean County Better Farming Association at a salary of $4,000 a year: "The farm adviser is worth all he gets."

On January 22, 1915, the Woodford county organization was completed, with 251 members. Officers were Howard Leonard, president; William H. Smith, vice president; James Smith, treasurer; and W. Frank Felter, secretary.

Other news in 1915: Manteno farmers built a limestone crusher; Frank Demaree, farm adviser in Grundy county, arranged to have office days in townships remote from the county seat; Albert M. TenEyck, Winnebago county, started a 4-page monthly newsletter. A little later, Farm Adviser Ed Heaton and County School Superintendent Royal T. Morgan started the Du Page Farm and School Bulletin.

In some counties, the farm adviser was considered a farm management expert, and he was expected to devote the major part of his time to that. In fact, one county limited the membership to 450, on the reasoning that no one man could handle more farms than that. This didn't last long, however. Gregory wrote in a *Prairie Farmer* editorial: "A County Farm Improvement Association should be open to any farmer who is interested."

In April, Gregory discussed a bill then before the Illinois Legislature which would give any county with a farm adviser $1,200 to help out. He commented: "The county farm adviser movement must draw a substantial share of its financial support from its members and other interested people in the county." (Governor Dunne vetoed the bill.) Farmers were feeling their strength through organization. The Chicago Milk Producers Association won their strike, and got 22 cents a hundred more for their milk, or a total of $8,000 a day more.

News items in June: A custom orchard-spraying outfit started in Will county. Farm women in Kankakee county organized a home improvement association and employed a home economics expert. Roy C. Bishop, farm adviser in Livingston county, discovered a fine deposit of marl in a field next to one on which a carload of limestone had been spread a few months before. On July 19, Macon county became the 19th in Illinois to hire a farm adviser.

Illinois was fortunate in getting top men to fill the job of farm adviser. Salaries were high enough to attract the best. Dean Davenport knew that the movement would bog down very quickly if poorly qualified men were hired. Many farmers were quite skeptical about the merits of the "new agriculture" that was getting so much notice all over the state. The University had the veto power over appointments. Probably the most important requirement set up was that the man must have had five years of experience after graduation from an agricultural college. It was natural, too, that University of Illinois graduates would be preferred during the early days, because soils work was a big feature of farm adviser work, and Illinois graduates would be familiar with the Hopkins system of soil building. However, as early as April, 1913, Ed Heaton, an Iowa State College man, and a native of Iowa, was hired in Du Page county. Requirements were so high though, that few could qualify for the jobs, and a few years later a number of counties had to wait for more than a year before a qualified candidate could be found for this important post. With salaries ranging as high as $4,000 a year, the jobs were very attractive, and there was no shortage of candidates. We should remember that a $4,000 job in those days was the equivalent of a $15,000 job in 1963.

In the July 1 issue of *Prairie Farmer* Gregory described the situation faced by men in the new job of farm adviser. He wrote:

"A good many people have been frankly skeptical about county demonstration work. Others have been over-enthusiastic, expecting the county adviser to do all sorts of fearful and wonderful things in his job of ushering in the agricultural millenium.

"But it is actual results that count, and in order that I might give *Prairie Farmer* readers an accurate idea of the results of this work, I made a visit to Kankakee county recently, where the adviser has been at work for about a year. Collier's (John S. Collier) principal lines of work are seed and soil improvement, and the work is done largely by personal visits to a man's farm, where his problems can be studied at firsthand.

"Such a plan takes a lot of time and hard work, of course, but Mr. Collier believes that one man well warmed up is worth half a dozen only slightly singed. The warming-up process is thoroughly done—so thoroughly done—that a man stands but little chance of escape once the county adviser gets on his trail.

"The county association is composed of a local association of 15 members in each township. On his application blank each member wrote down his promise to do certain things—put in five acres of alfalfa, build a silo, apply a carload of limestone or rock phosphate, or whatever it happened to be that he felt he could and would do during the coming year.

"And woe to the fellow who thought he could lightly escape the effects of his promise! About the time the limestone should have been applied Collier wrote John Smith, or whoever it happened to be, a letter. 'How about that limestone, John?' he would ask, and go on to suggest that it was high time that it was on the field. The chances were that John hustled around and ordered the limestone, and wrote the adviser to that effect. If he didn't hear anything from John for three or four days, however, Collier would sit down and write another letter—this time to Mrs. John. 'I wish you would take this matter up with John and get him to send for that limestone,' the letter would read. 'I'm mighty anxious to see John get a good stand of alfalfa this fall. Tom Brown down the road got his limestone spread two weeks ago.'

" 'We've got to have as good a stand of alfalfa as Tom Brown, if I have to spread that limestone myself,' Mrs. Smith would say.

"What could poor John do? The chances are that Collier has the name of his oldest boy on file, too, and will write to him next. So John goes to shoveling limestone. Obviously, the association is no place for a lazy man.

"The same follow-up system is used on the men whom the adviser visits. The first thing he does when he strikes a man's farm is to make a rough map of the place, indicating drainage, build-

36

ings, etc. On the same sheet is put down the crops grown on each field for several years past, the amount of livestock kept and manure produced, and any other facts which may be of value in prescribing for this particular case. At the end of the week the adviser writes a detailed letter to each man he has visited that week, repeating the advice he gave the man in person, and enclosing a copy of the map with the fields numbered and the soil types marked. He doesn't try to change a man's whole system of farming at once, but lays stress on a few of the most essential things. It may be that drainage is the most pressing need, or potash, or limestone and clover. Whatever it is, the letters keep coming at intervals until the man does the things he has been told. There's no getting away from it.

"About three hundred letters a week are sent out from the adviser's office in the Kankakee county courthouse, two stenographers being busy all the time. In addition to letter writing, the girls file bulletins and farm papers, arrange the adviser's schedule of visits, and care for all the routine details of the office.

"Last summer Collier worked by townships, visiting farmers in a neighborhood consecutively in order to save time. This year he is picking up the ones that were missed the summer before, which necessitates more traveling. There are emergency calls, too, and so popular has the adviser become that when I saw him the last of May his time was spoken for until the middle of August.

" 'Our two biggest problems are seed and soil improvement,' says Mr. Collier, 'and we are devoting most of our time to these points.'

"His work along these lines is having its effect. Over 400 cars of limestone were used in the county last year. There will be about 75 cars of rock phosphate used this year, or almost twice as much as the year before. Fourteen thousand dollars worth of clover seed was sown this spring by members of the association. There will be about 1,600 acres of alfalfa put in this fall. The association distributed $9,000 worth of muriate of potash to its members this spring. There is much peaty land in Kankakee county, where potassium is its greatest need. Along with the sowing of clover seed and the discriminating purchase of phosphate and potash, has come a marked decrease in the amount of mixed fertilizer used. Last year 56 carloads of mixed fertilizer were shipped into the county. This year only two cars have been reported so far.

"The stand of oats in Kankakee county is a great deal better this year than would have been the case if Collier had not been on the job with his follow-up letters. Some of the farmers, when they finally yielded to the pressure and tested their seed, found that it would test only about 25 per cent. Collier is also making an effort to get Kankakee farmers to raise an improved type of corn that will be especially adapted to their conditions.

"One incidental effect of the association is that the farmers have learned to work together. As a result, in several places in the county farmers have induced railroads to put in sidings where limestone can be unloaded and grain and livestock loaded. The saving of several miles in haul is worth a good deal to a busy farmer who is short of hired help.

" 'This siding saves me $30 on every car of limestone I unload,' remarked a Momence township farmer as we stopped to look at some of his peat land.

"In Manteno township the farmers are shortening the limestone haul and lessening the cost in another way. They have bought a portable crusher to run with a threshing engine, and will soon be prepared to grind stone right in their own neighborhood. The crusher cost about $500 and they figure they can grind the stone for about 40 cents a ton.

"In parts of Kankakee county much of the land is flat, making drainage one of the principal problems. The farmers are remedying this as fast as they can, however. The county surveyor estimates that at least $300,000 worth of tile will be put in this summer and fall.

"Last winter Collier held a one-week short course for the boys, and at the close organized them by townships into the Young Men's Country Club. Well up towards three hundred of the brightest farm boys in Kankakee county are members of this club. Just now nearly every one of the township clubs is organizing a ball team, and a series of Saturday afternoon games will be played throughout the county. At fair time the two leading teams will play a three-game series for a prize of $100 in cash. Sometime soon as many of the boys as can, and their fathers, too, will go down to Champaign on a special train to see the experiment station plots and fields. Next winter another short course will be held. This work of interesting the future farmers is going to do a great deal to raise the agricultural standards of Kankakee county.

" 'We're just plugging along,' Collier told me modestly as I was leaving.

"I could not help wishing that more counties were 'just plugging along' in the same way."

The program of work described by Gregory is not precisely like programs in other counties, but basically it is typical. Collier was unusual and unique. He was a man of strong ideas and he was resolute. He was later to become a "controversial" character in Farm Bureau circles, but he remained farm adviser in Kankakee county until he died in 1933.

Du Page county was a "dairy" county, and one of the things that most impressed Ed Heaton when he went to work as adviser on May 1, 1913, was that in many cases dairymen were spending too much money for commercial mill feeds. One of his first activities, then, was to try to get more grain with a high protein content produced on the farm in order to lessen the necessity for so much mill feed. "Make the farm feed the livestock," was his slogan, and he preached that doctrine wherever he went.

A glance at the county records indicates how successful his campaign became. In those days, corn was a fine crop for silage, but couldn't be depended on as a grain crop, due to the close proximity of Lake Michigan, which provided a sort of air conditioning for forty miles or so from its shores. The seasons were too short for growing the kinds of corn grown in those days. So, Heaton started a campaign for growing more barley for cow feed. In 1910, only about 30,000 bushels were grown in Du Page county (which had only nine townships) ; but after four years of effort, starting in 1913, the campaign had resulted in more than 500,000 bushels threshed, nearly all of it to be fed to dairy cows. A campaign for more alfalfa hay to take the place of so much purchased protein feed was carried on at the same time, with spectacular results. Clover acreage increased fifty-fold, and alfalfa by a lesser amount, because it was harder to grow.

Even more sensational results were attained in Kane county, where Farm Adviser Readhimer's campaign lifted barley production from 129,859 bushels in 1910 to 1,073,000 bushels in 1917. The farm adviser movement was going over in great style.

Chapter 5

I Double A

The farm advisers, though still a small group in 1913, lost no time in getting organized for exchange of information and experiences at their new jobs. Late in the year, Ed Heaton of Du Page county wrote to his fellow advisers to suggest that at the next extension meeting they organize an association. In December they did just that at Champaign, naming Jerome E. Readhimer of Kane county, president; Eckhardt, vice president; and Heaton, secretary-treasurer. John S. Collier of Kankakee county was the fourth farm adviser at the meeting.

Name selected was the Illinois Association of County Agriculturists. By mid-1914 there were thirteen members, meeting regularly twice a year, with special meetings called occasionally. Charter members, in addition to the officers named above, were: Charles H. Oathout of Champaign county, Lewis W. Wise of Iroquois, Delos L. James of McHenry, Ernest T. Robbins of Tazewell, Albert M. TenEyck of Winnebago, Henry Truitt of Peoria, Roy C. Bishop of Livingston, John S. Collier of Kankakee, Frank C. Grannis of Will, and D. S. Blair of Lake. (The Lake county organization was not recognized by the University, and didn't last.

A permanent organization was set up in 1917.) Charles J. Mann of Bureau county joined in 1914. It was customary for the members to take with them to the regular meetings two or three farmers from their respective counties.

Issues discussed are indicated by the resolutions adopted at the meeting in Champaign on January 28-29, 1915, with sixteen counties represented. The advisers asked that: hog cholera laws be enforced, importing (into the state) cattle with tuberculosis or other infectious diseases be stopped, all milk and creamery by-products be pasteurized, foot-and-mouth disease indemnities be paid from state and federal funds, a veterinary college be established at the University of Illinois.

All the following summer, the farm advisers, particularly Robbins, Heaton and Eckhardt, had been discussing the need for the county crop improvement associations to band together for mutual helpfulness. They were convinced that it was inevitable that within a few years matters involving state legislation would require united action by farmers, and further that if limestone and rock phosphate and seeds were to be purchased cooperatively, much better terms could be secured by pooling county orders to make up a huge volume.

Therefore, at their meeting in December, 1915, they instructed Ed Heaton, as secretary, to send invitations to farmers in the organized counties inviting them to attend the meeting of the Illinois State Association of County Agriculturists to be held in January at the University of Illinois.

Accordingly, a number of interested farmers showed up at the meeting on January 26, 1916. After consideration of routine business, a motion was adopted to the effect that Herman W. Danforth of Tazewell county take the chair while the matter of forming a state federation of county agricultural associations be considered by the advisers and farmers present. Danforth took the chair. After some discussion, Howard Leonard of Woodford county moved that the chair appoint a committee of five consisting of Danforth, two farm advisers, and two farmers, to consider the matter of a state association, and report at a later date. Eckhardt moved to amend the motion so that the committee would be made up entirely of farmers, leaving out the farm advisers. The amendment carried, and then Dean Davenport offered an amendment which would permit the committee to call in the farm advisers for consultation. This also carried, the amended motion was adopted, and arrangements made for the committee to report back at 8:30 that evening. The committee consisted of the following: Herman W. Danforth of Tazewell county, Mark McClure of Will county, Henry H. Parke of De Kalb county, Andrew Jackson Gilfillan of Iroquois county, and Howard Leonard of Woodford county.

At the appointed hour, in Room 903, Agricultural Building, the committee reported to the entire group which got right down to work, adopted the name "Illinois Agricultural Association," set the dues at $100 a year for each county association, elected Danforth president, and Leonard secretary of the temporary organization. Officers were instructed to go ahead and perfect the organization. Thus was set in motion the mightiest force that had ever appeared in Illinois agriculture. It was to bring profound changes for all farmers in Illinois. No arrangements for a permanent office or staff were made.

Farm paper editors were enthusiastic. "Who can foretell," asked the *Orange Judd Farmer,* "the power of such an organization of leading farmers of the state with hearts set on rural betterment, and with selfish interests far in the background?"

Prairie Farmer commented as follows:

"The work of organizing was done by the officers and representatives of the local associations with the help of the county advisers. It is planned to make the Illinois Agricultural Association a strong, statewide organization that will have the strength and the purpose to work for the interests of Illinois farmers in every possible way. There has been a great need of such an association in Illinois and farmers' interests have suffered for lack of it!

"The organizers of this new association are hard-headed, practical farmers. They realize that it will take hard work and good judgment to make the association live up to its possibilities. But

43

they are enthusiastically for it, and will spare no efforts to make it the real representative of the interests of Illinois agriculture. One of the most powerful effects of this association will be its wholesome influence on Illinois politics. While it will not be partisan in any sense, it will stand for better and more business-like state government. . . .

"Farmers can accomplish almost anything by working together.

"Let's all work together to make the Illinois Agricultural Association the greatest constructive force in the state."

The meeting to "perfect" the organization was held in the Farm Bureau office in the courthouse at Ottawa on March 15, 1916. A constitution and set of bylaws were adopted, permanent officers elected, and representatives of thirteen county associations signed up as members of the state organization; namely, Adams, Bureau, Champaign, De Kalb, Iroquois, La Salle, Livingston, Macon, Mason, McLean, Tazewell, Will, and Woodford. (Later, Adams county withdrew because of lack of funds, and De Kalb dropped out with no explanation, but both counties reaffiliated later.) Du Page county came in within three months, with others following soon after.

Permanent officers elected were: Herman W. Danforth of Tazewell county, president; Guy Carlyle (Lyle) Johnstone of McLean county, vice president; Howard Leonard of Woodford, treasurer; and Ernest T. Robbins of Tazewell, secretary.

Herman W. Danforth was the grandson of a Tazewell county pioneer who bought a large tract of swampy land in Iroquois county where the town of Danforth now stands. A law graduate of the University of Michigan, he practiced law for eight years before he went back to the farm in 1907. A strong believer in cooperative activities, he helped organize the farmers' elevator in Danforth and became its president. Later, he served as president of the Farmers National Grain Dealers Association. He was one of the founders of the Tazewell County Farm Bureau, and became its first president. He and Farm Adviser E. T. Robbins promoted the idea of a state organization of Farm Bureaus, and

44

Herman W. Danforth

Danforth was the outstanding choice for the presidency of the original IAA. He resigned within a year, to become president of the Federal Land Bank of St. Louis.

To the executive committee, Danforth named: John L. Keniston of Will county, Dan G. Reder of Bureau, and Henry H. Parke of De Kalb; to the legislative committee: John W. Kirkton of Livingston, Price N. Jones of McLean, and Merton Parker of Iroquois; to the organization committee: William M. Dwyer of Mason county, Thomas Wright Esmond of La Salle, and John C. Mies of Livingston; to the educational committee: Mark McClure of Will county, C. H. Root of Grundy, and Lorin Clark of Champaign.

In just over three months, on June 19, 1916, a special meeting of the IAA was called at Morrow Hall in the Agriculture Building at the University of Illinois. Action was taken to approve the Robey Bill, known as the Grain Trade Act, then before Congress. Roy C. Bishop, farm adviser in Livingston county, explained his plan for cooperative buying of feeder cattle and sheep. Danforth urged action to secure a pure-seed law at Springfield, and the legislative committee was directed to prepare a bill and try to get it through the legislature. A resolution was adopted in favor of repeal of the present law covering collection of real estate and personal property taxes by township collectors, in favor of a law placing the job of collecting in the hands of the county tax collector. Another resolution asked the Governor to appoint practical farmers to the State Livestock Commission, along with a competent veterinarian.

Beyond the above, records reveal little action by the IAA until March, 1917, when a meeting was held at Champaign-Urbana, and after considering routine matters, such as the cooperative purchasing of such things as typewriters, mimeograph machines, tires, and seeds, arrangements were made for the second annual meeting of the organization, to be held at the Jefferson Hotel, Peoria, on March 31, 1917.

At Peoria, nine of the eleven counties which had joined the IAA were represented, but it was reported that only five had paid

46

the membership fee of $100. It was reported that the Grain Trade Bill had been passed by Congress, and that a state pure-seed bill had been drafted, introduced and got out of committee with a favorable report. Dr. O. E. Dyson, state veterinarian, reported on bills he had prepared for the control of livestock diseases such as hog cholera, contagious abortion, and tuberculosis. County dues were reduced from $100 to $50 a year and John W. Kirkton of Livingston county succeeded Danforth, who had been named president of the Federal Land Bank of St. Louis. Secretary Ernest T. Robbins resigned in favor of Roy C. Bishop, farm adviser in Livingston county. Resolutions adopted favored the bill in the state legislature providing financial aid to counties employing farm advisers, and opposed any increase in freight rates unless such increases "have been proved justifiable and necessary."

John W. Kirkton, second president of the Illinois Agricultural Association, was born in Aberdeenshire, Scotland, the son of a roofer, or slater, as roofers are called in Scotland.

Kirkton's parents emigrated to America, and settled on the unfenced prairie near Gridley, Illinois. They bought 120 acres of prairie land in 1871 and from then on they were farmers. Part of the land was a buffalo wallow. The land had to be drained to be fully productive. As a boy, John herded his father's cattle on the prairie each summer. He had an innate love for livestock, and when he started farming for himself he developed a herd of pure-bred Shorthorns which he showed at county fairs, along with some pretty good Percheron horses.

Hugh L. Kirkton, a son of John, who still owns some of the land his grandfather bought in 1871, says that his dad loved the show ring, and was never happier than when he was showing livestock or judging it. (He became a licensed livestock judge in later years, and judged at county fairs over much of Illinois.) Hugh L. remembers well the early days of Farm Bureau in Livingston county. He remembers that his dad followed the Hopkins system of soil maintenance, and that he spread the first limestone used in the Gridley community. This event aroused a lot of comment, a few raised eyebrows, and even a little scoffing. But after John

John W. Kirkton

began to harvest lush crops of alfalfa which followed the use of lime and phosphorus, it wasn't long before "Lime, legumes, and phosphate" became standard practice in Livingston county. Roy C. Bishop, the first farm adviser in the county, became well known for his soils work.

John W. Kirkton accumulated 280 acres of land, which was farmed for many years by Hugh L. until his retirement, and is now operated by his son, Hugh Max. Hugh L., in commenting on how things have changed since his father's day, reports that Hugh Max often produces 125 bushels of corn to the acre, about double the yields of 30 years ago. Max has served on the board of directors of the Livingston County Farm Bureau. Hugh L. and Robert, another son of John W., both served as Livingston county Farm Bureau presidents.

Lyle Johnstone of Bloomington, first vice president of IAA, remembers John W. Kirkton well, as an outgoing, jovial person who got along well with people. Everybody loved to hear him tell stories, and he never disappointed them when he was presiding at a meeting. He knew his way around the legislature at Springfield. He and Roy C. Bishop played a big part in getting the legislature to pass the first pure-seed bill in 1917.

Another meeting of the IAA was held in Springfield on May 2, 1917, at which routine matters were discussed and everybody present called on Governor Frank O. Lowden at his office. The minutes of the meeting record contain no mention of war-created emergencies, although we had been at war since early in April.

At the next meeting, held in the Gold Room of the Jefferson Hotel in Peoria on July 6, it was reported that the new seed law that had been passed after the IAA legislative committee had labored valiantly in its behalf, had been found unconstitutional. (All other bills backed by the IAA had been passed with little trouble.)

Representatives of 16 counties were present, but only 14 county organizations had paid their dues. Six others were reported to be ready to sign up. In the minutes of this meeting, we find the first mention of the war. "An extensive discussion of the selective draft" was had. From the minutes: "It was decided that any action taken should be solely for the purpose of advising federal authorities as to existing conditions and to aid them in classifying those engaged in farming according to their relative importance.

The next annual meeting was held on April 15-16, 1918, at Springfield. Secretary Bishop reported that membership had grown to 23 county associations. He also reported that when the delegates called on Governor Lowden nearly a year before, the organization had offered its services to the state during the war emergency. He said further, in his report: "There are now fifty-one counties organized under the Smith-Lever Act. All of these counties should become members of the Illinois Agricultural Association."

Bishop's report shows that the IAA was getting into cooperative purchasing: "The purchasing committee has held six meetings during the year and contracted for the purchase of 23,000 tons of phosphate, 2,533 bushels of red and mammoth clover seed, 193 bushels of sweet clover, 610 bushels of alsike, 350 bushels of alfalfa, 300 bushels of timothy seed, 350 bushels of soybeans and 45,000 pounds of rape—making a cash value totaling $72,500."

Further on in the report we find:

"The usefulness of the Illinois Agricultural Association will be limited only by the measures the association takes for getting results. If the Illinois Agricultural Association means anything as a state organization or if its office is to have any power, this office must be well equipped and managed by the best qualified man or men that a reasonable amount of money and persuasion may command. The time has come when this step must be taken." Prophetic words!

War-created problems were discussed in some detail, and the county dues were restored to $100 a year. In the election of officers, Kirkton and Johnstone were reelected as president and vice president; Samuel L. Woodburn of Rock Island county was nominated and elected second vice president; and Gregory, *Prairie Farmer* editor, was nominated and elected third vice president. Leonard continued as treasurer, and Bishop as secretary.

Resolutions adopted pledged the organization to solid backing of the war effort, and gave support to the pending $60 million state bond issue for paved roads, to be paid off from automobile license fees.

The tempo of the organization movement was stepped up considerably in 1917, when the USDA undertook a campaign, with the full cooperation of the Extension Service, to organize county Farm Bureaus as a means of increasing food production. In early October of 1917, Walter F. Handschin, state leader of the farm advisers, announced that the USDA would pay $2,100 each year to any county with a Farm Bureau of 300 to 400 representative farmers, with assured financial support for a period of three years. Another $2,100 must be contributed locally. Another $1,500 a year of federal funds was made available to such counties for women's work in home improvement. The Extension Service promptly appointed organization specialists, as they were called, to help organize the counties. Those appointed were: William E. Hart of Marion, John C. Spitler of Montrose, Vernon Vaniman of Virden, Sidney B. Smith of Springfield, Charles Atwood of Peoria, and Walter Gaines of Crete.

Under forced draft, this program moved ahead so fast that competent men could not be found immediately to go to work in the newly organized counties. Some had to wait for a year or more for farm advisers. The great importance of the work as an adjunct to the war effort may be gauged from the action of the Woodford County Farm Bureau in making Farm Bureau services available free to non-members for a period of one year. Largely as a result of the work of the farm advisers, more than 2,500 Illinois farmers were now keeping business records. The Farm Bureau movement received a "good press" during those days. Wide publicity was given to results attained through soil improvement. For example, Andrew Jackson Gilfillan, president of the Iroquois county association, had followed directions of the farm adviser by putting lime and phosphate on a sandy field that would grow only 15 to 25 bushels of corn to the acre, and seeding it to alfalfa. The second year after seeding, this field yielded three big cuttings of hay, enough to pay good returns on a valuation of $200 an acre. Such results gave a tremendous impetus to the work. The Illinois Legislature passed a bill providing additional financial help to the counties for Farm Bureau work. George N. Coffey, assistant state leader of county farm advisers, was not overstating the situation when he announced that farmers were enthusiastically backing the movement only five years after its inauguration.

The county Farm Bureaus were assuming more responsibilities day by day. Eckhardt in De Kalb county wrote: "I want the cooperation of every farmer of De Kalb county in running every swindle to earth that shows up here. It is the duty of every member of the Soil and Crop Improvement Association to make such report." . . . Henry "Hank" Lloyd, farm adviser in Hancock county, reported that 95 per cent of the soils tested in his county were acid to some degree. . . . In another county, a "beef ring" was organized with twenty farmers, each contributing a beef animal so that members could enjoy fresh meat regularly. One member did the slaughtering, and got his meat in return. . . . Farmers were buying automobiles when they could get them. Among the makes advertised in farm papers were: the Velie (Moline), the King Eight (Detroit), the Reo (Lansing).

Near the end of the year, it was announced that Clinton county had won the distinction of having the largest charter membership, 410, of any Farm Bureau in the state. It was the second (to Randolph) to be organized in "Egypt." The movement was really getting into high gear.

Chapter 6

Full Speed Ahead

After the 1918 annual meeting, it was soon apparent that income at the rate of $100 a county was totally inadequate to finance the kind of a program of work that many leaders had in mind. All over the state, farmers and farm advisers soon realized that the new organization was doomed unless provided with enough funds to hire full-time men to work at state-wide problems—just as the county organizations had already hired men to work full time on a county basis.

Whenever farm leaders got together they discussed the problem. They soon became aware of a stern fact; namely, that it was urgently necessary to take decisive action at the earliest possible moment—or resign themselves to the prospect that the IAA would become just another organization that met once a year and passed a few resolutions.

No one was more keenly aware of the dangers than Editor Gregory of *Prairie Farmer,* Heaton and Eckhardt. These three spearheaded the drive for action, and they got plenty of support from a hard-core group of leaders of the county associations, now officially known as Farm Bureaus. There was plenty of opposition

—not too vocal at the time—that was sure to fight to the last ditch against what they considered grandiose plans to set up an organization that might spend as much as $100,000 of farmers' money annually.

Such a budget would seem inadequate in these days, but it was really big money at that time. It is revealing indeed to recall that Gregory himself had the idea that farmers would object to paying more than one or two dollars of state dues. It was Eckhardt, the dreamer and the dynamo, who finally convinced him that the kind of program they had in mind was possible only with a budget based on five-dollar dues, on top of the ten dollars that was generally paid to the county organization.

Eckhardt argued that the IAA, in order to survive, must provide service of the highest order to members; and that if such service were provided, farmers would be glad to pay for it, just as they cheerfully paid for the service they were already getting from the county organization. Once convinced, Gregory became a strong advocate, ably seconded by Howard Leonard of Woodford county and Lyle Johnstone of McLean county. It is true that as wartime incomes filled the pockets of farmers as never before, a five-dollar bill didn't seem as big as it had seemed a few years earlier. Still, there was stubborn resistance.

Late in 1918, leaders decided that the time had come to take positive action. Plans were made for a state-wide meeting at Peoria early in 1919, to revamp the IAA from top to bottom, provide for adequate funds, and clear the decks for action on a scale consistent with the dignity and importance of farming as a business and a way of life. The prospects were breathtaking and the hazards great, but the leaders of the movement had sublime faith in the project and were willing to take a calculated risk to win a prize of the first magnitude.

Everyone concerned knew that big things might be accomplished when the 1919 annual meeting was convened at the Jefferson Hotel in Peoria on January 21. When President Kirkton called the meeting to order, an air of expectancy was evident in the entire audience. Kirkton sounded the proper keynote in his opening address when he said, referring to the end of the war less than three months before: "Now we have met the enemy and they are ours and we come here today feeling that the time for reconstruction has come."

Delegates listened to many speeches by Eckhardt, Gregory, Dean Davenport and others. Eugene D. Funk, scion of a distinguished farm family in McLean county, made a powerful impression on them when he described how inadequately agriculture was represented at Washington during the war, when a government commission was arriving at the proper fixed price to announce on wheat. They knew for certain that farmers should be organized so that their voice could be heard in the national councils.

Finally, they got to the heart of the matter facing them that day, namely, the matter of financing the organization. That was a historic battle. Eckhardt and Gregory led the forces for a $5 fee for the IAA, to be collected from each member when he paid his dues to the county organization. It was nip and tuck for hours.

Many delegates had come instructed by their county Farm Bureaus to vote against high membership fees. Among them were Dudley H. Meyers, president of the Adams County Farm Bureau, and Samuel H. Thompson, another delegate from Adams county. Meyers was highly regarded in Farm Bureau circles, so much so that in 1930 he was one of the first men to receive the American Farm Bureau Federation award for distinguished service to agriculture. Thompson was coming into prominence through his service to agriculture in the state legislature. Both men heard the arguments, pro and con, and finally announced that they would vote for individual dues of $5 a year, and take the responsibility of getting the backing of the Farm Bureau membership at home. One by one, delegates fell into line, and when the vote was taken the proposal won by a decisive margin. On reconsideration, the vote was made unanimous. Good feeling prevailed from that time to adjournment, and practically all delegates went home convinced that they had made momentous decisions of enormous consequence to agriculture in Illinois.

Dave O. Thompson, farm adviser in McLean county, had made

55

an eloquent plea for action on a wide front when he made his speech dealing with the farmer's problems of marketing, transportation, finance and taxation. He fired many a delegate with enthusiasm for immediate action, lest present momentum be lost. Some say that his talk had a big influence on the next action, which was to find some way to provide "instant" cash to get going on the planned program right away. After considerable discussion, it was announced that pledge cards had been prepared, calling for delegates right there and then to pledge $100 a year for three years to supply working capital until a permanent dues system could be installed. Everyone hesitated. Then Charles E. Lock from Jersey county, an early graduate of the University of Illinois and a cattle feeder on a 450-acre farm, stood up and spoke briefly, somewhat as follows: "I've got three boys, one of whom is in France, and I want to give them a chance to be Illinois farmers. I want to be the first man to subscribe $100 to the fund to make possible this big association to stand for farmers' interests."

Those quietly spoken words broke the tension, and in less than thirty minutes a hundred delegates had marched up and signed pledge cards. (It is a matter of record that not one of the signers was ever called on to fulfill his pledge although the pledges were used as collateral for loans until money in abundance rolled in from members at $5 each during the next few months.)

The revised constitution and bylaws were presented, and approved by thirty "aye" votes against only two "noes." In further action, delegates elected Harvey J. Sconce, a big landowner in Vermilion county, to the presidency, and Jacob Calvin Sailor of Iroquois county to the vice presidency. (Offices of second and third vice presidents were dropped.) Howard Leonard was continued as treasurer, and apparently Dave O. Thompson agreed that day to become executive secretary, although he did not sign a contract until later. The delegates went home, convinced that at last the IAA was on its way.

Harvey Sconce of Vermilion county inherited a large tract of good land. After attending the University of Illinois, but not graduating, he returned to the ancestral acres, where he lived in

Harvey J. Sconce

a magnificent home. At the university, he had played left half-back on the football team in 1895, and right field on the baseball team in 1896. In 1919, when he became president of the IAA, he was still an athlete, although he had put on considerable weight. An anecdote related by one of his associates is quite revealing. It seems that at one Farm Bureau meeting he had with him an affidavits from the Vermilion county sheriff to the effect that on a certain winter day, following a fairly heavy snowstorm, Harvey Sconce did in fact run down and catch with his hands three rabbits. The oldtimer who tells the story said that Harvey seemed as proud of that achievement as he was of his football record. After his term as IAA president, he toured Europe and reported what he saw in a series of stories for *Prairie Farmer*. A Frank Lowden Republican, his labors in politics yielded little. The depression of the early thirties caught him with a number of unfortunate investments, and he lost all of his land. His former home has been converted into an institution.

Harvey Sconce was capable of great enthusiasm for a cause. He was one of the early advocates of research to find industrial uses for farm commodities. He became interested in a factory that turned cornstalks into paper that was good enough to use in farm magazines, and was so used to print an issue of *Prairie Farmer* in 1928. Now, 35 years later, the paper in that issue has stood the test of time better than the paper made from wood pulp in the same year. The flaw in the project was that the cost of processing the cornstalks was so high that the paper was never competitive with other papers. The result was that the project failed.

Sconce's business judgment may not have been good, but few people ever doubted that his heart was in the right place, or ever questioned his devotion to Farm Bureau.

The significance of the action taken at Peoria was immediately apparent to all thinking farmers. They realized that at long last they had something going for them that could, if properly managed, yield truly big returns. The issues discussed at the meeting and referred to the executive committee (board of directors) were issues that were irritating farmers at the time, issues that could arouse their feelings to fighting pitch:

1. An appropriation by Congress to make good the wheat guarantee for the 1919 crop.
2. Maintenance of the $17.50 minimum hog price until at least April 1.
3. Regulation of Argentine corn imports.
4. Investigation of embargoes on livestock shipments.
5. First roads to be built under the bond issue to be those most important as farm market roads.
6. Investigation of all bills affecting agriculture that may come before the present session of the Illinois legislature.
7. An amendment to the federal farm loan law to increase the maximum amount that may be loaned to any one person to $25,000, with some provision for increasing the percentage of the appraised value of the farm that may be loaned.
8. Repeal of the daylight saving law.

The leaders, especially Gregory, were exultant. In *Prairie Farmer* of February 8, he wrote:

"The annual meeting of the Illinois Agricultural Association at Peoria, January 21 and 22, was the most important meeting ever held in the State of Illinois.

"As a result of this meeting, organized agriculture takes its place beside organized labor and organized business. The Illinois Agricultural Association under the new plan will be strong enough to meet other organized interests on an equal footing, and to speak in a voice that will command attention. The Illinois Agricultural Association will not become a Non-Partisan League or be controlled by bolsheviks. It will not run amuck at every opportunity, nor start gunning for other interests. It will be a sane, sensible, businesslike organization.

"It will not hesitate to act promptly to protect farmers' interests whenever such action may be necessary. The meeting at

Peoria sounded the doom of the 'high wages and cheap food' program. It means that people will no longer willingly accept free trade in foodstuffs and high tariff for manufactured goods. It means that people will not go on working forever in the country on a 14-hour basis in order that people living in town can make a comfortable living in eight. It means that farmers will no longer be content to make four per cent on their money while the business man makes ten.

"There is to be a new deal. The cards are to be shuffled over. The farmer's watchful eye will be on everything that concerns his own welfare and that of the nation. For the Illinois Agricultural Association will not confine its work entirely to the things of the farm, but will take an active interest in everything that makes for better citizens and better Americans. This association will be the sanest, broadest, most progressive force for public welfare in the United States."

Frank W. Bill, then a young farm reporter for the Bloomington *Daily Pantagraph,* who died on March 6, 1962, after serving the *Pantagraph* for 45 years, must have been deeply impressed, because he wrote, in the issue of January 24, 1919:

"It is counted that this state meeting of farmers in Peoria . . . made a big place of history in agriculture. They made the greatest move for effective, powerful organization the farmers have ever attempted in this or any other state. That it was made at the identical hour when for the first time there was every assurance of success, and when the developments in agriculture demand it. And that it was made when to have failed in the unanimous action taken, would have been a step backward not to be recovered for years if at all. It is very much to the point that if these real practical farmers of many counties had not launched this same level-headed movement some wild and irresponsible organization would have been started which could do little good and much harm to the cause of agriculture.

"There has been much talk about farmers' organizing, and it has become much more definite and emphatic since the end of the war. But here is the real thing in a remarkable setting that promises practical success. For two days the men in the state meeting at Peoria discussed the matter with many positive and divergent opinions but finally they came to the unanimous agreement."

In a later story, it is noted by the *Pantagraph* writer, that every man in the McLean county delegation at Peoria signed a pledge card, including C. E. Yanney, a tenant farmer. Robert A. Cowles, who was later to render distinguished service to the IAA for many years as treasurer, also signed a pledge card.

To understand how widespread was the support given the new venture, one should read an analysis of the functions and opportunities of the IAA by Dean Davenport which appeared in *Prairie Farmer* on February 22, only a month after the decisive action taken at Peoria. The Dean was highly respected in the councils of agriculture, particularly for his integrity. His opinions carried great weight. Prefacing his statement with, "I am speaking personally, not officially," he wrote, in part:

"The Illinois Agricultural Association, like the County Farm Bureau, is not an association for holding meetings from time to time, though its members do get together. It is a body organized for business, being always 'on the job.' It is not a defensive organization looking for trouble. It is not negative but positive; that is, it exists not to prevent somebody from doing something objectionable, but rather to get desirable things done; and while I am sure it would be neither blind nor inactive in the face of impending adverse legislation or objectionable business practices, yet upon the whole and mainly it exists to develop agriculture as a business and along commercial lines.

"I am sure that this new agency for progress will not shirk any obvious duty or opportunity that may arise for serving agriculture, but yet upon the whole its great opportunity for service lies in undertaking what has never yet begun except in isolated cases—the development of agriculture in large ways as a commercial business.

"It would be easy to use this effective machinery for the purpose of buying and to some extent it will be so used without doubt, especially for agricultural commodities not satisfactorily handled by the trade; for example, farm seeds, fertilizers, and possibly certain classes of livestock. But wherever the business of merchandising has developed a satisfactory service, however great the temptation, it is not likely to be disturbed by this organization of farmers.

"When prices of all commodities are high and during the period of adjustment after war, the temptation is to utilize any organization at hand as a means of relief. This is what led to the Grange stores of the 70's, but I am sure that with that experience behind us, we shall not make the mistake of assuming that farmers can conduct the grocery and dry goods' business any more successfully than can men whose custom is trade.

"The business of the farmer is to produce and sell. At best he is not much of a buyer, and any great agricultural organization that assumes the buying of ordinary commodities to be its chief purpose in life will speedily spend itself and die from wasted energy.

"While this is true in general, the fact remains that farmers have not always been well served by the trade. The country over they have often been scandalously exploited, both in seeds and fertilizers—two exceedingly important commodities against which the individual farmer has no protection.

"In the meantime the farmer must take care of himself as best he can at some of the most dangerous points, and he will employ all available machinery to provide a safe supply until such time as the trade is able and willing to assume its natural and honorable duty of honest dealing.

"But it was not for this that all this machinery has been created. There is another and much more significant service to be rendered to agriculture, and that is by conducting production with some organized reference to the needs of consumption and the channels of trade—in plain terms, producing what is wanted and putting it into the world's markets in some systematic fashion, instead of growing what we may happen to produce and dumping it upon an unorganized and often an unwilling market."

The Dean went on to explain how the California Fruit Growers' Exchange had brought order out of chaos in the fruit markets; how growing sugar beets on contract had stabilized returns to farmers; and he implied that great opportunities loomed in the field of selling many farm commodities on contract, particularly high quality meats. It is somewhat significant now, more than forty years later, the American Farm Bureau Federation is now pushing contract selling as a major project.

Together, the Dean's statement and Gregory's comments constitute a pretty fair appraisal of what was in the minds of the farmers who set up the IAA. These men were meeting and acting, not in blind rage, with wild accusations against other groups—but in sober consideration of their problems. The Farm Bureau movement lacked the florid oratory and the scathing denunciations of others that accompanied the prairie fire of the Northwest known as the Non-Partisan League movement.

It is well to note that here in Illinois the rank and file of the Farm Bureau membership had little respect for such inflammatory movements as the Non-Partisan League. Their feet were on the ground, and they kept their heads on their shoulders. Like the barons who challenged King John at Runnymede, in 1215, demanding from a greedy and power-hungry king the rights of free men, redress of their grievances, and respect for their human dignity; like the American colonists protesting to an ill-informed and reactionary sovereign against the injustices that had been perpetrated against them—like these were the leaders of the movement that was crystallized at Peoria. They were not ragged and underprivileged people, but rugged and determined business men demanding economic justice. They had learned that the advantages and comforts that came with good times were very desirable, and they had made up their minds that they were going to find out what they could do to improve things—from good roads and electric lights to more stable prices for the things they produced. They deeply believed that they could, by their own efforts, do much to make country life as attractive as they knew it could be made through further technological progress and improved incomes. Raving and ranting, in exaggerated statements against other groups, sentiments verging on the revolutionary—these things were not for them. Rather they calmly set out to see what could be done, through united effort, to improve life on the farm.

Too much credit can not be given to the wisdom and restraint and plain horse sense that characterized their actions in the early days. As we look back over the history of the IAA, considering the many critical situations they faced, we marvel that so few costly mistakes were made. They truly builded better than they knew.

Chapter 7

Action Now

1919 and 1920

Flushed with success over the Peoria meeting, and provided with adequate finances, officers and the executive committee moved fast. Within two months, Dave O. Thompson, with nearly five years of successful experience as farm adviser in McLean county behind him, was hired as executive secretary, an office was opened in the Edison Building in Chicago on March 15, 1919, and the organization went into vigorous action on various fronts.

Most important for the future of the IAA perhaps was membership building. The American Farm Bureau Federation was soon to be organized, and the Farm Bureau movement was to sweep across the country like a prairie fire, with Illinois in the vanguard of the movement.

Vice President Sailor was employed to head the drive for new members. He promptly went to work by recruiting nearly fifty good Farm Bureau men from as many counties to act as solicitors at $10 a day and expenses. These men went to work like born crusaders to build the IAA up to fighting strength. The first drive opened in Lake county, and in a short time the organizers lifted the membership to 493. In Woodford county, the drive netted 891 members; in McLean, 2,040; in Logan, 884; in De Kalb, 2,024; in McHenry, 1,318; and so on. Topping all others was Iroquois county, with 2,739 members. In 32 counties worked by IAA solicitors, membership totaled 40,551. In 27 counties where the local Farm Bureau attempted the job without IAA help, memberships at the end of the year were only 6,549. In 12 other counties, efforts were under way to organize, and many members had signed up, but not reported to the IAA office. All in all, there were probably more than 50,000 Illinois farmers who had paid Farm Bureau dues in that first year. The IAA was off to a flying start.

In the field of legislation, the reorganized Farm Bureau scored a stunning success within the first few months of 1919. At the end of the 51st General Assembly, the results of farmer efforts were heralded in a *Prairie Farmer* story headlined "Farmers Get All They Ask For." *Prairie Farmer* also reported that fourteen important bills were passed with Farm Bureau support, along with eleven minor bills.

The greatest victory was a pure-seed bill to fill the gap left when the bill passed two years before was declared unconstitutional. To get it passed, Farm Bureau had to overcome the persistent opposition of almost the entire seed trade, which had a big stake in keeping Illinois the dumping ground for worthless seed, imported and domestic.

Of outstanding importance was the bill to license and regulate the commission merchants who, in the absence of any governmental supervision, particularly in Chicago, had been fleecing farmers out of vast amounts of money through shady practices.

One of the bills passed, appropriating $125,000 for a state limestone-crushing plant, was considered of great importance at the time, but it turned out to be a dud. Farm Bureau had to learn some lessons in those days, and that bill taught a great lesson, namely, that private industry can invariably do a better job at producing things than can a government-owned outfit. That lesson was never forgotten.

Everything considered, Farm Bureau leaders were greatly encouraged by the results of their first legislative efforts on a massive scale. They felt that at last the voice of the farmers at Springfield was being listened to with respect, and that was a tremendous change from the traditional situation in which leaders of labor and industry seemed to hold all the cards in the legislative game.

In his editorial comments in *Prairie Farmer,* Cliff Gregory, after describing how farm interests had been ignored in previous years, stated:

"This year the situation at Springfield was changed. Illinois farmers had competent experienced representatives on the ground, appointed by the Illinois Agricultural Association. These men took an active part in considering proposed legislation, framing bills, working with committees, and in lining up lukewarm members to support good measures. From the start most of the agricultural measures had easy sailing, compared with what similar measures have had in former years. Nearly everything of importance for which organized agriculture in Illinois asked was made into law.

"It should be a source of satisfaction, too, to know that these results have been accomplished quietly and with little flourish. Few enemies have been made and these were unavoidable. The whole matter has been accomplished by clean, businesslike methods, and Illinois farmers may well have a satisfactory pride in the achievement."

The prestige of the IAA was greatly enhanced by these developments at Springfield. The organization made remarkable progress in other fields, too. In summing up the 1919 achievements, Herman Steen, in *Prairie Farmer,* starts his story with this statement: "For the first time in the history of the state, the farmers of Illinois have an organization of their own, state wide in character, which is adequate to take care of the larger interests of the farm. This is the Illinois Agricultural Association, which, under the slogan of 'Organized for Business,' has grown in one year from an overhead office serving 35 farm bureaus into an institution which carries on its membership rolls the names of over 45,000 farmers who have paid $10 to $15 each. New members are being added at the rate of 300 per day.

The 1919 board of directors. Front row, left to right: J. W. Kinkton, J. R. Fulkerson, J. W. Robinson, Harvey J. Sconce, J. W. Thier, Z. M. Holmes, J. C. Gummersheimer. Back row: I. F. Gillmor, C. V. Gregory, J. P. Stout, Dave Thompson, Howard Leonard, J. W. Morgan, H. T. Marshall, A. A. Hill, G. C. Johnstone.

"Putting the Illinois Agricultural Association upon a business basis and perfecting its organization has been the outstanding achievement of a year of organization among farmers. Tremendous interest in this type of organization was generated in nearby states, and this was the nucleus around which the American Farm Bureau Federation was built in November."

After reviewing the work accomplished, Steen wrote further:

"The operations of the association during 1919 have cost over $100,000. About two-thirds of this has been used in perfecting the organization. It was soon found that the best plan was to employ a force of organizers in the field to explain the organization and to secure members. This work was put in charge of J. C. Sailor of Iroquois county, who had for years been a leader in the farmers' elevator movement. From a modest beginning in May, Sailor has now a well-oiled machine which covers two counties per week and adds 300 members or so to the list every day."

Gregory's comment: "The spirit of organization is taking strong hold of the farmers of America. Never have new farmers' organizations been formed so rapidly as now. These new associations promise much for the future. Wise leadership and careful planning will make the fulfillment of that promise certain. We can learn much from the experience of organizations which have already proved their success. . . ."

The IAA had indeed cut a wide swath during the first year after getting "Organized for Business." It was inevitable that the mushroom growth would lead to trouble later. Farmers had plenty of money in their pockets in 1919, but the deflation in prices in 1920 hit them hard. Many of them signed up in Farm Bureau for three years, giving postdated checks for the two following years. When the time came to honor the checks, there was plenty of trouble. Enthusiasm for Farm Bureau seemed to decline with farm prices. The ensuing difficult situation was handled with great skill, however, even though some of the members who refused to pay their dues were hailed into court. The fact that the organization survived this crisis with honor must be considered a high tribute to its innate strength. (The three-year membership system was dropped later, in favor of a continuing membership contract, under which either party to the contract could terminate it upon proper notice. The three-year plan was started in the early days, when a county would not be recognized by the USDA in the University Better Farming Association unless it had a certain minimum number of members, with financial support pledged for three years.)

The first livestock committee of the IAA, headed by Lyle Johnstone of McLean county, found its work cut out for it. The end of the war had knocked at least 20 per cent off the hog price, and the U.S. Armed Forces had canceled their contracts with the meat packers who had their cellars full of meat bought at high prices. To add to the confusion, the Administration at Washington was investigating the packers, hunting for evidence for use in anti-trust proceedings, and farmers were smarting under practices which had grown up in the central markets and which they believed needed correction. A definite recommendation for a hearing to consider these matters was made at the end of the year. The caution with which the committee moved, however, was typical of the conservative way that the IAA approached all of its problems.

"This recommendation," reported the committee, "is made with a view of arriving at a conclusion which will protect the livestock producers and insure the continuance of profitable conditions surrounding their business, and that without jeopardizing the interests of the consumers, the packers or other legitimate interests involved."

In another statement, the committee said, in part: "Widespread prejudice amongst producers and consumers exists because of the dominant position of the packers in the foodstuff business of the world.

"The best development and the best interests of the livestock industry have been hampered by the frequent agitations and investigations of the packing business.

"The result of every investigation has been an increased lack of confidence until the point has been reached when all concerned must choose between periodical, disastrous investigations caused by lack of public confidence and some form of Federal legislation regulatory of the meat packing business such as will restore and maintain public confidence."

The committee then recommended federal licensing of all packers, stockyards, commission men, handlers of poultry and dairy products, wholesale grocers, and even market-reporting papers, with the whole system administered by a "commission of five high-grade, competent men, to be appointed by the President of the United States, not more than three of whom shall be of the same political party." It was evident from the committee statements that the members fully realized that the packers had their own very real problems in adjusting operations back to a peacetime basis, and the committee members wanted to do all they could to prevent any serious hampering of the service to the livestock industry rendered by packers. They were out to correct abuses, but they wanted to be scrupulously fair to all concerned. The fairness manifested in this instance was to pay big returns in the years ahead.

That first year after reorganizing was one of intense activity. Lee J. Quasey was hired to head a claims department, later to become the transportation department, since the principal activity involved claims against railroads and other public carriers. Plans were laid to set up a livestock department, headed by the best qualified man available. The huge amount of clerical work, generated by the mushrooming membership made a much bigger staff mandatory, and the office was soon bursting at the seams. The staff was enlarged, work for the various departments was stepped up, and new activities were considered. The year might be considered a "shakedown cruise" of the young organization. Bigger quarters had to be secured.

At the annual meeting (the fifth) held in Peoria on January 13-14, 1920, Joseph R. (Uncle Joe) Fulkerson, chairman of the finance committee, reported assets of more than $500,000 with over $10,000 cash in the bank. He also reported that of the nearly $100,000 spent during the past year, some 71 per cent had been used for membership building. He added that this amount was

71

high, but that since the memberships secured had been for a three-year period, he did not consider the cost excessive.

In his presidential address, Harvey Sconce announced that he would not be a candidate for reelection, since he had been invited to work in the campaign of one of the candidates for the Presidency of the United States. Howard Leonard of Woodford county succeeded him. (Dudley H. Meyers, president of the Adams County Farm Bureau nominated Samuel H. Thompson of Adams county but Leonard won by a considerable majority.) Zealy M. Holmes of Peoria county was named vice president, and George A. Fox of De Kalb county, treasurer. Dave O. Thompson began his second year as executive secretary.

Howard Leonard brought a different kind of personality to the IAA presidency. Leonard helped organize the Woodford County Farm Bureau and was a charter member. As an energetic farmer, he was one of the natural farm leaders to emerge from this early period.

Born near Tremont in Tazewell county where he grew to manhood, Leonard moved to the Woodford county farm near Eureka which he farmed for 40 years. He attended Eureka College and married Clara McGuire, daughter of a Eureka grain dealer. The Leonards had four children, two of whom survive.

Leonard had worked hard in the early days of the IAA organization and had served as IAA treasurer since its founding in 1916. On the board of directors, he had been a member of the organization committee.

After his election to the IAA presidency, he was named to the board of the newly formed American Farm Bureau Federation. Although the IAA presidency had not yet become the full-time job it is today, Leonard spent two or three days a week in the Chicago office.

After leaving the IAA presidency in 1923, Leonard continued to make speeches for the IAA and worked in organizing county Farm Bureaus throughout the state. In 1923 he helped organize and was the first chairman of the National Livestock and Meat Board. In 1941, he became Director of Agriculture for the State

Howard Leonard

of Illinois by appointment of Governor Dwight Green. He held that post until his death in 1945.

Pursuant to its policy of hiring top-grade men to head the various departments, the executive committee engaged W. G. Eckhardt, farm adviser in De Kalb county, as director of the grain marketing department. Eckhardt had done an outstanding job as seed corn administrator during the war, and it was conceded that he knew more about grain marketing than anyone else available.

Eckhardt began work on May 1, 1920, soon after the executive committee had approved a program outlined by the grain marketing committee consisting of Robert N. Clarke of Stronghurst, Albert A. Hill of Decatur, and Edwin G. Stifle of Robinson. The committee, in working out its program, had leaned heavily on the counsel of representatives of the Farmers Grain Dealers Association. In fact, the meeting at which the bulk of the work had been done was held at the office of the secretary of the FGDA, Lawrence Farlow, in Bloomington.

Since all hands agreed that Illinois farmers by themselves could do little to influence grain prices, Eckhardt immediately called a conference of Farm Bureau representatives of the Midwest states at Chicago on May 12 and 13. At this conference, it was agreed that farmers must own and operate the county elevators, and also a sales agency, in order to make their influence felt. At a series of 15 meetings in Illinois the plans were explained to farmers. At all meetings, farmers were enthusiastic for the plans.

Meanwhile, James R. Howard, president of the American Farm Bureau Federation, had been consulted, and he cooperated to the fullest extent by calling a meeting of all farmers' organizations interested in grain marketing, to be held at Chicago on July 23 and 24. At this meeting the "Committee of Seventeen," which was to make history of a sort, was appointed, and Eckhardt was a member. This committee was directed to "consider, formulate, and submit hereafter for consideration, a definite plan of organization whereby all organizations of grain producers can conduct cooperative grain marketing through one or more central organizations or grain exchanges, or such other solution of the cooperative marketing problem as may be approved by such committee . . ."

The committee went right to work by hiring a staff to work out the data necessary to intelligent procedure. "The appointment of this committee," reported Eckhardt at the 1921 annual meeting of the IAA, "I consider the most progressive and concrete step forward in the past hundred years for agriculture." He predicted that by spring a definite plan would be forthcoming. (Forces set in motion by the committee were to lead to disaster within two years in the failure of the U.S. Grain Growers. Of that, more later. Eckhardt resigned from the IAA to become treasurer of USSGG in 1921.)

During 1920, the fruit and vegetable committee, made up of Charles F. Kiest of Anna, Frank Dieckman of South Holland, Alvin O. Eckert of Belleville, and Albert B. Leeper of Lima, had hired Charles E. Durst of the University of Illinois to head up the fruit and vegetable department, starting work early in 1921.

John R. Bent, director of the phosphate-limestone department, reported that he had had difficulties in disposing of the 50,000 tons of phosphate contracted for in 1920, and that a smaller amount would be negotiated for in 1921. He also reported unsatisfactory progress on the projected limestone-crushing plant being built by the State of Illinois at the state penitentiary at Chester.

J. C. Sailor, director of the organization department, was able to report another sensational year. Membership had more than doubled, to a total of 107,700. Farm Bureau was a smashing success. Although there were to be setbacks, and soon, the organization had become so much a part of the daily life of Illinois farmers that its future was never in much doubt. It had "arrived."

IAA prestige had steadily increased, more farmers were taking an interest in activities at the state level, and it was found necessary to go to a bigger city for the 1921 annual meeting. Chicago, with plenty of hotel space, was selected, and the LaSalle Hotel was named as convention headquarters. At that meeting, on January 13 and 14, officers and members could look back on the preceding year with satisfaction. Membership stood at 107,628, total income at $420,679.83. A dizzy pace had been set. Some of the older heads were apprehensive. "Uncle Joe" Fulkerson of Jersey county, reporting as chairman of the finance committee, sounded a word of warning: "There are many bumps ahead that we do not know about, and we cannot run with safety without a brake. . . . When you look over the report and see that our Association has spent last year a little over $386,000, we wonder whether the finance committee will remind you of the epitaph on the departed motorist's tombstone, which reads:

"Here lies John Blake,
Tread softly as you pass;
He thought his foot was on the brake—
But it was on the gas."

Mr. Fulkerson went on to say: "I hope to see the day come in the near future when the IAA may have a hundred thousand dollars invested in U.S. government bonds, which could be put up as collateral at a moment's notice. This idea of collecting dues and tying them up may not be very popular with the members down home, but it is good business. Think it over."

It should be noted here that among the changes made in the constitution and bylaws at the 1920 meeting, was one which limited the elective offices to those of president and vice president. Secretary and treasurer were to be appointed from then on.

In 1920, a number of departments had been set up and staffed. Plans had been made to go in heavily for marketing activities. Department heads were as follows: William G. Eckhardt, grain; Chris Larsen, dairy; Charles E. Durst, fruit and vegetable; John R. Bent, phosphate-limestone; Herbert W. Mumford, livestock; Lee J. Quasey, claim and service; and Edgar L. Bill, publicity.

Edgar L. Bill was a son of the well-known farm writer, Arthur J. Bill of Normal, editor of the *Farmer's Voice,* and farm editor of *The Daily Pantagraph* in Bloomington. Young "Eddie" was tuned to the same wave length as Dave Thompson. He was able and resourceful, and he saw to it that the sensational story of the Farm Bureau movement got into most of the daily papers and all of the farm papers in Illinois. He also arranged to have Farm Bureau speakers appear at non-farm meetings wherever possible, to let business men particularly know what organized farmers were up to in Illinois.

When Bill resigned in 1922 to join Dave Thompson in organizing Homestead Films, he was succeeded by Lynn J. Montross, who later became a successful novelist. Succeeding him was Harry C. Butcher who later went into radio and became a vice president of Columbia Broadcasting System. During World War II, he became a captain in the Navy, and was assigned foreign duty as aide to General Eisenhower. At the end of the war he wrote "My Three Years With Eisenhower."

Others to serve in the IAA publicity department included George Thiem, who later attained journalistic fame by twice winning a Pulitzer prize with the Chicago Daily News; Caspar L. "Cap" Mast, now president of the Millers' National Federation; George C. Biggar, now general manager and part owner of Radio Station WLBK, De Kalb; James H. White, who has had a fine career as part owner and assistant to the president of a farm paper in Denver; James C. "Scotty" Thomson, who is now editor of Prairie Farmer; and Creston Foster, news service director for the AFBF. Butcher, Thiem, Montross, and Mast are all listed in Who's Who in America. This array of talent reflects the enlightened personnel policies early adopted by the IAA and its affiliated companies. It tells us much as we search for reasons for the smashing success of this great venture of Illinois farmers.

Officers and executive committee were agreed that the best man available should be hired for any particular job, and they did not hesitate to pay salaries big enough to attract such men. It was generally considered that this policy paid off in quality of service rendered. Professor Herbert W. Mumford (head of the Animal Husbandry Department of the University of Illinois, and later Dean of the College of Agriculture) was persuaded to become head of the livestock department, and livestock men all over the state regarded it as an achievement of the first order that the organization was able to enlist the services of such a distinguished educator.

Professor Mumford went to work on February 16, 1920, and by the end of the year had a large staff working on a comprehensive survey of every phase of livestock marketing. He had enlisted the services of such men as Francis M. Simpson, Lee Devine, L. L. Corrie, E. M. Clark, Charles A. Stewart, and John C. Watson—the same John C. Watson who won fame in later years as head of the IAA activities in the field of public taxation. In fact, early in 1921, Watson was named IAA statistician, and it was not long until he was devoting practically full time to taxation.

The work of Mumford and his staff was concerned with basic conditions in marketing livestock, and the results were to have a heavy impact on the industry. It is apparent that he had decided that the free and open market for farm animals was the best system known, everything considered; and therefore centered his activities on improving marketing operations within that system.

The newly organized American Farm Bureau Federation, under its first president, James R. Howard of Iowa, very quickly initiated nation-wide activities in this field. Howard appointed the livestock marketing committee of fifteen, which was to make history by organizing the National Live Stock Producers Association, with headquarters in Chicago. Before the year was out, this association had a cooperative "producers" commission agency in operation at National Stockyards, East St. Louis. This was the first of many agencies set up in major markets all over the United States. Most of them are still in operation today. In these activities, the IAA and the American Farm Bureau Federation were plowing new ground. They were pioneers in the true sense, and this work was to have a tremendous impact on the marketing of livestock throughout the country.

In commenting on these developments in his report for 1921, Professor Mumford wrote, in part:

"The Live Stock Marketing Plan, national in scope, as rapidly as it can be put in force, is entirely practicable and is worthy of the support of every livestock man not only in Illinois but throughout the entire country. The degree of benefit that results from the operation of this plan will be directly in proportion to the extent to which it is supported by livestock producers. It points the way in which a national voice in livestock affairs and by which significant and permanent improvement in livestock marketing may be brought about. Neither it nor any other plan can be of real service unless it is widely patronized and loyally supported."

Chapter 8

Organized For Business

At the seventh annual meeting of the IAA in Springfield, January 11 and 12, 1922, Howard Leonard was reelected president. Samuel H. Thompson of Adams county, who had been a member of the executive committee, was elected vice president, succeeding Zealy M. Holmes. Thompson had rendered valiant service to agriculture in the state legislature; he knew precinct politics, and even in those days he was a patriarchal figure, tall, slightly stooped, with gray hair and mustache. The father of seven children, he lived just across the road from the house in which he was born, and he farmed some 500 acres of land. He was destined to become one of the revered leaders of Farm Bureau.

The year 1922 marked a fundamental change in the IAA at the administrative level. Dave O. Thompson had served as executive secretary under a contract for three years, ending early in 1922. He "ran the show" as the executive officer. There was no question of renewing the contract, because he had told the other officers frankly that he did not feel that he was the person to lead the organization further along the road that the IAA must follow in the years immediately ahead. That road was indicated by

81

the slogan which had been adopted: "Organized for Business." Thompson regarded himself as primarily an educator. He did not relish becoming involved in the affairs of business. He had done his job well as farm adviser in McLean county, and he reveled in getting the state organization under way. He loved promoting a good cause, but he clearly perceived that the IAA would soon be deep in business ventures involving millions of dollars. He felt that he had completed the job he had set out to do, namely, getting the organization under way, and now he wanted to get out and get into something better suited to his temperament and his tastes. The executive committee had been doing some sober thinking after Thompson's decision became known. Members of the committee had come to the conclusion that administrative decisions, as well as policy decisions, should be the responsibility of the president, who was elected by the membership. Therefore, they had sponsored a change in the constitution and bylaws to bring this about. This change meant that the president would have to serve on practically a full-time basis.

George A. Fox gave up his post as treasurer to succeed Thompson as secretary, and Robert A. Cowles of Bloomington became treasurer (on a per diem basis). Cowles was, in the finest sense, a gentleman. Of overpowering integrity, tall, dignified and urbane, he was as meticulous in dress and behavior as he was in scanning a bookkeeper's report or a financial statement. No one who has ever served the organization was more of a perfectionist. His insistence on proper structure in any business set up by the IAA was to prove of inestimable value in the ensuing years. His hairsplitting could become exasperating to his associates, but his essential "rightness" could never be questioned. He became a tower of strength to the burgeoning complex of the IAA and affiliates that was taking form.

In its program of activities during 1921 and 1922, the IAA gave cooperative marketing developments a big place. This was entirely natural, since it reflected a very real trend in agricultural affairs. Herman Steen, who wrote a book on cooperative marketing which was published in 1923, has said that two great waves

82

of sentiment swept across the country, culminating just after World War I—one of them for farm organizations, and the other for cooperative marketing. Steen himself was caught in the latter, as he left the managing editor's desk at *Prairie Farmer* in 1923 to become secretary of the Indiana Wheat Pool. The wave was further reflected by the passage of the Capper-Volstead Act by Congress in 1922. This Act freed bona fide farmer cooperatives and labor unions from prosecution under the anti-trust laws, and permitted cooperatives to agree on uniform prices, something that corporations could not legally do. Senator Arthur C. Capper of Kansas sponsored many farm measures of which the Capper-Volstead Act was the most far-reaching.

The IAA in these years provided help in organizing cooperatives, loaned money to many, and gave widespread publicity to such ventures. Many individuals accorded undue merit to cooperative action as a means of virtually solving the farmer's economic problems. In fact, it might fairly be said that Herbert Hoover himself, to judge by his speeches and actions as President of the United States, put too much reliance on this principle as a means of assuring prosperity to farmers. The principal farm measure that he advocated and signed into law was the Agricultural Marketing Act of 1929, which in operation fell far short of what he seemed to expect of it.

The IAA, along with the American Farm Bureau Federation, went "all out" for the "co-op" movement. Many of the enterprises sponsored by the organization are functioning well today, but others fell by the wayside. The biggest failure was probably the U.S. Grain Growers, which was organized with great fanfare and publicity, as well as solid backing by farm groups in 1921 but in 1922 it was in deep trouble. Farm Bureau leaders tried to save it by reorganizing when it was in the red by more than a quarter of a million dollars. Down it went, and with it went the hopes and dreams of William G. Eckhardt, the man who had done so much for the farmers of De Kalb county and the early IAA.

The outcome of IAA ventures in livestock marketing was quite different. The National Livestock Producers Association, created in late 1921 largely through Farm Bureau efforts, brought tangible results to farmers almost immediately. This nation-wide group founded the Producers Livestock Commission Association, East St. Louis, Illinois, which opened for business on January 2, 1922, and within days it was handling 25 to 40 carloads of livestock daily. Soon "Producer" agencies were to open in Chicago and Peoria, as well as in Indianapolis and Buffalo, Cincinnati, Denver, Salt Lake City, and many other cities.

There are those who contend that the farmer-owned livestock-selling agencies operate just as independent commission men operate and so do little to improve market conditions; but there is little doubt that the "Producer" agencies have brought much-needed, and wholesome competition into the markets. This competition certainly has helped to keep commission charges down to reasonable figures. The same may be said with equal certainty with respect to cooperative activities in grain marketing. Few unprejudiced observers would deny that commission charges for selling grain have been kept down by the additional competition. The co-op interests did not become unduly discouraged by the failure of U.S. Grain Growers. More failures followed, but today a good share of all grain produced is marketed through farmer-owned elevators and cooperative sales agencies on the big markets.

It should be pointed out here that exemption from income taxes is apparently not essential to co-op success. The big farm co-ops fathered by the IAA do not operate with income tax exemption; neither does the GLF, famed co-op organized by the Grange, the Farm Bureau, and the Dairymen's League of the New York milkshed. Owners of such organizations, who are farmers, take justifiable pride in their achievements in creating business enterprises that can compete with the best independents without the advantage of income tax exemption.

As subsequent chapters will clearly show, many of the business affiliates sponsored by the IAA have become spectacular successes. The story of these enterprises is truly an epic of American enterprise.

The year 1922 brought some bumps in the road that had seemed so smooth the year before. Dues collections dropped from

$441,239.68 in 1921 to $362,460.30. Considerable trouble had been encountered in enforcing membership contracts that had been signed for three years in 1919 and 1920. This situation reflected the farm depression that had begun in 1920, following wartime conditions. Farmers had far less money to spend, some of them were in serious difficulties on account of land purchases at high prices, and some felt that Farm Bureau was slow in producing results that could be realized in terms of money by the member. It is a tribute to the basic soundness of the organization, and to the skill and judgment of officers, executive committee, and key employees that this crisis was weathered in good shape, and that the vast bulk of the $150,000 or so of back dues that was outstanding in early 1922 was finally collected—and without generating too much ill will in the counties.

A policy of retrenchment was adopted, the budget for 1923 was pruned down to realistic size, and all hands went resolutely to work to carry the young organization forward to the goal that they had so hopefully set for themselves three years before. George E. Metzger, a Purdue graduate, who had served as assistant farm adviser in Macoupin county, was brought in as director of organization-publicity, started an intensive publicity program designed to keep farmers informed about Farm Bureau and its objectives, which proved very effective. Furthermore, he arranged for schools of instruction for solicitors in 38 locations. A total of 5,536 people attended these schools. From that time on, the bulk of the soliciting of new members, as well as the renewing of past membership contracts, was done by farmers themselves, rather than by paid solicitors. This change in method brought about great economies in building and maintaining membership.

Metzger was to become one of the all-time stalwarts of Farm Bureau in Illinois. He spoke with vigor, at times with machine-gun rapidity, and with great earnestness. He was a worthy successor to J. C. Sailor, the man who had commanded the early "flying squadrons" of organizers who had built the membership to such high levels in 1920 and 1921. George remained on the job until March 1, 1950, when he moved to his Indiana farm, where he carries on as these words are written, at the age of 73, doing

George E. Metzger

all his own work on a farm of substantial size, but in his own words, "not overworking" because he has his work so fully mechanized.

To indicate the range of activities of the IAA in the business field during the early twenties, the record shows that the service-claim department recovered more than $15,000 for members on freight overcharges or damage in transit during 1921; that nearly 500,000 pounds of wool had been handled in 1919; that cooperative dairy marketing organizations had been set up in Jo Daviess, Stephenson, Adams, and Madison counties; that six egg marketing groups were functioning; that the Illinois Fruit and Vegetable Exchange at Centralia was handling 75 per cent of the early apples and peaches produced in the state; that the onion-set growers were organized in Cook county, where 80 per cent of the onion sets grown in the entire country were produced—all of this before the end of 1922. Early in 1921, to house the growing staff, larger quarters were leased in the Transportation building, 608 South Dearborn Street, Chicago. Headquarters remained here until the IAA moved into its own building at 43 East Ohio Street, Chicago, in June, 1947.

The year 1922 was to see another significant development, a full-scale attack on the problem of taxation. John C. Watson was nominally the IAA statistician, but in 1922 his major concern was tax assessments of farm land. In May, 1922, the IAA published Watson's pamphlet, "Taxation of Farm Land in Illinois," which revealed that the Illinois Tax Commission had arbitrarily raised the assessed valuation of farm land for state taxes in many counties to such an extent that farmers were forced to pay increased state taxes amounting to $786,219 in 1919, 1920, and 1921. The thing that irked farmers was that the increased assessments were applied *only* to farm land. It was shown further that the Tax Commission assessments were often used by local tax officials as an excuse for raising assessments for county and local taxes also. It was obvious that farm land was being discriminated against. This was probably a natural development, since prices paid for farm land had risen sensationally during and immediately after the war.

Sales as high as $500 an acre had been recorded. What was overlooked was the fact that wartime prices had dropped with a sickening thud, and that farmers faced higher production costs while farm prices fell to disastrous levels.

The studies that Watson published precipitated a fight to the bitter end with the Illinois Tax Commission. The end was a farmer victory, and a tremendous increase in prestige for the IAA.

Watson went about the work most methodically. Whenever a survey was completed in a county, the figures were sent to the county Farm Bureau for use in backing up its arguments with the county board of review. In one county, the board of review reduced the total assessed valuation of farm lands by $2,435,830, and in another county the board of review abandoned a contemplated increase of nearly $800,000 as a direct result of Farm Bureau intervention. The Farm Bureau won these battles simply because it never went into action without incontrovertible facts to support its plea.

This phase of the tax work culminated at a hearing before the Illinois Tax Commission in November, 1922. The outcome was startling to many people. In summing up the victory, the *IAA News Letter* for December 28, 1922, reported, in part:

"Decreases in equalized state land valuations which amount to a reduction in farm taxes of $557,550.00 for 1922 or approximately twice the sum spent by the IAA during the year for all projects, are announced by the Illinois Tax Commission.

"This amount, combined with the raises in valuations for 1921 and 1922 which were prevented, makes a grand total of $1,072,050, which has been saved farmers in land taxes during the past two years, a sum approximately four times as large as the amount spent by the IAA for all projects in 1922.

"The IAA and the county Farm Bureaus were the first and only organizations in the history of state taxation to appear before the Illinois Tax Commission for taxation justice for the farmer."

It was obvious that the new organization was making good in a big way. The Farm Bureau was indeed proving itself a good "hired man" for the farmer.

Chapter 9

The Scene Shifts
1923-25

At the eighth annual meeting in Chicago, January 17 and 18, 1923, events occurred that were to have profound effects on the future of the IAA. Vice President Samuel H. Thompson was elected president, succeeding Howard Leonard; Alvin O. Eckert of Belleville became vice president; and Earl C. Smith of Detroit was named to the executive committee for the first time. Thompson was to become one of the foremost advocates of national legislation (the McNary-Haugen Bill) to stabilize farm prices; and Earl Smith was to succeed him as president and to remain in that office for twenty years—a period during which he became the principal architect of the structure and policy of the IAA.

Samuel H. Thompson was born on August 18, 1863, near Quincy, Illinois. As a boy, he went to country school during the winter and worked on the farm at other times. In talking about the early days, Mr. Thompson often told of driving 12 horses in a circle to supply power for the threshing machine in use at the time. In later years, he and his brother Alex operated a steam threshing outfit for the neighborhood "ring" for a number of years. He remembered well the walking plow and cultivator, as well as the advent of the self-binder.

Samuel H. Thompson

The public career of this pioneer began in 1885, when he became a tax collector, and continued work on his father's farm. He later served as road commissioner and supervisor. In 1916, he was elected to the Illinois General Assembly. In 1889, at the age of 26, he married Miss Lemmie Dickhut, and the young couple immediately bought an 80-acre farm, going into debt for the entire cost, $6,000. They prospered, and soon began to add to their acreage, which eventually increased to more than 500. The Quincy airport today occupies 160 acres of land that the Thompsons owned.

Four boys and three girls were born to Sam and Lemmie Thompson. They lived to celebrate their golden wedding in 1939. In 1945, Mrs. Thompson died of shock two hours after the death of a daughter, Miss Florence Thompson.

Thompson became president of the Broadway Bank of Quincy in 1918 and he was always proud of the fact that the bank survived the great depression without difficulty. His banking experience was of great value to him when he served as president of the IAA, and later, of the American Farm Bureau Federation.

During Thompson's first year as president, Professor Mumford, having completed his task in livestock marketing, returned to the University as Dean of the College of Agriculture, and Charles A. Stewart, his assistant, succeeded him.

By action of the executive committee, the name of the statistical service bureau was changed to the department of taxation and statistics, with John C. Watson as director. Watson was able to report a grand total of estimated real estate tax reductions of $3,963,773—$1,800,000 county and local, and $2,163,773 state, over the past three years.

Under President Thompson, work of the various departments was expanded and improved, cooperative marketing activities were stepped up and the overall program of the organization seemed to settle into a fairly consistent pattern.

The Producers' agencies were going great guns, and plans were under way for invading other markets. Francis M. "Fanny" Simpson, general manager of the National Livestock Producers' Association, reported that the six agencies then in operation had handled 20,719 carloads of livestock in the first five months of the year—more than they had handled during the entire previous year. That total represented 8.5 per cent of all receipts in those markets.

The Illinois Fruit Growers' Exchange joined a nation-wide sales agency, the Federated Fruit and Vegetable Growers, Inc., with 150 sales offices. Charles E. Durst soon resigned as director of the fruit and vegetable department to accept a job with the sales agency, and was succeeded by Albert B. Leeper.

Arthur D. Lynch, widely experienced in dairy marketing, succeeded Chris Larsen, who resigned to become Dean of Agriculture at South Dakota State College. Lynch worked energetically to establish co-ops in more markets, and to organize more farmer-owned creameries.

Co-op enthusiasts were jubilant when Governor Len Small signed the so-called "Co-op" bill legalizing co-op contracts on June 22, 1923. The bill was passed over rugged opposition, but the farm forces easily prevailed. The House vote was 99 to 47.

The disorganized and reorganized U.S. Grain Growers was still floundering. Ed Cunningham of Iowa, the new president, finally gave up, taking the easy way out by accepting appointment to the Federal Reserve Board, early in May.

The cooperative organizations set up by the IAA frequently got into trouble—often financial trouble. Some mistakes had to be corrected, and the IAA supplied the legal assistance needed to reorganize on a sounder basis. This happened to the dairy co-ops in Rock Island and Stephenson counties. The Egyptian Seed Growers had to be reorganized. In this work Donald Kirkpatrick, a young attorney who had come from Ohio to assist Newton Jenkins, became a prominent figure, so prominent in fact that when Jenkins resigned a year or so later to run for the Senate, "Kirk" was quickly made director of the legal department. In 1923, he spent 49 days in East St. Louis, reorganizing the Illinois-Missouri Milk Producers Association. He was destined to become one of the key men on the IAA staff for many years. He, with the

Donald Kirkpatrick

help later of Paul Mathias and Harry Meloy, handled legal matters involved in the creation of the IAA affiliates which have been so spectacularly successful.

During 1923, Watson pushed his tax work with increasing zeal. He could speak pretty plainly when the situation demanded it. He had a particularly stormy meeting with the board of review in Vermilion county, where he found that farm real estate was assessed at 45 to 50 per cent of actual value, while town and city property was assessed at only 25 to 40 per cent of real value. When the board of review members showed distinct coolness toward his request for equalization, he said: "Are you going to permit one class of property to pay more than its share of taxes? If so, why did you take your oath of office?"

Thanks to the energy of George E. Metzger, four new county Farm Bureaus were organized during 1923, even though a great deal of time had been given to collecting dues for past years. When the annual meeting was held in Galesburg, January 16-17, 1924, the books showed 60,569 paid-up members. It was a big drop from the 95,007 of the previous year, but considering the prevailing economic conditions, the wonder is that the loss was not even greater.

Fortunately, the budget had been pruned considerably, and the IAA lived within its income by a considerable margin.

Harmony reigned at the convention. Sam Thompson was re-elected president, and Chauncey B. Watson of De Kalb county was named vice president. Fox continued as secretary.

The year 1924 was to see a shift in emphasis in the work of the IAA. At the convention, delegates had reaffirmed their faith in cooperative marketing, but before long the organization was to get into one of the hottest fights in its history over federal legislation, a fight from which Sam Thompson was to emerge as one of the great farmer advocates for national legislation designed to stabilize grain prices. From this time on, the IAA was to put major emphasis on federal "programs" for agriculture.

Chester C. Davis had left the IAA to go to Washington to work full time with George N. Peek and Hugh S. Johnson (fathers of the idea of "parity") in getting before Congress the bills which were to be called the McNary-Haugen Bills. Peek and Johnson were farm implement manufacturers (Moline Plow Company, Moline, Illinois) who crusaded for "Equality for Agriculture" just after World War I. In 1921, Peek was discussing their plan, which involved selling surpluses abroad at world prices in order to maintain a fair domestic price. A reporter remarked that his plan needed a good slogan. Peek said quickly: "Equality for Agriculture," and henceforth the battle was fought under that standard.

Senator Charles L. McNary, a lawyer from Salem, Oregon, who served continuously in the Senate from 1918 to his death in 1944, was deeply interested in the Peek-Johnson plan, and he became its champion in the Senate. (In 1940, McNary was candidate for the vice presidency, running mate of Wendell Willkie.) The House champion was Gilbert N. Haugen of Northlake, Iowa, a congressman from 1899 to 1933. All five bills based on the Peek-Johnson plan, which were introduced from 1924 to 1928 bore the McNary-Haugen label. Secretary of Agriculture Henry C. Wallace was a strong advocate of the plan.

The IAA fought for the first McNary-Haugen Bill, which had been endorsed by the executive committee of the American Farm Bureau Federation. It provided for an agricultural export commission and a government-owned corporation with capital stock of $200 million. The idea was to buy enough wheat, for instance, to keep domestic prices stable at a profitable level, then dump the surplus abroad for what it would bring. It was to be financed by an equalization fee paid by the farmer on whatever he sold. In speaking to the executive committee during the debate, Sam Thompson said:

"I don't believe in political remedies as a rule, but this bill looks like an honest effort to overcome the emergency problem. . . . As I see it, the bill is a national compulsory pool with the whole cost of operation on the farmers. It is not paternalism, but does take care of the emergency."

The die was cast. The course had been set that was to be followed for many, many years. Within a few weeks, Thompson suggested to Gray Silver, Washington representative of the American Farm Bureau Federation, that he call Midwest Farm Bureau leaders and others interested to Washington to plan a campaign to get the McNary-Haugen Bill on the legislative calendar. The campaign was carried out, but both *Prairie Farmer* and *Wallace's Farmer* later charged Silver's efforts were not very vigorous.

On March 6, 85 county Farm Bureau presidents met in Chicago and unanimously passed a resolution practically demanding that their congressmen and senators get busy and pass the bill. The county leaders were really on fire. Sam Thompson found himself leading a crusade. He spoke often and vehemently on the subject. He carried on a long debate with Congressman Henry T. Rainey of the 20th Congressional District, who sincerely felt that the bill was a mistake, and would be vetoed if passed.

On April 8, 1924, President Thompson wrote a long letter to President Coolidge, pleading with him to support the bill. Thompson was not fighting alone. Farm forces all over the Midwest were working hard. IAA Treasurer Cowles was one of the ablest of his lieutenants. He made a talk over Radio Station WOC, Davenport, Iowa, that stirred many farmers to action in behalf of "farm equality." He made many trips to Washington to help out there. Other members of the IAA staff were making speeches for the bill, and the information department was promoting the cause in every way possible. George Fox spoke at many meetings. Many businessmen joined farmers in demanding "equality" for the farmer. Petitions signed by all sorts of people rained down on Congress. Support for the bill was impressive.

When some congressmen expressed doubt regarding the grassroots support of the legislation, Frank Barton, chairman of the IAA legislative committee, appealed to Farm Bureau leaders all over the state, and in less than a week had secured 58,000 signatures to a petition, directed to the President of the United States and the Congress, asking for approval and early passage of the McNary-Haugen Bill. After that, few legislators had any doubts about how Illinois farmers felt about the issue.

All efforts were unavailing; on June 3, Congress rejected the legislation by a decisive margin. This setback only renewed and strengthened the determination of the Farm Bureau and other forces. Plans were laid to renew the fight the following year.

* * *

The year 1924 saw the beginning of an IAA service that was to affect profoundly the course of the IAA. In studying the reasons for failure of farmer-owned grain elevators and other businesses, IAA investigators had concluded that the principal cause of failure was sloppy accounting. They further determined to do something about the situation by organizing a cooperative auditing association called the Illinois Agricultural Cooperative Association. George R. Wicker, an accountant with wide experience in Minnesota, was employed to manage it, and Vernon Vaniman of Virden, was hired as field man. Vaniman, was serving as assistant state leader of Extension work, and he undertook the work on leave of absence from the University of Illinois. He never went back to Extension work, and he became one of the key staff men in various activities of the IAA for many years. Later, he did membership work for the American Farm Bureau Federation, continuing until his sudden death while on a speaking trip.

The new service was an instant success. By the end of the year auditing service was being rendered to 112 clients, 49 of which were farmers' elevators, along with 39 county Farm Bureaus and 24 other cooperative groups. Four accountants were working, and a branch office was opened at Springfield. It is probably safe to say that the reliable and efficient auditing service provided was one of the greatest factors in the success of IAA-sponsored business ventures from that time on.

* * *

From the beginning, the IAA showed great interest in problems of education. In the early years, it was apparent that the organization lacked facts upon which to base any program of action. In 1924, therefore, the educational committee employed George W. Willett, a high school principal from LaGrange, to undertake a comprehensive survey of the entire public school system and laws relating to it. Ten thousand questionnaires were sent out to find out exactly what farm people wanted in the way of schools, what they were getting, and what changes in existing laws were desired. When the questionnaires were processed, it was discovered that most farm people were opposed to consolidated schools, largely because of poor roads. It was immediately apparent that any further extension of consolidation must be approached carefully, even though eventual consolidation seemed almost inevitable. It was well that this problem was approached cautiously, as will be seen in later developments. Later in the year, John Watson and J. H. Whisnand of Coles county were asked to serve on the advisory council to the state educational commission. Further developments will be discussed in a later chapter.

The IAA did a great piece of work in 1924 by helping to stop in its tracks a plan to create another cooperative known as the Grain Marketing Company, following the failure of U.S. Grain Growers. The plan had the backing of the American Farm Bureau Federation. In fact, Gray Silver, Washington representative of the AFBF, was named president of the new company, and John Coverdale, secretary-treasurer, with full approval of the AFBF board of directors. The IAA, with help from the Indiana Farm Bureau and a few others, showed the plan up for what it was, namely, a scheme under which a number of old-line grain companies would unload their properties upon the new cooperative at a price far in excess of their true value. This was one of the few occasions when the IAA had to oppose the AFBF. At the time, it seemed likely that the IAA would withdraw from the national organization, but cool heads prevailed and the breach was healed.

The phosphate-limestone department continued its good work in maintaining quality standards, in finding economical sources, in advising county Farm Bureaus on all matters including storage methods and the possibilities of developing farmer-owned plants for producing agricultural limestone. Nearly 260,000 tons of limestone were handled cooperatively during the year, out of the total used in the state of 500,000 tons. This latter amount was about one-quarter of all agricultural limestone used in the whole USA.

On March 3, 1924, a project long under consideration was completed by organizing the Illinois Farm Bureau Serum Association. The farm advisers had been vaccinating hogs for members for a long time, and they taught farmers how to do the work themselves. This situation led to a real tussle with the veterinarians, who objected to farm advisers and farmers doing work that veterinarians considered their own and exclusive job. The farmers won the battle. Before the year was out, 46 county Farm Bureaus had purchased at uniform prices no less than 20 million cubic centimeters of serum. As was the case in so many other business services later to be provided by the IAA, this development came in response to demands by members.

One of the most constructive pieces of work done in 1924, was its support of area testing of cattle for tuberculosis, which resulted eventually in Illinois becoming free of bovine tuberculosis. Arthur D. Lynch of the dairy department, C. A. Stewart of the livestock marketing department, and his successor, William E. Hedgcock, who had been farm adviser in Peoria county, took the lead in this work. Later, M. H. Petersen was employed to head a department, the T.B. eradication department. The IAA fought for and secured reaffirmation and enforcement of the order by the state veterinarian requiring a 60-day retest of all cattle brought into the state for dairy or breeding purposes. A move for a state appropriation to indemnify owners of reacting cattle was pushed to success in 1925, when the legislature appropriated $3 million for T.B. eradication. Results were reflected in the fact that at that time, one-fourth of the entire federal appropriation for indemnities was allotted to Illinois.

* * *

At the tenth annual meeting, held in Champaign, January 15-16, 1925, Sam Thompson was re-elected to his third term as president, and H. E. Goembel of Hooppole, Henry county, was named vice president by a vote of 76-74, over Earl C. Smith.

It was another harmonious meeting. Action of the leaders was solidly endorsed by the voting delegates, and the move to pull out of the AFBF was stopped, but the delegates adopted a stinging resolution, as follows:

"Be it resolved that we look with exceeding disfavor upon any evidence of the attempt of those of the present or past administration to play politics or use the influence of the American Farm Bureau Federation to further any commercial or selfish interests; that we do not favor disruption of the American Farm Bureau Federation and the establishment of a precedent of a withdrawal, believing existing evils may be corrected to better advantage from within the organization and that we recommend continued support of the American Farm Bureau Federation at this time.

"We therefore, direct the officers and executive committee to use every prerogative at their command to the end that the American Farm Bureau Federation shall purge itself of all evil influences that seem to exist at this time."

That was blunt language that could not be misconstrued. Farm Bureau leaders in other states were not in full accord with the Illinois attitude toward what was going on in the AFBF, but many were not satisfied with things as they were. The showdown came at the 1925 convention of the AFBF in Chicago. President Bradfute was a candidate for reelection, and Sam Thompson became the candidate of the "reform" group. Vice President Edward A. O'Neal was also a candidate, but the battle was between Bradfute and Thompson. After seven inconclusive ballots, the insurgent group won by the narrow margin of 24 to 19. Everybody knew that the AFBF course was firmly set now. The new leadership would scrupulously avoid questionable promotional activities and throw its full strength into the fight for enactment of the McNary-Haugen Bill when Congress met early in 1962.

* * *

Many Farm Bureau oldtimers will remember 1925 as the year in which a tiny acorn was planted in the insurance field. That acorn has now developed into one of the sturdiest oaks in the Farm Bureau forest. For a number of years, Farm Bureau members had been wondering aloud why the IAA could not do something about the prevailing unsatisfactory situation with respect to fire insurance on farm buildings. There were hundreds of little farmers' companies, run largely by farmers in their spare time. Rates were low, but practically nobody was out selling. If you wanted insurance, you went to the local agent and bought it. Furthermore, the little companies were handicapped by a state law which limited the amount of coverage that could be written on any one risk. The result was that most farm buildings were woefully underinsured. As soon as the facts were revealed, the IAA insurance committee, made up of George F. Tullock of Rockford, I. N. Hosford of Hamilton, and Otis Kircher of Danville decided that here was indeed a golden opportunity for the Farm Bureau to render service of outstanding value to members. It was obvious that what was needed was a reinsurance company to spread the risk. Accordingly, they called a meeting in Chicago on December 27, 1924, of representatives of the Illinois Association of Mutual Insurance Companies, and 12 mutual companies. The idea of a reinsurance company was unanimously endorsed, and everybody went to work to make it a reality.

At the first meeting of the new company, The Farmers Mutual Reinsurance Company, on February 10-11, 1925, in Springfield, C. A. Asplund of the Svea Mutual of Orion, Illinois, was elected temporary president, with George A. Fox, 1st vice president; E. J. Carmody of Towanda, 2nd vice president; and W. B. McFarland of Hoopeston secretary. The IAA, under contract to promote the new company, immediately named Vernon Vaniman as field man. Within a short time, Vaniman had committees at work in 67 counties, and 385 volunteer workers had turned in insurance applications amounting to $751,000. The IAA agreed to underwrite expenses for the first year, estimated at $5,000, and to provide office space and the required reserve fund of $10,000. Cowles was named treasurer. All legal requirements having been met, a charter to do business was issued on November 17, 1925. We will watch the acorn grow as this story continues.

Chapter 10

Finding the Pot of Gold

In farming, as in all other pursuits that man undertakes, the secrets of success or of failure are often hidden behind long established customs and practices. Only by careful study of interrelated factors can such secrets be revealed. It is probably well that this is so, because the prize that we value most is the one that has been won at the cost of very great effort. There is no satisfaction in life greater than the sense of achievement that permeates the very fiber of his being when, after long and persistent effort, a man realizes that he has whipped a problem that taxes to the limit every resource that was his to command. Then, truly, such a man's "cup runneth over."

The early soil and crop improvement associations that were forerunners of the Farm Bureau were set up primarily to enable farmers to do a better job of farming. New knowledge in soil fertility, in plant and animal breeding, in disease and pest control, in animal nutrition, and in a dozen other fields had been unearthed by research institutions; but putting this new knowledge to work on farms proved to be a slow, and sometimes discouraging business. In Illinois, fortunately, the Farm Bureau became, by design, a mighty right arm of the Extension Service in harnessing the inherent power of new ideas and putting it to work on the farms so that it might yield better farm living for the people. The unparalleled success of the team effort of researcher, extension worker, the local organization, and the farmer himself is now legendary. In half a century, Illinois agriculture has been transformed. It is probably true to assert that we have made more progress in this field since 1912 than in all preceding history. Some of the knowledge that was applied in this impressive achievement was not even new. Marcus Terentius Reatinus Varro, the learned Roman who is reported to have written some 620 books, wrote in 36 B.C. about the virtues of lime in the soil (in "Rerum Rusticarum libri tres"). He didn't know why lime helped the soil, but he knew that it did help it. When we started using limestone in Illinois, we knew much more about it than Varro did, and we put that knowledge to work. (I refer again to the fact that Illinois farmers came to use annually one-fourth of all the agricultural limestone used in the United States.)

As farmers proceeded to apply new methods of production and management, it became apparent to leading farmers and people in agricultural colleges and the Extension Service that something more was needed. Farmers who had the best of crop yields or the finest of livestock often asked why it was that neighbors whose yields were much poorer or who had low-grade livestock seemed to do equally as well.

For a number of years, the U.S. Department of Agriculture and some of the agricultural colleges had been studying management problems by making farm management surveys of 100 or more neighboring farms. The Smith-Lever Act of 1914 gave a big boost to this work. They were trying to find the facts underlying the success or lack of it on certain farms, considering the farm as a business unit. Professors George F. Warren of Cornell University, Andrew Boss of the University of Minnesota, and Walter F. Handschin of the University of Illinois, were all pioneers in this work.

Probably the first Illinois farm management survey was made

104

in 1910 by Joel Coffey and John J. Yoke in a cattle-feeding section in Hancock and nearby counties. It was a project of Professor Mumford, then head of the Department of Animal Husbandry at the University of Illinois. The form used was long and involved, and much information was obtained in narrative form. No summary was made. These studies were not complete farm management surveys. The principal purpose of the survey was to locate farms on which to study costs of production later.

A year later, Professor Handschin, who had been doing cost studies in Minnesota, was brought in to head up farm economics studies in Illinois. Studies began in 1912 in Hancock and Franklin counties, under the division of Livestock Farming of the Animal Husbandry department. John Wells of De Kalb county, a 1911 graduate, helped Handschin organize the project. Dana H. Stevenson, an Illinois graduate in 1912, and a native of Hancock county, agreed to act as fieldman until someone could be found to replace him. A student, J. B. (Jerry) Andrews, went to Franklin county about August 1, 1912, with Handschin to start the record-keeping there. He remained until school started, then made monthly trips to check records with the cooperators. After graduation in June, 1913, he went to Hancock county as a full-time fieldman. C. A. Hughes, later a farm adviser, also served briefly as a fieldman.

Dairy production costs were studied as early as 1911, when Wilbur J. Fraser headed the Dairy Husbandry department, with Frank A. Pearson, later of Cornell University, as fieldman.

The first farm management survey in Illinois based on complete farm financial and production records was carried on in Tazewell county by H. F. Williams, E. B. Brossard, Earl Moffitt, and M. C. Wilson of the USDA, with Jerry B. Andrews assisting. The records studied were for the year ending March 1, 1914. Ernest T. Robbins was the farm adviser in Tazewell county.

Williams and Robbins organized the survey record forms into a simple account book which was published by the Tazewell County Farm Bureau and the Tazewell County Bankers Association in 1915. It was used by several Tazewell county farmers and was the basis of some of the 200 survey records obtained in Illinois in 1915. It was one of these books kept by William H. Smith, vice president of the Woodford County Farm Bureau who lived on the county line between Tazewell and Woodford counties that first drew Martin L. Mosher's attention to the Illinois work when he came to Woodford county in January, 1916.

One of Handschin's associates was H. C. M. (Harold) Case, a young man who had had farm experience and who had worked with farm people after graduation. Case saw a challenge in problems of farm management. To prepare Case for his assignment as farm management extension specialist, Handschin sent him to Wisconsin, where he helped three other men in making surveys of some 75 farms near Oshkosh. Professor D. H. Otis of the University of Wisconsin had developed a rather complicated system of farm accounting. Each farmer kept his own records, with the help of a fieldman who visited him once during the summer.

Case returned from Wisconsin with the conviction that any system of accounting, to be successful, must be simple and practical for the farmer following prevailing farm practices. Otherwise, farmers would simply not use it. Handschin agreed with him. After returning from Wisconsin, Case's first assignment was to go to Grundy county, where Frank Demaree, during his first year as farm adviser in 1915, had helped a large group of farmers make inventories of their business, using survey blanks developed by the USDA and Cornell University. Case helped each farmer bring his record up to date. He did the same thing in Tazewell county, calling on farmers who were using simple account books. Inventories were available from the survey study made in 1914, which helped a great deal. In Champaign county, a typical farm survey study was made of some 75 farms, depending on checkbook stubs, incomplete records, and memory of the farmer himself. More than a hundred survey records were closed, and these were studied closely by Handschin and Case.

It soon became apparent that farmers had little confidence in records that depended on memory or incomplete data. But when a farmer had set down all his transactions in a simple account book, along with an inventory at the end, there was no appeal from it. It had to be accepted.

It was not only his own record that was valuable to the farmer. Of greater importance was the fact that a number of farmers keeping records in the same community provided the basis for comparing one farm with others in the same area, all with similar weather and market conditions. Much depended on interpreting the record in the light of conditions on that particular farm. If his hog operation was less profitable than his neighbor's, he wanted to know why. It might be that the neighbor raised eight pigs per litter, while he raised only six. It might be that his neighbor kept his pigs free of intestinal parasites, while he did not. The neighbor might have fed a better ration, grown out and fattened his pigs faster to get them sold ahead of the market glut.

Case and Handschin immediately set about to devise a simple account book adapted to a practical analysis of the farm business. This book was available for the 1916 season. Mosher had left county agent work in Clinton county, Iowa, at the end of 1915 to become the first farm adviser in Woodford county, Illinois. He had planned a farm management survey in cooperation with Sam H. Thompson (no kin to the IAA President Thompson), USDA farm management demonstrator for Clinton county in 1916. When he heard of Case's work he invited him to come to Woodford county to start some farm records. Case's visit was a momentous one. He found in Mosher a keen and analytic mind, methodical and patient, deeply impressed with the possibilities of farm records as a tool for improving farm practices. Then began the long association of two men who have had most rewarding careers in farm management work.

(This association was interrupted in 1919, when Henry C. Taylor persuaded Case to go to Washington, D.C. for two years —on leave from the University of Illinois—to serve as farm management extension specialist for 33 northern and western states. As Case recalls it, Taylor counseled him: "Regardless of anything else you may do, Case, I want you to popularize farm accounting.")

The outgrowth of that farm accounting venture, started in Woodford county in 1916, was to become the most outstanding project of its kind in the world. Within a relatively few years, Illinois farmers were keeping about half of all the farm accounts in the United States. So popular did it become that in 1962 just about ten per cent of the commercial farmers (with gross incomes of more than $10,000) now belong to the Farm Bureau Farm Management Service, which was set up when the demand for accounting service outgrew the manpower and facilities of the Extension Service in 1924. The increase in farm incomes growing out of this project is simply incalculable. The most telling proof of its value is the fact that only rarely does a man drop out of the Association, once he is in.

The Woodford county project of 1916 was duly completed, and it created so much interest among Farm Bureau members that by 1918, when Mosher needed an assistant, one of the requirements to the job was experience in farm accounting. Rollo D. Shaffer was hired, and the accounting work became a major Extension project. By 1920, it had become such a fixture in the county that it was set up on a five-year basis. The Woodford County Farm Bureau and the University of Illinois agreed to back it, sharing the cost of supervising and summarizing a hundred account books per year for the next five years. Paul E. Johnston, a University of Illinois graduate with considerable experience in farming, came in as assistant farm adviser with the responsibility of representing Farm Bureau in the joint venture.

The project grew like a rolling snowball. Similar work was under way in seventeen other counties. In 1922, Mumford returned to the University of Illinois as Dean of the College of Agriculture, after a two-year leave during which he laid the foundation for a cooperative livestock marketing system for the Illinois Agricultural Association. He gave solid support and impetus to the work. At this time, Case returned from his sojourn in Washington and an additional year of graduate study. In the same year, when death came to Professor Handschin, the Dean appointed Case as his successor. Case, in turn, persuaded Mosher in 1923 to leave

Woodford county to join the University staff as a specialist in farm management, so that his talents could be utilized over a wider field.

By 1924, it became apparent that some changes would have to be made in Woodford county the following year, when the five-year agreement between the University and the Woodford County Farm Bureau would end. Demand for the service was too big to be carried on under the old plan. The University was spending as much as could be justified on the basis of the value of the project as a research and Extension operation, especially when there were insistent demands from other counties for similar help. Case and Mosher had been giving the matter a lot of thought. Gradually the idea of a cooperative farm management association developed. They tested it out by calling on about thirty farmers in Wood-ford, Livingston, Tazewell, and McLean counties, and asked them if they would be willing to pay half the cost of keeping their accounts, provided the other half could be handled in some other way. They were much encouraged by the enthusiastic reaction of the great majority of those interviewed. They were particularly impressed by the response of William H. Smith, a pioneer Farm Bureau member and record-keeper in Woodford county. Smith had done as much as any other man in the state to develop the Farm Bureau in his county and later throughout the state as he helped in the reorganizing of the IAA following the historic meeting in Peoria in 1919. He was a man of substance, of great integrity, and influential with his neighbors. He was enthusiastic. Louis C. Schertz, another good farmer, said the service was worth $50 a year to him, and that he would even pay $100 a year for it rather than be without it. He figured that he was able to increase his annual income several hundred dollars by what the records revealed about his farm operation.

In October, 1924, a meeting was held in El Paso to discuss the entire matter. The farm advisers of Woodford, Livingston, Tazewell, and McLean counties each brought two or three leading farmers. Dean Mumford, Case, and Mosher came from the University. The IAA sent Secretary George A. Fox. Byron Colburn, a local banker, represented the county bankers' association. The idea of a farm management association was heartily endorsed. Recognizing the county Farm Bureau as the principal supporter of Extension work, Dean Mumford suggested the name "Farm Bureau Farm Management Service" which was tentatively adopted. Mosher was given the task of organizing the new group, and he got busy right away by meeting with the Farm Bureau boards in each county, all of which officially approved the project. The Tazewell and Woodford county boards agreed to pay $5.00 toward the fee of each member; the Livingston county board arranged to pay all but $5.00 of the cost; and the McLean county board agreed to solicit membership, but insisted that each member should pay his own way. No time was wasted. In November, members began to sign up for the service for a three-year period. The first man to sign up was, fittingly enough, J. Frank Felter of Woodford county, who was among the first to start keeping records in 1916. As he signed, Mosher, seeing his and Case's dream come true, remarked: "We should have a camera here—this may be worth recording." The signing took place in the Farm Bureau office in Eureka. Other early signers were William H. Smith, Howard Leonard—later IAA president, and John Voorhees of Woodford county. Voorhees set a notable record during his farming days by keeping records continuously on the same farm and the same acres for 38 years.

Thus the pioneer Farm Bureau Farm Management Association was launched. Officers of the Association asked that Mosher become the fieldman. Dean Mumford and Professor Case, anxious to see the venture succeed, agreed to release him. The work went ahead as planned. All concerned knew that the service might stand or fall on the results achieved during the first three-year period, a sort of "shakedown cruise." There was no need to worry. When the contracts expired in 1928, the Association was solidly established. A reorganization took place, and 175 members agreed to sign up for another three years. Mosher left to return to the University where he directed the project until he retired in 1950. Jerry Andrews became fieldman. A period of remarkable growth ensued.

By 1929, the number of cooperators jumped to 420, and Wilson A. Herrington, with years of experience as farm adviser behind him, came in to assist Andrews. By 1931, there were 820 cooperators, with four fieldmen assisting them. Forest Fisher, farm adviser in Wabash county, Illinois, came into western Illinois in 1930, and Joseph B. Cunningham, farm adviser in Noble county, Indiana, came to the Illinois Valley area in 1931. The Association was a sensational success. The great depression dealt it a sickening blow, but didn't knock it out. In 1933, only two fieldmen with help from the state office were needed to look after 430 cooperators in 14 counties. The comeback was slow and gradual. By 1941, there were three fieldmen working with 675 cooperators in 23 counties. Soaring farm prices during World War II made it mandatory for farmers to have accurate records for income tax purposes. Jumping to 1954, we find a membership of 4,400, employing 24 fieldmen in 89 counties. In 1963, nearly 6,000 members (some in every Illinois county) kept 34 fieldmen busy.

Cost of the service rose with the steady inflation which followed the war. By 1953, members were paying a minimum of $41 a year on farms of 100 acres or less, up to $70 on 580 acres, with an extra $2 for each additional 40 acres. Those fees are certainly reasonable charges for very high-class service. It's hard to see how it could be rendered at any lower cost.

It's hard to estimate the value of the service to a member, but fieldmen can tell you of dozens of instances in which members have increased their incomes by more than $1,000 a year by correcting weaknesses in their operations revealed by the records. Both Case and Mosher, now living in retirement in Urbana, feel that the promises they saw in farm accounting half a century ago have been richly fulfilled. They recognized a great opportunity when they found out by studying farm surveys that the incomes of two neighbors, growing identical crops on the same types of soil, and feeding the same kind of livestock, could and did vary as much as $5,000 to $10,000 a year, with variations due directly and unmistakably to organizational and operational practices which they had adopted and to the thoroughness with which they

111

had applied them. The lessons taught by the record books were persuasive because there was no way to argue with the facts revealed. The verdict of the books was final, and the only way to change it the next year was to improve the faulty practice.

The men who pioneered in this work really caught the tide at flood stage. Many factors contributed to its success. The interest and activity of most farm advisers were important factors in its success. As I have remarked earlier in this book, these men were the line sergeants in the forces that were battling for an improved and more rewarding agriculture. They were men in whom both University official and farmer could place their trust and confidence. Also the fieldmen and Extension Service workers rendered service of a high order. High in the list would be Johnston, Andrews, Handschin (all deceased), Robert R. Hudelson, Joseph B. Cunningham, W. A. Herrington, Roy L. Donovan, Foster F. Elliott, and many others. And always there was support and encouragement from Deans Mumford, Henry P. Rusk, and the present (1963) dean, Louis B. Howard. Never in the history of the Extension Service and county Farm Bureau have the University and the local farm organizations worked together more happily and to greater good purpose.

Chapter 11

The Battle for Equality

When the IAA annual meeting assembled in Champaign on January 21, 1926, delegates had one responsibility above all else —naming a president to succeed Sam Thompson. Earl C. Smith of Pike county, who had served on the executive committee for three years and was chairman of the finance committee, had given a good account of himself. All his associates recognized his business acumen, he was admired for the firmness of his convictions, he knew his way around in the political arena, he was a highly successful cattle and hog feeder, and he was just the right age— close to 41. He won over Frank Barton of Livingston county, 126 to 64. After the election, he spoke briefly. Regarding policies, he said tersely: "I have been a hearty supporter of the policies of the past administration and contemplate no changes at this time."

Thus began a 20-year career as leader of the strongest state Farm Bureau in the country. Smith and his associates were to build the IAA and its affiliates to dizzy heights. The IAA was to become the wonder and the envy of most other Farm Bureaus. Eventually it became the pattern from which many, many other Farm Bureaus were developed, from coast to coast.

There was to be no departing from the philosophy of the slogan, "Organized for Business," but Smith was always careful to remind his associates that business was not the main reason for organizing. Business services were viewed as an adjunct, and a useful one, but he insisted that the big, over-riding job of a farm organization was to speak authoritatively for farmers in local, state, and national councils. What farmers needed most, Smith argued, was a *national policy* on agriculture. He often pointed out that this country, almost from the beginning, had had a very definite policy with respect to industry—one of encouragement—while agriculture had to shift pretty much for itself. It was true that agriculture had been encouraged by the Homestead Act, and had been magnificently provided for in terms of education and research by establishing the Land Grant College system, the Experiment Stations, and the Extension Service. But this was not enough, said Smith, and, furthermore, the dignity and importance of agriculture were not recognized by the public. The disparity, as he saw it, between industry and agriculture had been accentuated because industry had grown great under the privileges accorded it through the benefits of corporate organization, the tariff system, and in many subtle ways that were not always apparent. Industry, it seemed to many besides Smith, had grown to maturity but had refused to be weaned, and was really fattening, to some extent at least, at the expense of agriculture. (In this connection, it is interesting to note that Alexander Hamilton, father of the protective system that was adopted to build the country through industrialization, had admitted that agriculture would not be helped through the protective system, and that some way should be provided to offset any disadvantages that it might suffer. Unfortunately, the federal government has been struggling with that problem for the past 35 years, and seems no closer to a solution than it was in Hamilton's day.

With Smith leading the IAA, and Sam Thompson at the helm of the American Farm Bureau Federation, and with farm-minded Frank O. Lowden of Illinois a fair possibility as Republican candidate for the Presidency two years later, many Farm Bureau leaders firmly believed that the years immediately ahead held the prospect, if not the promise, of better things ahead for farmers.

Earl Clemmons Smith was the son of William T. Smith and Annie Clemmons Smith, only child of William A. Clemmons, a pioneer farmer and livestock feeder in Pike county. William T. Smith was a college professor who once taught at what is now Illinois State University at Normal, Illinois. In 1888, because the family physician advised the family to move to a warmer climate, on account of Mrs. Smith's health, they moved to Harriman, Tennessee, where Mr. Smith engaged in the real estate business. He built a business building, the Smith Building, which still stands in Harriman.

Earl C. Smith grew up in Harriman, along with a sister, Vera M., and brothers, Vincent V., Hugh M. A., and Virgil W. The other children, as befitted the children of a college professor, all received good educations. Vincent went into the public utility business, and Hugh became a highly successful physician in Knoxville, Tennessee. Vera, a gifted musician and vocalist, became Mrs. Culan V. Biddle, and lives today in Knoxville. Virgil died soon after World War I, as a result of disabilities incurred in the war.

Earl refused to conform to the family pattern. He rebelled when school authorities directed him to study Latin. His dad told him that he was on his own from that time on. He went to work for a wholesale grocery firm in Chattanooga. By the time he was sixteen years old, he was promoted to a job as traveling salesman. This achievement by one so young, was noted in the Harriman newspaper. Later, he worked as traveling salesman for Armour and Company. This experience was to stand him in good stead. On a visit to Vincent, who lived in Indianapolis, Earl was out walking when he noticed a sign on a small grocery and meat market, announcing that the business was to be sold at auction. Earl looked over the stock with a practiced eye, and mentally appraised its value. On the day of the sale, he was there, and when it was apparent that it was going to be sold at a real bargain price, he bought it. He ran the business for a year with the help of a butcher, then sold it, and came out of the deal with some $5,000 in cash. He was not yet twenty-one years of age.

The story of how he accumulated enough capital to buy the grocery and meat market is an interesting one. When he first went to work, he spent all of his income, a lot of it foolishly, in his dad's opinion. His father gave him a man-to-man talk on the necessity of saving, and as an incentive he offered to give him outright $50, provided Earl would save $50. He started to save, but it was hard going. He said later that it was just about the hardest job he ever undertook. But he succeeded. He turned the cash over to his Dad, who then wrote out a note for $100, and signed it. Then he said: "Now, Earl, if you will save $100, I'll match that." This system of doubling his capital appealed to the young man, and he redoubled his efforts. How much he accumulated in this way is not known, but he had enough by the time he was twenty to handle his first substantial business deal.

The Smith family usually spent their summers at the Clemmons farm. Earl began to think about becoming a farmer. He couldn't forget that Grandfather Clemmons had accumulated a fortune largely by buying hogs, feeding them out, then taking them by barge on the Illinois River to market in St. Louis. Earl's mother tried to discourage him, but in 1907 she agreed to let him handle the farm to find out if he really liked it. In 1909, he married Mary J. Sanderson. A year later, on August 1, 1910, when he was twenty-four, he signed a lease which specified in great detail just how the farm was to be operated. Not more than 100 acres were to be cropped each year, and not more than 40 acres of grass was to be mowed for hay to be fed on the farm, "the object being to build up the land as much as possible." No land was to "be put to corn more than two years until it has had at least two years of grass, unless by written consent of the party of the first part."

In case grassland was plowed up, "a like number of acres of land shall be sown to timothy and clover by said second party at his own expense."

Earl also agreed to "fill all washes and ditches, and stake same,

Earl C. Smith

or plant willows in them where needed, also to break land so as to prevent far as possible land washing."

Also: "Said second party may have dead or down timber for his own use for cook stove for himself only, no live standing timber to be cut for firewood, but he may have tops of timber cut for posts, same to come off lands of Mrs. Smith."

Cash rent of $1,100 a year was to be paid, half on March 1 and the balance on August 1 of each year. Acreage leased was more than 500.

Earl and Mary prospered from the beginning. (This period was the so-called "parity period" in agriculture.) The years of World War I were particularly rewarding. The culmination, for Earl, came in 1919. He had fed out hundreds of cattle which sold at truly high prices. It was then that Earl paid off his last debts, and he never went into debt again. At his death, he owned just under 500 acres. For many years he had looked after farms owned by his brothers and his only sister. He kept detailed farm records. He knew within a fraction of a cent how much it cost him to produce a pound of beef or pork. He was regarded as one of the best farm managers in Illinois, and was made an honorary member of the Illinois Society of Farm Managers and Appraisers.

The Smiths had no children, but there were around 40 nieces and nephews who regarded the Smith farm as their "second home." They always found sympathy and sound counsel there when they had problems, and affection in abundance.

Earl C. Smith was often considered anti-labor. He did think that labor, in the years after World War II, was asking, and getting too much. But he had some ideas that were far from being anti-labor. For example, in his convention speech in 1945, when General Motors Corporation was defending the theory that automobile industry profits should not be used as a gauge by which to set the wages of labor, Smith said that workers should receive "reasonable living wages," and management "reasonable returns for capital invested." "After meeting these requisites," he said, "would it not be well to consider an allocation of remaining profits to capital, to management, and to workers in proportion to their contribution to final results?"

In a letter to Senator Paul M. Douglas of Illinois, Earl C. Smith commented on the controversy over fixed versus farm price supports as follows, in part: "The attention of the country has been largely centered on the question of 90 per cent price supports versus flexible supports, and many people including some farmers seem to think that this is the major question. As you well know, this is far from true. Either one could be effective if properly and fully administered and either one will fail to the extent that we fail to get production substantially in line with demand."

Earl was an outstanding businessman. He had the first Buick franchise for Pike county, and held it for many years. He made arrangements with Zimmerman Brothers, who ran a garage in Pittsfield, to handle repair work for his customers. He held the franchise until the custom of taking in used cars as part payment for new ones became general. Earl wanted no part of this, and he sold the franchise to the Zimmermans. For his personal use, Earl never bought any car except a Buick.

Mary Sanderson Smith died suddenly on March 21, 1949, in the 40th year of their marriage. Earl's next marriage, in 1951, was to Mrs. Eula Sanderson, widow of Mary Smith's brother. She died in 1955. Four years later, on March 26, 1959, Earl and Mrs. Eda B. Hunter nee Simmons, widow of Harold F. Hunter, were married. Two years later, on June 30, 1961, Earl C. Smith died.

It was apparent early in 1926 that the Farm Bureau forces, led by Thompson and Smith, had gathered a lot of support for their drive for federal farm legislation. Many business groups, and many newspapers put their shoulders to the wheel, and before long a battle royal was in progress. President Coolidge and his Secretary of Agriculture, William M. Jardine, were strongly opposed to the McNary-Haugen Bills, so strongly opposed that they caused another bill to be written, called the Tincher Bill, which would set up a federal farm board and appropriate $100 million to lend to cooperatives, in the hope supporters of the McNary-Haugen bills could be induced to compromise.

The Farm Bureau forces were in no mood to compromise. The IAA, at its January convention had gone on record in favor of the principles of the Dickinson Bill, which differed little in substance from the McNary-Haugen Bills. The bill which was finally introduced was called the Farm Board Bill, but later known as the Haugen Bill. It would create a federal farm board charged with the responsibility of keeping close tab on market prices, and whenever surpluses seemed to be driving farm prices below fair levels, it was empowered to remove or withhold from the market any "surpluses above domestic requirements," in order to maintain prices at fair levels.

President Coolidge had addressed the convention of the American Farm Bureau Federation in 1925, and had condemned in no uncertain terms all proposals which would involve the Government in buying and selling, or in price-fixing, direct or indirect. He did promise to look with sympathy on any farm relief measure "designed in accordance with sound economic principles." He said further: "I propose actively and energetically to assist the farmers to promote their welfare through cooperative marketing."

President Coolidge drove home his argument by adding: "Moreover it (meaning a government agency going into buying and selling) would apparently destroy cooperative associations and all other marketing machinery, for no one can compete with the government. Ultimately it would end the independence which the farmers of this country enjoy as a result of centuries of struggle and prevent the exercise of their own judgment and control in cultivating their land and marketing their produce."

This caused the McNary-Haugen forces to intensify their efforts. They were determined to push through Congress a measure that would set up machinery capable of lifting from the market the heavy surpluses that were having such a depressing effect. In the opinion of the leaders, the Government itself was the only agency capable of accomplishing this. The Farm Bureau forces also were insisting on the equalization fee as a means of supplying the money needed, so that the stigma of paternalism could be avoided. What they wanted was a "self-supporting" piece of legislation. The odds were against them, but they went at the job with hammer and tongs.

It was all to no avail. The Haugen Bill was beaten in the House, 212-167, in May, 1926; and within two months the Senate was to vote down similar legislation, 45-39. President Coolidge was still in firm control. The opposition of the industrial East, or that part of it east of Indiana and north of the Ohio River, was reflected in the vote in the Senate. Only one "aye" vote was recorded from this area.

These developments widened the breach between Farm Bureau and the Administration. Earl Smith, in a signed article in the *IAA Record* of July 1, 1926, paid his respects to the entrenched interests, as follows: "It is quite surprising to note in a careful analysis of the vote on these bills before both houses, that those who have most enjoyed the fruits of protection are unwilling for farmers to share with them its benefits." And an editorial in the August issue stated plainly: "We are just a bit skeptical even now about the prospects of securing any worthwhile legislation to make the farmer's dollar worth as much as the other fellow's, until after 1928 . . . ." It was obvious that farmers were becoming disenchanted with the so-called "American protective system."

These events foreshadowed political developments which culminated in the historic break of Midwest farmers with the Republican party in 1928, and then the landslide to the Democrats in 1932. That was just one of many precedent-shattering results of the nation-wide depression touched off by the stock market break of 1929.

When Congress reassembled early in 1927, it lost no time in coming to grips with the surplus problem. Congressmen and senators, egged on by large segments of industry and the press, as well as farmers, quickly passed identical bills, the McNary Bill in the Senate and the Haugen Bill in the House. The big reason for the farm victory in 1927 was that lawmakers from the South had undergone a change of heart. In 1924, during the first battle, the South was not particularly interested in surplus legislation because the price of cotton had remained high in comparison with prices of other farm products. In response to an average price of 18.2

cents a pound in 1925, however, southern planters had put in a huge acreage in 1926, with the result that the average price of the 1926 crop dropped with a thud to 10.9 cents. The growers "got religion" quickly, got on the bandwagon in a hurry, and demanded action now at Washington. That was why the McNary-Haugen Bills were passed with relative ease in 1927. In Farm Bureau circles, the Midwest and the South joined forces for the first time. It was an historic occasion.

But they had not reckoned with the stubbornness of Vermont-born Calvin Coolidge. Recognizing the importance of the issue, the President meticulously explained the reasons why, in several thousand words, he felt compelled to veto the bills on February 27, 1927. The "silent" Mr. Coolidge wasted a lot of words in marshalling his arguments, but he used only a few to outline his chief objection. He wrote: "The chief objection to the bill is that it would not benefit the farmer. Whatever may be the temporary influence of arbitrary interference, no one can deny that in the long run prices will be governed by the law of supply and demand." That statement might well be pondered by the present national Administration, which is attempting to apply "arbitrary interference" to the economics of agriculture to a degree never attempted and hardly contemplated during the past thirty years of "farm programs." Maybe Mr. Coolidge had something there. A lot of water has gone over the dam and under the bridge in that thirty years, but our blessed lawmakers seem no nearer a solution to the problem of stabilizing farm prices by government fiat in 1962 than they were in the 69th Congress so long ago.

No question about it, Farm Bureau was becoming a formidable power. Though it foreswore partisanship, it was a factor in the political world. It stirred up many a hornet's nest in national affairs as well as in state matters. In the latter category was the tempest aroused by George Wicker, director of business service. Concerned mainly with auditing, Wicker had made a survey of 65 farmers' elevators, which plainly indicated that among the causes of failure of such cooperatives, sloppy accounting and easy credit and unsound business practices stood out very conspicuously. Some of those with vested interests professed to be insulted. At a meeting of the Illinois Farmers Grain Dealers Managers Club, held in Dwight, those present adopted a resolution:

"We deplore and strongly condemn the activities of the Illinois Agricultural Association, who directly and through their subsidiaries have seemingly made a strong effort to inject themselves into the farmers elevator movement. . . .

"We hereby ask the directors of our state association to pass resolutions setting forth the fact that the Illinois Agricultural Association and its subsidiaries are in no manner connected with the farmers elevator movement, have no right to talk for it or to give out any statement concerning any of its activities. . . ."

Some of the managers had apparently been hit where it hurt.

Such untoward occurrences only served to throw additional light on the messy situation which prevailed in many farmer cooperatives, and it wasn't long until the auditing service provided by Wicker and his associates became one of the most valued services of the IAA. At the end of 1926, there were 212 clients, 97 of them farmers' elevators. Because it met a very great need, the auditing service grew fast, and it did, in truth, put many a shaky enterprise solidly on its feet, and well on its way to enduring prosperity.

* * *

Many "coming events" were casting their shadows before in that year of 1926. The young Farmers Mutual Reinsurance Company had a most satisfactory year, and future prospects were rosy indeed. Success in this field intensified demands by members for service in the field of automobile insurance. Farmers who owned cars were badly under-insured. They generally had to pay the same rates that all others paid, even though farmers in those days drove their cars little except in their own communities where risks were low. They had felt for years that they were subsidizing the car owner in the high-risk areas, and they were asking the IAA to do something about it.

Things came to a head on October 8, 1926, in Chicago, when the executive committee and the county Farm Bureau presidents in joint session voted unanimously to set up an automobile insurance company to be owned and operated by the IAA, with service limited to members. The executive committee had authorized such a venture a month before, and this meeting ratified it with great enthusiasm.

This action was not taken without thorough preparation. For months, Vernon Vaniman, fieldman for the reinsurance company, had been talking with members about automobile insurance, and he and IAA General Counsel Kirkpatrick had done enough spade work to convince them that here lay a golden opportunity. Earl Smith, ever the cautious operator, had insisted on slow and careful procedure. It was therefore agreed that no money be collected until a large number of bona fide applications for insurance had been secured. Anyone who knew Vaniman can understand how he reacted to the challenge. Working with his usual vigor, he set committees to work in all organized counties, and early in 1927, no less than 3,290 applications had been received. An application for a charter was made, and on April 27, 1927, the auto company was licensed as the Illinois Agricultural Mutual Insurance Company.

A premium deposit of $10 was required from each applicant, along with a policy fee of $5, plus a $10 surplus share contribution. Charter members thus contributed $25 the first year. The fact that more than 3,000 IAA members eagerly signed up was a tribute to the unbounded confidence of the members in the IAA and its leadership. It was a magnificent testimonal, and later events were to prove abundantly that the confidence of the members had not been misplaced. J. P. Gibson was named manager, to be succeeded by Ara E. Richardson, who held the position until he became manager of the Country Life Insurance Company.

These years were not years of notable expansion of membership, which held steadily above 50,000; but they were years in which service to members was being expanded with breathtaking speed. Services were provided because members demanded them. For example, cooperative purchasing of limestone had proved highly successful, and members were asking why the same prin-

Vernon Vaniman

ciple could not be extended to the purchase of other supplies, petroleum products, for example. Already a number of county Farm Bureaus had formed companies to distribute petroleum products at substantial savings. This was very important to farmers, since the tractor was fast becoming the major source of power on farms, and more and more farmers were buying trucks. In 1923, the Hancock County Farm Bureau had pioneered in this movement, with great encouragement from J. H. "Hank" Lloyd, farm adviser who had been with them since 1915, and who had started this do-it-yourself business by teaching members to vaccinate their own hogs. They pooled their orders for serum. The advantages of volume purchases were being convincingly demonstrated.

Frank E. Fuller, farm adviser in Marshall-Putnam counties, had been talking with fellow advisers in his area about the possibilities of Farm Bureaus getting into this field, and at one meeting he brought evidence of success attained by farmer-owned companies in the upper Midwest. Several of the advisers were deeply interested. They went home and began to promote the idea. The results were soon seen in tangible form, because by the end of 1926 the Marshall-Putnam County Oil Company, the Knox County Oil Company, the Ford County Service Company, the Edgar County Supply Company, the Coles County Supply Company, the McLean County Service Company, the Montgomery Farmers' Oil Company, and the Menard County Farmers' Supply Company were doing business, and the De Kalb County Agricultural Association, primarily a seed distributing agency, had started distributing petroleum products. One big reason for farmers taking so readily to such projects was that in those days a lot of inferior oil was being sold, causing much dissatisfaction and unnecessary expense to tractor owners. It seemed to farmers that the oil companies assumed that any old oil was good enough for tractors. The importance of quality-control had been demonstrated over and over again, and members in these counties had resolved to take control through their own companies. With eight county companies engaged in the business, it was inevitable that eventually they would pool their orders. That development came very quickly, as will be seen presently.

Chapter 12

A Steady Hand at the Helm

We now move into a period of steady development. Growth in membership was to slow down during the depression years soon to come; but business services were added and expanded, and the organization maintained a strong financial position through thick and thin. It had matured. Its "character," if you may apply this term to an organization, was formed. The man who did most to mold that character was Earl C. Smith. He had the men he wanted in key places, he knew he could depend on them, and he moved into new ventures with the utmost confidence.

Smith was liberally endowed with business acumen. A gifted calculator, he always added two columns of figures, rather than one. He could absorb the important facts in a financial statement within minutes, and furthermore he could judge the potentials of a business proposal with uncanny accuracy.

Earl Smith was also a good judge of men. He did not hesitate to select men with little experience to undertake a job, provided they measured up to his standards with respect to character, industry, integrity, and habits. He gave many young men their big chance to develop, and a high percentage of them went on to fine careers in IAA affiliates or with other companies.

The men Smith depended on most heavily in these years in creating the structure of IAA were Bob Cowles, as treasurer, Donald Kirkpatrick as general counsel, and George Metzger as organization director, and he depended on Vernon Vaniman, for whom he had real affection, in a rather special field. Smith considered "Van" a promoter par excellence, and loved to challenge him by giving him a hard assignment. Vaniman usually came through. Smith knew the special gifts of each man, and he was careful to give no one an assignment unsuited to his abilities or his inclinations. In this way, he avoided many troubles that could have developed in this burgeoning empire. Smith was not without his "blind spots," and it is possible that some men suffered injustices at his hand; but judging on his entire performance, one is bound to conclude that he managed the array of talent at his disposal with superlative skill. The evidence is all in the record.

The opportunity which came early in his administration for the IAA to organize a company through which the county groups could pool their orders for petroleum supplies must have appealed to Earl Smith as a splendid opportunity. Sentiment in the counties had grown so strong by this time that it was only a question of when to get started. A committee representing the nine county Farm Bureaus already in business met repeatedly with IAA officials to work out a plan, and Kirkpatrick and his assistants were busy working out legal details of the proposed setup. It was an exciting venture. The Knox County Oil Company had handled $130,000 of business in its first year, and paid patronage refunds of $7,866. It owned five bulk plants and 13 service stations. It was apparent that the surface had hardly been scratched. Possibilities for the future seemed unlimited.

After months of discussion, the nine county companies finally agreed on a plan, and application was made for a charter. The charter was issued on March 7, 1927. The name of the new company was the Illinois Farm Supply Company.

Mountainous tasks loomed ahead. One that could not be put off was to develop specifications for gasoline, kerosene, high quality lubricating oils and greases. Two top petroleum engineers were employed to do this job. Other county groups were clamoring for help in setting up supply companies, promotion and advertising plans had to be worked out, administrative problems by the dozen had to be resolved—in short, all the puzzles confronting every new venture had to be worked out. Accounting and insurance services were provided by the IAA as a matter of course.

The Illinois Farm Supply Company (now FS Services, Inc.) was (and is) owned by the county supply compaines through issuance of common and preferred stock; but there was an issue of "B" stock, all of which was held by the Illinois Agricultural Association. This stock carries voting privileges, so that the IAA itself had the means necessary to prevent any action which might be considered detrimental to the parent organization or to farmers generally. This arrangement was devised to maintain forever its status as a Farm Bureau affiliate. The founders looked ahead a long way in providing this safeguard.

* * *

In 1927, the IAA had a busy time at Springfield. It was strong enough to block the new gasoline tax measure until it was amended to give rural districts a fair share of the proceeds of the two-cent levy. The bill finally passed and signed by the Governor provided that one-half the proceeds be used in the counties at the discretion of county boards, and further, that gas tax funds could be used to pay principal and interest on county road bonds issued for the construction of state-aid roads built under state specifications. It provided further that such funds could be used to replace taxes for state-aid roads, then levied against property. This represented a great victory for the farm forces.

A determined fight for a state income tax was waged, but it was a losing battle.

One of the big accomplishments was passage of the grain storage bill, under which grain could be stored on the farm in state-sealed bins, and the warehouse receipt used as collateral for loans. This legislation was to be tremendously useful a few years later, when federal commodity loan programs were launched.

The IAA was able to kill a bill in this session that would have prevented farmers from vaccinating their own hogs with the double treatment.

John Watson continued his great work in securing equalizations between farm and urban real estate. In Knox county, the board of review voluntarily reduced farm assessments by 25 per cent when the Farm Bureau presented the evidence to prove that farm property was unfairly taxed. Boards in Stephenson and Champaign counties were recalcitrant, however, until a hearing was held in Chicago on October 6. After Watson had presented his case, the State Tax Commission admitted he had proved his case. The Champaign Board apparently accepted the decision, but did nothing until the commission ordered it to act. The Stephenson county board held out until the State Tax Commission practically gave it an ultimatum: either reduce assessments on farm property by 24 per cent or raise Freeport assessments by 30 per cent.

These tax cases did a great deal to prove the value of farm organizations, but unfortunately farmers did not rush to join the Farm Bureau, since member and non-member were benefited equally.

It would be well at this point to review the work done by the IAA in response to demands from members for help on dairy marketing problems, which are always complex and difficult to handle. Arthur D. Lynch had been working since 1922, aiding in organizing cooperative groups to sell whole milk or butterfat. He started as Chris Larsen's assistant and succeeded him when he resigned. By the end of 1927, there were eleven bargaining associations or "cream pools" for farmers producing butterfat.

In 1926, Farm Advisers Wilfred Shaw of Peoria county, Henry A. DeWerff of Woodford county, and Ralph Arnett of Tazewell county, asked the IAA for help in solving the milk marketing problem in the Peoria milkshed. After many conferences, the Illinois Milk Producers Association was set up, and it made history. The big thing achieved was agreement with distributors that all would pay the same price for milk of like test and like quality, and that all milk would be paid for on the basis of use, with milk for fluid consumption bringing the highest price of the three classes provided for. Producers were happy when the results of the first year's operations were tabulated. They had received an average price of 20 cents a hundred pounds over the previous year's prices. Wilfred Shaw was named IMPA manager in 1928. Shaw was to move on to IAA employment in 1935, and eventually (1950) to become secretary, a position he held until his retirement in 1962.

In 1927, dairymen around Bloomington followed the Peoria pattern in organizing the McLean County Milk Producers' Association, with Forrest C. Fairchild as manager. Ara E. Richardson and Lynch had a hand in organizing the Pure Milk Association in the Chicago milkshed in 1926, which is still operating in 1963. This cooperative brought relative peace to a market that had been plagued for years by bitter arguments between producers and distributors. The IAA also helped producers organize in other areas, as we will see later. The help given the producers by the IAA was largely instrumental in bringing about a fair solution to the marketing problem. Cream marketing during these years was the province of Frank Gougler, IAA director of produce marketing. He gave a lot of time also to finding better ways to sell poultry and eggs.

* * *

Turning to the political arena once more, the McNary-Haugen Bills were passed again by Congress, by 204 to 121 in the House and by 53 to 23 in the Senate. On May 23, President Coolidge vetoed the measure for the second time, as expected, thus insuring a new alignment of political forces in the Midwest. Farm Bureau forces immediately prepared for the national party conventions, hoping to get the right kind of farm planks in the platforms.

The Republican convention at Kansas City only added to the sense of frustration that Farm Bureau forces already felt. The ultra-conservatives were still in control of the party. The platform adopted was totally unsatisfactory to Farm Bureau. As Earl Smith

131

said: "Summed up, it fails utterly to recognize the fundamental problem facing agriculture. . . ."

At Houston, the Democrats, recognizing the opportunity to win over a large segment of the farm vote, adopted a farm plank much more to the liking of the farm forces. Quoting Smith again: "The agricultural plank in the Democratic platform adopted at Houston covers the essentials of a national farm policy more completely than any platform previously adopted by a political party. . . ."

As it turned out, platforms had little to do with the outcome of the election, which was decided on other issues. With Herbert Hoover President, Farm Bureau leaders expected to get from Congress a federal farm board and a stabilization corporation, and encouragement to cooperatives, but little that would come to grips with the underlying problem.

The Farm Bureau was doing poorly in its attempt to get government help for farmers, but it was doing mighty well in its self-help activities for farmers. Before the end of 1928, nearly 11,000 automobiles had been insured in the Farm Bureau company—a sensational record for a company not yet two years old. The reinsurance company, only a year older, had $13 million of fire and tornado insurance in force, plus $4,600,000 of farm crop hail insurance, a service first offered in 1926.

The volume of business of Illinois Farm Supply Company, in its first full fiscal year, which ended August 31, 1928, amounted to $677,818.07, practically all of it in petroleum products. Several of the 16 county companies making up the company received patronage refunds of more than $1,000. Members knew that this was just a small beginning. They looked ahead to great things, and they cherished the results that were accruing to their efforts at self-help. Here was something tangible. It helped where farmers needed help. Here was something they could control. It was quite different from going, hat in hand, to political leaders to ask for legislative help. It did a lot to improve the morale of members, and it added immensely to the prestige of the Illinois Agricultural Association.

As a group, Farm Bureau members developed great confidence in their organization and in its leadership. Earl Smith had their profound respect. He had firmly established himself as a great leader. They moved ahead with self-assurance that was almost cockiness. They knew that they were well on the way to great achievements.

The venture into the fire insurance field in 1925 and auto insurance early in 1927 were a revelation to members. With these projects well under way, many of them wondered aloud if they could not be similarly successful with life insurance. Demands for life insurance service were so insistent that the matter was discussed in detail at the annual convention in 1927, whereupon President Smith ordered an intensive study to determine just how well farmers were being served in this field. The survey revealed one thing with crystal clarity: farmers were woefully under-insured. Few had enough life insurance to cover their mortgage indebtedness. Furthermore, it seemed that few insurance agents were trying to insure farmers, and that most agents knew little about the insurance needs of farmers. Many agents pushed endowment policies as a means of saving even for farmers who were heavily in debt. What such a farmer most needed was protection for his family until he had his big debts paid off. It was believed that agents working for the farmers' own companies and knowledgeable as to the problems of the farming business could best serve farmers in planning insurance programs tailored to their individual needs.

The upshot of the survey and much discussion was that the IAA board of directors in 1928 authorized the setting up of a legal reserve stock life insurance company, contingent upon: (1) Subscriptions for $40,000 first preferred seven per cent accumulative stock to be sold to Farm Bureaus and Farm Bureau members; (2) Pledges for $3 million of insurance by January 1, 1929. Here indeed was another challenge for Vaniman. He and his cohorts in the counties, inspired by the spectacular success of their previous insurance ventures, really went to town this time. By December 15, 1928, they had secured pledges of $82,000 for stock, and no less than $8,000,000 for the first special participation policies. This was a stimulating experience for the organizers. They knew without any question that farmers were eager to buy life insurance that met their needs, and that the potential of their company was tremendous. County Farm Bureau presidents met at Decatur on December 27, 1928, to approve the plan unanimously. It was a mere formality for the voting delegates to the IAA meeting to give final approval. In fact, policies had already been printed, and the Country Life Insurance Company was ready to do business. The first policy was mailed out on February 1, to Sam S. Davis, farm adviser in Piatt county. Larry A. Williams, an experienced insurance executive, was hired as the first manager.

A word about the relationship of the new company to the IAA is in order here. The Illinois Agricultural Holding Company was organized by the IAA to own all Country Life Insurance Company common stock, so that the IAA itself would always have control. Under the law, it was not permissible to limit sale of policies to Farm Bureau members only, but Farm Bureau control is assured by this arrangement.

To understand how completely the business activities of the IAA were (and are) coordinated and controlled, we should here look back to October, 1926, when the Illinois Agricultural Service Company was chartered as a wholly-owned subsidiary of the IAA. Directors, five in number, were to be elected by the executive committee (now the board of directors) of the IAA. In the beginning, the IAA president, secretary, treasurer, business adviser, and head of the legal department, made up the board. It is an administrative corporation, whose job is to render business advisory service to all commercial or semi-commercial activities sponsored by the IAA. Around the IAA office, it has been called the Service Board, or the Management Board. The boards of directors of the IAA and of the commercial companies make policies. As a coordinating body, it has rendered supremely important service in keeping the entire complex of IAA and its affiliates moving ahead as a team, rendering service to members.

The scope of responsibility of the Illinois Agricultural Service Company may be gauged by the fact that in 1929 it was administering the affairs of the Illinois Agricultural Cooperatives Association, Illinois Agricultural Mutual Insurance Company, Farmers' Mutual Reinsurance Company, Country Life Insurance Company, Illinois Farm Supply Company, and the McLean County Milk Producers' Association. Since all of its board members are officers or full-time employees of the IAA, it can usually be called into session on short notice, and decisions can be reached quickly. The commercial companies pay fees for services rendered sufficiently high to pay for the time devoted to the service by the board of directors.

Not all Farm Bureau members considered the commercial ventures as unmixed blessings. There was apprehension in many places that the IAA itself would become so involved in commercial business that it might conceivably neglect its principal business, which was to give farmers a voice in local, state and national affairs affecting their welfare.

Earl Smith could appreciate the danger, and often spoke frankly about it. The dangers were real enough to impel Organization Director Metzger to state the case in his report for 1929. In enumerating the problems of membership acquisition, he listed three, then said:

"Fourthly, membership acquisition to some extent in some counties has been handicapped by the income to the Farm Bureau from commercial or semi-commercial sources. I refer to such income as insurance commissions, part of the rent of the Farm Bureau office paid by subsidiary companies, etc. Apparently a number of our county organizations have chosen to balance their budgets from income from this source rather than from membership fees. I am calling attention to this matter because I believe it may result very disastrously to the membership in the state organization, should it be followed by any considerable number of county organizations." Metzger was a man of convictions and he did not hesitate to express them. He had put his finger on a vital issue that needed sober consideration. How it was finally resolved will be told in a subsequent chapter.

This situation was remedied to some extent by the general acceptance, starting late in 1933, of the Uniform Cooperative Agreement between county Farm Bureaus and IAA. Then, in 1935, the Illinois Legislature passed a law requiring that all insurance agents be licensed. To leaders everywhere, it was unthinkable that county Farm Bureaus should go into the insurance business, so to speak, and a new plan was adopted with practically no opposition. Under the new plan, individual agents were licensed. They continued to have their offices in county Farm Bureau offices with rent and stenographic expenses paid by the companies under a service agreement. Furthermore, they had to agree not to advertise their insurance as "Farm Bureau" insurance, but instead advertise in the name of the insurance companies they were representing. The new arrangement had a most salutary effect on both insurance agents and Farm Bureau. It was a real forward step.

Chapter 13

Sweet are the Uses of Adversity

The issue of farm relief had been clear-cut in the 1928 national election. The Republican party had rejected the Farm Bureau proposals in favor of a milder approach, and had elected a President. Therefore, Mr. Hoover was duty-bound to sponsor legislation based on the platform promises. There was nothing Farm Bureau could do except to help work out the best possible program within the limits of the platform.

President Hoover called a special session of the 71st Congress soon after inauguration. After many weeks of debate and official hearings, Congress enacted the Agricultural Marketing Act. It was approved on June 15, 1929. As the name indicates, it was primarily an attempt to encourage cooperative marketing, providing a revolving fund of $500 million to be loaned to cooperative marketing associations. The Act was to be administered by an eight-man board appointed by the President. It also provided that cooperative associations could take out price insurance upon payment of insurance premiums, so that the co-op would not lose too much money in case of price declines. A stabilization corporation was to be set up to buy any unsalable surpluses.

It would serve no good purpose to discuss in detail the operations of the Federal Farm Board. Suffice it to say that Mr. Hoover appointed as chairman, Alexander Legge, president of the International Harvester Company, a man of outstanding ability, whose integrity was above reproach. Vice chairman was James C. Stone of Lexington, Kentucky, a founder of the Burley Tobacco Growers' Association, and a highly respected leader in cooperative marketing. C. B. Denman, president of the National Livestock Producers' Association, was appointed to the board as livestock representative. Other members were: Carl Williams, editor of the *Oklahoma Stockman and Farmer,* representing cotton; Charles C. Teague, president of the California Fruit Growers' Exchange; W. F. Schilling, president of the Twin City Milk Producers' Association, St. Paul; Charles S. Wilson of New York, who was to represent the fruit interests of the northeastern states; and Samuel R. McKelvie, farm paper publisher of Nebraska, whose special province was wheat. Arthur M. Hyde of Missouri, Secretary of Agriculture was an *ex officio* member. Legge was to resign within two years, to be succeeded by Stone. McKelvie and Teague also resigned later, to be replaced by Sam H. Thompson, president of the American Farm Bureau Federation, and Frank Evans of Utah, former general counsel of the AFBF.

Legge soon announced that loans would be restricted to marketing agencies owned and controlled by farmers. "Organize if you want help," was the word that went out. If agriculture could be helped by cooperative marketing the board was determined to make the most of the machinery available.

Unfortunately, plans did not work out well. Soon to come was the stock market break and a long-continued and world-wide erosion of commodity prices. As always happens when easy money is available, the revolving fund sort of melted away as conditions got worse. Some cooperatives were "bailed out" of trouble for a time; but in early 1933, after the board had been quite inactive for a year, the entire project was liquidated, and even more ambitious farm relief projects were undertaken by the Roosevelt administration.

Returning to the IAA, we find its own affairs booming. By

the end of 1931, the Association was leasing 15,000 square feet of office space (an entire floor) in the Transportation Building at 608 South Dearborn St., Chicago. Quite a change from the two rooms and 364 square feet occupied when the first Chicago office was opened in 1922! No less than 137 people were now employed. The bulk of these were needed to carry on the office work, under the direction of Office Manager C. E. Johnston, who had succeeded John H. Kelker, whose duties as manager of the Farmers Mutual Reinsurance Company now required all of his time.

Those were years of adversity in many ways, but the organization and its activities seemed to thrive on it. For example, Illinois Farm Supply Company made steady progress. In its fifth year of operation ending August 1, 1931, the Company handled more than $5 million worth of petroleum products, serving 47 county supply companies. Farmers had invested $929,772 in those 47 companies. They owned 120 bulk storage stations and 351 truck tanks. By 1935, total volume of business of 60 county service companies was to grow to $8.4 million, with patronage refunds to members amounting to $180,000.

Illinois Farm Supply Company, as well as the other commercial enterprises sponsored by IAA, added greatly to the prestige and renown of the parent organization. As was indicated earlier, one of the big reasons for going into the oil business was that farmers were not satisfied with the quality of the petroleum products then being distributed by some companies. From the beginning, Farm Supply adhered rigidly to high quality specifications, and every effort was made to give members the kind of service they expected from their own organization. Unlike many farmer cooperative groups organized earlier, Farm Supply did not give easy credit to its patrons, and it did not cut prices. With men like Smith and Cowles running things, it was certain that these twin pitfalls would be avoided at all cost. Smith and Cowles were dedicated to the belief that farmers wanted good quality and service, and were willing to pay for it. They believed also that farmers would appreciate having their business run efficiently. Events were to prove conclusively that they were as right as rain.

Members took great pride in their institutions, and it wasn't long until dividends received on their enterprises supplied all the evidence they needed that the capital supplied by them was being judiciously handled. For example, the Iroquois Service Company, organized in 1931, was able to pay patronage dividends amounting to $9,600 in 1934. To dramatize the payment, it was all made in silver. The coins were piled high on a table at annual meeting time as tangible evidence of success. That meeting was a memorable occasion in Iroquois county. To say that it enhanced the loyalty and devotion of members is to make a gross understatement. Members became rugged, aggressive defenders of the Farm Bureau and its affiliates.

Leaders did not hesitate to invade new fields. In 1931, for instance, they undertook an experiment in the use of soybean oil as an ingredient of paint that was to prove epochal. By 1954, to look ahead 20 years, four million gallons had been used.

* * *

At this time, remarkable gains had been made in the insurance field. By January 1, 1931, the Illinois Agricultural Mutual Insurance Company, only three years and nine months old, had received 25,674 applications for auto insurance. And 16 months after it had opened its employer's liability division, 1,550 members had applied for policies to protect them against claims made by their employees. The financial statement showed assets of over $600,000. The company was growing by leaps and bounds.

Comparable gains had been made by the Farmers Mutual Reinsurance Company. By 1935, 10 years after organizing, the record shows that 33,855 fire, 23,412 windstorm, and 32,724 crop hail policies were in force, representing a 16-fold increase in volume of fire insurance over the amount in force at the end of 1926, and a 6-fold increase in crop hail insurance, these being the only types of policies handled in 1926. J. H. Kelker was the manager in 1935.

The story of the early years of the County Life Insurance Company, founded in 1929, is a saga in itself. Under the management of L. A. "Larry" Williams, it was making giant strides. Efferves-

cent, imaginative, and untiring, Williams had the gift of elo-
quence. He could lift an audience out of its chairs by his inspiring
talks. He could, and did, talk as enthusiastically about Farm
Bureau as he could about insurance. He inspired his agents with
crusading zeal, a zeal that was reflected in new records almost
every year. He had able lieutenants in the field. Dave Mieher,
Clarence Ramler, and B. E. Mosier, who supervised the work of
the agents most effectively. In 1935, they set a sensational new
record by selling $19,877,113 worth of life insurance, bringing
the total in force to more than $80 million. You run out of super-
latives when trying to describe the brilliance of such a record,
made in spite of the fact that the country was still deep in the
Great Depression. Williams that year was made director of acquisition for all of the IAA insurance companies.

Dave Mieher was to succeed Williams years later as manager,
and to go on from there to manage the highly successful Southern
Farm Bureau Life Insurance Company. Others who went on to
rewarding careers with other insurance companies include: Paul
L. Laffey, Howard Reeder, Frank V. Wilcox, Paul Edwards, Don
Teare, Carl Peterson, Duane Kuntz, Al Grauer, Vern Holland,
and John Weaver. Peterson and Weaver became presidents of
big companies.

* * *

In 1929, the Illinois Produce Marketing Association was organized to coordinate the sales activities of local associations,
many of which had been set up to sell cream and eggs cooperatively as well as to find ways to improve quality, and to improve
marketing practices generally. Frank A. Gougler had been director of the Produce Marketing department of the IAA, and he
had made up his mind that greater volume was the key to lower
marketing costs, hence the state-wide association. By 1930, thirty-
one local associations were selling their cream to the state association, and volume of cream sold under contract had risen to
nearly 5 million pounds.

The above plan showed spotty results for a time, but in 1933
the state association was dropped and the Illinois Producers

Creameries set up in its place. Buttermaking began in plants at Davenport (Iowa), Peoria, and Bloomington in 1933, and by 1935, plants had been established at Galesburg, Champaign, Carbondale, Mt. Sterling, and Olney, and the Davenport operation moved to Moline. J. B. Countiss, sales manager, reported total output of the eight plants at 6,106,929 pounds. The product was marketed in standard cartons labeled "Prairie Farms Butter." The entire dairy manufacturing business was to undergo severe shocks within a few years, the effects of which will be recounted later. A lot of study was devoted to the problems of egg marketing, but little was accomplished.

Not all Farm Bureau business became successful. The Soybean Marketing Association was organized in late 1929, with James Henry "Hank" Lloyd, a veteran farm adviser from Hancock county, as manager. More than a million bushels of the 1930 crop were pooled. Loans from the Federal Farm Board and the Federal Intermediate Credit Bank financed storage operations. Business increased by a half in 1931 and 1932, but price levels were falling steadily, and the virtual failure of the soybean crop in 1933 gave the organization a knockout blow from which it never recovered.

In 1931, times were not good, but they were good compared with the times that were to follow within two years. The Hoover farm program had not proved itself, but activities in the field of cooperative marketing had been stepped up with Farm Board money, and the Hoover Administration was hoping that it could stabilize the grain market. The Farm Board in 1929 had sponsored a giant grain marketing agency, the Farmers' National Grain Corporation (another U.S. Grain Growers?), and during 1930 it had attempted to hold the line as wheat prices dropped all over the world. The Farmers' National itself was getting over-extended, and therefore the Grain Stabilization Corporation was created to take over the stabilization job. Freed of the stabilization burden, Farmers' National announced early in 1931 that it had made a "profit" of $666,266.84 during the fiscal year ending February 28, 1931, and it continued its operations for a number of years. Nevertheless, on June 30, 1931, the Federal Farm Board, through the Grain Stabilization Corporation, found itself in possession of 257 million bushels of wheat. Sam Thompson faced this situation soon after he had taken his place on the Farm Board on May 1. The Farm Board faced a hopeless situation. It finally was dissolved, within two years, and Mr. Thompson returned to his home in Quincy.

When Mr. Thompson was appointed to the Farm Board, Edward A. O'Neal, automatically moved from the vice presidency of the AFBF to the presidency, Charlie Hearst of Iowa became vice president, and Earl Smith moved into Hearst's place on the AFBF board. Smith was soon to replace Hearst upon the latter's death, as vice president, and the team of O'Neal and Smith were to make history for the American Farm Bureau Federation for a 10-year period.

The deepening depression took its toll. By 1932, sales of limestone and phosphate had fallen to such an extent that Director John R. Bent of the phosphate-limestone department was released, after many years of loyal and effective service to the IAA. The department was revived in 1937, with John R. Spencer as director until 1946. It was reactivated in 1948 as a soil conservation department, to be changed later to a natural resources department. Financial problems were acute, even for a well-financed organization like the IAA, in 1932.

While the Farm Board was having its troubles, the IAA was attempting to do something about grain marketing problems in Illinois. It organized the Illinois Grain Corporation in February, 1930, with Harrison Fahrnkopf, another experienced farm adviser who had joined the IAA staff in 1928 as director of grain marketing, in charge. The Illinois Grain Corporation became a regional member of the Farmers National Grain Corporation, and continued to utilize its marketing facilities for a number of years.

Illinois Grain stockholders consisted of farmer-owned grain elevator companies. By 1935, membership had grown to 199, and grain handled, from both members and non-members, totaled

10,309,000 bushels, 90 per cent of which came from members. This was considerably less than had been handled in 1933 and 1934, but volume was considered satisfactory.

The depression made heavy inroads on membership lists. Many farmers failed to pay their dues. Bank failures added to the general distress. Membership dropped from 60,076 in 1930 to 54,355 in 1933, in spite of valiant efforts by George Metzger and his staff of organization men. Considering the depressed conditions, the wonder is that it didn't drop further. Morale was at a low level in the county organizations. Accurate records were not being kept. When dues were collected, the IAA share was not being sent in with any regularity. Membership records in some counties were in wretched shape. Clearly, something had to be done. The entire IAA staff met for two days to consider the problem, and out of this meeting came a plan to place definite membership responsibility on one man in each county, authorize him to appoint lieutenants, and organize a fall mobilization campaign to collect past-due membership fees and sign up new members. These county directors of organization were to be paid on a commission basis.

The plan was presented to a state-wide meeting of county Farm Bureau presidents and boards of directors at Decatur on September 18, 1933, and received practically unanimous endorsement. The state was divided into three regions, with a director in each, appropriate publicity campaigns were launched, some 200 community meetings were held to stir up enthusiasm, and everybody went to work. Results were most gratifying, with 4,400 memberships sold, and more than 6,000 delinquent members restored to good standing. This all-out drive did more than build up membership—it did a lot to restore morale in the counties. Organization workers and members too, faced with declining membership, got a new appreciation of how much Farm Bureau meant to them and made up their minds that it was worth real sacrifice to keep the organization going, and strong enough to render its accustomed service to members.

144

It helped a lot also in improving relations between the IAA and the county Farm Bureaus, relations which had been too loose, too hit-or-miss, too lacking in uniformity as between county organizations. For some time the organization department, with a lot of help from Vernon Vaniman, who was devoting most of his time to insurance matters, had been working on the problem. The result was a document which amounted to a contract between the IAA and the county Farm Bureau in which the rights as well as responsibilities of each party were clearly outlined. When signed by officers, it became a binding agreement as to collection of dues, sending the IAA share to the IAA office, and the keeping of membership records. In the document, the company organization agreed to accept responsibility for building membership, with one man directly in charge.

Within a few months, every county Farm Bureau in the state, with one exception, had signed the agreement, known as the Uniform Cooperative Agreement, and a new era in relationships was under way. Thus was inaugurated a membership-building movement that continued for twenty-one consecutive years. In only two of those years did any year's membership fall below the mark of the preceding year. It was destined to push membership above 200,000. Other factors were involved in this remarkable advance. Most of the business services, such as in fire and auto insurance were limited to members; and in others, dividends and patronage refunds were paid only to members. These services were so successful that members were reluctant to give them up, once they had made use of them. Furthermore, the Farm Supply Company employees and insurance salesmen proved themselves effective boosters for Farm Bureau. It was not long before many members figured that the savings made through business services were so great that they simply couldn't afford not to be members of Farm Bureau. This was a mighty factor in maintaining membership in the parent organization.

Meanwhile, important staff changes had been made. In 1930, Alfred R. Wright of Varna, a substantial farmer with banking interests, succeeded Frank D. Barton as vice president, to remain until 1935, when he was named assistant treasurer, a post he held with distinction until he resigned in 1946. Talmage DeFrees of Smithboro succeeded him.

Vernon Vaniman, who had done much of the work in building membership in late 1933, was named organization director for 1934, and George Metzger devoted full time to his job as secretary. However, in 1935 Vaniman left to become organization director of the American Farm Bureau Federation, and organization responsibility again reverted to Metzger. Since it was apparent that the two jobs were too much for one man, Paul Mathias (who came to the organization in 1933 as assistant to General Counsel Donald Kirkpatrick,) was named corporate secretary with full responsibility for IAA records, and Metzger became field secretary and director of organization. Mathias became general counsel for the IAA in 1950, and holds that position as this book is being written.

Vaniman had rendered service of tremendous value to the IAA, not only in organization work, but also, as reported in other chapters, in getting the insurance companies and other business enterprises started. He was a born promoter. Nevertheless, IAA officials agreed to release him for greater responsibilities in the national field, where he worked with state Farm Bureaus with great effectiveness until his sudden death on November 30, 1948.

It should be remarked here that in all IAA activities, the organization men in the field were depended on to do spadework in all IAA projects. In stock-selling campaigns for new businesses, in rounding up crowds for special meetings, in helping to run meetings, including the IAA annual meetings, in performing "chores" of any kind, the organization men in all counties were always willing and dependable workers. They have been, in truth, the shock troops of the IAA.

Chapter 14

Democrats Wrestle
with Surplus

Turning now to political developments, the years between the Farm Board failure and the Supreme Court decision ending acreage controls in early 1936 were years of feverish experimentation by the Roosevelt administration. Soon after taking office, Franklin D. Roosevelt confronted one of the worst crises in American history. Bank failures and bankruptcies became epidemic, millions were out of work, and public morale was at a deplorably low level.

Roosevelt regarded amelioration of farm distress as one of the most important items on his agenda. Before he was inaugurated, he had acceded to the pleas of midwest forces, principally Farm Bureau forces, on the appointment of a Secretary of Agriculture. Farm Bureau forces wanted Henry Aagard Wallace, Iowa farm paper editor and a man deeply learned in many fields. A great geneticist, he was also informed on monetary matters and meteorology. He had the confidence of midwest farmers.

Early in his administration, Roosevelt conferred with farm leaders and promised that he would sign any bill designed to stabilize farm prices, provided they come to agreement among themselves on what should be done. No time was wasted. More than fifty so-called "farm leaders," largely farm organization officials and farm paper editors, met in Washington soon after the inauguration and quickly agreed upon principles to be embodied in a new farm law. A bill was written, and considered by the House, which adopted it by a vote of 315 to 98 on March 28. On April 28, the Senate passed the bill, and it was approved by the President on May 12. Name of the bill was the Agricultural Adjustment Act of 1933. The law under which farm programs are carried on today is still that Act, which has been amended considerably. Roosevelt named Chester C. Davis, who had been director of grain marketing for the the IAA until he resigned to devote full time to Washington activities on behalf of "farm relief," as production administrator of the new Act. George N. Peek, retired farm implement manufacturer of Moline, who had led the battle for the McNary-Haugen Bill for the committee of 22, was named administrator, with Charles J. Brand, former chief of the Bureau of Markets, as co-administrator. Jerome Frank was general counsel. With Wallace Secretary of Agriculture, and with almost the entire farm press completely sympathetic, the new experiments to restore the purchasing power of farmers certainly started out under favorable auspices.

Henry Morgenthau, Jr., New York farm paper publisher and a leading businessman, was assigned to take over the moribund Federal Farm Board's activities. Morgenthau gathered together the pieces left from the wreckage, including the assets, and transformed the whole into the Farm Credit Administration. By October, 1933, no less than $15 million in farm mortgages had been refunded, thirteen new banks for cooperatives were set up, and a massive program for refinancing farm loans of all kinds was set in motion. Under the new law, the Federal Land Banks were authorized to issue not more than $2 billion in farm loan bonds on which both principal and interest were to be guaranteed by the government of the United States.

Farm credit was the most pressing need, and it got first attention. Soon, however, action came on the production-control front. Plow-up campaigns were started for cotton and tobacco, and six million pigs were slaughtered for grease and tankage in 1933 in order to reduce pork supplies in hopes of raising prices. The announcement of a 45-cent-a-bushel non-recourse loan on corn brought cheers from Cornbelt farmers.

Plans for a 20 per cent reduction in corn acreage for 1934 were being formulated, and tied to them was a plan to reduce pig farrowing by 25 per cent. Costs were to be met through processing taxes. A cotton program would be ready early in 1934, and prices for fruits and vegetables and dairy products were to be improved by marketing agreements. Taken altogether, these efforts soon took on the proportions of a national crusade.

The story of the first non-recourse corn loan in 1933 is most dramatic. Illinois farmers had been borrowing money on stored corn, due to the fact that the IAA had sponsored a warehouse act in the Illinois legislature, providing that warehouse receipts could be used for collateral. IAA President Smith believed very strongly that in this emergency the federal government should make loans on stored commodities available to all farmers, and he discussed the matter with Washington officials, particularly with Henry T. Rainey of Carrollton, speaker of the House of Representatives, who had served in Congress for thirty years. Smith made a talk on September 13 over WLS, Chicago, discussing the idea, and he asked farmers to write or wire their congressmen, backing the idea. (The Agricultural Adjustment Administration had already announced a 10 cent loan on stored cotton.) He was in Washington later, only to find that Illinois congressmen had heard from only a few farmers on the issue, and were therefore unconvinced that farmers needed such loans. Smith immediately called Metzger, IAA organization director, who suggested that if Congress needed proof of how farmers felt about it, the IAA should call a state-wide mass meeting to discuss it. Smith, discouraged by the meager response to his WLS appeal, was reluctant, but finally agreed to the plan. Metzger enlisted the help of all county Farm Bureau presidents, who responded enthusiastically. Arrangements were completed for the meeting in the Caterpillar Tractor plant in Peoria for September 27, 1933.

President Smith invited Rainey to be the principal speaker. Other speakers listed were President Edward A. O'Neal of the American Farm Bureau Federation, State Senator Simon E. Lantz, Clifford V. Gregory of *Prairie Farmer,* and others. By noon on the appointed day, the 5,000 chairs that had been provided were filled, and 3,000 more farmers were perched on tractors, boxes, or on any object that offered support. Many had to stand, the crowd was a good-humored one and well-behaved, but there was no mistaking the fact that they were there to demand action from their elected representatives in Washington. The air fairly crackled with excitement. While waiting for the meeting to begin, Joseph H. Checkley, farm adviser in Logan county, led the enthusiastic crowd in community singing. The vigor of the singing reflected the feelings of the farmers.

President Smith was at his best in his introductory remarks. He described what the new administration had already done in behalf of farmers. He assured the audience that there was no partisan politics in those efforts. Referring to President Roosevelt, Secretary of Agriculture Henry A. Wallace, Chester Davis, and George N. Peek of the AAA, he said: "These men are our friends. Let's not criticize them but let's be helpful and constructive. . . ." Referring to the crop-control program, he said that the idea is repugnant to farmers, and he said further that, "it is repugnant to me, but we have no other choice so long as foreign demand for our surplus is all but gone." Then he discussed the big issue, the proposed corn loan. Remarks by O'Neal, Gregory, Lantz and others about the necessity of government action in many fields to meet the critical economic situation were cheered to the echo. Congressman Rainey was plainly impressed. He had the crowd with him when he arose and said: "I have never, in all my experience as a public speaker, addressed a more thoughtful, earnest, large audience than this . . . ," and he won them completely when he closed his address by saying: "I am following the leadership of Earl Smith, Ed O'Neal, Clifford Gregory, Henry Wallace and those great farm leaders. They are going the right way, and you will go the right way if you join with me and follow along with them."

Edward A. O'Neal, Henry A. Wallace, and Earl C. Smith

151

The crowd didn't realize it at the time, but the fact is that the fate of the proposed corn loan was decided by what went on at Peoria. They responded with a ringing affirmative vote when asked if they wanted a corn loan. Speaker Rainey immediately sent a long telegram to President Roosevelt, reporting the sentiment of Illinois farmers and reiterating his conviction that an early announcement of a loan plan would do much to restore confidence among Cornbelt farmers. Smith, tremendously encouraged, went to Washington immediately to confer with Administration officials. Wallace had already approved a loan plan for corn, but he was inclined to think that 35 cents a bushel would be the upper limit. Smith argued earnestly for 50 cents, but would compromise at 45 cents. The issue was taken to the President. As Smith related the incident later, Roosevelt listened to him attentively, and finally said, with a twinkle in his eyes, something like this: "Well, Mr. Smith, we might as well go broke at 45 cents as at 35 cents. The loan will be 45 cents."

I am certain that Smith regarded that moment as one of the greatest in his career. He knew that announcement of the loan would give a tremendous lift to morale among farmers, strengthen their confidence, help them pay their debts and buy all sorts of goods and services. He regarded that moment as the turning point in moving agriculture out of the depression. Official announcement of the 45-cent corn loan was made a few weeks later.

Before the commodity programs could be readied for 1934, George Peek resigned, largely because he and Henry Wallace could not agree, and Chester Davis took over as administrator. By herculean efforts and many a short cut, programs were actually set up and were in operation for the 1934 crops of corn, wheat, cotton, and tobacco.

It is a temptation here to discuss in detail the operation of the various programs in 1934 and 1935, but it would hardly be appropriate in a book about the Farm Bureau of Illinois. The IAA gave solid support to the AAA program, and helped Chester Davis and Henry Wallace in every way possible. IAA leaders generally believed that in this program at last, had been found a way to stabilize farm prices.

There was trouble ahead, however. The programs worked, after a fashion, in 1934 and 1935; but on January 6, 1936, the Supreme Court, by a six-to-three decision, declared the essential features of the AAA program, namely the power to levy processing taxes and the power to enter into acreage reduction contracts with farmers constituted coercion by economic pressure, and were therefore unconstitutional.

That ended the acreage control experiment for the time being; but resourceful lawyers found ways to go about the job legally, the AAA was amended in 1938, the Department of Agriculture was again in the business of curtailing acreage.

The IAA and the American Farm Bureau Federation were solidly behind Henry Wallace and the Administration in getting the new farm program which grew out of the amendments to the Agricultural Adjustment Act of 1933, which were adopted early in 1938. Earl C. Smith made numerous speeches defending the Act, and advising farmers to cooperate in every way to make it effective. In his address at the IAA annual meeting in January, 1939, he lauded the objectives of the new program, while admitting that the system of allotting corn acreage left something to be desired. He advised farmers to quit quibbling over little things and try to make the law work. "If we are to preserve and improve the AAA of 1938," he said, "it now appears necessary for all of us to become more active in support of efforts to bring about a much better understanding on the part of all farmers of the purposes and of the opportunities under the law." Delegates to the convention adopted a resolution endorsing the legislation.

Cornbelt participation in the program was not general in 1938, 1939, and 1940; and when we got into the war in late 1941, Claude R. Wickard of Indiana, who had succeeded Henry A. Wallace as Secretary of Agriculture when the latter was elected Vice President in 1940, found himself with the greatest accumulation of food and fiber in history. This he considered a blessing, and he predicted food would win the war and dictate the peace.

During the war, no farm production controls were in effect, except for tobacco, and for some years afterward there was no need for acreage allotments, since all of our surpluses were needed

153

to rebuild a war-ravaged world. So, for national administration and for Farm Bureau, the issue of production control remained dormant for several years. But Earl C. Smith remained a rugged advocate of controls, even after he retired in 1945 after twenty years as president of the IAA, right up to his death in 1961.

During these years, the business services provided through the IAA, thanks to conservative management, close attention to costs, and rigid auditing practices, were flourishing. President Smith referred to them in his 1937 convention address: "Although largely developed previous to and during depression years, each company continues without debt of any kind or character and, with the exception of the Illinois Livestock Marketing Association, each company has its capital intact, has met all capital obligations, in many cases has returned large patronage dividends, and in addition, has added substantially to its surplus."

Chapter 15

Days of Depression Pass

As I have indicated in previous chapters, the IAA affiliated business institutions grew reassuringly during the depression, and membership problems were subjected to hard study. Farm Bureau members were intensely loyal. By 1933, membership had dropped less than ten per cent since 1930. In 1933, it stood at 54,355. The next year showed a gain of more than 10 per cent, and by 1940, it had grown to 70,453. Net farm income had risen from $2.68 billions in 1933 to $4.68 billions in 1940, for a gain of 75 per cent. Many Illinois farms had been re-financed during this period. The country was still far from prosperous. Unemployment stubbornly refused to drop below nine million. The outbreak of World War II in 1939 had stimulated business to some extent, but its full force was not to be felt until 1941.

In 1933 and 1934, government checks had been of material assistance to Illinois farmers. It was estimated that Illinois farmers would get $40 million in corn-hog payments in 1934, and $2.6 million in wheat payments, along with some $45 million in corn loans. Contrary to the general impression, crop-adjustment payments never were a big per cent of the farm income, usually five or six per cent, and the top was about 7.5 per cent in 1939.

The IAA, with Smith at the helm, was a rugged defender of the farm program sponsored by the New Deal. He invited his close friend, of Chester C. Davis, administrator of the Agricultural Adjustment Act, to address the IAA convention at Danville on January 5, 1934. Davis reported that plans were under consideration for a beef cattle "program" designed to improve cattle prices. Voting delegates to the convention, in a clear-cut resolution, approved the principles embodied in the Agricultural Adjustment Act of 1933, and went beyond mere approval by continuing: "We further urge that immediately upon the levying of processing taxes upon any basic agricultural crops, equivalent increases in import duties on all foreign commodities that compete with such basic agricultural commodities be imposed, as is provided for and authorized in the Agricultural Adjustment Act." They pledged their cooperation and support to Secretary of Agriculture Wallace and AAA Administrator Davis.

In his convention address, President Smith took care to say that he considered current government efforts to stabilize farm prices as emergency measures only. He said that permanent solution to the problem rested primarily on: (1) increasing exports; (2) finding new industrial uses for farm commodities; and (3) restoring large areas of marginal lands to the public domain. "Owners of fertile farm lands," he said, "must not longer than necessary be asked to keep idle large portions of their respective acreages." Today, nearly thirty years later, those words have a curiously familiar ring. All of the remedies suggested have been tried, and one wonders how much has been accomplished, even though billions of dollars are being spent each year.

Farm income was increasing in these years, in spite of searing drouths in 1934 and 1936. In his address at the IAA convention in Quincy on January 30, 1935, President Smith pointed out that although the 1934 corn crop was 35 per cent less than in 1933, its farm value was 46 per cent greater, and that while the pork produced in Illinois was 12 per cent less than in 1934, its farm value was 45 per cent greater. To President Smith, this was proof that farmers must control market supplies in order to stabilize prices.

Voting delegates to the convention were much intrigued with the notion that some of the corn crop could be used profitably by converting it into alcohol to be blended with gasoline for motor fuel. All over the Midwest, this idea caught fire and Congress was bombarded with requests for action. The idea sounded plausible, and it was not discredited until it was found that distillers could not pay more than 25 cents a bushel for corn if the resulting alcohol were to compete with alcohol made from blackstrap molasses. It was also discovered that one gallon of alcohol would cost more than the nine gallons of gasoline in the mixture. The idea was finally discarded, but for years it was hotly debated. Many of the speeches made in its behalf were as inflammatory as the fuel mixture itself.

Producers of corn and hogs apparently were convinced that government efforts to control production were bearing fruit, for in the corn-hog referendum on whether to continue the program in 1936, they voted six-to-one for continuation. Within months the Supreme Court decision invalidating the processing tax was to wreck most of the program of production control, but that situation was later cleared up when Congress passed the Agricultural Adjustment Act of 1938.

On January 6, 1936, the Supreme Court had announced its decision, and the IAA convention at Decatur opened on January 29. The decision overshadowed everything else discussed by the delegates. The talk indicated that farmers were particularly incensed because of the stipulation that some $200 million in processing taxes were to be returned to the processors who had paid it. Farmers regarded this as a windfall to the packers, because they believed packers had passed the cost on to consumers in the form of higher prices, or had collected it from farmers in the form of lower prices paid for live hogs.

The delegates said in the resolution on farm programs: "Study and experience both before and after the enactment of the Agricultural Adjustment Act have fully convinced farmers of the imperative need for such legislation. . . ." And further: "The right of the American farmer to receive for his products prices which will give him average purchasing power in line with the prevailing price levels of industry and labor cannot be questioned."

Within a month of the convention, on February 25, 1936, Congress was to adopt amendments to the Soil Conservation Act of 1935, which permitted the continuance and expansion of payments to farmers for conservation practices. Commodity loans, of course, were not affected by the Supreme Court decision. Then, early in 1938, Congress enacted the Agricultural Adjustment Act of 1938, which provided production-control features pretty much as they had been in the old program. Then began the accumulation of surplus commodities which presented the Federal government with a problem that would have been gigantic except for the outbreak of war in Europe. The war "bailed out" Secretary of Agriculture Wallace on this one, and the problem did not again become serious until after the Korean War.

In 1936, there was no need for farmers to curtail production. Nature did it with a drouth that was almost a duplicate of the one in 1934. In fact, reduced volume of commodities going to market caused farm prices to rise gradually, and by the summer of 1937 most of them had practically reached the parity level.

Under these circumstances, the sense of urgency that had actuated farmers in their deliberations on ways to lift farm prices was modified to some extent, but President Smith overlooked no opportunity to keep the issue alive. An editorial in the June issue of the IAA RECORD faithfully reflects his ideas, as follows: "The farm problem will not be solved until the farmer exercises as much influence and is as effective in fixing prices on his products as are the folks he buys from.

"The AAA, organized agriculture's most ambitious and successful efforts thus far to influence prices, is gone. Soil conservation, another approach at preventing the accumulation of price-depressing surpluses, is here. How effective the new program will be is still a question. Farmers will write the answer. . . ."

Delegates to the 1937 IAA convention in Chicago (January 28-29) adopted a firm resolution in favor of additional national legislation designed to stabilize farm prices by bringing production into fair relationship with effective demand. The Supreme Court decision a year earlier had shocked Illinois farmers, but it had not in the least dulled their determination. They believed that Congress could provide legislation that would stabilize farm prices, and they were demanding just that. President Smith was the spokesman for organized agriculture in Illinois, and everybody knew it.

During 1937, Congress dallied on considering the new control legislation, but in August, when the crop estimates were published, huge crops of cotton and corn and wheat were predicted, it finally got off dead center and attempted to pass the bill. But it was not until February 10, 1938, that the House passed it, to be followed by the Senate four days later. It came close to meeting Farm Bureau specifications, and Secretary of Agriculture Wallace termed it "the most constructive farm legislation which Congress has ever adopted." Smith thought it would stabilize livestock prices as well as grain prices. Speaking at Peoria on February 19, he said that "instability in price levels of feed grains is the cause of price swings in livestock prices. When corn is selling at parity or around 80 cents and hogs are bringing eight cents or less, feeders will market them at 190 or 200 pounds instead of feeding longer. This will decrease pork production and produce better meat which will lead consumers to eat more of it."

President Smith proved to be a poor prophet. Guessing what farmers will do under certain circumstances is not unlike trying to guess the stock market. In 1938, with lots of corn on hand from the 1937 crop, farmers produced enough hogs to depress the average price from $9.50 in 1937, to $7.74. In 1939, it dropped to $6.23, and in 1940 to $5.39. The low price discouraged production in 1941, and the average price rose to $9.09. In 1942, with a war on and government appealing for more hogs with minimum prices guaranteed, came a big increase in production which sold at higher prices. In 1943, hog producers proved what could be done under a crash program by producing the stupendous quantity of well over 25 *billion* pounds (live weight)of pork which sold at an average price of $13.70. Due to the insatiable post-war demand for meat, hog prices rose to an average of $17.50 in 1946, and to $24.10 in 1947.

If anything was proved by this record, it is that if farmers have an attractive price incentive, they will automatically respond with huge production. It matters not whether the incentive comes from the free play of market forces, or from government itself. The record is only too clear on this point, to the great embarrassment of the Federal Government which has offered to buy all the market will not absorb of several commodities. The free play of economic forces in cattle, hog, and poultry markets have done a better job of regulating production than have government controls in the regulated segments of agriculture; but the lesson that is there for all to see is largely overlooked in our mad rush to have a benevolent Federal Government guarantee everybody security and prosperity. Now we are in position to ask ourselves, to paraphrase St. Mark: "If the salt loses it savor, wherewith shall it be salted?"

There should be no question in anyone's mind about what Smith considered the No. 1 job of a farm organization. He often said with convincing earnestness that it was more important to see that farmers got a good price for their corn than it was to save them a few cents on a gallon of gasoline. In fact, he said on more than one occasion that 90 per cent of the obligation of a farm organization consisted of the responsibility to develop sound national policies for agriculture.

In his address at the 1938 IAA convention in Springfield on January 27, President Smith said: "When we adopt policies which will maintain farm commodity prices at fair levels, we will have found the key to national welfare, contentment, and prosperity." He went on to say further: "When completely organized, agriculture will still be in the minority but it can be a very powerful minority in preserving American institutions that have proved their worth, in putting down special privileges, and securing an equitable distribution of the national income. . . . Since the turn of the century, both American business and organized American labor, with the sanction or the approval of government, have secured an ever-increasing portion of the national income without regard to the relative position of agriculture. We should not forget that maladjustment between agriculture and these groups has resulted in large part from federal laws, tariffs, corporate controls, agreements and labor monopolies or restrictions. Equitable readjustment must be effected at an early date if any reasonable degree of prosperity is to be assured and the essential principles of a democracy preserved."

During the period under discussion (1932-1940), the IAA was very busy with state legislation. In 1933 and 1934 a strong position was taken in favor of legislation to limit taxes on tangible property to one per cent of fair cash value, except to retire bonds or to pay bond interest, but no progress was made in this field. A sales tax bill assessing a tax of three per cent on retail sales, was held unconstitutional in 1933, and the legislation enacted in its place a so-called "occupational tax," which was, in effect, a two per cent sales tax. The purpose was primarily to pay relief costs, and to reduce taxes on tangible property. This tax, now grown to $3\frac{1}{2}$ per cent, is in effect at the time of writing these words. This tax did result in eliminating the state tax on real property ($5.00 for each $1,000 of assessed value). By 1935, this tax was yielding more than $60 million a year. In 1960, it yielded $357,158,287, and in fiscal 1963, $543,341,480!

The objective of the IAA tax work has been, not only to keep taxes in bounds, but also to spread them properly, so that no segment of the population escapes paying something near its fair share. Repeated efforts have been made to amend the revenue article of the state constitution, which was adopted in 1818 and revised in 1870. The "uniform clause" in the section on taxation has been the stumbling block to tax reform. Providing as it does that all property shall be assessed at the same proportion of value, it has led to practically universal failure to report intangible property to the tax assessor. In Chicago, automobiles are not reported to the assessor, but the city imposes a vehicle tax which is presumed to make up for the loss. Another disadvantage of the clause is that it has led to great opposition to a state income tax. The IAA has repeatedly advocated adoption of an income tax as one means of broadening the tax base, and it has had the support of labor groups, educational groups, and others, but such efforts have never been successful. Real tax reform will probably not come until the revenue article of the state constitution is rewritten.

The big tax problem in the period under discussion was to meet bills for relief of the unemployed. Special session after special session of the state legislature was called, and various expedients, including diversion of road funds into relief channels, were resorted to in order to meet the rising costs.

While he devoted much of his time to national farm legislation during this period, President Smith enthusiastically directed the commercial enterprises fathered by Farm Bureau. He had plenty to be proud of. The Farm Supply Company in 1940, for example, was furnishing essential supplies to 64 county service companies and 78 other cooperatives. The county service companies could report in 1940 accumulated surpluses totaling more than $2 million, and patronage dividends returned to farmers amounting to $1,537,000 annually for the past three years, or more than 100 per cent on their capital investment. Petroleum products distributed amounted to more than 100 million gallons in 1940.

During 1940, Country Life Insurance Company sold more than $20 million worth of life insurance, bringing the total in force to more than $153 million. The Illinois Agricultural Mutual Insurance Company had 85,864 automobile insurance policies in force. The Farmers Mutual Reinsurance Company had fire, windstorm, and crop insurance in force amounting to more than $250 million. The Producer creameries were selling more than 6 million pounds of butter. The marketing agencies were doing well. The Farm Bureau in Illinois was doing quite well, thank you. In his foreword to the 1940 annual report, President Smith wrote. "Membership in the Illinois Agricultural Association at the close of 1940 was the highest in more than seventeen years. The records disclose that without exception the departments of the Association and its associated organizations continued a healthy growth in volume of business, in savings and in service to its members. Never was the organization in a better financial condition."

The IAA and its associated companies were indeed out of the depression.

Chapter 16

The War Years

The silver anniversary of the founding of the IAA was celebrated with appropriate ceremonies at the convention in St. Louis, January 28-31, 1941. A special edition of the IAA RECORD, with silver cover, was issued, with a brief history of the founding and growth of the organization. A record-breaking crowd of some 6,000 people came, including many of the oldtimers who had played important parts in developing the Farm Bureau in Illinois to its position as the biggest, most powerful, and best-financed in the whole United States. It was a year of jubilee. Membership was approaching 75,000.

In his address at the convention, President Smith paid tribute to the vision and resourcefulness of the pioneers who laid the foundation for the present structure, now grown so great, and reviewed the principal events in the twenty-five years of growth. He reported that the IAA and the twelve IAA-sponsored state-wide cooperative organizations now had assets of more than $20 million. More than $5 million had been returned to members as patronage dividends, and more than $5 million had been added to surplus accounts. "This measures the organization," he said, "only from the standpoint of the activities that can be reflected in dollars and cents. When considered from the standpoint of the primary purpose, that of providing broad representation of farmers' interests in social, economic, and political affairs, we can, at least in a limited way, truly visualize the real value of the organization and the service it has performed."

President Smith was deeply distressed because federal laws enacted to stabilize the farm economy were not working too well. He was inclined to believe that the situation was the result of saddling the Secretary of Agriculture with too many responsibilities. Costs of administration were becoming indefensible, and duplication of efforts as between agencies was developing. "On repeated occasions," he said, "the most direct and constructive criticism has been made to men in highest positions of authority with recommendations for correction of the growing difficulties. Not only has nothing been done to correct the situation but in many cases conditions are becoming more serious and acute. In many sections farmers are becoming confused and losing confidence in the ultimate effectiveness of these national programs."

It must have hurt Smith to make these remarks, because from 1933 on, Farm Bureau and the Franklin D. Roosevelt Administration had worked almost as one force, in writing farm legislation and seeing it through Congress. But the honeymoon was definitely over. The ostensible break had come over the drive that Secretary of Agriculture Wallace had made to have the Department of Agriculture take over the Federal Land Banks and make them, in effect, government credit institutions. In the opinion of Farm Bureau leaders, this move was simply a part of a general trend in the Administration toward further domination of agriculture by the Federal Government, which meant, to Farm Bureau leaders, bureaucracy rampant. It was beginning to dawn on many that "partnership" of an organization with government is likely to become quite one-sided, with the citizen organization the silent (and impotent) partner.

It might have been expected that when Claude R. Wickard of Camden, Indiana, succeeded Wallace as Secretary of Agriculture, peace would be restored, but it didn't work out that way. Wickard was a Farm Bureau member, an excellent farmer, and had had long experience in the administration of the farm program in the Midwest states. But his ideas coincided precisely with those of the Administration, and the breach was not healed. He did not attend the convention at St. Louis, nor was he represented. The only Washington man on the program was Chester C. Davis, now a member of the National Defense Advisory Commission.

The existing unpleasant situation was reflected in the resolution on farm programs adopted at the convention. The resolution applied to the so-called "action agencies" of the USDA, which administered the AAA, crop insurance, marketing agreements, the Commodity Credit Corporation, the Soil Conservation Service, and the Farm Security Administration. The resolution pointed out that these agencies were administering federal funds of more than $1 billion and had payrolls aggregating more than $65 million annually, and went on as follows: "The Illinois Agricultural Association, in line with the declared policy of its national organization, the American Farm Bureau Federation, insists that the Congress now in session, for the purpose of efficiency and economy, perfect a reorganization of these so-called agencies; that in this reorganization, duplication and overlapping be eliminated; and that a complete reorganization be made in Washington with the extension of such coordination into the several states, counties and local communities.

"Now is the time to reorganize the line and now is the time to coordinate these forces. Specifically, to accomplish this objective, we propose the creation by Congress of an independent five-man, non-partisan administrative board appointed by the President, the membership of which would represent agriculture. This board should report periodically to the Congress and to the secretary of agriculture or through the secretary of agriculture to the President. . . ."

In another resolution, the delegates demanded a similar board to administer the farm credit agencies. No question about it, the delegates were plainly worried about the prospect of federal domination of all of agriculture. In another resolution, delegates said that they saw no need of substantial changes in the Agricultural Adjustment Act of 1938, but that commodity loan levels should be raised to be more in line with new conditions.

Now the fat was in the fire. Farm Bureau and Wickard were to clash repeatedly later. On April 3, 1941, Wickard announced support prices for hogs, butter, poultry, and eggs, without consulting his advisory committee of which Smith and O'Neal were members. O'Neal quickly pointed out the the minimum hog price of $9 a hundred was below the parity price of $9.24, and Smith said that the minimum prices would almost certainly become maximum prices, and thus prevent farmers from receiving parity prices. Furthermore, Wickard released the brakes on corn production by announcing that farmers who wished to do so could raise their corn acreage to normal without penalty. Smith felt sure that this action would certainly keep corn prices below parity.

Other events followed quickly. On May 26, President Roosevelt signed a bill raising all commodity loan rates to 85 per cent of parity, a figure previously suggested by Farm Bureau. And on July 1, the President signed the bill extending the life of the Commodity Credit Corporation. The really important thing about this bill was a rider attached to it which provided that for any farm commodity for which the Secretary of Agriculture asked increases in production, the support price would be 85 per cent of parity. This rider was known as the Steagall Amendment, and the commodities involved became known as "Steagall" commodities. More than a year later, the Stabilization Act, October, 1942, raised supports to 90 per cent of parity, and provided specifically that such supports should be continued for two years following the end of the war. (This was to arouse endless controversy after the war because Congress repeatedly extended the two-year clause, which led to government taking title to mountainous piles of farm commodities.)

By August 30, 1941, farm prices, due to war-created demands for farm products, had risen practically to the parity level. Then, in December, came the attack on Pearl Harbor by the Japanese.

The entire economy was put on a war footing. Acreage allotments on all crops except tobacco were eliminated. Every effort was made to increase, rather than decrease production.

One of the events that took place at the 1941 IAA convention, which was to be important to the organization, was the election to the IAA board of directors of Charles B. Shuman of Moultrie county. He was 33 years old, operated 450 acres of land, had served as president of his county Farm Bureau for four years, had been a 4-H Club leader for 10 years, was a director or officer of several cooperatives, had Angus cattle and Duroc-Jersey hogs, grew some hybrid corn, was married and the father of three sons. He was destined to succeed Smith as president of the IAA four years later, and to succeed Allan B. Kline as president of the American Farm Bureau Federation in 1954.

The IAA in 1941 demonstrated once again why it is important that farmers be organized. Immediately upon adjournment of the legislature in July, the Illinois Department of Finance announced that effective August 1, 1941, the state sales tax would be applied to sales of breeding stock, and also to livestock feeds. The new regulation was not based on any change in the law, but upon a recent State Supreme Court decision affecting sales of seed. Representatives of IAA and others interested promptly requested a hearing, and asked that the ruling be held in abeyance until a hearing had been held. The request was granted, the hearing held, and the tax was imposed. The IAA went to work, and soon filed suit in the Circuit Court of Sangamon county. The case, along with others filed at the same time, was never tried, but early in 1942 the Department of Finance announced that effective January 7, it would revert to the old rules under which breeding stock, feed and seed sales would be exempt from the tax. Had the tax been imposed, it would have cost Illinois farmers between $600,000 and $800,000 a year.

In 1941, the IAA held two annual meetings. For very good reasons, the end of the fiscal year had been changed from December 30 to September 30, and it was decided that the annual meeting should be held reasonably soon after that date. November

25-28 were the dates selected, and Springfield was the place. A host of problems were to be considered. We were not yet in the war, but we were heavily involved in lend-lease operations. We were backing the allied cause with everything we could do, "short of war." The USDA was organizing a drive for increased production of hogs, dairy products, vegetables, soybeans and other oil-producing crops. As war demands for all kinds of goods mounted, fear of a skyrocketing price movement and consequent inflation became general. The board of directors of the American Farm Bureau Federation had already asked the federal government to impose selective price controls in order to keep the economy on a sound basis.

Convention delegates, as expected, adopted a resolution asking for price controls "on any commodity for which an inadequate supply threatens to cause an undue price rise, and providing for comparable restriction of wage rate increases within affected industries."

Price ceilings on farm commodities should be set at "not less than 110 per cent of parity, thus giving free play in the price level of farm products between a government-supported 85 per cent of parity minimum and such a 110 per cent of parity maximum, thereby protecting both producers and consumers of agricultural commodities by assuring substantially a parity relationship."

On federal taxation, the delegates recommended recapture of all excess profits resulting from defense activities, and that any abnormal increase in salaries or wages be paid only in the form of defense bonds or certificates, not negotiable until the emergency had passed.

At the annual meeting, all commercial affiliates were able to report thriving business, the result primarily of very satisfactory prices of most farm commodities. Demands for everything were zooming upwards. Chester H. Becker, reporting for the first time as manager of the Illinois Farm Supply Company, noted that, "we have encountered serious difficulties in purchasing certain commodities." Insurance sales were booming. Prairie Farms butter sales were up 13.93 per cent, and profits were up 88 per cent. The war boom was on.

All through 1942, war-created problems multiplied in respect to manpower, selective service, price ceilings, priorities, transportation, and a dozen other categories. When delegates assembled in Chicago on November 17 for the 28th annual meeting, 66 young staff men from the IAA and affiliates, many of them holding positions of great responsibility, had entered the armed forces. Many adjustments had to be made. Business went on at accelerated tempo. President Smith reported: "Without exception, the Association and all the business services connected with it have not only successfully met all necessary changes, but have expanded their services and improved their respective financial positions. It is particularly pleasing to note that during the year, 16,831 new members joined the ranks of the organization, bringing the membership in the Illinois Agricultural Association to 85,808 for a 19-year high. This is as it should be, for never in the history of the Nation have farmers as individuals or as a group been confronted with more serious problems and responsibilities."

President Smith, reporting on the leaders' spring meeting at Springfield on April 10, wrote (in part) as follows: "It was the overwhelming opinion of the 1,000 leaders assembled that the best way to protect the basic principles of agricultural legislation and the meritorious phases of national farm programs would be for farmers now to demand retrenchment in the field of agricultural appropriations together with a great reduction in administrative machinery.

"In other words, it was the prevailing opinion of the leaders that with price levels of agricultural commodities approaching, and in some instances exceeding parity, there is no justification for a continued demand for large appropriations such as have been secured by organized agriculture during recent years.

"This is equally true in the activities of the Farm Security Administration. Every thoughtful farmer realizes that with satisfactory prices for agricultural commodities, the need and requirement for easy credit is greatly reduced.

"Over all, a retrenchment policy of this character would call for a drastic curtailment of activities in the administration of these farm programs with consequent reduction in administrative costs running into tens of millions of dollars. Such a retrenchment policy would also permit approximately 100,000 farmers who have been engaged in the administration of the various farm programs to give a great deal more of their time to active farm production which the nation now requires."

Any way you look at it, the above sentiments represented plain common sense, the calm voice of reason. With farm prices at parity, why was there any need of government payments? Needless to say, such sentiments struck no responding chord in Congress, nor in the bureaucracy which administered the various farm programs. Plenty of notice was given in the press of the Farm Bureau campaign to reduce profligate waste in administration of the Farm Security Administration; but hardly anyone today remembers that at the same time Illinois farmers were asking for comparable reforms in the administration of programs for commercial farmers. Ironically enough, reform did come in the Farm Security Administration; but little was done in the other field, where much greater savings could have been made. The upshot was that Farm Bureau was tagged in many publications as being against the "little farmer."

A big issue between Farm Bureau and the Administration was on the question of releasing government-owned commodities at prices below parity. Farm Bureau took the position that with livestock prices at or above parity, there was no good reason for keeping grain prices below parity, particularly because grain prices at parity levels would still leave the feeder plenty of margin for profit. The Administration prevailed, but no problem was solved; and within months the Administration was deep in a complicated system of subsidies designed to keep consumer prices down so as to lessen demands for increased wages.

It is worthy of note that in his address at the 1942 annual meeting, President Smith spoke plainly and forcefully on the subject of the dangers of inflation. "Why," he asked, "do we not tackle inflation at the point of its basic cause?" He pointed out that national income had increased at least $34 billion in two short years. "This large increase in the national income is largely the result of war activities and conditions," he said. "Should we not amend our revenue measures so as to recapture at least a very substantial part of this abnormal increase in the earnings and income of the American people? This increase is caused by war conditions and should be recaptured and used by the government in meeting war expenses.

"I fully appreciate that we do not like to think in terms of increased taxes but I believe that a serious tax consciousness on the part of every individual in America would be the best way to impress upon government officials the necessity of reasonable economy in managing the affairs of government. I also believe that if the government recaptured this abnormal increase in the earnings of the citizens, it would be the most effective way to curtail the abnormal increase in the demand for commodities, which, in essence, is the basic cause of inflation. This could all be accomplished with only a small part of the expense and the number of government employees that will be required if we depend upon price controls and rationing to reach the same ends."

In the above, Smith went right to the heart of the matter. The trouble with his suggestion as to how to prevent inflation was that it was too simple. Furthermore, it had no political appeal. Put into effect, it might alienate voters. And so the Administration took the politically expedient course, one that permitted concealment of the true cost for years through "control" of prices, with the bill finally presented to all citizens in the form of a dollar that was worth less than fifty cents twenty years later.

By 1943, the Administration was rationing many foods, and its program of keeping retail food prices low through subsidies was in full swing. The first subsidy announced was on butter. Then came cheese, bread, sugar, vegetables, and potatoes, and finally beef, pork and lamb. At the annual meeting in Chicago, November 16-19, IAA members condemned consumer subsidies in strong language, and the voting delegates, in resolution, said plainly: "Illinois farmers are unalterably opposed to consumer subsidies. They belive that such subsidies are unwarranted in fact, are highly inflationary in effect, are prone to establish for postwar periods false standards of fair farm prices, and are decidedly unjust in burden on present and future taxpayers."

Delegates also again asked that appropriations for carrying out the purposes of the Agricultural Adjustment Act be reduced. Underlying this resolution was the conviction that farmers should be permitted to earn fair incomes through fair prices, not from low prices plus government payments. Especially critical was the resolution on price control, as follows, in part: "The administration of the price control law by the Office of Price Administration has not been in accordance with the intent of Congress, and has seriously disrupted the production of vitally needed food and other agricultural products. Many of the rules and regulations affecting agriculture appear to have been devised by persons with little respect for the law, with very little knowledge of agriculture, and with even less regard for the interests of the producers of farm products. These regulations have been unnecessarily numerous and needlessly complex, and many of them have done little or nothing to control inflation. On the contrary, they have operated to create confusion and uncertainty; to disrupt the orderly and efficient processes which have been developed over the years for the production and marketing of agricultural products; to encourage unnecessary and inefficient practices; to increase the number of middlemen and add to their profits; to widen unduly the marketing margins between producers and consumers; to discourage honest attempts to comply with the law; and to promote evasions and violations of price ceilings and rationing orders."

In other words, the whole job of rationing and price control had been horribly bungled.

Farm Bureau membership had increased to more than 100,000 in 1943. It was a fitting time for the members to honor President Smith for his eighteen years of outstanding leadership. Eloquent tribute was paid to him by Vice President Talmage Defrees, and on behalf of all ninety-seven county Farm Bureaus, Harry Munch and Harry Gehring, presidents of the Macon and Knox county Farm Bureaus presented him with a huge grandfather clock. Then, presidents of the other county Farm Bureaus marched up to shake

172

100,000 membership mark was reached in 1943 and announced on WLS Dinner Bell Program. From left, Dave Thompson, Prairie Farmer editor; O. D. Brissenden, IAA organization director; Mr. Smith; and Art Page, conductor of the radio program

Mr. Smith's hand and present to him tributes prepared by their county Farm Bureaus. President Smith, visibly affected by this outpouring of admiration and respect, responded briefly, ending with: "All I can say is thank you and God bless you." (When Smith died in 1961, his will provided that the clock be given to the Illinois Agricultural Association. It stands today, along with an oil portrait of Mr. Smith, in the Earl C. Smith Memorial Hall of the new IAA building in Bloomington.)

During the fall and winter of 1943-1944, farmers were wrestling with many problems, as rationing became tighter and shortages of many materials developed. One of the most vexing situations existed in the marketing of hogs. A floor of $13.75 had been placed under the price, and hog growers had responded magnificiently with a pig crop of something over 123 million head. In fall and winter, stockyard and slaughter facilities were taxed to the utmost. One trouble was that the guaranteed price applied only to hogs weighing 200 to 270 pounds. Farmers who fed their hogs to a weight of 265 pounds, for example, found that they could not get them to market for weeks. They either had to reduce feed to keep the hogs from going above 270 pounds, or continue feeding usual rations and so push the hogs out of the price-support range. In either case, the feed would be practically thrown away. The 270-pound maximum seemed silly to farmers, because lard was one of the commodities that was in very short supply. As a result of plain mismanagement by the Office of Price Administration, the hog marketing situation was the most chaotic ever experienced in this country. It was a good example of what usually happens when government undertakes to substitute government fiat for natural market forces. It left a bad taste in the mouth of the man who had to accept less than the floor price because of factors beyond his control.

Moving with tortoise-like speed, the War Food Administration in January, 1944, finally extended the price floor to hogs weighing up to 300 pounds, and removed restrictions on farm slaughter. The latter did not help much, because farmers were required to collect ration points on any dressed hogs sold. An easy way to solve the problem of the market would have been to suspend ration-point requirements on pork. Consumers, with plenty of money in their pockets, would certainly have gone on a pork-buying spree if this had been done, and markets would have been cleared quickly. But Washington will seldom do anything in a simple way. The WFA continued to stumble along, hoping that the problem would go away. At one time it was estimated that 300,000 hogs were held over in all markets. Hogs weighing below 200 pounds and over 300 pounds were selling readily at prices between $11.75 and $13. This was galling to farmers who had increased hog far-rowings on the basis of a guarantee of $13.75.

Early in 1944, former Congressman Marvin Jones of Texas, now War Food Administrator, announced that the $13.75 floor would continue until October 1. After that date, the floor would be dropped to $12.50 for hogs weighing from 200 to 240 pounds. (This was later raised to $13.00 on all weights up to 270 pounds.) Disillusioned by government mismanagement of the hog program in 1943, farmers bred some 5 million fewer sows in 1944, thus cutting pork production by some 25 per cent.

All through the war, the IAA had protested against the cheap-food policy followed by the Administration, but to no effect. In the light of later developments, it is interesting to note the reasons why Illinois farmers were so firmly opposed to food subsidies. As summarized by the IAA research department, food subsidies:

1) Increase the national debt.
2) Are inflationary in effect.
3) Are unjustified from the consumer standpoint.
4) Will increase the burden of taxes in postwar years.
5) Are subject to the most undesirable political abuses.
6) Tend to establish low standards of values for farm products.
7) Lead to the socialization of agriculture and other industries.
8) Deny to farmers the right to receive the full value of their products in the market places.

As the year went on, it became apparent that the Allied forces had gained the upper hand in the war, and the extreme tensions of 1943 began to relax. At the 1944 IAA convention, much was said about postwar planning. President Smith in his annual address once more reiterated his belief that basic crop prices must be stabilized through government control of production. To stabilize livestock, Smith ventured to suggest that the marketing agreement section of the AAA could be utilized.

During the early months of 1945, problems incident to price control, rationing, shortages, and so on continued to vex farmers, but it was apparent that the war was near the end. People began to give serious thought to postwar problems. The IAA devoted a lot of attention to state legislation. A major achievement was securing the adoption of a law changing restrictions on the adoption of constitutional amendments. The law, as finally passed, provided that:

1) Amendments to three articles of the constitution instead of one may be submitted by the same session of the General Assembly.

2) An amendment of the constitution can be adopted by the favorable vote of two-thirds of those voting on the proposition, as well as by a favorable vote of a majority of those voting in the election.

3) Votes upon future amendments to the constitution shall be cast on a separate ballot or in a separate column on the main ballot.

Getting this legislation through was cause for jubilation because it was believed that it would open the way to several badly-needed amendments to the constitution. However, when the proposition was submitted to voters in the 1946 general election, it had to be voted on under the old rules, namely, that to be adopted, it had to carry a majority of those voting in the election, and it lost, by three votes to one. The discouraging thing about the result was that while a majority (more than three to one) of those voting on the proposition did vote in favor of it, more than half of those voting did not vote at all on the proposition.

The IAA also was largely instrumental, in the 1945 session of the legislature, in getting a state appropriation of $15 million for the improvement of rural roads.

Important school legislation was passed. Most important was the school survey law which is described in detail in another chapter. Also, state aid in the form of flat grants was increased from $13 to $19 per pupil for elementary schools, and from $2 to $4 for high schools, and the maximum state contribution to the cost of pupil transportation was raised from $15 to $20 per pupil. Special equalization aid for needy schools was raised from $1,048 to $1,200 per school for rural schools. Another useful bill passed was one making needed changes in the program for control of Bang's disease in cattle.

President Smith had been busy for some months as chairman of an American Farm Bureau Federation committee charged with the responsibility of formulating postwar agricultural policies. On August 28, the report was submitted to the board of directors of the AFBF, and it was accepted. The heart of the report was that there was at that time no necessity for any substantial change in existing laws with respect to farm price supports authorized by Congress.

(On October 28, 1945, Howard Leonard, president of the IAA from 1920 to 1923, died in Springfield, where he had served as state director of agriculture since 1941.)

The IAA convention in Chicago, November 26-29, marked the end of an era in Farm Bureau, an era that very properly could be called "the Smith era." If any man has ever left his stamp on an organization, it was Earl C. Smith. Other men had made great contributions to the development of the Farm Bureau in Illinois—notably Treasurer Cowles, General Counsel Kirkpatrick, Field Secretary Metzger, and Vernon Vaniman—but it was Smith who captained the team. Smith's judgment in picking men to manage the numerous IAA affiliates was almost flawless. Once Smith had placed a man in a position of authority, he loaded him with responsibilities, and held him strictly accountable for results. This policy had paid off in truly sensational progress of many affiliates.

President Smith had planned to retire some years earlier, but after the war broke out, he decided to see the organization through that trying period. Once peace had come, Smith made his decision quickly. He was fifty-nine years old, and in fairly good health, but he did not feel up to the task of meeting postwar problems. That was a job for younger men. "I have great reverence for graying hairs," he told the delegates, "but I know, as every man knows, and I can speak without being misunderstood, that young men usually furnish the initiative and zeal for driving ahead. It takes great vigor as well as sympathetic understanding to inspire people to do things."

Talmage Defrees, who had served as vice president for 11 years, also retired, as did Alvin O. Eckert of Belleville, Albert Hayes of Chillicothe, and W. A. Dennis of Paris—all of whom had rendered long service as board members. The retirement of so many oldtimers accentuated the feeling among delegates that this was the end of an era.

In announcing his decision, President Smith assured his hearers that he did not plan to go into business or politics, and that he had no desire for further honors. "I have been given all the honors that anyone could possibly want or desire—the honor of representing this great body of the finest people on earth, the farmers of Illinois," he said, and added: "And I think to take any other kind of position would be to belittle the wonderful position of leadership and the opportunities for service I have enjoyed here."

At the convention, Charles B. Shuman of Moultrie county, now 38 years old, was elected to replace Smith, and Floyd E. Morris of Sangamon county succeeded Talmage Defrees as vice president. Morris had been elected to the IAA board of directors the previous year, after he had served on the IAA schools committee previously. He operated a 330-acre livestock and grain

Charles B. Shuman

farm, and had been county chairman of the Agricultural Adjustment Administration activities in his county.

Shuman lived on his own 46-acre farm near Sullivan, and also operated his father's farm of 456 acres adjoining. In addition, he owned a farm of 230 acres which he had bought from his grandmother's estate, but he rented that one out. He was graduated with honors from the University of Illinois in 1928, and remained to take a master's degree a year later, after which he went home to manage his father's farm. In 1933, Shuman and Miss Ida Wilson, a mathematics teacher in the Sullivan High School, were married. He bought a home and 46 acres of land nearby where he and his bride started life together. At the time of his election to the IAA presidency, the Shumans had four children, three boys and a girl.

Chapter 17

Shuman Leadership

When Charles B. Shuman took the helm that had been held so steadily by Earl C. Smith for twenty years, his closest associates in Farm Bureau must have known that "something would have to give." A man of firm convictions, and never reticent about expressing them, Shuman had let it be known that he was something less than enthusiastic about price-fixing as a panacea for agriculture. He certainly was not an all-out advocate of production control, as Smith had been. He had openly voiced his disapproval of the practice of making federal payments to farmers for so-called "soil conservation" payments. He regarded such payments as thinly-disguised handouts which were justified during the long depression, but could not possibly be defended during the war years when farm prices and farm income were well above parity. This judgment was backed by many farmers who were beginning to express doubt as to the propriety and practicability of making payments for practices that were well established and had proven profitable. Those concerned with future policies of the IAA knew that Shuman would work tirelessly for policies which he considered just, but would not carry the banner for policies he did not believe in.

In his first convention address as president, in 1946, Shuman said: "Farmers believe in full production and they would certainly prefer not to return to the specific crop acreage control programs of the past. However, farmers know that prices supported at 90 per cent of parity without any program for keeping production in balance with effective demand could result in huge surplus accumulation. Excessive production and surplus accumulation would be wasteful of soil resources as well as disastrous to price levels. Much of the surplus production in the past has come from increased grain acreage at the expense of proper land use and conservation practices. Consideration should be given to coupling the support price program with an effective soil conservation plan. Much public support could be had for a plan that would assure those producers who conserve the soil a parity price for their products."

Reading those lines today, one realizes that Shuman's fears about ruinous accumulation of surpluses were only too well-founded. The Federal Government did maintain prices at levels that, without effective control of production, resulted in government holdings of farm commodities to the extent of a $9 billion investment. Thus was created one of the most serious, and most baffling domestic problems that the government faces today, after nearly thirty years of alleged government control of production. The problem is no closer to solution today than it was when the first adjustment act was passed in 1933.

As far as the question of IAA policy was concerned, the situation was quickly eased late in 1947, when Allan B. Kline of Iowa was elected president of the American Farm Bureau Federation to succeed Edward A. O'Neal of Alabama, who had led the organization for 16 years. Kline was a highly successful farmer, but he was more than that. Possessed of a keen and inquiring mind, he was well-informed in economics, and he was an eloquent speaker. He was destined to lead a crusade against the pricing and production-control policies of the Federal Government for seven years. The state Farm Bureaus, with some reservations in the tobacco and cotton states, went along enthusiastically with Kline.

and Farm Bureau became known as the most rugged opponent of the kind of government controls that were in effect.

Shuman, who had earned a master's degree in agronomy at the University of Illinois, had always backed the idea of a farm program based on the principles of soil conservation, went all the way in supporting Kline in his efforts to get more flexibility into the pricing and production-control features of the program. At the 1947 IAA convention, delegates paid due respects to the features of past programs that had been of real value, but they said in resolution: "It would not be advisable to press for the extension on a permanent basis of war emergency programs designed to promote exceptional production by high price supports. We will give careful study to all proposals for modification of our agricultural legislation to determine not only their impact upon agriculture but also their effect upon the nation as a whole."

It was apparent to the delegates, as it was to farmers everywhere, that there was no easy solution to the so-called "farm problem," but they backed the moderate approach with respect to prices. Kline continued his efforts, and he was backed so firmly by Shuman that when he resigned from the AFBF presidency in 1954, Shuman was the logical man to succeed him. Shuman is now recognized, as Kline was, as the most effective opponent of price-fixing and production-control policies of government.

Reverting now to other problems faced by Shuman when he assumed the IAA presidency, administrative problems were formidable. The organization was still growing with phenomenal speed. In 1946, membership had increased by 15,174 to bring the total to a new high of 130,825. Business of the affiliates, almost without exception, was growing at a comparable, or even faster pace. The inflation brought about by the government policy of paying too much of the cost of the war by borrowing made it necessary to raise salaries of the employees of IAA and affiliated companies. All business had to adjust to the age of inflation. The increasing membership required expanison of services and hard work just to keep abreast of the fast-moving economic changes. Staffs had to be enlarged. It was an era of tremendous growth accompanied by "growing pains." The end of wartime price ceilings, production payments to dairymen and other expedients brought new and vexatious problems. It was a time for "agonizing reappraisal." The services rendered to farmers by the affiliated companies were meeting with ever-increasing acceptance. Business in the three insurance companies had increased during the war years by amounts ranging from 40 per cent to more than 100 per cent. The business of the Farm Supply Company had grown by leaps and bounds, and in 1946 the company paid out more than $1 million in patronage dividends. Facilities had to be expanded to meet new demands, and shortages of many things, together with new and higher wage scales created grave problems. In his convention address in 1948, Shuman referred to the huge increases in business of the affiliated companies, and the greater responsibilities they must shoulder. Then, referring to the IAA itself, he said: "The Illinois Agricultural Association itself is in excellent financial condition. However, expenses have been increasing at a much more rapid rate than has income. This same situation faces many of the County Farm Bureaus. Either income must be increased or services now deemed essential must be eliminated."

On top of all other problems, there was a gnawing one that was eventually to be solved by disrupting the intimate relationship between Farm Bureau and the Extension Service in Illinois which had existed since the earliest days of Farm Bureau. This relationship which had been in effect from the appointment of the first farm advisers, had proved mutually satisfactory to Farm Bureau and Extension; but as Farm Bureau grew in numbers and influence, other organizations began to complain that a government agency should not "show favoritism" to any one farm organization, but should treat them alike. A joint committee representing the U.S. Department of Agriculture and the Association of Land Grant Colleges and Universities was set up to make recommendations as to the future course for the Extension Service in agriculture and home economics. The Committee's report, issued in 1948, carried the following statement: "Though close cooperation (by the extension service) with general farm organizations is highly desirable, formal operating relationships with such organizations are considered detrimental to the public interest." The late Henry P. Rusk, then dean of the College of Agriculture of the University of Illinois, was a member of the committee. He filed a "statement of exception," which was filed with the report. The report was accepted by the USDA, and became USDA policy henceforth.

It should be reported here that in a number of counties the work of running the county Farm Bureau had become so heavy that a man had been appointed to manage all Farm Bureau affairs, leaving the farm adviser free to devote full time to his extension and educational activities.

The IAA met the situation by taking steps to change the contracts between county Farm Bureaus and the Extension Service and also to change the method of Farm Bureau support of Extension work. Under the new plan, instead of giving the farm adviser office space, stenographic help, the use of an automobile, and other benefits, the county Farm Bureau henceforth made an annual contribution to the University of Illinois, to be used in Extension activities. Thus, the Farm Bureau contribution toward Extension work continues, but it is made in such a way as not to be offensive to other organizations, which, after all, can do the same thing if they so desire. Some hard feelings resulted from the change, but the change had been ordered by the Secretary of Agriculture. In most counties those concerned decided to make the best of a troublesome situation. All of this took time and study.

The financial arrangements between the Extension Service and Farm Bureau are still in effect today. However, county Farm Bureaus became hard pressed to meet the increased costs of Extension Service while at the same time properly financing growing Farm Bureau programs.

Therefore, in the 73rd session of the Illinois General Assembly in 1963, a bill was introduced which would allow the Extension Service to seek financial support through the county board of supervisors. The bill was passed with the support of Farm Bureau and the Extension Service.

Prior to the passage of the 1963 law, Extension Service support through county tax funds was limited. The new law authorizes county governments to increase financial support to the Extension Service. The maximum amount of financial support is based on the total county population—the higher the population, the more funds that can be contributed to the Extension Service. In the event that county funds are not available, the board of supervisors after approval by referendum in the county, can levy an annual extension education tax.

By 1953, the IAA had a plan which has since become general throughout the state. A secretary of organization manages the Farm Bureau. The farm adviser has his office in the Farm Bureau building, but the Extension Service pays the office rent, and provides stenographic service and transportation from funds provided largely by Farm Bureau. The addition of another man to the county Farm Bureau staff in the county has meant added expense, but in most counties membership dues had to be raised anyway as a result of the fall in purchasing power of the dollar. In most counties appropriate action has been taken to keep the organization in sound financial condition. It should be understood that the new phase of Extension relationship does not disturb direct Farm Bureau sponsorship of 4-H club work in the county. This goes on as it has gone on for fifty years. In fact, practically all Extension work goes on with its usual effectiveness, and all concerned seem to find the new arrangements fairly satisfactory.

Shuman, as soon as he became president, took up the cudgels which Smith had wielded against what they considered unnecessary and unjust subsidies to consumers. In the March, 1946 issue of the IAA RECORD, Shuman wrote, in part:

"Every time the housewife goes into the grocery store, Uncle Sam goes in with her and pays part of the cost of her purchases with money from the federal treasury. Money raised by taxation is going by the billions to reduce the price of food through these consumer subsidies so that the best paid people in the world may buy their food below actual cost."

A month later he paid his respects to price control: "Ordinarily prices tell us when a commodity is plentiful and we use it freely. Other times prices tell us there is a scarcity and we use less of the commodity. Today we use too much food or eat too much meat because price falsely says, 'Go ahead, there is plenty.'

"Does price control check inflation? Most of us, remembering the experience of World War I, think of inflation in terms of soaring prices. Today we know that legal prices can be arbitrarily held down and at the same time we can have inflation through lowering of quality, tie-in sales, barter, black markets and other devices.

"Full production is the only way to prevent disastrous inflation. That full production will come only when there is reasonable price incentive. Your organization has not asked for an abrupt end of the controls over price, but we have insisted that a definite schedule for removal be incorporated in any legislation extending O.P.A. The end must come within a matter of months—not years!"

The end of food price control and rationing did come rather soon. It came, not because the Administration wanted it to come, not because Administration leaders had suddenly seen the folly of it, but because, as Secretary of Agriculture Clinton P. Anderson explained, the local ration boards were resigning at the rate of 150 a week. It was simply impossible to enforce the regulations.

As I have indicated, the IAA was faced with internal problems of grave importance. Membership had grown sensationally from 70,000 in 1940 to around 124,000 in early 1946. With so many members demanding more service than ever before, with shortages in manpower and materials hampering things at every turn, and with the necessity of revising wage and salary standards quickly, IAA problems were formidable. Prompt action had to be taken.

One urgent necessity was additional office space. In the Transportation Building, some 56,000 square feet of office space was occupied, plus a lot of storage space; and it was grossly inadequate. Purchase of a building had been contemplated for some years, but rentals were low in the Transportation Building, and decision had been deferred. Now, the time for action had come. At a special meeting in Springfield on March 22, 1946, delegates unanimously approved the purchase of the American Bankers' Building at 43 East Ohio Street, Chicago, with rentable floor space of more than 80,000 square feet. Moving day did not come for more than a year and by that time even more space was needed. The Illinois Farm Supply Company moved into rented space at 100 East Ohio Street.

Early in his administration, President Shuman directed the urgent attention of the board of directors to the wage and salary problem. Sweeping action came within months. IAA affiliates were faced with the imminent loss of key employees because of opportunities for much greater financial reward outside the IAA group. First step taken was to evaluate and grade the jobs, then find what other companies in the same business were paying. Expert consultants were employed, whose reports indicated unmistakably that IAA was far behind its competition in salary range, and not even in the running with respect to retirement programs because no such system had been instituted. Upgrading of salaries began within months, and pension systems studied. By 1946, a pension plan was adopted, to become effective in January, 1947. Thus, within two years, it might be said that IAA salary and wage policies had been completely and realistically overhauled to meet new and drastically changed conditions.

The staff was working under 16 department heads. There was wide diffusion of responsibility. In order to coordinate the work of the departments, they were drawn together in three divisions; namely, organization and information, under Field Secretary George E. Metzger; general services, under Ivan E. Parett after June 1, 1947; and marketing, under Lawrence L. Colvis.

The division of general services was the catch-all division. It included research, safety and public health, rural school relations, soil conservation activities, property taxation, veterinary medical relations, and road improvements. The entire system has undergone considerable realignment since then. Now, the work is distributed as follows: the departments of personnel, general office, and corporate records are under IAA Secretary Charles S. Mayfield; investments, controller, and treasury are under Director of Finance Kenneth D. Carpenter; legal, stock records, local government, property taxation, natural resources, and legislation are under General Counsel Paul E. Mathias; organization, young people's activities, family activities, and records service are under Secretary of Organization Charles E. Alexander; publications, radio-television and graphic production are under Secretary of Information William W. Allen; and livestock, grain, dairy, agricultural promotion, fruits and vegetables, and lockers are under Secretary of Marketing Walter B. Peterson; research and library departments are under Leonard Gardner, assistant to the president.

The post-war years were years of dramatic development of most IAA affiliates. Illinois Farm Supply Company sales in 1948 jumped $13,000,000 over 1947, to a total of $44 million. During the year, it bought outright one oil-refining company and another in cooperation with two other midwest cooperatives, and started construction of a new fertilizer plant and a feed mill. The Illinois Livestock Marketing Association doubled its business, to a total of more than $30 million. The insurance companies compiled new records.

An interesting item from the 1947 IAA convention: In resolution the delegates said that they would not oppose removal of taxes on yellow margarine, provided only that it be sold under labels clearly identifying it as oleomargarine.

In his 1948 convention address, President Shuman endorsed the principle of flexible farm price supports in the amendments to the Agricultural Adjustment Act which the 80th Congress adopted late in the session.

One of the minor activities sponsored by the IAA with most gratifying results is a project first undertaken in 1948, under which ten medical students each year who lack the resources to complete their education are granted loans up to $5,000 (at two per cent interest), provided they will agree to enter practice and remain for five years in a rural community to be selected by the board of directors of the fund. The town which is the center of the community must be one with a population of not more than 5,000. The student must agree to repay the loan in annual installments, starting seven years after receiving the loan. The seven year interval permits the student to complete his internship.

The program was started in cooperation with the Illinois State Medical Society, which put up half of the $200,000 fund, and with the College of Medicine of the University of Illinois, which agreed to keep ten admissions open for the students recommended. (The student may also enter some other medical school, but in such cases, the student himself must make arrangements for admission.) There has been no need to increase the size of the fund so far, and there is no indication that there will be any such need in the near future. The board of directors of the fund consists of three representatives of the Illinois State Medical Society and three directors of the IAA. Secretary at the beginning, and until just before his retirement from the IAA staff in 1961, was Ivan E. Parett. Since then, Roy E. Will, assistant secretary of the IAA, has held the post.

By 1962, more than 50 doctors had completed their education under the program and were in practice; while 59 students, interns, or doctors in military service were preparing to practice. Greatest amount of money on loan at any one time has been $172,500. Repayments are now sufficient to keep the program going without further contributions from the sponsors.

One of the interesting sidelights on this venture is the fact that Dr. Jack Gibbs, who practiced for six years at Havana, and Dr. Thomas Bunting of Pittsfield, two of the early recipients of loans, are now representing the Society on the board of directors of the fund. This happy circumstance indicates that the program has reached maturity.

While the primary purpose of the program is to help needy students, there is a subsidiary purpose, which is to help students who have their own resources to gain admission to medical school, but because of marginal grades have not been able to gain admission. So great is the need for doctors in rural areas that the University of Illinois College of Medicine is willing to take a few students who fail by a small margin to meet the admittedly high grade standards, provided they can secure the endorsement of the board of directors of the fund. It should be clearly understood that such students must meet the same standards of performance that all others do when they finally do get into medical school. The faith of the fund directors in the men they have recommended in this category has been richly justified, for only a very small percentage have failed scholastically.

The applicants for loans are most carefully screened. First, they must be recommended by the county Farm Bureaus in their home county, and by the county medical society. Then, all must take the standard medical college admissions test. The test score is made available to the board when personal interviews are conducted. Applicants must have completed four or five years of pre-medical study. A life insurance policy covering the amount of the loan and with the fund as beneficiary, must be taken out.

It was soon discovered that penalty clauses were needed to insure compliance with all provisions of the contract, including the obligation to practice at least five years in a rural community selected by the board of directors of the fund. The penalties are really severe, in case a student defects from the program. He must repay the loan, with interest at seven per cent, and also pay a penalty of $5,000. For a non-loan student, the penalty is $3,000. The justification for the high penalty is that if a student defects, he will have deprived a more deserving student of the advantages of a loan and a community will have lost the badly needed services of a doctor. The students admit the justice of the penalty, and readily agree to having it included in the contract. The record shows that not once has it been necessary to exact the penalty. In only one case has there been a monetary loss, and that was a case in which the student suffered mental disturbances which barred him from medical practice.

The need for the program is plain, for at this moment there are more than ninety rural communities in Illinois that badly need the services of a resident doctor. Some, of course, could not support a full-time doctor, but there are many others that could. There is a real and pressing need for general practitioners in those areas.

Both Farm Bureau and the Medical Society are highly pleased with the results of this venture. More than fifty Illinois communities now have adequate medical service which they probably would not otherwise have had; and within a short time more than a hundred physicians will have been launched upon rewarding careers. It's hard to see how the investment of $100,000 by each sponsor could have been put to better use in the field of public service.

During the 1949 session of the Illinois Legislature, the IAA fought for an increase in the gasoline tax from three cents to five cents a gallon; but the bill was defeated. However, many of the recommendations of the 1944 IAA School Report were enacted into law.

On October 8, 1949, Herman W. Danforth, first president of the Illinois Agricultural Association, died at his home in Danforth, Iroquois county, at the age of 77 years. He had seen the organization grow from a handful of members to 167,000.

Late in the year, Congress reversed its action of 1948 by going back to fixed price supports at 90 per cent of parity for basic crops through 1950. The IAA and the American Farm Bureau Federation had opposed the action. In his address at the IAA convention, President Shuman reiterated Farm Bureau's opposition to fixed price supports. He also paid his respects to the Brannan Plan for stabilizing farm prices, under which farmers would have to depend on an annual appropriation by Congress for a good share of their income. He regarded it as almost infamous. Delegates backed him in resolutions on both issues.

Late in 1949, several changes were made in the staff setup. The office of vice president was made a full-time job. (This change was not destined to be permanent, and was reversed two years later when Floyd E. Morris was succeeded as vice president by Otto Steffey). Donald Kirkpatrick retired as general counsel, to be succeeded by Paul E. Mathias. Ivan E. Parett was named secretary of public relations, and John K. Cox succeeded him as secretary of general services. Wilfred Shaw returned from the American Farm Bureau Federation, where he had been secretary-treasurer, to succeed Mathias as IAA secretary.

In 1950, the controversy over fixed price supports grew hotter. Writing in the April issue of the IAA RECORD, President Shuman said, among other things: "Immediately after the end of the war we should have launched a program to encourage adjustment of production to cope with changing demand conditions.

"Acting under the compulsion of political expediency, the administration and Congress have moved in the opposite direction. Continued high government supports for field crops have discouraged the expansion of livestock production and resulted in huge accumulation of storage stocks. Shiny, new grain bins dot the landscape and only an unusually short crop can save us from a dangerous situation."

Shuman said that maximum use should be made of the current program, but that administration should be improved, and the law changed. He suggested that: "Careful study should be given to the suggestion that production be adjusted by allocation of a soil conservation base rather than a crop acreage allotment to each farm. Perhaps this type of program could be tried experimentally as an alternate to the specific crop control plans now in effect."

On March 1, 1950, George E. Metzger retired as secretary of organization after 28 years of service to the IAA, to his farm near Kewanna, Indiana. (He is still farming as these words are being written.) He was honored at a testimonial dinner on February 16, and presented with gifts by his associates. He was succeeded by Oscar D. Brissenden, who had been director of organization since 1939. Charles S. Mayfield, who had been Brissenden's assistant, became director of organization.

In his convention address in 1950, Mr. Shuman sharply criticized the trends in farm programs. Among other things, he said:

"Through amendment and administrative rulings, we are far removed from the original intent of the farm program legislation. Certainly neither farmers nor the Congress contemplated the present huge federal agricultural bureaucracy with the expenditure of millions of dollars in administrative costs and subsidies during periods of high farm income. I would suggest that we in agriculture take the lead in reducing government non-defense spending by supporting drastic reductions in farm program expenses. I am convinced that agriculture would not be seriously damaged by suspension of practically all government farm program activities and expenditures in these periods when our prices approach parity. Not only would we have additional millions for national defense but farmers would be in a much better position to request accelerated assistance in periods of anticipated price collapse. By getting our own house in order, we would be in a much better position to insist that all other economic groups reduce their demands for special government assistance. Implementation of this suggestion would be simple in that no change in basic law would be required—merely a reduction in appropriations . . . Industry, labor and agriculture have turned to government for assistance in maintaining prices at profitable levels. We have forgotten that for every new guarantee we must inevitably sacrifice some degree of freedom. I am convinced that dependence upon government by any group for special economic assistance, except in extreme emergency, is unsound and can only lead to a larger and more powerful bureaucracy and in the end to complete nationalization of all enterprise. I hope that the Farm Bureau organization will take the lead in reversing this trend toward the socialistic state . . .Socialism is just another word for big government with all of its dangers and costs . . ."

Mr. Shuman also suggested that it would be a wholesome thing for agriculture if Secretary of Agriculture Charles F. Brannan, author of the "Brannan Plan" for stabilizing farm income, could be removed from office. Convention delegates adopted a resolution which was the most outspoken so far adopted by the IAA in criticism of farm program developments at Washington. Here it is in its entirety:

"During the past year, the U.S. Department of Agriculture has made a determined effort to impose upon agriculture a farm program that, if enacted, would have discouraged efficiency and penalized individual initiative.

"We also protest the growing tendency of the Department of Agriculture to impose official thinking upon the people whom they are appointed to serve and deplore the use, for this purpose, of governmental organizations set up to administer existing programs.

"Furthermore, we are concerned about the growing tendency to accept, as permanent programs, measures orignally designed to combat the effects of deflation or to prevent the recurrence of a depression. This attitude is not confined to farmers but is found in every segment of our population from the recipient of public assistance to representatives of great industries.

"We urge that such programs be eliminated or sharply curtailed, and we accept responsibility for our full share of an overall economy program."

How things had changed! Twenty-five years earlier, IAA President Sam Thompson was one of the leaders of a crusade for the McNary-Haugen legislation. In 1933 Earl C. Smith had been one of the most articulate and forceful advocates of the first Agricultural Adjustment Act. Now, in 1950, IAA President Charles B. Shuman and AFBF President Allan B. Kline were emerging as the two most outspoken champions of less government control in agriculture. It would be dishonest to pretend that Earl C. Smith, living in retirement on his Pike county farm, approved of all this. He had always contended that the failure of farm programs to accomplish what had been expected of them, and the frightful cost, were due to poor administration, largely because of the vested interest of the government bureaucracy. On this issue, he had deep convictions, and he was true to them to the last.

Charles B. Shuman was just as firm in his convictions. He had toured Europe in the summer of 1950 after attending the meeting of the International Federation of Agricultural Producers, and he was shocked by what he saw. When he returned, he wrote, in the IAA RECORD:

"In attempting to become economically self-sufficient, the

small nations of Europe have built the trade barriers and restrictions that effectively throttle international trade. These national barriers have been one of the causes of the recurrent wars.

"Certainly these barriers to trade are today helping fix upon the people a permanently low standard of living. National pride is a fine thing but where it results in attempting to isolate and maintain an uneconomic unit, it can only bring misery to the citizens who must divide the limited number of jobs and the smaller quantity of consumer goods available.

"All over the world the same old unsound nationalistic programs are being brought forth again. Russia has its iron curtain. England's austerity program is designed to reduce imports and equalize incomes.

"Sweden subsidizes its uneconomical flax industry by government price support. Switzerland is fortifying her mountain passes. Only in France and Germany did we find real evidence of definite efforts to break down the trade barriers and avoid extreme nationalism.

"American farmers have a tremendous interest in helping to reduce the barriers to world trade. The 'too many people' of Europe would quickly consume our surplus agricultural production while we could well use many of the products of their skill and art.

"If goods and services could flow more freely between nations there would be a need for every person in the world in some type of productive work."

(The impact of the above on the reader will be accentuated if he will stop and consider the sensational economic changes that have come about in some of the very nations Mr. Shuman refers to, as a result of the creation of the Common Market. He really called the turn in that case. The enormous possibilities of economic progress through freer trade that he envisioned are being richly fulfilled after only four years of operation, with still greater possibilities ahead as trade barriers are further reduced. Charles B. Shuman, as readers know, went on to become the president of the American Farm Bureau Federation in 1954. Under his leadership, the AFBF set up an agricultural trade center in Rotterdam, Netherlands. Also, the AFBF launched a nation-wide campaign to promote better nutrition—especially for teenagers.)

On state issues, the IAA won a major victory when voters approved the so-called "gateway amendment" to the state Constitution which provided henceforth that in any referendum vote, a two-thirds majority of those *voting on the amendment* will decide the issue—or, as under the old rules, a majority of those voting in the election. This arrangement would make it much easier to amend the Constitution in the future.

With the Korean War going on, President Shuman in the January, 1951, issue of the IAA RECORD, again advocated greater production, minimum restrictions on prices, heavier taxation, and reduced non-defense spending. He wrote, in part: "I am convinced that we, in agriculture, should abandon all allotment and production restriction programs for the duration. . . . It is more logical to recapture wartime profits through taxation than to throttle production with price controls. . . . Organized labor should be willing to lengthen the basic work week to a minimum of 48 hours. . . . We can win if we are prepared to sacrifice and work."

Farm Bureau efforts to encourage Congress to reduce government spending met with little success in 1951. The American Farm Bureau Federation advocated a reduction in the appropriation for conservation practice payments from $285,000,000 to $150,-000,000, but it failed by a few votes to get the necessary majority. (Both Illinois senators, Paul H. Douglas and Everett M. Dirksen, voted for the reduction). The refusal by Congress to cut this appropriation proved beyond all doubt how deeply the farm issue was involved with politics. Even though the largest farm organization urged the reduction, most lawmakers were still convinced that farmers generally wanted to get checks from Washington, whether deserved or not. At the time, farm prices were at 100 per cent of parity.

By 1952, although demand for certain commodities, stimulated by the Korean War, had given another boost to some prices, it was evident that supply was catching up with demand. Wheat was piling up in government storage. In his convention address, Mr. Shuman again emphasized his conviction that the best farm program would be one that provided price supports at what might be called a "stop-loss" level, not an incentive level. He favored a standby program—one that would be geared in only when farm prices were threatened with collapse. "Unless farmers are willing to live under a completely regimented economy," he said, "the only basis for a farm program in the future is to support farm prices against disastrous collapse. . . . There is nothing in either ancient or modern history which indicates that farmers would be better off under a government price fixing and control system than they are under a free enterprise system."

Convention delegates backed President Shuman by adopting a resolution asking for a stand-by program, with flexible price supports, and based largely upon sound principles of soil conservation.

Some readers may recall that when the Korean War broke out in 1950, Congress enacted the Defense Production Act of 1950, and that ceiling prices on some foods were imposed. Enforcement seemed to be only half-hearted, however, and the Act was amended repeatedly until there was precious little left of it by 1952. The American Farm Bureau Federation referred to it in a statement in late 1952 when Price Stabilizer Tighe E. Woods proposed a "rollback" on retail ceiling prices on beef, stating that such action would only "make a bad matter worse." Further: "Mr. Woods refuses to recognize the elementary facts that price controls never have worked on meat, that meat supplies are more than ample and that there is no basis whatsoever for his efforts to continue to keep the livestock and meat industry under his bureaucratic thumb."

Needless to say, the IAA heartily endorsed the AFBF statement. The Farm Bureau was truly fed up with government meddling with farm affairs. That did not mean, in many instances, that individual farmers felt that way. In 1953, the long period of lush prosperity for beef cattlemen began to fade. A feeder who had bought steers at $35 per cwt. and sold them after fattening at $28, wrote to President Shuman to suggest that government should fix minimum prices for farm products. Answering him, Mr. Shuman told him that farmer experience with OPA and OPS "certainly demonstrates that government pricing is unworkable." He said further: "Wheat, cotton, corn, butter and oilseed crops are supported and are all in serious trouble with huge surpluses.

"On the other hand, the producers of hogs, eggs, potatoes, fruits and vegetables have renounced high rigid price supports, have taken adjustments and are in a relatively healthy position . . ."

Internally, the Farm Bureau was going through a period of severe strain. Member dues had been at $15 a year since 1919. County Farm Bureaus had generally had plenty of money for whatever they decided to do, until the postwar inflation had seriously reduced the buying power of the dollar. Fifteen dollars would pay for little more than half the service it bought in the 1920's. County Farm Bureaus began to raise dues here and there, but many years were required to get readjusted to new conditions.

By convention time, November 16, 1953, the IAA could point with pride to a membership of nearly 200,000, considerably more than double the nearly 95,000 who belonged only 10 years before.

The meeting was a harmonious one, and delegates condemned in resolution the high support prices which had resulted in heavy accumulation of unsalable surpluses, suggesting that flexible supports be substituted for corn, beginning with the 1955 crop. (The 90-per cent-of-parity support had been extended through the 1954 season by Congress.) It was evident that the Commodity Credit Corporation would soon possess an inventory valued at nearly $6,000,000,000!

A new Secretary of Agriculture, Ezra Taft Benson, appointed by the newly elected President, Dwight D. Eisenhower, was in office during 1953, and everybody knew that he was against the high-support policies of the previous Administration. He had served notice soon after taking up his official duties that farmers could expect less cash from the government during his tenure of office. It was not until February 15, 1954, however, that he took any very big step in this direction. On that date, he announced that price supports on dairy products would be lowered from 90 to 75 per cent of parity. He pointed out that in one year, the government stockpile of dairy products had grown from the equivalent of 1.44 billion pounds of whole milk to the equivalent of 8 billion pounds, and he thought it was time to call a halt. Butter was priced out of the market, actually, except for the luxury trade. Per capita consumption was only about half of what it had been in pre-war days. Practical Ezra Benson couldn't see much sense in producing for government storage. The announcement aroused a storm of criticism, but it did discourage production, and the time was to come when for months at a time, the government did not have to buy any butter. (The government inventory of dairy products was pretty well liquidated during the Eisenhower administration, but as soon as the Kennedy administration took over, Benson's successor, Orville L. Freeman, raised dairy supports, and soon the government was spending at the rate of half a billion a year in buying surplus dairy products.)

Early in 1954, the IAA board of directors approved a project to promote increased use of dairy products in Illinois outside of Chicago. This was the first of a series of food-promotion campaigns which the IAA was to sponsor, in cooperation with processors and distributors.

On June 7, at a special delegates' meeting in Springfield, members rejected a proposal to raise IAA individual dues from five to seven dollars a year. Since the proposal involved a change in the IAA constitution, a two-thirds affirmative vote was required for adoption. Those voting "for" numbered 90,105½, while 74,943 voted "against." The majority was far short of the 110,032 needed. (In 1957, dues were raised from $5 to $6 and in 1959 to $7.)

During 1954 the IAA staged a campaign in favor of a proposed amendment to the state constitution to compel the General Assembly to redistrict the State for election purposes. This effort failed, as affirmative votes fell short of the required two-thirds of those voting. A similar campaign two years later was successful, and we did secure reapportionment.

200

Congress, during the summer of 1954, amended the basic Agricultural Adjustment Act to provide for flexible price supports on all basic farm commodities, and eliminated the possibility of imposing marketing quotas on corn. A feature of the new law was the extension of the Agricultural Conservation Program for two years, with transfer to states as quickly as state laws would permit.

The 83rd Congress also enacted a law expanding social security coverage to farmers on a mandatory basis. This move was opposed by the Farm Bureau. Among the provisions of a revised tax bill was one permitting farmers to deduct soil and water conservation expenses in income tax returns, and another allowing them to charge off depreciation on farm buildings and machinery at a faster rate.

Later in the summer occurred an event which illustrates how difficult it is for government to control gross farm production. Due to severe drouth in many sections of the country, Secretary of Agriculture Benson announced that for 1955 the "total acreage allotment" provision of the farm law would be set aside. That meant that as long as farmers and ranchers complied with their individual crop allotments, they would be permitted to plant their other acres to any other crop, ostensibly to permit them to grow feed for their livestock. It meant that Cornbelt farmers could plant soybeans on acres taken out of corn. Curtailing corn production resulted in simply shifting land from one crop to another.

At the convention in Chicago, November 15-18, delegates adopted a resolution calling for acreage allotments on a soil conservation base and elimination of allotments and marketing quotas on specific crops, and gradual adjustment of price supports on feed grains and soybeans to permit these commodities to move freely through normal trade channels. "The paramount objective of Farm Bureau," they contended, "is full parity of income for farm people with minimum reliance on government. The first move toward achieving this objective is to shift the emphasis from government price supports and acreage controls on individual commodities to a program based on market needs."

President Shuman, after nine years in office, was reelected for another one-year term. The standing ovation he was given was ample evidence of approval of his leadership. Otto Steffey was reelected to serve his fourth year as vice president.

A month later in New York, at the convention of the American Farm Bureau Federation, Charles B. Shuman was elected president of the national organization, succeeding Allan B. Kline who retired on advice of his doctor. Shuman, a strong supporter of the Kline philosophy of less government in agriculture, was the logical man for the job. He is still on that job today.

A few days later, the IAA board of directors elected Otto Steffey president. A livestock and grain farmer in Henderson county, Mr. Steffey had been a Farm Bureau member for 35 years, and had been an IAA board member since 1934. During the depression, he bought enough land to bring his holdings up to 370 acres. He fed out some 100 head of cattle each year, and raised 400 to 500 hogs. As vice president, Mr. Steffey had served as chairman of the finance committee, as well as chairman of the resolutions committee. Before becoming vice president, he had served more than 30 years on the organization-publicity committee of the IAA board. He was thoroughly familiar with all phases of IAA operation, and well-grounded in Farm Bureau policies. He had a record of never having missed a board meeting.

In his younger days, Otto Steffey played baseball with the Henderson County Farm Bureau team. He served as president of the Farm Bureau baseball league for many years and his interest in baseball was one of the moving factors which led him to become interested in the Illinois Farm Sports Festival to which he made a noteworthy contribution.

His interest in baseball is probably the foundation for one of his major contributions to Farm Bureau. In baseball he learned the importance of the team effort. He brought this same interest in team effort when he assumed the presidency of the IAA. Implementation of a staff reorganization which resulted from a man-

202

Otto Steffey

agement study done in the last year Shuman served as president was Otto Steffey's first task as president. He accomplished the task well and added materially to the morale and tone of the Farm Bureau team.

Chapter 18

1955-1963

During the summer of 1955, Illinois wheat growers demonstrated their dissatisfaction with government controls by failing
to give a two-thirds vote in favor of marketing quotas on wheat.
This action was the more significant when you consider that at
that time most eligible farmers didn't take the trouble to vote in
the wheat referendum. Reasons for their indifference were many
and complex, but they boiled down to a what-difference-does-it-
make attitude. Often it was simply a matter of a choice of two
evils: accept acreage allotments, marketing quotas, penalties, and
high price supports—or accept the same allotments, lower price
supports, and no penalties. Therefore, in effect, the cards were
stacked in favor of a "pro" vote. Often, barely one-third of those
eligible took the trouble to vote.

Illinois farmers were deeply concerned over the threat of huge
surpluses of feed grains that could be grown on land diverted
from crops under acreage allotments. At the 1955 IAA convention in Chicago, November 14-17, delegates demanded regulations
that would limit crops on such acres to soil-conserving crops only,
not to be grazed or harvested. They also asked for suspension

of acreage allotments on corn, and for changing the price-support range to 60-90 per cent of parity for all basic commodities. Again they called for a minimum soil conservation base for each farm, with eventual removal of all restrictions on land outside this base. Delegates were alarmed at the mounting cost of storage of government-owned commodities, which was at that time about a million dollars a day.

A number of state-wide problems were matters of concern at the time. It was in 1955 that the IAA and the Extension Service in Illinois began to change the historic relationship that had existed from the beginning. Secretary of Agriculture Ezra Taft Benson had issued a memorandum in November, 1954, under which county agricultural agents (farm advisers in Illinois) could no longer accept free office space, salary, transportation, or other expenses directly from a farm organization. There were other provisions, all of which meant that Extension work in Illinois was no longer to be carried out through the Farm Bureau. The steps taken to meet this situation have been recorded in a previous chapter.

It was in 1955, too, that it became certain that an IAA affiliate, Prairie Farms Creameries, was headed for trouble, due to the lessening importance of butter in the dairy economy, which was moving toward a whole-milk basis.

The growing importance of Farm Bureau campaigns to increase consumption of animal products and improve diets was highlighted in late June, 1955, when the Du Page County Farm Bureau, in cooperation with the Pure Milk Association, arranged with four "Flying Farmers" to use their own planes to release over several towns 1,800 balloons bearing the message, "June is Dairy Month," and reminding consumers that milk and dairy products were a good buy. Some were retrieved as far away as 25 miles. Reports indicated that the stunt was highly successful.

In October, the IAA, in cooperation with the American Farm Bureau Federation and the 99 county Farm Bureaus, put on a state-wide meat promotion campaign. Quarter-page advertisements were run by the IAA in most Illinois newspapers in cities of more than 50,000 population, and many county Farm Bureaus ran ads in smaller newspapers. Experience gained in this drive encouraged county Farm Bureaus to raise funds locally to carry on promotions annually in later years.

At policy development meetings during the summer, the most pronounced trend in farm sentiment was clearly in the direction of a "soil bank" type of program. Many farmers seemed to be convinced that the most practical, as well as the most economical plan to stabilize production and prices, would be for the government to rent enough land from farmers to eliminate heavy surpluses, without any acreage allotments for individual crops. Most farmers believed that if as much as 50 million acres could be taken entirely out of production, the whole problem would be solved. A somewhat similar plan had been tried under the first AAA in 1933, when rental costs were very low. Nobody really knew, in 1955, how much it would cost under post-war conditions of inflated currency and inflated land values. Anyway, the idea seemed to be gathering many adherents. At the 1955 convention, delegates asked for strict control of diverted acres, as noted previously, but did not go as far as some soil-bank proponents wanted to go.

Charles J. Elliott, operator with his son, Kenneth, of a 360-acre grain and livestock farm in La Salle county and a Farm Bureau member for 41 years, was elected vice president, a post that had been vacant since Otto Steffey moved up to the presidency.

In his convention address, President Steffey touched on a subject that had been simmering for years in the minds of many members, and which was shortly to arouse sharp controversy, namely, a move away from Chicago as IAA headquarters. He did not recommend moving, but he asked members to study the situation carefully before making up their minds. He also recommended raising IAA dues to $6 on October 1, 1956, and to $7 two years later. Member dues to the AFBF had been raised 25 cents a year in 1953, and another similar raise was to become effective on December 1, bringing the total to $1.00 a member. The additional cost of 50 cents a member would cost the IAA $100,000 a year. It was obvious that IAA dues must be increased, and delegates voted to follow President Steffey's suggestion.

The AFBF in 1955 adopted a resolution calling for a soil bank program under which government would rent enough land from farmers to keep production in line with demand. What irked farmers most about previous programs was the fact that Washington officials had permitted farmers to plant and graze or harvest other crops on land taken out of crops which had been under allotments. Early in 1956, the Senate had a new farm bill written, but it fell far short of the requirements that had been outlined by farmers at the AFBF annual meeting. In order to crystallize farm opinion, President Steffey called a mass meeting at Peoria for February 20, which attracted some 11,000 farmers. Steffey said plainly that the Senate bill was a farce, largely because it provided for no control over diverted acres. "Lack of control over diverted acres," he said, "has been a major factor in depressing prices of corn, hogs, and cattle. Under the original version of S. 3183, wheat and cotton farmers could divert part of their land to the production of corn, soybeans, sorghums or other feed grains."

After hours of discussion, it was apparent that farmers at the meeting were overwhelmingly against any bill which failed to provide control over diverted acres, and were strongly in favor of a soil-bank plan which would take a real big chunk of land out of production. Steffey, now certain of grassroots backing, headed for Washington, where, with 15 other Farm Bureau members and AFBF help, he was able to get a number of amendments to S. 3183, introduced. The situation was reminiscent of the McNary-Haugen days but this time the Congress was Democratic. (While Congress debated the issue, on April 20, 1956, Samuel H. Thompson, who had led the McNary-Haugen forces thirty years before, died in Quincy at the age of 92.)

Congress did enact a bill, but it contained a provision for a two-price system for wheat and higher supports for feed grains, and President Eisenhower promptly vetoed it. Without knowing what Congress would finally do, farmers started planting corn.

Finally, late in May, Congress did pass a bill, and President Eisenhower signed it. It provided for a two-part soil bank program. The acreage reserve part of the program offered producers of "basic" crops, cotton, rice, tobacco, corn, wheat, and peanuts, an opportunity to reduce production with one-year agreements. The conservation reserve encouraged the retirement of cropland for a three- to 10-year period. In 1956, corn farmers could become eligible for price supports at $1.50 by planting within the acreage allotment established under the old allotment program, or by planting within their corn base and placing an acreage equal to 15 per cent of the corn base in the soil bank program, either in the acreage reserve or the conservation reserve. Those who did not comply with this requirement would have price support at a lower level as designated by the Secretary of Agriculture. The law was passed too late for extensive participation in 1956, but even so, some 5.5 million acres of corn land was put in the soil bank that year.

One weakness of the new law, as Farm Bureau members saw it, was that while it did provide for payments-in-kind in return for underplanting of acreage allotments, it also provided cash payments as an alternative. Farm Bureau believed that a good start could have been made in liquidating the heavy stocks of surplus grain held by the Commodity Credit Corporation, if its recommendation had been followed.

At the 1956 IAA convention, members were shocked by the sudden death of Vice President Charles J. Elliott, who had been elected to office only a year before. He collapsed just after he he had presided over the open session of the resolutions committee and died later the same day.

In the farm policy resolution, delegates reaffirmed their faith in the soil bank type of farm program, but called for a number of changes which they believed would make it more workable and effective. They also urged every effort to expand foreign trade, and recommended stepping up of activities under Public Law 480, under which foreign currencies could be accepted in payment for surplus farm commodities. They urged extending for at least two more years the three-year period authorized, and a substantial addition to the appropriation of $3 billion. Getting rid of the surpluses was becoming really expensive.

At the same time, delegates deplored the trend toward "concentration of all powers in the federal government." They added: "If this trend continues, we will have increased federal requirements applicable to our schools, federal labor legislation outlawing state right-to-work laws, federal legislation fixing water rights and the control over water, and federal control of our highways and of similar state governmental functions."

At the end of the convention, President Otto Steffey had been reelected, and William J. Kuhfuss, Angus breeder from Tazewell county, was named to succeed the late Charles J. Elliott as vice president.

On December 11, 1956, Cornbelt farmers went to the polls to vote in referendum on whether they wanted a 51-million-acre soil bank base program for corn, or a simple acreage allotment program with a 37-million-acre corn allotment for the commercial corn area. As in marketing quota referenda, a two-thirds majority was required to change over to the soil bank plan. In the Cornbelt, acreage allotments won, because only 61.2 per cent of the vote was for a change. In Illinois, however, farmers voted for the soil bank base by 53,669, to 12,985. It was obvious that they were fed up on acreage allotments.

Earlier in December, more than a hundred Farm Bureau people had assembled in Chicago to study the process of distributing food in a big city. Officials of meat-packing companies, chain stores, independent food stores, restaurants, hotels, and other outlets for meat arranged tours for the visitors, who planned to utilize knowledge of distributional processes gained on this trip in pushing promotion in their own communities. Emphasis was on animal products. Reason for this is the simple fact that by far the most effective way to use up corn and other surplus feed grains is through greater consumption of meat, dairy, and poultry products. People living on a bread, beans, and potato diet, such as Great Britain adopted during the war years, will consume the products of a relatively small acreage of cropland. But on a diet rich in meat, milk, eggs, and poultry, the same number of people will utilize the production, indirectly, of five or six times the number of acres as they would on the simpler diet. Hence the emphasis on animal products. The better diet costs more than the other, but people like it better, and in the United States, people enjoy relatively high incomes which enable them to eat better. Farm people understand this situation, hence are willing to contribute their money and their time to push campaigns for greater consumption of animal products.

In March, 1957, Farm Bureau members from many states went to Washington to call on their congressmen and senators to let them know their views on legislation affecting farm people. Sixteen people from Illinois were in the group. How much good was accomplished no one knows, but ever since, Farm Bureaus everywhere have given more attention than ever before to ways of getting members closer to those who represent them in Congress.

The week following the visit, a bill to give Cornbelt farmers a corn program featuring a soil bank base, rather than the old and discredited acreage allotment plan was voted down in the House; but 14 downstate Illinois congressmen voted for it, which was encouraging, while seven Chicago congressmen voted against it.

On May 25, 1957, Henry H. Parke, one of the founders of the De Kalb County Soil Improvement Association, forerunner of Farm Bureau, died at his home in Sycamore at the age of 81.

By IAA convention time, Congress having taken no significant action on problems affecting the corn grower, delegates reiterated their request for legislation establishing: a minimum soil conservation base, permitting unrestricted use of forage or soil-conserving crops grown on the base acreage, substantial government payments to encourage shifting of additional acres to conservation crops (not to be grazed or harvested), freedom of use of all other crop acreage, more flexible price supports, and orderly liquidation of government-owned surpluses.

In January, 1958, farmers in four states, Illinois, Nebraska, Tennessee, and Maine were given the opportunity to submit "bids" indicating at what price they would enroll their whole farm in the Conservation Reserve program for a 5- to 10-year period. All "bids" in Illinois, Nebraska, and Tennessee were rejected because most of them were much higher than the payment rates offered under the regular Conservation Reserve program. Some 350 Maine bids covering about 20,000 acres were accepted because the payment rate was not too much greater than the regular Conservation Reserve rates.

The question of the office location had been simmering for many years. During the administration of Earl C. Smith, agitation in favor of moving the office out of Chicago was strong enough to cause the board of directors to authorize a detailed analysis of the problem. A study was duly made and a report submitted which indicated unmistakably that, everything considered, Chicago was the best location for the IAA office. Availability of office help was a big factor cited in favor of Chicago. Many IAA officials, but particularly Earl C. Smith, were convinced that the reasons for staying in Chicago were so compelling that the office would always remain there.

Agitation persisted, however, with the result that Real Estate Research Service, a firm specializing in such matters, was employed to study the situation and make definite recommendations. It was obvious at this time that the IAA building at 43 East Ohio Street was totally inadequate to meet future needs. The study resulted in a definite recommendation for the purchase of a bigger office building in Chicago.

The board of directors gave continuing study to the problem of additional office space during ensuing years, and in 1957, authorized the purchase of two lots on Grand Avenue, just across the alley from the IAA building. As soon as the lots had been bought, a committee was set up to conduct studies on the feasibility of erecting a building. The committee consisted of President Steffey (chairman), Vice President William J. Kuhfuss, Edwin Gumm, Earle B. Johnson, and Frank L. Simpson. This action was taken at the board meeting held in October, 1957.

We now move on to the board meeting held on February 19,

20, and 21, 1958 in Chicago. After discussion of the problem of additional office space, Vice President William J. Kuhfuss moved: "That the Illinois Agricultural Association board of directors recommend to the voting delegates that a new home of ample size (approximately 240,000 square feet) to house the Association and affiliated companies, be built."

After the adoption of the motion it was agreed that the voting delegates should be assembled at Springfield, Illinois, on March 24, 1958, to consider and act on the proposal to build a new home and to borrow not to exceed $5 million for the purpose. Further discussion resulted in the adoption of a resolution directing that the proposed new building be erected on the recently purchased lots on Grand Avenue.

The voting delegates met in Springfield on March 24 and authorized the board of directors to "construct, lease, or acquire a home office building and to borrow up to $5 million for the purpose."

It was promptly moved that the proposed building be located "in a mid-state location." After a spirited discussion, the vote was taken and a new building in downstate Illinois was approved.

Before action could be taken to carry out the directive of the delegates, members everywhere were stunned when they learned of the sudden death of President Steffey at his home on May 15, 1958, slightly more than three years after he had succeeded Charles B. Shuman as president. Mr. Steffey had enjoyed good health, and was not aware of any heart weakness, but he died within a few minutes after being stricken, just after breakfast with Mrs. Steffey, as he was preparing to leave for a meeting in East St. Louis. Mr. Steffey had been a "team player" in Farm Bureau giving his best to any job that was ever assigned to him, and it was a matter of deep regret to his many friends that his career was cut so short. As a memorial to him, his friends and associates immediately set up a scholarship fund to be used to finance college educations for young men and women who would otherwise be unable to go to college.

Otto Steffey was the first IAA president to die in office. Hundreds of Farm Bureau leaders from throughout the state attended funeral services for the farm leader held in Stronghurst. His eulogy, a fitting description of the man, said, "To lead people, he walked with them hand in hand."

According to the IAA constitution, the IAA board of directors may elect a new president in case of death. They acted promptly and named William J. Kuhfuss, who had served as vice president for less than two years, Edwin Gumm of Knox county was named vice president. Since he had heavy responsibilities at home, it was necessary for Kuhfuss to make sudden adjustments to permit him to devote full time to Farm Bureau, but considering the burdens of the office, it was mandatory that he do so.

Kuhfuss lived on the farm on which he was born in Tazewell county which he operated in cooperation with his brother, Alvin. He was graduated from Illinois State Normal University in 1934, after majoring in science and agriculture. In college he won three letters in football and four in baseball. The two brothers, over a 20-year period, developed a prominent Aberdeen-Angus herd with some 70 brood cows, and they customarily raised about 400 hogs. They followed good soil conservation practices, and developed their farm, now extending over 800 acres, to a high state of pro-ductivity. The brothers showed cattle at many fairs, and William Kuhfuss became a director of the Aberdeen-Angus Breeders' Asso-ciation. In 1935 he was married to Elizabeth Storm, daughter of a minister in Minier. Four children, Karen, Linda, Thad, and John, all of whom have participated in 4-H club work, complete the Kuhfuss family. In 1951, Karen showed the grand champion heifer at the Illinois State Fair, and Thad showed a first-place winner at Springfield, placed second in the junior steer class at the International and third in the open class.

Edwin Gumm was a dairyman who spent 25 years building up a dairy herd on his farm south of Galesburg, and then, in 1947, sold the herd and began raising hogs and feeding beef cattle in partnership with his only son, John, who had just returned from army service.

The new officers had their work cut out for them, taking over

William J. Kuhfuss

as they did just as the organization faced the tremendous job of pulling up stakes in Chicago, finding a site and erecting a building downstate, moving staff members to the new location, and then finding replacements for those employees who simply could not move out of Chicago. It was a heavy assignment.

Erecting a new office building in a downstate location now became project No. 1 for the IAA. President Kuhfuss appointed George E. Merker, Jr., of the legal staff to the job of relocation coordinator. The Fantus Factory Locating Service, Chicago, was employed to survey a number of downstate cities and report to the board of directors with recommendations as to site. After intensive study of the problem, Bloomington was recommended as the Fantus downstate choice in a report on October 6. The question was settled in just over six months after the decision was made at Springfield. The architectural firm of Graham, Anderson, Probst, & White was already at work on building plans.

The coming move to Bloomington created other tough problems. It was necessary to hire and train new employees, and there was no room in the IAA building in Chicago for that. It was necessary to transfer a good deal of work to Bloomington long before the new building would be ready for occupancy. Arrangements were made with Illinois Wesleyan University to meet this difficulty. New buildings were erected on the campus, and basements of existing buildings were leased to the IAA, and were occupied by IAA employees for several months until they could move to the new building. When you consider that more than 800 new employees were hired and trained before the move, you can appreciate the magnitude of this problem.

On May 15, 1960, on-the-job-training began in quarters made available by Illinois Wesleyan University. In late May, certain units of Illinois Farm Supply Company and the insurance companies were moved into the new fieldhouse at Illinois Wesleyan. By mid-July the second of the new buildings on the campus was ready. By the end of July, some 70 per cent of IFS operations had been moved.

In January, 1960, building plans were approved and in Febru-

216

Exterior of new IAA building, 1961

Attending dedication ceremonies of new IAA building are wives of early Farm Bureau leaders; Left to right: Mrs. Howard Leonard, Charles B. Shuman, Mrs. Earl C. Smith, William J. Kuhfuss, Mrs. C. J. Elliott, and Mrs. Otto Steffey

217

County Farm Bureau presidents brought soil from their counties to be blended in planting area of new building courtyard to symbolize the intermixing of ideas, influences, and efforts of Farm Bureau members.

218

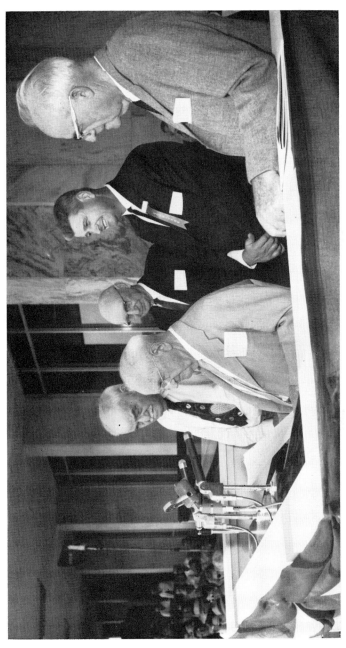

Oldtimers at building dedication ceremonies. From left: John Gummersheimer, "Uncle Joe" Fulkerson, Lyle Johnstone, William J. Kuhfuss, and Dave Thompson

Charles B. Shuman addressing dedication crowd

Board room in IAA building

220

ary a contractor was selected—Sherman Olson, Inc., of Chicago. Ground was broken on February 22, 1960. Construction work went ahead without a setback through spring, summer, and fall, and by November 4 the new building was enclosed. Work continued without letup, and on April 27, 1961, the first offices were occupied when the Illinois Agricultural Auditing Association and the Illinois Farm Bureau Serum Association moved into their new quarters. The offices of the IAA itself were moved the week of June 27. By October, the building was fully occupied. The building had been built for $350,000 below the budget and completed months ahead of schedule—an achievement of the first order by Sherman Olson, Inc.

The building was dedicated, with appropriate ceremonies, on September 7, 1961.

The three surviving members of the first IAA board of directors—Guy Carlyle "Lyle" Johnstone, "Limestone John" Gummersheimer, and "Uncle Joe" Fulkerson—were honored, along with Dave O. Thompson, first IAA secretary.

An assembly room in the new building was dedicated to the memory of Earl Clemmons Smith for his 20 years of service as president. In the room hangs an oil portrait of Smith, and there, too, stands the grandfather clock that members once presented to Smith at an annual meeting.

Mr. Smith had passed away on June 30, 1961, a few weeks after he was stricken with a heart attack. He died at his home in Pike county only a few hours after President Kuhfuss and Oscar Brissenden had called on him to ask his permission to dedicate a meeting room in the new IAA home to him. Deeply touched by this tribute to him, he readily assented and said: "You know my heart is in the IAA, and to it I gave the greatest effort of my life."

The memory of Otto Steffey is enshrined in a time capsule which is sealed in a block of Colorado marble, mounted at the entrance of the new building. It was paid for by donations from members in memory of Mr. Steffey, who was IAA president at the time the decision was made to erect the new IAA home at Bloomington.

The capsule is to be opened in the year 2016, one hundred years after the Illinois Agricultural Association was organzied. It contains microfilm copies of the original articles of incorporation and bylaws of the organization; list of those present and officers elected at the meeting on March 15, 1916, at Ottawa when the IAA was actually established; list of all IAA presidents, 1961 board members, and all members in good standing in 1961; along with a copy of the 1961 annual report of the IAA, and a record of the meeting at Springfield on March 24, 1958, when the voting delegates authorized construction of the new building at Bloomington. Additional material included provides a fairly complete record of how the organization came into being, what it undertook to do, and how well it succeeded.

Vice President Edwin J. Gumm, in conducting the time capsule ceremony, said: "The supreme worth of every individual who contributed to the Farm Bureau philosophy is recognized in this dedication."

The principal address was made by Charles B. Shuman, president of the American Farm Bureau Federation and a past president of the IAA. Some 12,000 people attended the dedication.

On August 9, 1958, George A. Fox of Sycamore, one of the Farm Bureau founders, who served the IAA as treasurer and later, secretary, died at the age of 81. The oldtimers were dropping off, one by one.

Meanwhile, Congress had enacted the Agricultural Act of 1958, which provided that farmers in the commercial corn area could vote in referendum for their choice of two programs—either for continuance of the existing program of acreage allotments with supports at 75 to 90 per cent of parity, depending on supply, or for doing away with allotments entirely, and accepting price supports at 90 per cent of the average market price of corn received by farmers for the preceding three years, or 65 per cent of parity, whichever might be higher. More than 70 per cent of the eligible voters favored a new program. This had been expected, since acreage allotments had been ignored by the great majority of Cornbelt farmers in 1958.

At convention time, November 16-19, 1959, government investments in farm surpluses totaled nearly $9 billion. Delegates adopted a farm program resolution calling for sweeping changes in the basic farm law. It was proposed that farmers would vote, in referendum, upon a proposed three-year program under which it would be mandatory for every farmer to keep a specific per cent of his land in soil-conserving crops, not to be pastured or harvested. No restrictions would be imposed on the use of land over and above that required to be in soil-conserving crops. In other words, no acreage allotments. Reasoning behind the resolution was as follows: Surpluses are now unmanageable. Voluntary compliance has not worked. It is time for every farmer to help carry the burden of crop reduction. Let all farmers vote, and if two-thirds or more favor the proposition, then all must comply.

This proposal was duly sent to the resolutions committee of the American Farm Bureau Federation, which rejected it. Then, at the delegate session, President Kuhfuss moved that the proposal be submitted to the AFBF board of directors for study and appraisal. This motion was tabled after short debate. Many of the delegates were of the opinion that any system of mandatory controls would be rejected in referendum and that it would be a waste of time to try it. This was the end of what was probably the most "radical" proposal on farm programs ever adopted by the IAA.

In 1958, the IAA engaged in an intensive campaign to head off a proposed $248 million bond issue for state welfare and educational buildings. While admitting the need, the IAA took the stand that it should be met by broadening the tax base, instituting needed economies in government, and going on a pay-as-you-go basis. The bond issue failed in the November election. However, two years later, in 1960, voters accepted this method of financing building needs in approving a $195 million bond issue for state universities and a $150 million bond issue for state welfare institutions.

At the 1960 convention, delegates again asked for a farm program based on the principles of soil conservation, and for effective use of payments-in-kind in rewarding farmers for taking land out of production. They also asked for support prices at levels which would permit movement of farm products into consumer markets, with supports limited to those farmers who reduced acreage. A month later, IAA officials had the satisfaction of seeing the substance of this resolution adopted by voting delegates to the American Farm Bureau Federation at Denver. It has come to be known as the cropland retirement program and Farm Bureau forces failed, in 1961 and 1962, to get Congress to pass a bill based on it. In 1961, Congress adopted a "temporary" feed grain program, plus a mutilated version of the Cochrane-Freeman Omnibus Bill. These laws brought about reduced acreage of corn and feed grains, but at very high cost to the government. Over-all reduction in volume of grain produced was far below expectations. In 1962, Congress adopted the Administration's farm bill, considerably amended from its original form.

This new law provided for a one-year extension of the 1961 and 1962 type feed grain program, a one-year emergency wheat program for 1963 and for a referendum on an extremely controversial multiple-price certificate wheat plan for 1964 and thereafter.

On May 21, 1963, wheat farmers throughout the U.S. went to the polls to cast their ballots on this wheat program, knowing their vote could have extremely significant implications on all farm programs. If the multiple-price certificate plan was approved by two-thirds of those voting, farmers would be faced with a mandatory program of acreage allotments, marketing quotas, marketing penalties, and land diversion. Under this program, the price support loan level was to be set in relation to feed prices and world wheat prices. In addition to the price support loan, a farmer would receive certificates for his proportionate share of the wheat used for food in the U.S. and a certain part of the export wheat as determined by the Secretary of Agriculture. The certificates would bring the total returns of this part of a farmer's wheat to about $2.00 a bushel. If farmers rejected this program, price supports would be set at 50 per cent of parity, about $1.25. Farmers desiring price supports would have to comply with their allotments. However, there would be no marketing quotas, marketing penalties, certificates, or mandatory diversion.

The wheat certificate plan was rejected by a majority of the farmers voting in the referendum. It was a stunning setback for all those in government and out who believe that agriculture must be managed by government through control of production and price.

The defeat was truly decisive, because no state in which wheat is a major commodity gave the plan the necessary two-thirds majority. In Kansas, leading wheat state, 57.4 per cent of those voting turned thumbs down on the plan. Minnesota, Missouri, and North and South Dakota came close to ratification, but failed by a narrow margin. In Illinois, over 70 per cent of those voting, voted "no."

The defeat was the more satisfying to Farm Bureau and other forces which had been fighting against rigid price and production controls, because Secretary of Agriculture Freeman had conducted an all-out campaign, predicting horrible economic repercussions for wheat growers unless they voted for strict regimentation. Freeman told farmers that a favorable vote would assure wheat farmers of $700 million more annual income.

Freeman's forces left no stone unturned in seeking a victory. They staged massive efforts in cotton and tobacco states, telling farmers that if controls on production were ended on wheat, it would be only a question of time until cotton and tobacco programs would also be scuttled. That their work was effective in those states is shown by the fact that the following states gave the plan a two-thirds majority: Kentucky, Georgia, North Carolina, Tennessee, and South Carolina. The irony of this situation is that wheat is not a major crop in any one of those states.

Both President Kennedy and Secretary of Agriculture Freeman announced that they thought farmers had made a mistake, and Freeman hinted broadly that they would come back into the fold before too long. Furthermore, Canada was shortly to sell some $500 million worth of wheat to Russia, thus practically eliminating the wheat surplus problem for Canadian farmers. On top of that, the Administration at Washington authorized the sale of nearly 200 million bushels of U.S. wheat to Russia. That action is something to ponder over, because Russia, considered by many to be our worst enemy, will be helping us with two of our serious economic problems, the wheat surplus and our unfavorable balance of payments.

Chapter 19

Sine Qua Non

There is a Latin phrase, *sine qua non*, for which there is no satisfactory equivalent. It means "without which not," and is used to designate things vitally essential to proper functioning. There are many *sine qua nons* in the structure of the IAA, "without which not" it could have reached its present position of eminence. Some of these get little public notice, but all have made tremendous contributions to Farm Bureau progress. In this chapter we will discuss a few of them.

ILLINOIS AGRICULTURAL SERVICE COMPANY

In 1963, as we look back fifty-one years to the organization of the first soil and crop improvement associations, we witness an impressive example of what farmers can accomplish by working together. The entire complex of IAA and affiliated companies represents a new way of life, in a sense, for the more than 195,000 families which make up its membership. During the pre-Farm Bureau days, most farmers felt that they were fighting uphill battles against forces that seemed to have most of the advantages on their side. Farmers believed that they, and they alone of the various occupational groups, were subject to blind economic forces; while other groups apparently had been able, largely through organization, to control to a significant degree the economic forces with which they had to contend. The big industrial corporation, the tariff laws, and the big labor organizations are examples which immediately come to mind.

As the Farm Bureau developed throughout the nation, farm people found that they too could fight effectively at Washington for national legislation in their own interest; and they found also that they too could form great commercial enterprises, some of which could render better service at lower cost than could the business entities which had previously served them. This led to a remarkable change in attitude by farm people on the questions of public policy and farm business services. It led to what might be called a massive boost to the morale of rural people. Instead of standing on the sidelines, and as some extremists contended during the early days, "taking submissively the crumbs which fell from the banquet table" at which others were feasting, farmers found themselves in the thick of many a battle on the tax front, the farm price front, the education front, and many others. They were no longer isolated from their fellows. They had closed ranks, created powerful leaders; and they were fighting as a group for what they considered economic equality. They found the fight exhilarating, and they labored tirelessly to extend and enhance the gains that had rewarded their early efforts.

In the picture in 1963, you see nearly all of the real farmers of Illinois banded together in an organization which carries a great deal of weight as it speaks for them on public policy through which they control commercial enterprises of great magnitude which return to them, as owners, extremely satisfactory profits.

The fact that this great establishment has been held together and kept on an even keel through so many years is puzzling to many people. It should be said at once that it has not been easy. Grave and threatening problems have faced the leadership at all times. It is admitted that mistakes have been made, that substantial losses have been sustained in some commercial ventures—but viewing the operation in perspective, one's verdict on total results can be only a most favorable one.

One of the principal keys to success in keeping the whole movement unified has been the Illinois Agricultural Service Company, which was set up on October 7, 1926 to supply management services to the growing IAA affiliates. General Counsel Donald Kirkpatrick, who was serving as secretary of IASC in 1929, in making his annual report as secretary, termed the organization a "balance wheel" for the commercial activities of the IAA. It was and is a wholly-owned subsidiary of the parent organization. In the early days, it was commonly called "the service board." In discussing its function, Kirkpatrick wrote:

"Under the direction of the several boards of directors of the commercial service companies, the service board has managed, as corporate manager, the following companies:

1. Illinois Agricultural Mutual Insurance Company.
2. Farmers Mutual Reinsurance Company.
3. Country Life Insurance Company.
4. Illinois Farm Supply Company.
5. Illinois Agricultural Cooperatives Association.
6. McLean County Milk Producers Association.
7. Champaign County Milk Producers Association.

"The active manager of each of these companies is under the immediate direction of the service board, being employed by the service board with the approval of the respective boards of directors.

"The service board appears at this time to have established the following functions in the organization:

1. An immediate and continuing supervisory and advisory direction of active managers of commerical service companies.
2. Expeditious group decision on administrative business matters.

3. Segregation of administrative detail from policy matters and reference of policy problems to respective boards of directors.

4. Maintenance of proper balance and relation of commercial activities of the Association to other departmental activities.

"It is legally necessary in most commercial activities to set up a separate corporate entity, in all cases it is highly advisable, but this does not mean that separate corporate entities and their resulting separate boards of directors are other than members of one happy family with management that is unified and all working to the common end and all persons connected therewith, soldiers of a common cause. The service board is one of liaison units in our organization."

As indicated earlier in this book, it had been arranged that the IAA owns voting stock ("B" stock) in all affiliates, which assures control. The advent of the "service board" assured further safeguarding of commercial activities from possible exploitation against the wishes of the farmer owners. In the early days, when both Farm Bureau and the infant affiliates were feeling their way cautiously, it could be said that the IASC was a dominant influence in the affairs of every affiliate. Boards of directors of affiliates were often inexperienced in business affairs, and they depended heavily on the counsel of the ISAC. There is general agreement today that this happy arrangement was a big factor in getting new businesses under way and in shielding them against costly mistakes.

Directors of the "service company," as it is commonly called, are elected by the IAA board of directors. The president of the IAA has always been the president of the service company. In 1963 the board consisted of William J. Kuhfuss, president, IAA; Charles S. Mayfield, IAA secretary; Paul E. Mathias, IAA general counsel; Kenneth D. Carpenter, IAA treasurer and director of finance; and Walter B. Peterson, IAA secretary of marketing.

For a long time, policy and management decisions of affiliates were very closely supervised by the service company; but as officers, boards of directors, and management personnel of affiliates gained experience, the role of detailed direction gradually shifted to one rather of coordination and counseling. Experience proved the best results in a business come when a competent manager is hired, given responsibility, and then held strictly accountable, rather than by watching over his shoulder all the time with respect to details.

At first glance, one might conclude that this situation could seriously complicate matters for a manager because he is responsible to two groups, his own board and the service company. In practice, however, this has not proved to be generally true. On the contrary, managers have usually found it distinctly helpful to have a set of "ground rules" provided for them. With such guide lines agreed on, if a manager ever gets out of bounds on some activity, he simply cannot plead that he didn't know the rules. On the other hand, managers have generally found that they are encouraged to exercise all the ingenuity they possess to adopt innovations and improved practices, so long as they are within policy and likely to improve business. In this respect, the service company has simplified, rather than complicated, the manager's problems.

After thirty-five years of experience as the principal coordinating agency in the IAA and affiliated companies, the service company rarely has to confront a problem that is wholly new. There will be angles to any new problem that relate it to previous problems that have been met. The overwhelming opinion among present IAA leadership and the management group of the affiliates is that if the service company had not been set up in 1926, it would have become mandatory very shortly thereafter to create something like it. It is simply unthinkable to suppose that businesses of the size attained by many of the affiliates could possibly have remained in orbit around the IAA for so long, if the gravitational pull of the parent organization, the IAA, had not been continuously maintained, and strong enough to offset other powerful forces, trying relentlessly to pull them off into other solar systems. Farm Bureau members today can be thankful that the early leadership of the IAA had the wisdom to provide the safeguards that have proved so effective over a long period of years.

* * *

LEGAL AFFAIRS

Frederick H. DeYoung of Chicago was the first director of the legal department of the IAA (1920 and 1921), and he was succeeded by Newton Jenkins in 1922. Jenkins left to go into politics, and his assistant, Donald Kirkpatrick, succeeded him in 1924. Kirkpatrick was to stay until his retirement on January 1, 1950, when his assistant, Paul E. Mathias, took over as general counsel.

As the Farm Bureau affiliates developed, need for establishing a solid corporate structure soon became obvious.

The early days filled with zeal of promotional efforts gave way to the more tedious task of establishing business practices which could stand the test of time. Playing a leading role in this work was Mathias who joined the Illinois Agricultural Association in August of 1933, as assistant to Donald Kirkpatrick. Mathias was born and raised on a farm near Rochester, Indiana. He did his undergraduate study at the University of Chicago and continued to receive a law degree in 1927. He joined the Legislative Reference Bureau of the State of Illinois and spent seven years working with legislators in drafting bills, many of which became laws of the State of Illinois. This intimate contact with the lawmaking procedure was to stand him in good stead when later he became a member of the IAA staff.

His first job was as an attorney in the legal department but his ability over and above his legal competence was soon recognized, and he became corporate secretary and assistant general counsel. Much of the legal work in connection with the establishment of the corporate structures of many of the affiliates as they are known today has been done by Mathias.

As a long time member of the Illinois Agricultural Service Company, his business talents have played a major role in the solid

Paul E. Mathias

structure of the IAA affiliates. He has been a major contributor to the success of these companies over the years.

In addition to his work in the legal and business fields, he has had the major responsibility for state legislative programs, has played an important role in the IAA's national legislative program, and has at various times supervised many of the program functions in the IAA.

As of 1963, the legal staff consists of Mathias, Harry Meloy, Joel McNulty, George E. Merker, William M. Goebel, Lawrence Eaton, and Albert J. Cross, who also heads the department of local government. (George E. Merker devoted full time to a special assignment as relocation coordinator during most of 1960 and 1961.) All are qualified to practice law in Illinois.

The broad scope of the legal department is indicated by the following excerpts from its annual report in 1962:

"The legal department is a service department. It assists in the work and projects of other departments and companies. It does not initiate new or independent projects of its own. The department serves the Illinois Agricultural Association, the county Farm Bureaus, the affiliated state-wide companies, and their local member companies.

"The department advises concerning corporate matters and legal problems that arise in day to day operation. It prepares articles of incorporation, by-laws, stock certificates, and membership agreements and amendments and revisions thereof. It prepares and revises contracts for the affiliated companies and generally advises concerning corporate matters and procedures. Settlement of certain of the claims of Country Life Insurance Company and Country Mutual Insurance Company are reviewed in the department. The department also assists with the preparation of policy forms, endorsements, and similar documents for the insurance companies. A great deal of time is devoted to review of documents in connection with the investments of the insurance companies.

"During the past year, the consolidation of several dairy companies into Prairie Farms Dairy, Inc. was completed. The consolidation of several producer agencies, Illinois Livestock Marketing Association and certain local member companies, into Illinois Producers Livestock Association also was completed and became effective during the year. FS Services, Inc. was incorporated under the laws of Delaware and Illinois Farm Supply Company and Farm Bureau Service Company of Iowa were merged into FS Services, Inc., effective September 1, 1962. These mergers and consolidations are time consuming, involve a great deal of detail, and have required a considerable portion of time of members of the legal department.

"A manual dealing with the Fair Labor Standards Act and its application to the state-wide companies and their local member companies was prepared. A considerable amount of time was devoted to labor matters and labor negotiations, wage and hour law questions, unemployment compensation, social security questions, and similar matters.

"The department also considered a number of questions arising out of the sales tax law and the use tax law.

"Personnel of the department have served on numerous committees of the organization during the year.

"The department does not attempt to give assistance upon personal legal problems of the individual Farm Bureau members. It does advise on legal problems which are of general interest. Members with individual legal problems are advised to consult competent local attorneys for assistance."

It should be added that the general counsel also has charge of the departments of legislation, local government, stock records, natural resources, and property taxation.

* * *

FINANCE DIVISION

As the IAA and its affiliates have grown, the size and complexity of the problems facing it have increased in proportion. As anyone can well imagine, financial problems became pressing immediately after the reorganization of the IAA in 1919. First treasurer following the reorganization was George A. Fox of

Sycamore, one of the key men who made notable contributions to Farm Bureau progress during the formative years. He was transferred to the office of secretary in 1922, and was succeeded by Robert A. Cowles of Bloomington, who remained treasurer until his retirement in 1948. Both men were sound and conservative in their financial policies. Both knew and respected the value of a dollar, and Cowles, particularly, was a perfectionist. He was never satisfied with anything less than perfection in his financial reports. Together, these men set the standards and created the great tradition of sound financing that became part of the grand tradition of the IAA.

By 1934, the IAA insurance companies were taking in so much money that the job of investing the funds was a major problem. From the beginning, the investment policy had been ultra-conservative. The big bulk of the funds was used to buy federal, state, or municipal bonds, and high-grade industrial bonds. Decisions on what to buy were made by IAA Treasurer Cowles and his associates, with advice from bankers and others. Vice President A. R. Wright of Varna, who was a banker as well as a farmer was frequently consulted on these matters, and he soon demonstrated his knowledge and skill in the investment field. In 1935, he was made assistant treasurer and assigned special responsibility for investing funds of the insurance companies.

Changes in investment policy have come about very gradually. Wright made a beginning in bringing about a greater diversity in the investment portfolio, but those changes were minor in comparison with those made later. In 1949, for example, old precedents were shattered when some 10,000 shares of preferred stocks in industrial and utility companies were purchased. Later, some cautious purchases were made of top quality common stocks, but amount invested is still severely limited. About one-third of all insurance company assets in 1963 is invested in mortgages. Another third, roughly, is invested in industrial and utility bonds. Only about eight per cent of the funds are invested in U.S. government bonds. The interest rate earned on investments has gradually risen from only 2.6 per cent in 1947 to 3.81 per cent in

236

1957, and to 4.37 per cent in 1963. Returns per dollar invested have increased 68 per cent in sixteen years!

The responsibilities of the IAA treasurer today are vastly different from those of 1922, when Robert A. Cowles was paid on a per diem basis presumably because the job did not warrant a full-time employment. Consider the fact that each year in these times the IAA treasurer has the responsibility of investing more than $36 million for the insurance companies. In addition, the insurance companies have more than $286 million in assets, most of it tied up in investments which must be constantly reappraised for soundness and profitability in an ever-changing economic climate. The IAA itself has assets exceeding $3 million.

The IAA treasurer in 1963 truly has a complex job on his hands. Kenneth D. Carpenter, treasurer since 1957, is director of the finance division which is made up of three departments—treasury, investments, and controller, with 38 employees. The investment department alone requires the full time of six people. Jay T. Nelson is assistant treasurer, and Florence Wilson is assistant to the treasurer. Vernon D. Ogren is director of investments, and William H. Beam is controller.

The finance division is faced with problems of borrowing as well as lending. The rapid growth of affiliates such as FS Services, Inc., involves long-term financing new feed mills, new fertilizer plants and other facilities. Observers might assume that new facilities could be financed largely out of earnings; and it's possible that this might be done except for the fact that this company can find much more profitable uses for its funds. A factory building, for example, can be financed through a bond issue or long-term mortgage at a relatively low interest rate. It would not be good policy to put FS money into it, when the money can be put into other facilities needed to expand the business and earn two or three times the rate that a mortgage yields.

Insurance company money, on the other hand, is generally invested in mortgages and bonds at low interest rates because insurance companies are restricted by law to some extent, and by business prudence generally to investments in which the hazard of loss is very low. For example, new apartment houses are regarded as a suitable investment for insurance companies, but would not even be considered for FS funds.

The business of the IAA and its affiliates has become big by any standard. The annual report of the finance division in 1958 indicated that accounts were maintained in 33 banks, and that receipts and disbursements aggregated $100 million, with 2 million items deposited and 500,000 checks processed. Comparable statistics for today would be much larger. It would be utterly impossible to handle financial operations of this size successfully without the help of men of the highest qualifications, men who are specialists in some field of finance. The record is solid proof that the high standards set by George A. Fox and Robert A. Cowles in the early days have been well maintained through the years.

* * *

INFORMATION AND PUBLICITY

I have referred briefly in previous chapters to IAA emphasis on keeping the public, as well as the members informed on activities and policies of the organization. The fact that four of the early information directors are now listed in "Who's Who In America" is evidence enough that IAA officials went after top-grade men to staff the information department.

The official publication since 1921 has been the IAA RECORD, a monthly publication of 24 or more pages, printed on good paper. (It started as a quarterly, but in 1926 became a monthly.) The IAA RECORD has won many prizes for excellence in journalistic practices.

In the early days, a film library was started to supply appropriate films for showing at local or county Farm Bureau meetings. This service was extensively used for many years. As late as 1949, for example, the library contained 438 reels of film, covering 273 subjects. Films were provided for 829 programs during the year. In 1953, the first IAA movie was made, and enjoyed wide popularity for a number of years. Also, a film of the Illinois Sports

Festival was made, along with another, dealing with hail damage to crops, which was sponsored by the Country Mutual Fire Company. A series of slide films dealing with marketing problems was also undertaken. For three years, the information department produced a television show, "Farmtown, U.S.A.," which was telecast from Chicago. In 1956, a filmed monthly TV series was inaugurated for use of downstate TV stations. A number of movies were produced for IAA affiliates. Changing conditions resulted in modification or dropping of much of the film work during the next few years. The film library was discontinued in 1959, due to lack of demand, which, in turn, was due to the decline in number of local Farm Bureau meetings held.

As of 1963, production of sound tape and slide films, as well as TV news-clips dealing with Farm Bureau events, is a big feature of the IAA information program. Radio tapes are sent weekly to some 60 downstate radio stations.

Every effort is constantly made to keep the newspapers and wire services fully informed on the activities of the IAA and the affiliated companies through news releases.

Of all the responsibilities shouldered by the information department, high on the list has always been the obligation to keep the members fully informed. The IAA RECORD goes to each member, but it is only one of many channels of information now utilized. County Farm Bureaus constantly receive from the state office informational material for local use in their own publications, the local press, and radio and TV stations. This work has been greatly intensified in recent years, as county organizations in great number have put full-time organization men on their staffs. These men carry primary responsibility for local publicity and public relations activities. Press packets, radio and TV tapes, slide films, and news releases are sent to them regularly. They have at their command all of the materials needed to keep Farm Bureau in the public eye at all times.

All of the above activities amount to a massive effort, using all methods of communication, to keep Farm Bureau members and the general public abreast of all Farm Bureau developments. All this requires a staff of eight men, headed by William W.

Allen, secretary of information. James C. Tippett is director of publications, Richard L. Wright is director of radio-television service, and William E. Clark heads the graphic production department.

It seems in order to report briefly on how the IAA RECORD is financed. No advertising has ever been accepted, except from the affiliated companies. The affiliates advertise regularly, and thus provide a substantial part of the funds needed to support the publication. The IAA itself provides the balance.

The information department has never been slow to adopt new methods and techniques in the field of communications. For example, in 1961, when Farm Bureau was pushing its cropland adjustment program, an audio-visual presentation—a series of full-color 35 millimeter slides with tape-recorded narration and background music—was used to explain the issue. Some 48 copies were sent to Farm Bureau leaders in the state for use in meetings.

To keep the public informed as to the policies and activities of the IAA, the information department must keep in close touch with all purveyors of news at all times. When major agricultural issues are under consideration, special efforts are made. In 1962 a series of action conferences were called to mobilize Farm Bureau forces for national legislative activity. To help local news media, newspaper, and radio and television personnel in each city where a meeting was scheduled were invited to a breakfast at which the Farm Bureau position was outlined. As a result, new stories and radio and television broadcasts dealing with the meetings were notable for their accuracy. It was quite apparent that those who prepared them were well briefed on the issue. Also, considerable editorial comment was generated, much of it favorable. Such efforts are time-consuming and expensive, but they have proved well worth while.

Over the years, demands for service have increased to such an extent that the services of a full-time commercial artist and a full-time photographer are now required. Service is rendered in these fields, not only to the IAA but also to county Farm Bureaus and IAA affiliates. Staff members are called upon to handle all sorts of assignments in helping out the county Farm Bureaus; for instance, to produce a pageant dramatizing the development of a county Farm Bureau over a period of fifty years.

In the summer of 1962, an institutional movie, "The Farm Bureau Story," was produced. It depicts the role and functions of the Farm Bureau and the affiliated companies. The 20-minute production, in full color, was written, produced, and photographed by the staff of the information division.

A new radio feature called "Capitol Comment" was offered to radio stations in 1963. It is a five-minute commentary on state and national legislative issues, and is being used by 46 stations.

Press packets containing Farm Bureau news are sent to county Farm Bureaus weekly for use in their own publicity activities. During sessions of the Illinois General Assembly they also receive a feature entitled "Dateline Springfield" to keep them up on legislative happenings. This column also goes to 32 newspapers and three radio stations which requested it.

Through 1956, the publicity department had operated as a part of the organization division. A management study that year determined, however, that the publicity department and the departments of public relations and research should be combined into a full division to be called the information division.

C. S. Mayfield, who was secretary of organization, became acting secretary of information. In late September, 1956, Russell Van Cleve resigned and William W. Allen was named director of publicity.

Then, in February, 1958, John L. Lacey was named secretary of information. Lacey, who had served on the American Farm Bureau Federation information staff for 22 years, served the IAA until February, 1960. On Lacey's retirement from the IAA, Allen was promoted to the secretary of information post.

* * *

ORGANIZATION DEPARTMENT

Since the obvious advantages of belonging to Farm Bureau are so great, it might be assumed that it should be an easy matter to maintain the membership at its 1963 strength of some 195,000. It is true that an organization of a sort could be maintained in

Illinois without continuing effort to maintain and extend membership. But that is not the kind of organization that was envisioned at the beginning, and it is not the sort of organization that Farm Bureau leaders want today. Leaders learned in 1923, when a third of the 1922 members dropped out, that it is never safe to rest on the oars in this work. To use a parallel from the business world, the time of greatest peril to a business comes when it has reached the top in its field. Bitter experience has proved time and again that then is the time when promotion, advertising, and better service programs must be stepped up rather than curtailed. There is too much at stake now to risk a falling off of business. When the top is reached, it often takes more effort to hold top position than was required to get there.

Farm Bureau learned this lesson in 1923 and it has never been forgotten. It learned another lesson too, and that is that farmers who are members themselves are the most effective "salesmen" of the Farm Bureau idea. That is why today, after half a century of experience, the IAA organization department does not even consider staging a membership campaign without "teams" of members playing the leading role.

Throughout the history of Farm Bureau in Illinois, strength and substance has been added to the organization largely by farm men and women who believed in themselves, in their neighbors, and in the future of American agriculture. Imbued with the conviction that farm people thinking and working together could accomplish tasks that could not be performed by individuals working alone, they have indeed achieved greatly by pooling their strength. Countless individuals told their neighbors why they had joined Farm Bureau, and impressed them with their vision of the future. The result has been a steadfast loyalty that has brought tremendous achievements. It goes without saying that leaders and staff members were important in carrying out the jobs that members have outlined for them.

It can be said that ever since 1921, the work of maintaining the organization has been done according to carefully devised and definite plans which required salesmanship of the highest order on the part of organization men. A broad understanding of the issues, along with the ability to present them with conviction, has been the first essential quality in those seeking to do organization work. For the organization worker, equitable membership quotas and realistic dues-collection procedures have encouraged him to maximum effort. These are some of the factors in the rise of the Illinois Agricultural Association to its present commanding position as the largest, and by all odds, the most powerful state Farm Bureau organization in America.

Tremendous enthusiasm and determination were developed among the workers, both volunteer and professional, when the big drive for 100,000 Farm Bureau members in Illinois was undertaken in 1943. The goal was barely reached in 1943, but in the ensuing years, membership zoomed to such an extent that by 1950, organization department workers began talking confidently of eventually reaching a goal of 200,000. In 1953, a drive for the new goal was conducted, and it went over the top. In just ten years, IAA membership had doubled!

Oscar D. Brissenden, who retired from the IAA in 1963, had a notable career in the organization department for twenty years before assuming other responsibilities as special assistant to the president in 1952. In the latter capacity, he traveled widely, and addressed many Farm Bureau meetings in all regions. Now in retirement, he keeps busy with his farms in Clay and Livingston counties.

All of the IAA organization directors, starting with and including George E. Metzger, have recognized the member himself as the key person in building and maintaining Farm Bureau. Following Metzger, were Vernon Vaniman, Oscar D. Brissenden, Charles S. Mayfield, and Charles E. Alexander—all stalwarts who have had notable careers in Farm Bureau. District organization men of long tenure who have carried out the policies in the field with excellent results include Harry B. Claar, L. B. (Burl) Hornbeck, Emmett Keim, Asa B. Culp, John C. Moore, Thomas Smythe, and John C. Howlett, the last four of whom are now deceased.

The job of membership building is now vastly different from what it was even a dozen years ago. After World War II, greatly increased activities of county Farm Bureaus simply required more manpower. For a number of years, membership work in the county was placed in the hands of a man called the county organization director (COD). As time went on, however, it became evident that most county organizations needed someone to carry out, under the direction of officers and board of directors, not only the entire county Farm Bureau program, but also the program of the state organization. The answer to this problem was found in creation of the job of secretary of organization, hired and paid jointly by the county Farm Bureau and the IAA. These men are now the key men in Farm Bureau activities at the county level.

The county Farm Bureaus have changed with the times, and have gained in efficiency. Dues of current members are collected in large part by simply sending a notice through the mail. A second notice is often necessary, and sometimes a third. If the member does not pay up then, he is dropped from membership.

There is a steady and relentless attrition of membership due to death, retirement, sale of farm, and other causes. In these days when the average size of farms grows so rapidly, it is something of a problem to maintain the number of members in any county. In some counties, it involves signing up almost every farmer who is eligible to membership. It is a matter of considerable pride in many counties that a difficult feat has been practically accomplished. "Potential" members are now becoming scarce in every county. And that situation is probably the greatest tribute that can be paid to the organization men and the members who have been responsible for it.

The organization department in 1963 is headed by Charles E. Alexander. Assistants are Frank Chambers and Theron Summers. Kenneth L. Cheatham directs young people's activities, and Emmett Keim looks after membership records, after long experience as a district fieldman. The family activities department has been without a director since the resignation of Miss Coena Blair in July, 1963. Cullen B. Sweet, assistant director of organization, died in February, 1963. District fieldmen are G. W. Blanchard, G. W. Hagaman, H. A. Hiltbrand, William Isle, Floyd Nethery, and Earl Eubanks.

Chapter 20

Plucking the Goose

According to the old French axiom, the collection of taxes should be handled as you pluck a goose, the aim being to get the greatest amount of feathers with the least amount of squawking by the goose. In 1921, farm owners were doing plenty of squawking, primarily because they thought they were being de-feathered a lot more severely by tax collectors than were other people.

Prior to the reorganization of the IAA in 1919, farm people had found no effective way to make their collective voice heard in councils in which public policies were adopted. On the subject of taxes, individual farmers could protest to the county boards of review, and sometimes they got relief from assessment inequities, but as far as participating in the making of tax policies for the state as a whole was concerned, farm people felt that they were out in the cold.

It was inevitable, therefore, that when the IAA was reorganized and adequate funds were provided for group action through the $5 individual membership fee, there would be strong demand for action on the tax front. In 1919, the quadrennial revaluation of real estate had been based largely on the sensational increases in land prices, which in turn had been based on wartime prices for farm commodities. There had been no corresponding increase in prices for urban real estate, hence it was farm land that took the brunt of the increased taxes that had to be collected to meet rising costs of government. (At that time, Illinois had a state tax on real estate.)

By 1921, farm owners were in a belligerent mood, because the bottom had dropped out of farm prices in 1920. Farmers contended that they were being forced to pay wartime taxes out of incomes that were at a depression level. The IAA legislative committee in 1921 undertook to fight for an amendment to the revenue section of the state constitution. That was a losing fight, but in the course of it, George A. Fox, then IAA treasurer, asked John C. Watson, head of the IAA statistical bureau, to undertake a study of the methods followed by the Illinois Tax Commission.

It was found that in 1919 the Commission had "equalized" taxes by adding some $55 million to the farmers' tax bill, and in 1920 had added another $112 million. Clearly, it was time to act. On December 14, 1921, IAA and county Farm Bureau representatives appeared before the Commission in a public hearing. It was the first time in Illinois history that such a thing had been done. Farm Bureaus in many counties had been working for reductions through boards of review, and tax officials everywhere were fast becoming aware of Farm Bureau.

The Illinois Tax Commission was evidently impressed by the case the farm forces had made in the 1921 hearing, because in 1922, instead of adding to the assessed valuations fixed by the county boards of review, it had ordered a decrease for the state amounting to $68,945,061. This reduction, plus valuations lowered by county boards of review resulted in Illinois farmers paying approximately a million dollars less state taxes on farm land in 1921 and 1922 than they would have paid if the 1920 valuations had been allowed to stand. Much of the reduction came about simply because farmers, through Farm Bureau, had made effective protests based on facts uncovered by Watson.

It should be noted here that county Farm Bureaus were very active. In nine counties in 1923, for example, hearings were held before the assessors when they received the assessment books and were instructed as to their duties by the county treasurers, who by virtue of their office were the supervisors of assessments. Information disclosed by the Farm Bureau investigations previously made was presented in full, and in eight of the nine counties either complete or more nearly complete equalization of farm and city real estate was made. In twenty-four counties, hearings were held before county boards of review. In about half of the counties, complete equalization was achieved, and in most of the others partial correction of inequalities was made. In only a few counties did members of review boards resent the action by Farm Bureau. Usually, they welcomed the hearing and did their best to make proper adjustments.

The really big achievement came in 1923, the year of the quadrennial revaluation of all real estate. Farm Bureaus were ready for it, armed with statistics supplied by Watson. Changes made in revaluation, plus changes that had been made in 1921 and 1922, meant that farmers the next year had their taxes, state and local, cut by some $4 million. Member investment in Farm Bureau dues was paying big returns.

Since Watson was now devoting practically full time to tax matters, the name of his department was changed to the department of taxation and statistics. The IAA and Watson himself were now well-known throughout the state. In 1923, Watson and John L. Whisnand of Coles county, head of the IAA education committee, were appointed to the advisory council of the Illinois Educational Commission which was set up by the 1923 legislature. This led to much work at Springfield on both educational and tax matters, and very soon Watson became one of the IAA staff men at Springfield, speaking for the IAA on all matters under the direction of the legislative committee consisting of Sam Thompson of Quincy, Frank D. Barton of Cornell, and Arthur C. Everingham of Hutsonville.

The year of 1923 was a year of continual controversy with the Illinois Tax Commission. In six counties, boards of review refused to equalize valuations between farm and urban real estate. The Commission promised to order reassessments in these counties, but failed to do it. Watson pressed the chairman for action, but got nowhere. Finally, the chairman of the Commission resigned. The year ended with only about half as much accomplished as could have been accomplished if the Commission had acted with firmness.

A happy ending did not always result after Farm Bureau intervention. In Madison county, the review board refused to equalize, even though it admitted that farm land was assessed at 60 per cent of its value while urban property was assessed at only 40 per cent of its value. Nearly 200 landowners refused to pay their taxes and asked, through the Farm Bureau, to be heard on their claim that assessment of their land was discriminatory. A test case was brought, and the farmers lost. On appeal, the Illinois Supreme Court upheld the decision on the basis that judgment must be sought by each taxpayer, rather than by the group. The interesting thing about the decision was that the Supreme Court agreed with the farmers that farm lands were in fact assessed at a higher ratio to value than were urban lots.

At the request of county Farm Bureaus, Watson undertook to survey county finances in several counties. In two counties serious irregularities were disclosed, which, in one case, led to legal action against the appropriate officials.

In 1924, the Illinois Educational Commission, after months of study, came to the conclusion long before reached by IAA officials, namely, that real tax reform could be attained only by amending the revenue article of the Illinois Constitution. The Commission teamed up with the IAA in asking the State Legislature, in 1925, to approve a resolution in favor of submitting an amendment for referendum of the people in 1926. (In spite of an all-out campaign by the IAA for a favorable vote, the proposal did not carry.

By 1926, Farm Bureau members were backing the tax work so enthusiastically that in many counties local Farm Bureau officials and committees were on a do-it-yourself basis, with little help from the IAA except in special cases. Watson and his staff, with a lot of help from George E. Metzger, director of organization, had worked so effectively and with such spectacular results that there was no need to urge members to get interested in tax projects. They really rallied around this project and made their influence felt in practically every county.

In 1927, the IAA legislative committee and staff worked hard on a state income tax bill which the Illinois Senate passed but the House killed in the final hours of the session. Farm Bureau forces helped to get the first Illinois gasoline tax adopted at the same session. Two years later, in 1929, IAA forces again prevailed upon the Senate to pass a similar bill, and the House killed it by the close vote of 72 to 69. The IAA had become a real power in Springfield.

One of the county Farm Bureaus that made tax history in 1929 was the Champaign organization. In that case, 194 farm owners had filed a bill in equity against county officials for improper assessments, but there was some dispute as to jurisdiction which caused the Champaign County Farm Bureau to ask for a hearing. When it was held, the Farm Bureau was so bitterly attacked by attorneys for the county taxing officials that the Farm Bureau asked the Illinois Tax Commission to assume jurisdiction and determine the facts. The Commission readily agreed, and sent a representative to the county. This man found the facts substantially as the Farm Bureau contended they were, and upheld the Farm Bureau, whereupon the county officials gave up, admitted the inequalities charged, guaranteed proper action by the board of review, and even paid the court costs and attorney's fees of the 194 complainants. That case did a lot to enhance the prestige of Farm Bureau in Champaign county, and it put plenty of backbone in Farm Bureau tax committees in other counties.

Nearly all the county Farm Bureaus were active in tax matters in 1931, a year of quadrennial assessment. Values had dropped substantially, due to the stock market crash and omens of the coming major depression, hence revaluations downward were general, not only in real estate, but also in personal property. In fact, personal property assessments in the state, with Cook county excluded, dropped more than $142 million below the 1930 assessments. Value of all land and improvements, with Cook county excluded, dropped some 16 per cent, or more than $268 million. By 1932, Watson believed that, generally speaking, there was not much disparity in assessments of different classes of real estate. Accordingly, Watson and his staff encouraged county Farm Bureau tax committees to direct their efforts to bring pressure to bear on local tax officials when budgets were being made up, in the hope of reducing public expenditures. These efforts were quite successful. There was no way to measure the savings effected, but it was thought to run into the millions.

Early in 1933, the state legislature passed an occupational tax bill (in effect, a sales tax), which was quickly declared unconstitutional by the Illinois Supreme Court. Guided by the Court decision, the legislature passed a second bill which became law, but failed to provide funds to meet the huge need for unemployment relief (chiefly in Chicago). In this emergency, a special session was called in October, and a bill to levy state taxes of $38 million to meet relief needs was passed. However, a companion bill provided that a bond issue of $30 million, to be paid off by gasoline taxes, be voted on in referendum at the 1934 general election. In case voters approved this idea, the $38 million tax levy would be abated. (The bond issue got a favorable vote in 1934.)

The year of 1933 was a busy one for the members of the IAA legislative committee. They stayed at Springfield a good deal of the time. They had been so well impressed with the work of a young state employee of the Legislative Reference Bureau that he was offered a job as assistant to Donald Kirkpatrick, general counsel for the IAA. The young man, in turn, was impressed by the constructive policies of the IAA, and he accepted the job and went to work on August 1. His name was Paul E. Mathias, and he was destined for a long and rewarding career with the IAA. He was to succeed Kirkpatrick when he retired at the end of 1949 as general counsel.

The IAA in 1934 advised farmers to vote in favor of the $30-million bond issue as the lesser of two evils. It took a firm stand, however, against further diversion of gasoline taxes. In 1935 the IAA lost out in an attempt to get the legislature to pass a resolution amending the revenue article of the state constitution to limit any tax on property to not more than one per cent of valuation, and to give the legislature the power to tax any other objects and subjects of taxation. The two-thirds affirmative vote necessary to pass such a resolution was not forthcoming. The sales tax was now producing more than $40 million for state purposes and $20 million for relief purposes, so that no state levy on property was necessary. It was estimated that this situation saved Illinois farmers at least $6½ million a year.

In 1937, a very troublesome tax case was finally disposed of when the board of review consented to reduce valuation of farm lands in Madison county by $3,500,000, or about 20 per cent. Another event of that year was the appointment of Bert Vandervliet as assistant to Watson. Vandervliet, a recipient of a Rockefeller fellowship at the University of Cincinnati, had served a two-year internship in public administration at the Cincinnati Bureau of Government Research, and after graduation was doing research work for the Illinois Commerce Commission. In some work involving the Rural Electrification Administration, he met Watson who introduced him to Herman Danforth, first president of the IAA. He was to remain for many years, and to become head of the tax department in 1946.

Watson did his best to keep Farm Bureau tax committees and members well informed on tax tissues. In his annual report for 1938, he stated: "Taxpayers should remember that their property taxes are now all local or county in nature. Most property taxes are spent within a few miles of the property upon which they are levied. Property taxpayers, therefore, have it within their power to oppose and perhaps to prevent unfair or oppressive property taxes. . . .

"Unless the Farm Bureau tax committees and rural taxpayers give considerable attention to the persistent increase in taxes on rural property, such increases are likely to continue until they reach the burdensome height which they had prior to and early in the depression. This is a matter which deserves the careful attention not only of county Farm Bureau tax committees, but also of the taxpayers themselves in the various taxing districts. Unless the local taxpayers look after their own interests in respect to the burden of taxation, they have no right to complain and cannot rightfully expect any other organization or persons to protect them. . . ."

In the late thirties it was apparent that something must be done soon about rural schools. A survey made by the tax department revealed that of the 10,000 one-room rural schools in 1937-38, nearly 40 per cent had an average daily attendance of not over 10 pupils, and that about 13 per cent had an average daily attendance of not over six. It was certain that some sort of reorganization of rural schools was coming. In 1939 and 1940, conferences on school problems were held at the IAA annual meeting.

In 1942, responsibility for tax work was placed in a new department of research and taxation, with Lawrence H. Simerl as director. Watson stayed on as adviser on school and tax problems. By 1943, preoccupation with war-created problems, plus wartime prosperity, caused farmers and Farm Bureaus too, to neglect tax problems. Watson devoted a great deal of time to digging up information needed by the recently appointed committee on school problems. The IAA sponsored the so-called "Gateway Amendment" designed to make it easier to amend the state constitution, but it failed to receive the necessary two-thirds vote of both Houses of the General Assembly.

In 1945, the General Assembly, in spite of the opposition of the IAA, enacted tax legislation destined to have far-reaching consequences. The new law, to become effective on January 1, 1946, directed the state department of revenue to raise property assessments in each county to actual cash value, and to reduce most tax rate limitations by 50 per cent. Since there were wide disparities in the way assessors arrived at their valuations in different counties, it was obvious that previous inequalities might be increased still further unless uniformity of assessment methods could be achieved. County Farm Bureaus buzzed with tax activities in 1945. No less than 62 of them asked the research and taxation department to prepare detailed reports on the situation in the respective counties, with suggestions as to how to obtain a more equitable distribution of the burden of property taxation, and for controlling the expenditure of public funds. Eventually, reports were prepared for all 102 counties. The state department of revenue had the responsibility of taking the reports of county assessors and county boards of review, and adjusting them to the new regulations.

The new Revenue Act authorized the state revenue department to administer an equalization program, primarily to achieve a measure of equity in the distribution of state grants-in-aid. As a result, state-aid was greatly increased in southern counties, particularly where property assessments had been much higher than in the richer counties. However, average county-wide assessments were never adjusted to full value. The first year, they averaged about 75 per cent. Since then, property values have risen steadily, without a corresponding increase in assessments; so that now the average assessment is about 50 per cent of actual value. A decision of the Supreme Court in 1946 removed the traditional limits on tax rates, so that many counties did raise rates.

In 1946, research and taxation were divided into two separate departments, and Bert Vandervliet, who had worked under Watson from 1937 to 1942, was employed as director.

The following years saw intense activity in the tax field, not only as a result of the new practice of presumably assessing property at full cash value, but also because of the quadrennial reassessment in 1947. Farm land had zoomed in value during and since the war, and the cost of public services had risen dramatically, particularly in the case of schools. There was some tendency for individuals to blame the new assessment practices for the rise, but it was only one of several factors responsible, as Vandervliet continually pointed out to delegations from county Farm Bureaus which sought help. In fact, the new plan rendered great service in providing a greater degree of uniformity in assessments than had existed in the past—which was one of the big objectives of tax reform. The fact that it did magnify serious inequalities of long standing served a good purpose in that it stimulated many individuals and groups to take positive action.

The real trouble was right at home, with too many inexperienced assessors and too little direction. Since property tax money is all spent at home, it is the responsibility of taxpayers in their own areas to see to it that their money is spent efficiently. It is true that the so-called "Butler" laws enacted in 1946 made it *possible* to have excessive tax rates, but it was the local officials who made up the budgets and filed the tax levies. Performance of many local officials was so bad that citizens demanded that the General Assembly in 1947 reinstate some of the more restrictive controls over local taxing officials, which had been abolished by the 1946 legislation. Such legislation was passed, with IAA support.

In 1947, Governor Dwight Green appointed a special tax committee to prepare proposals for reinstatement of tax rate limits. Paul Mathias of the IAA was a member. Bert Vandervliet of the IAA was a member of the subcommittee which drafted the basic formula by which tax rate limits were imposed. This formula was accepted by the legislature, and it was the basis for limiting the taxing power of every local governmental unit in downstate Illinois for many years. Since then, many units have been freed from strict adherence to this formula, but many are still subject to it.

Inefficient assessing was the target of the General Assembly in 1949 when it enacted a law providing for county supervisors of assessment, which was declared unconstitutional about six months after all appointments were made, and before it had a chance to become effective. In 1953, a similar law was enacted and is still in effect.

In 1951, the department of property taxation was transferred from the general services division to the general counsel—a logical move, since tax problems always involve legal questions. Also the department was assigned the responsibility of assisting in preparing tax schedules for about 75 commercial companies affiliated directly or indirectly with the IAA—a task that required the bulk of the director's time from March 1 through September. Property involved is worth many millions.

During these years, more county Farm Bureau tax committees were at work, and were digging more deeply into tax problems than ever before. In a few counties, certified public accountants, brought in to make detailed studies of the tax and fiscal situation, revealed unbelievably bad practices involving issuance of non-referendum bonds to retire accumulated debt, fund transfers of questionable legality, assessment irregularities of untrained or politically-motivated township assessors, inferior budgetary practices, ineffective control of expenditures, and even plain venality on the part of some officials. The more you dig into the public business, the more you are convinced that it is generally carried on with shocking inefficiency. If a county supervisor of assessments is appointed, he can't be effective unless the county board of supervisors cooperates with him to the fullest extent. If he makes an honest effort to assess property fairly, there may be people of influence in the county who object to having the job done properly because they know that their own property is very greatly under-assessed. Anyone or any group that undertakes to bring about reforms soon discovers that the task is a hard one, precisely because so many people or businesses in a community have their own vested interests at stake.

Many students of tax problems have begun to wonder if upholding the principle of local control is not kicking back on the people. Maybe it would be better if we permitted the state to set up technical qualifications that any candidate for assessor, for example, was required to meet before he could run for office. The state sets up standards for school teachers and county highway engineers; why not for jobs that require just as much skill, training, and experience in another field of public service? One thing seems clear, and that is that the public business has become big business, even in small counties, and it is up to the people to find some way by which that business can be carried on efficiently.

In his annual report for 1955, Bert Vandervliet wrote:

"The need for improved assessment administration within the

counties and townships still represents the basic defect of the Illinois assessing system, and until our local assessment officers develop the capacity and fortitude required to freely exercise their broad powers impartially, any expectation for marked improvements in this field of activity represents little more than wishful thinking. The achievement of any semblance of uniformity in property assessments within most of the counties necessitates numerous radical adjustments in a sizeable proportion of all local assessments within such counties, and until such severe adjustments are accomplished in a systematic and impartial manner, the existing maldistribution of the total cost of local government will persist."

During the past forty years, the IAA has helped the county Farm Bureaus to bring about equalization in assessments of real property, and in a few cases to expose unsavory situations in local government; but the basic difficulty is in sloppy and inefficient work in the townships and counties. Inequalities of assessment between urban and rural real estate have been generally wiped out, but the *system* of assessing is inefficient and obsolete, just as is our system, generally, of local highway maintenance.

Work of the department of property taxation had so enormously increased during the fifties that in 1960 James Greer, formerly supervisor of assessments in McLean county, was brought in to help carry the burden; and early in 1961, Ellis Wheeler, formerly auditor of Macon county, was added to the staff. With this expert help, the department has been able to render a wider range of service to county Farm Bureaus. One relatively new activity has been for the county Farm Bureau to call to public attention the personal-property tax delinquencies in the county. In a number of counties, this work has stimulated tax officials to make a determined drive for collection of such accounts. In furtherance of this work, the department, in collaboration with IAA organization men, has examined and reported on the situation in about half the counties in Illinois. In a number of cases, the collection of personal taxes was not rigidly enforced, and in some, collections were practically on a voluntary basis. It was rather surprising, but in practically all cases county tax officials gave their solid cooperation in such projects. Some even requested and obtained from county boards, authorization for the employment of additional personnel in their offices or in the state's attorneys' offices to devote full time to the program. This experience constitutes convincing evidence that the administration of the personal property tax can be substantially improved. It is estimated that during 1961 and 1962 delinquent tax-collection programs initiated by IAA and the county Farm Bureaus in 15 counties have resulted in the collection of an additional $750,000 in taxes. How much of this amount would have been collected if Farm Bureaus did not take the initiative is impossible to estimate, but it's a good bet that the bulk of it would not have been collected. Delinquencies are always high in incorporated areas.

Out of all the experience that Farm Bureau in Illinois has had in working on the perplexing problem of taxation comes the conclusion that the outmoded revenue section of the state constitution must be amended before a tax system that is just and equitable to all taxpayers of the state can be realized. This, so far, has proved impossible to achieve.

Chapter 21

Membership and
Livestock Marketing

Membership in the IAA was to fall from 60,000 in 1930 to 54,355 in 1933, but substantial progress was being made in many ways. Caution was the watchword, but nevertheless at the annual meeting in 1931, Earl Smith reported that IAA affiliates had done a $6 million business in the previous fiscal year. In his convention address, he said that it was no time to start new enterprises, but rather a time for strengthening those now in operation.

A year later, in his foreword to the annual report, he wrote: "The great economic unrest prevailing throughout the world in 1931 made it increasingly difficult to serve agricultural interests, but the Association has met all obstacles and continued its forward stride to better serve the real needs of farmers.

"Notwithstanding these difficult conditions, the Association and its affiliated companies closed the year in splendid condition and entered the year 1932 better equipped than ever to continue the fight in behalf of economic justice and equality of opportunity for the farm people and the Nation."

George Metzger, reporting as director of organization, announced that the old three-year membership contract had been discontinued in 74 counties, and replaced with a "one year, continuing contract." He felt that the new type of contract would do much to stabilize membership. He had able men carrying on membership work: Clare Bradford in District I; Oscar D. Brissenden (son of the revered Leslie F. Brissenden of Clay county) in District II; R. J. Hamilton in District III; John C. Moore in District IV; Asa B. Culp in District V; L. B. Hornbeck in District VI; H. H. Walker in District VII; and Leslie F. Brissenden in District VIII. All these men served ably for many years. O. D. Brissenden was later to become director of organization, and still later, special assistant to the president until his retirement in 1963.

The IAA affiliates were making steady progress. The advantages of large-scale purchases by members are well illustrated by the work of the Illinois Farm Bureau Serum Association. In 1931, the Association bought for its 73 member counties more than 49 million cc. of hog cholera serum, about a 50 per cent increase over the previous year. As a result, handling charges per unit were so low that commissions charged member counties were cut in half early in 1932. Furthermore, because of the huge volume handled, the Association was able to buy its supplies at rock-bottom prices.

A big factor in building membership in the early days was the possibility offered to improve marketing systems through united action. By 1930, it had become apparent that changing conditions in livestock marketing had to be met with constructive action by the livestock marketing department. The meat packers had established buying points in livestock areas, so that they could buy from farmers and ship direct to their slaughtering plants, thus bypassing the central markets. Farmers feared that reduced competition at the central markets could have a bearish influence on price levels. Another change of far-reaching consequence was that the truck was superseding the railway car as a carrier of livestock. These two developments had seriously reduced the business of the local shipping associations, and half of the 500 associations that once existed had simply given up. This was a tough situation to face.

Ray E. Miller, director of the livestock marketing department, moved quickly. He undertook to meet the situation by organizing county or district associations to replace the old local associations. It was hoped that increased volume per association would give new life to the shipping association idea.

It should be recorded here that Federal Farm Board money and marketing counsel were available to help. Under the aegis of the Farm Board, the National Live Stock Marketing Association had been set up to serve the cooperative selling agencies. It included in its membership all the members of the National Live Stock Producers Association. The next logical step, it seemed to IAA people, would be to band the county or district selling associations into a state-wide association. Proposed in 1930, it became a reality when the Illinois Livestock Marketing Association received its charter on March 4, 1931.

The new association, with a huge potential volume of business under its control, could ship direct to packers if that course seemed advantageous, or it could consign to the Producer agencies on the central markets. It might seem that it could thus weaken the Producer agencies by selling direct; but leaders seemed to feel that a lot of hogs were going to be sold direct regardless of what was done, and that the cooperative agencies had better get into the act or lose the business entirely. At any rate, the step was taken. A sales office was opened at Decatur on October 7, 1931, with Robert W. Grieser in charge. During the first month, with four member units in operation, the Association handled 47 carloads of livestock. During fiscal year 1932, with eight member units, business increased to 2,029 decks. It was off to a good start. Volume for 1933 was 2,983 decks; for 1934, 2,831 decks; for 1935, only 1,308 decks. This sudden reduction in volume was attributed largely to "intense competition from local buyers, packer buyers, auctions, etc."

In point of fact, there were more reasons for the reduced volume, and the time came when the big reason had to be recognized. The shipping associations were simply selling hogs on consignment. The owner had to wait for his money; while he could sell at an auction, or to an order buyer, or to a packer and get his check upon delivery of the hogs.

In all of its commercial ventures, IAA officials learned early that a cooperative institution must "meet the competition" in order to survive. A Farm Bureau member will not patronize a cooperative business unless the service rendered is satisfactory. Early recognition of this hard fact of business life is one of the big reasons why most of the businesses established by the IAA have been highly successful, some of them spectacularly so. All over the country you can see the wreckage of cooperative business ventures which were founded on the false assumption that member loyalty will insure success in almost any enterprise. This assumption has led a number of farm organizations into unwise projects. It is highly important for farm organization leaders to know which fields to stay out of. One rock upon which some organizations have foundered is the farm implement business. It seems that IAA officials in Illinois used a high degree of prudence in following a policy outlined about as follows: "Do not go into any business unless you can be sure that agencies in that field are not presently rendering the kind of service that farmers are entitled to; and if you do go into this field, be sure that you can render good service at a fair price."

The Illinois Livestock Marketing Association, after operating at a loss in 1935 gave serious thought to "meeting the competition," and early in 1937, three of the five surviving units changed over from the consignment plan to one offering both consignment and "cash on the barrelhead" plans. That same year sales of feed, through contract with the Illinois Farm Supply Company, begun tentatively in previous years, amounted to 1,490 tons.

The cash market proved popular, and by 1938 business handled amounted to 2,012 decks, mostly hogs. Sam F. Russell, farm adviser in Adams county, had become manager, with H. W. Trautman sales manager in Decatur. Further changes in the setup seemed necessary, and reorganization and reincorporation were accomplished in April, 1940. Sam Russell remained as director of livestock marketing and manager of the Serum Association. Traut-man succeeded him. Livestock handled was 1,649 decks.

The war brought its tough problems of manpower, price con-trols, shipping regulations, and many others. Volume of business rose in 1942 to a new record of 220,000 head of livestock handled through the Decatur office, and in 1943 to 242,727. In 1944 and 1945, volume slipped badly, due to price floors and price ceilings. Post-war recovery was fast, and volume has increased over the years. In 1961, the Association handled 821,944 market hogs, 17,523 market cattle, 11,676 feeder cattle, 12,223 market sheep, and 45,527 feeder pigs. Lawrence L. Colvis has been manager since 1952, when business had become so heavy that H. W. Traut-man had to devote full time to his duties as sales manager.

With the steady decline in importance of the central markets, the Producer agencies lost business in proportion. The meat pack-ers had been de-centralizing their operations to such an extent that the central markets had lost the dominant position they held for so long. This situation led to a step that probably should have been taken ten years earlier—a giant merger in 1960, involving the Illinois Livestock Marketing Association and seventeen of its member companies. This was followed in 1962 by another signifi-cant step, that of consolidating ILMA and the Producer agencies in Chicago, Peoria, and Springfield. New name of the consolidated organization is Illinois Producers' Livestock Association, with headquarters in the old Producer offices in Chicago with Colvis in charge. Now, at long last, all Farm Bureau livestock marketing has been consolidated in one agency. It is believed that the new setup will result in added economy and efficiency, and will enable the one agency to meet new conditions most effectively. Time will tell if these hopes can be realized.

Farmer-owned agencies seem to be in a good position to spon-sor innovations and improvements. For example, the decline in importance of animal fats has led to attempts to encourage the creation, so to speak, of a new type of hog, one with less fat and more lean meat in the carcass. The task is not an easy one. The geneticist and the breeder are heavily involved, as well as the feeder, the packer, and the consumer, whose verdict is final. Several attempts have been made to develop what is called the "meat type" hog. Definite progress has been made. In fact, the Illinois Producers' Livestock Association is well into the business of supplying feeder pigs of approved type to feeders. The pigs are produced (about 150,000 annually now) under contract, by cooperating breeders. This inaugurates a new step in livestock marketing. It is the first instance in Illinois of a marketing venture in which there is a formal contract between farmer and marketing agency. More than 10,000 sows are now under contract, and the program is expanding rapidly. To induce feeders to go along, higher prices are paid for the finished meat-type hogs. Assistance in financing and supervision of production practices is included in the contract. Should this business develop as it is expected to, it will constitute a long forward step in the direction of meeting the drastic changes that have come about in consumer demand as a result primarily of the suspicion on the part of the medical profession that too much animal fat in the diet may be responsible in part, for the fearful increase in atherosclerosis and allied diseases in recent years.

The farmer must accede to demands of consumers in matters of this sort. And it is the responsibility of the farmer cooperative to take the leadership in changing production practices accordingly. This responsibility also represents a great opportunity because the cooperative organization directed by the owners, seems to be in a unique position to encourage its members to tailor their products to meet consumer demand, and incidentally to get the high dollar for their products. (The feeder pig program now brings more money into Southern Illinois than the peach crop.)

The importance of livestock marketing to the Illinois farmer may be gauged by the fact that in 1959 the ILMA had 22 local associations as members, and that gross sales of livestock through these associations amounted to $40,461,103.00. More than 900,000 hogs were sold for members.

The advantages of selling through the Association, particularly for the small producer, are many. When a farmer takes his hogs to the local association, they are immediately sorted and graded. All hogs falling in one grade are assembled in one place, and the manager quickly knows how many truckloads of that grade he can offer for sale that day. Buyers are interested in large-lot hogs that are uniform in type and grade. If a farmer goes into an open market with a truckload of hogs of three or four grades, and all are "lumped off" at one price, he is quite likely to be penalized for the lack of uniformity in his shipment. The buyer can buy a number of such lots, then assemble them in grades and sell them at a substantial profit to himself. The cooperative association, the seller's own agency, renders this service to the farmer member, and preserves whatever profit has been made for the farmer himself. Added to this advantage is the confidence the producer has in his own agency. He has the feeling that his hogs or cattle are in good hands, and that he will share in any profits that may accrue from this system of bulk handling of livestock.

In the old days, before Producer agencies were set up in the central markets, the farmer felt more or less helpless when he took his livestock to market. He knew that many "scalpers" were making good incomes by buying small lots of livestock from different consignors, then sorting and grading them in uniform lots and selling them at good prices. He always felt that he was at a disadvantage in the livestock market.

The creation of the Producer agencies soon after World War I reflected farmer dissatisfaction with current marketing practices. Most farmers sensed that sharp practices were all too prevalent in the "yards," but that as individuals there was little that they could do about it. Thus it is easy to understand why the reorganized IAA went to work so energetically in 1920 to do something about improving conditions in livestock markets. Members demanded action. The story was the same in other states, hence it was a relatively easy matter to get almost unanimous support for the plan to set up Producer commission associations in major markets.

The Producer agencies thus started out with solid support from the country, and generally they did well. In many of them, it was not long before they were handling one-fourth of all receipts. Some had trouble with inexperienced help, and some of them got into real trouble; but generally they performed well, and for at least thirty years they were a factor to be reckoned with in the principal markets. The decline of the big central markets has drastically altered the picture, and it led, as indicated previously, to the consolidation of the Producer agencies in Chicago, Peoria, and Springfield with the ILMA.

One who has watched these developments in livestock marketing for the past forty years must be impressed with the fact that the advent of farmer-owned marketing agencies has been a big help to the farmer in the sense that having his own agency on the market has given him a much better understanding of the workings of the market. He knows that through his agency he is represented on that market, and is in fact a part of that market. He knows that to the extent that his own representatives in the market are competent, he will get a fair deal. He no longer feels that he is an outsider when he goes to market. This factor alone is enough to justify all the effort and money that has been put into the livestock marketing projects that Farm Bureau has sponsored. They have done much to maintain solidarity in the ranks in Farm Bureau.

Chapter 22

Sharing the Risk

The founding of various insurance services has already been noted. It seems appropriate at this point to look more closely into these ventures, and to tell the story of the remarkable developments that grew out of small beginnings.

The Farmers Mutual Reinsurance Company, founded in 1925, enjoyed steady growth. By 1927, 67 small farmer-owned companies had signed specific reinsurance contracts. The company was too small to carry all of its risk, hence a good deal of it was ceded to other companies as a safety measure. In fact, the company merely acted as a broker in the early years, for the most part. Overhead was low. John H. Kelker, controller of the IAA, acted as assistant secretary and manager, and Vernon Vaniman was fieldman. Robert A. Cowles was treasurer. Volume of business increased rapidly. By 1927, volume of crop hail insurance amounted to $3,981,500.

At this early date, extensive efforts were being made to prevent losses. Farm Bureau meetings were held to discuss fire prevention. In De Witt county, Farm Bureau set up a plan under which every Farm Bureau member's property would be inspected for fire hazards. National fire prevention week was observed with appropriate activities. Purchase of lightning rods and fire extinguishers was encouraged.

By 1928, business was booming. Early in the year, windstorm, cyclone, and tornado insurance were added to fire and hail coverage, and by the end of the year a total of $14 million of insurance was in force. The following year, the total increased to $25,150,105; and in 1930 to $40,940,000. By 1933 it jumped to $58,854,952, to $96,339,873 in 1934, and to $117,974,306 in 1935. The company was just over ten years old!

Acquisition was in charge of Vernon Vaniman until April 1, 1935, when he was transferred to other duties. At that time the IAA insurance service department was established with Larry A. Williams as director of insurance acquisition and service for all three IAA insurance companies. Thus Farm Bureau insurance agents had a full line of insurance to sell. In 1937, Williams, also manager of Country Life Insurance Company, resigned and was succeeded by Dave C. Mieher, who had been a fieldman under Williams.

In 1938, all fire and windstorm policies were rewritten on a non-assessable, participating basis. Rates under the new policies were guaranteed. The response to this change was most gratifying.

Business continued to zoom to new records almost every year. By the end of 1940, it was definitely "big business," with $250,-582,692 of insurance in force. During the year, two steps forward were made. A graduate agricultural engineer was employed, with two assistants, to inspect insured property and recommend safety measures; and the writing of new business was limited to Farm Bureau members. The latter step made very little difference, because most people insured were members anyway; and it was felt that members would have more pride in the company when they knew that it was a Farm Bureau project in its entirety. Furthermore, it was believed that those insured would be more likely to take appropriate safety precautions when they were aware that any losses sustained were coming, in part, out of their own pockets. Charles M. Seagraves was in charge of the IAA safety department.

The war years were difficult. Practically all safety work had to be discontinued because of travel restrictions and limitations on manpower. Nevertheless, steady progress continued. By 1945, just twenty years after its founding, the Company had more than $305 million of insurance in force. In addition, more than $94 million of hail insurance was written during the year. It had paid dividends to members amounting to $1,644,439.60; and its total assets were $5,280,649.52. No wonder members were proud of their company!

On February 1, 1946, the name of the company was changed to Country Mutual Fire Company. The unprecedented farm prosperity was reflected in steady growth to $530 million of insurance in force, plus $147 million of crop insurance in 1948. At the end of 1948, John H. Kelker reached the age of retirement, and Darrell L. Achenbach succeeded him as manager. A Christian county farm boy, Achenbach, after graduation from Taylorville high school, worked on the home farm, then for an electric utility company, later for a bank, and finally got a job with the Farm Credit Administration at St. Louis. This work gave him valuable experience and a wide acquaintance among farmers, principally in Illinois. On one occasion, he examined the affairs of a Production Credit Association in Charleston. Charles B. Shuman was a member of the board of the Association. In late 1948, Shuman, as IAA president, was looking for a successor to Kelker and he remembered young Achenbach, who by that time was manager of the Fox Valley Production Credit Association at Geneva, and offered him the job. At this writing, in 1963, only 14 years after he started in the insurance business, he has the responsibility of managing all of the insurance activities of the IAA.

By 1951, insurance in force topped $1 billion for the first time; and by 1953 it had jumped to $1,424,181,103, plus $432,719,586 in crop hail and additional peril insurance written that year. Total dividends to members since organizing amounted to the amazing total of $12,528,517.88. To state that dividends returned to policy-holders were satisfactory is to under-state the case. To be explicit, the dividend on a fire insurance policy in 1953 amounted to 25 per cent of the premium paid for that year!

It is a matter of considerable pride to IAA directors that more farmers in Illinois have hail insurance on growing crops than do farmers in any other state. The Farmers Mutual Reinsurance Company (now Country Mutual Insurance Company) pioneered in offering low-cost hail insurance to members in 1926, and the response was most gratifying. At present, some 40 per cent of all crop hail insurance in Illinois is carried by Country Mutual. Rates charged are comparable with those of other insurers, but each year there is a patronage refund amounting at times to 40 per cent of the premium. Policyholders generally are confident that they are getting this insurance at rock-bottom cost, hence they continue to buy it year after year. There have been years in which more than 50,000 policies have been issued.

We will now move forward to 1956, the last year of Country Mutual Fire Company's separate corporate life, since on January 1, 1957, it was merged with Country Mutual Casualty Company. At the end of its separate corporate existence, it had $1.9 billion of insurance in force; it had reduced the average fire rate from 47.7 cents per $100 of insurance in 1949, to 37.6 cents in 1955; and it had returned dividends to policyholders in 31 years amounting to $15,695,317.23.

Some of the reduction in cost must be credited to the fine program of fire prevention carried on over the years, and a lot of it to modernizing office work through punch-card equipment and other electronically-controlled machines. Added business could be taken on with limited increase in office help.

Spectacular success had also been attained in the field of automobile insurance. The IAA, yielding to the demands of many county Farm Bureaus, set up the Illinois Agricultural Mutual Insurance Company in 1927. Decision to go ahead with automobile insurance was made at a meeting of the IAA executive committee and the county Farm Bureau presidents at Chicago on October 8, 1926. Demand from members for auto insurance had been so insistent that there was not a dissenting vote when the question was put before the meeting.

Donald Kirkpatrick and Vernon Vaniman, who had realized long before that the Farm Bureau members would eventually insist on their own auto insurance service, had devoted months of study to the problem. Now they were ready with a plan. A premium deposit of $10, policy fee of $5, and a "surplus share" payment of another $10, would be collected from each applicant to provide working capital and to meet legal requirements. (The law required a surplus of five times the maximum risk.) Maximum risk of $10,000 would be for public liability in any single accident. To cover losses, every policyholder would pay his share each six months. The first board of directors would consist of the IAA executive committee. The county Farm Bureaus would accept applications.

Vernon Vaniman went to work, and within a short time he had county and township insurance committees at work, familiarizing themselves with the plan, and generating enthusiasm for the new project. The goal was 5,000 applications from Farm Bureau members on hand before launching the company. By the time of the annual IAA convention in Peoria, January 26-28, 1927, no less than 44 county Farm Bureaus were hard at work, trying to secure their quotas of applications; namely, 20 per cent of the members for charter policies. One of the most popular features of the tentative policy was the agreement to pay the insured the actual value of the car lost through fire or theft, rather than paying on the basis of annual theoretical depreciation.

By annual meeting time, success of the undertaking was assured. J. P. Gibson, Jr., of Chicago, who had spent ten years in the insurance business since his graduation from Beloit College, was hired as manager. Vernon Vaniman was given the responsibility of field operations, assisted by Ara E. Richardson. The Illinois Agricultural Mutual Insurance Company was chartered on March 28, 1927, and opened for business April 1. By April 6, there were on file more than 3,000 signed applications. On April 8, directors of the new company voted to offer insurance on oil trucks owned by Farm Bureau supply companies. Business increased so fast that four more office workers had to be hired to help the one person who had been processing applications. It was obvious that this insurance project was a smash hit. By July 8, twelve counties had exceeded their quotas, with Winnebago in the lead with 347 policies, and La Salle second with 242. Before the company was a year old, it had received 7,200 applications for policies. A sensational record.

In 1928, Ara E. Richardson succeeded Gibson as manager. In 1929, in response to broad demand, the company started writing employers' liability policies, and sold 1,088 during the year. County Farm Bureaus represented the insurance companies, and hired salesmen, but consideration was being given to coordinating the acquisition of all IAA lines of insurance through individual general agents. The business was getting really big. Policies sold in 1929 amounted to 7,951, and the following year, 6,563.

By the end of 1932, when the Company was less than six years old, 36,249 applications for automobile policies had been received, together with 1,966 for employers' liability policies. It had a surplus of $475,593.59. Loss ratio was gratifyingly low. A continuous program for safer driving was carried on.

In 1933, the Company started insuring 4-H club calves. The same year, in lieu of the initial surplus share payment of $10, buyers could choose a small surplus assessment. During the first year of this arrangement, 97 per cent of the buyers of insurance chose this plan. During the year, rates on commercial trucks were doubled to make it more consistent with the risk involved.

By 1934, it was evident that driving practices of farmers were changing. Farmers were driving further away from home, driving more in congested traffic, and maybe driving faster. Driving was more congested in all areas than ever before. In 1928, the number of accidents amounted to only 13.9 per cent of the number of policies in force; by 1934, it had risen to 22.2 per cent. Nevertheless, the business was thriving. Admitted assets rose to $1,148,761.97, and surplus to $579,636.46.

This company had made remarkable strides in eight years, and Country Life was now well established. Many reasons can be found for the remarkable growth made, but one factor stands out above all others. That factor was simply that farmers considered these companies their own. Generally, they promoted them effectively by word-of-mouth with evangelical enthusiasm. It is probably unfair to the insurance industry to maintain that in those early days farm people were skeptical to a considerable degree of the "fine print" of insurance policies, but such a feeling did exist. With accident insurance policies, for example, many thought that so many limitations were written into them that it was hard to qualify for indemnity payments.

In auto insurance, the IAA company was one of the first to included a non-owner provision in its policy. In the country, it was common practice to borrow a neighbor's car, and farmers really appreciated having protection when they were driving a car they didn't own, or if the hired man was driving theirs.

Another help in the early days was a clause in the policy giving protection in case of collision with stationary objects. Most other policies and our first ones paid indemnities only in cases of collision with moving objects. The Farm Bureau agents, most of whom were farmers working part-time, learned very early just what sort of protection farmers wanted. It was their reports to supervisors which led to the new company offering policies that seemed to be "tailor-made" for farm people. Farmers were quick to buy such policies.

Another great help was that the agent selling Farm Bureau insurance could supply policies to meet any and all needs. IAA companies were among the first to provide "one-stop" insurance service, and they were properly rewarded for doing so.

In 1935, both the old "surplus share" and "surplus fee" features were dropped, and a new "cash premium policy" was substituted for all policies in force. All of the surplus and premium deposit money due to policyholders was returned to them—a total of $266,746.54. A 10 per cent dividend was also declared on policies in effect for more than 2½ years. These moves proved popular with policyholders. The rising loss ratio was recognized by small increases in rates. The company redoubled its efforts to develop more skilled drivers. The state department of insurance, after examining the company, summarized its findings as follows: "The company is strong financially and has made splendid progress as is evidenced by the comparative statement included in this report. The company is prompt and fair in its loss payments and investments are of excellent quality." The company was given an "A" rating by Best's.

The entire agency setup had to be revised in 1935, when a new insurance agent licensing law was adopted by the State of Illinois. Farm Bureaus were dropped as general agents, because under the new law they would be classed as commercial institutions if they continued to sell insurance, and would lose their identity as educational institutions. Thereafter, the insurance companies made contracts direct with general and special agents, with the approval of the county Farm Bureau, and the Farm Bureau was compensated for clerical work, office space, and other expenses incurred. These changes materially improved the whole situation.

The company was growing steadily, but so was the accident rate, which rose to 40 per cent in 1937. By 1938, assets had surpassed $2 million, of which more than half was surplus. During that year, the dividend policy was changed. Policyholders with policies in force thirty months would get a dividend of 10 per cent, while those with policies in force for five years would get 20 per cent. Policies in force numbered 65,899.

World War II brought many problems involving manpower, travel restrictions, gasoline shortages, etc. The impact of suddenly changed conditions is reflected dramatically in some of the company statistics. For example, in 1941, the ratio of loss and loss expenses to earned premium was 67.4 per cent. And in 1942, this ratio went down to 53.9 per cent. This made possible a substantial addition to the surplus account. Ara E. Richardson, manager of the company, attributed this largely to slower, and therefore safer driving. The smaller loss ratio permitted the payment of special dividends of $369,957.55, in addition to regular dividends of $325,779.92. The dividend amounted to approximately 90 per cent of the six-month premium due from the policyholders. Their happiness over owning their own insurance company was greatly enhanced. At the end of the year, assets exceeded $3 million and 98,790 policies were in force.

In 1943, with no new cars being built, it might be expected that insurance sales would decline. Not so. Due largely to the fact that Farm Bureau membership was expanding rapidly, the company actually wrote 582 more auto policies than in 1942. Ratio of loss to premium remained low, and again a whopping special dividend was declared, this time for $658,760.17, in addition to regular dividends of $367,539,751.

It has been the practice of the company to improve service to members in every possible way. In 1944 a new employers' liability policy was offered which broadened coverage to give the insured general liability protection against claims arising out of the business operations of farming, as well as those arising out of and in connection with his personal activities and maintenance of his home. It also provided for medical expense payment to an injured employee regardless of the liability of the farmer for such injury. Liability insurance had become one of the necessary expenses of farmers who employed help.

By the end of 1944, the Company had 12,103 liability policies in force. It was another big year for the company. The year of 1945 brought the end of the war and the easing of many restrictions. This was reflected in the loss ratio, which went up to 56.69 per cent. It was another very profitable year. Dividends, regular and special, amounted to $990,249.59. A total of 129,621 auto policies were in force, and total assets had climbed to $4,103,019.95.

The return of peace was accompanied by a return to free-and-easy driving habits, higher speeds, heavier traffic; and the result was a shameful rise in the loss ratio to 80.44 per cent. It became necessary to increase rates on two forms of coverage. The name of the company was changed during the year to Country Mutual Casualty Company. In 1947, Frank V. Wilcox became manager, when Richardson moved to Country Life as manager.

The early post-war years were years of golden prosperity. Farm Bureau membership grew by leaps and bounds, as did the insurance business. In 1949, for example, the company sold more than twice as many auto policies as it did in 1944, and regular dividends paid exceeded $1 million. The loss ratio was still distressingly high, at 63.25 per cent. More Illinois cars outside of Chicago were insured in this company than in any other company. It was setting a dizzy pace. In 1951, it paid its largest special dividend of $1,636,893.27. It was one of the first ten U.S. companies in auto insurance.

If anyone thinks that it was an easy job, with only simple problems to meet, in maintaining the high eminence reached by the company in 25 years, that person is badly mistaken. The early success of this operation was based mainly on the fact that the farmer in the early days was truly a preferred risk, and that therefore his insurance risks could, and should be carried at relatively low cost. The outstanding success attained by the company proved this without question.

This success attracted wide attention, and other companies finally came around to the practice of adjusting rates to the risks involved. That meant harder competition for the farmer-owned company. Furthermore, another element was now accentuating the problem. Better roads, larger school districts, more freedom for young people, and many other factors were operating to wipe out lines between country and town. Farm cars were being driven more and more outside the state, into bigger cities with more congested traffic. These factors were rapidly eroding the preferred risk status of the farm family.

On top of this, people with only a remote interest in agriculture were joining Farm Bureau, partially at least to get the advantages of low cost auto insurance. In his annual report in 1953, Manager Wilcox put it this way: "We now find ourselves developing experience upon farm risk highly diluted with non-farm risk. The situation is no longer that of a large enough farm group to absorb the non-farm group without increasing the price of insurance of the farm group. At the same time we find the insurance industry outside of Farm Bureau for the first time in its history developing an experience upon true farm risks. . . ."

The IAA had already done something about this problem. At the IAA convention in 1951, the voting delegates had approved a rule under which no county could offer certain commercial services to associate members (those interested in agriculture, but non-farmers) beyond ten per cent of its farmer membership. In the early days, associate membership was extended to such people as farm advisers, teachers of vocational agriculture, employees of Farm Bureau, rural pastors, and similar groups. By 1950, it was apparent that persons were taking out associate memberships mainly to get the advantages of commercial services, creating a situation that was far from desirable, hence the new rule. Farm advisers, Farm Bureau employees, hired men, and teachers of agriculture are exceptions to the rule, however, so that no hardship has been imposed on those who, though not actual farmers, are contributing to the advance of agriculture.

The Country Mutual Casualty Company operated under that name for the last time in 1956, because it merged with the fire company on January 1, 1957. Name of the merged companies is Country Mutual Insurance Company. As of September 30, 1956, the old company had 287,478 vehicles insured, and a record high of $2,896,367.79 was returned to policyholders as dividends. Only 8.2 per cent of the premium income was required for administration. It was one of the most efficiently operated insurance companies in the United States. In 1956, losses paid to or on behalf of policyholders exceeded $10 million. Admitted assets were approaching $25 million. What a change from 1935, the first year that regular dividends were paid, when admitted assets were just over $1 million and dividends amounted to $33,395.90!

The insurance business, like any other, is making changes to meet new conditions. Country Mutual, following the recent trend toward "package" policies, is now offering such a policy, the Farmowners policy, which protects the home and its contents, farm buildings, and personal property from losses due to fire, windstorm, or other catastrophe, and also gives comprehensive liability protection. In three months after its introduction, more than 6,500 policies were sold, indicating that it will be very popular.

A second significant change involves rates on automobile insurance. From now on, the rate you pay will depend on your accident rate. The company was founded partly as a protest against flat rates for all policyholders, whether urban or rural, and its experience has proved without question that lower insurance rates were justified for farmers simply because they had fewer accidents.

Now, policyholders are grouped according to their accident records. The careful driver will be able to "earn" a lower rate than his neighbor who seems to be "accident-prone," will have to pay. Each starts with a basic rate which will be increased with each auto claim paid by the company according to an escalator formula. Conversely, for each year without a claim being paid, the rate is reduced. The lowest rate is 30 per cent below the basic rate. Company officers are convinced that this variable rate is the fairest way yet devised to allocate losses due to accidents among policyholders.

In 1963, for the first time, policies were made available to members who had commercial interests other than farming. The insurance protection from these new lines now make it possible for Farm Bureau members to not only protect their farm and farming operation with Country Mutual but also protect, through their own company, business enterprises other than farming in which they have an interest. These policies provide liability protection to all forms of commercial operations, fire insurance on all types of buildings which are used for many purposes, and workmen's compensation for employees of these businesses.

Chapter 23

Organized for Safety

Country Life Insurance Company started operating in early 1929, after it had been approved by the IAA board of directors and county Farm Bureau presidents at a meeting in Decatur on December 27, 1928, and voting delegates to the IAA annual meeting in Danville on January 31, 1929, officially authorized it. It was necessary to sell preferred stock in the amount of $50,000 to Farm Bureaus and members, and to get pledges for $3 million in life insurance policies in order to start. The IAA itself put $125,000 into the new company. These requirements were far exceeded when subscriptions for preferred stock totaled $82,000, and insurance pledges to the amount of $8 million were on hand before the annual meeting. The first policy was issued to Sam S. Davis, farm adviser in Piatt county, on February 1, 1929. Before the charter policy campaign had ended, a total of $12,580,000 of life insurance had been sold.

Thus off to an auspicious start, Manager Lawrence A. Williams took full advantage of the momentum attained by enthusiastic acceptance by farmers. In ten months of day-and-night activity, eighty county Farm Bureaus staged insurance banquets, and a lot of them were addressed by Williams himself. Some 17,000 people attended these functions, and many of them bought insurance. Life insurance in the amount of $19,535,500 was in force by the end of the year. Things worked out just as expected. A lot of sales were made over-the-counter at Farm Bureau offices when members simply came in to say that they wanted to buy life insurance. The new company had no experienced agents. They were mostly farm people who had become interested in insurance. In working out plans, IAA officials had figured that with a ready-made clientele made up of woefully under-insured, successful farmers, little salesmanship would be needed on the part of the agent. They were right. The agents learned fast, however, and many of them went on to become successful agents. In fact, quite a number discovered that they were natural-born salesmen, and were soon producing at very creditable rates.

The following year, more effort was required to sell insurance, and a lot of time was required to select agents, give them the rudiments of selling techniques, and get them started. Two state-wide schools were held, attended by general agents at their own expense. Nearly 500 of the 1,300 agents enrolled in a correspondence course, and about 100 of them completed it. Country Life carried a heavy schedule of advertising in the IAA RECORD, and many promotional programs were staged to call attention to this new insurance service. Since state laws did not permit restricting life insurance sales to Farm Bureau members, appeals were directed to non-members as well as to members.

During the first year, no term insurance had been sold, but in the second year, sensing a real demand for such policies, the company offered them on a special basis under which the county Farm Bureau would get applications from 100 members so that they could be handled on a wholesale basis. These policies proved quite popular, and undoubtedly contributed a great deal to further sales of insurance, since the term policies could be converted to other types of policies at any time within the life of the policy, which was 12 years.

During 1930, volume of business increased over 80 per cent, admitted assets increased some 250 per cent and reserves nearly 500 per cent. L. A. Glover, well known actuary, after reviewing the record of the first two years, reported, in part: "From the standpoint of business written and paid for, I believe its record is without parallel." So good was the record, in fact, that a special dividend was paid to all policyholders a year before there was any obligation to pay a dividend. This action did much to enhance the prestige of the new company. Acquisition and administrative costs were remarkably low. It was apparent that the company was headed for a great future.

By the end of 1931, there were 1,100 producing agents employed, many of them on a part-time basis, who sold some $13 million of insurance. Assets doubled. The company made the largest gain of any Illinois insurance company during the year. With more than $44 million of insurance in force, death claims amounted to only $130,000 for the year. In 1931, the custom of holding a Country Life agents' convention was inaugurated, with 400 in attendance. The agent's bulletin, CLIC, which heretofore had been mimeographed, was put out in printed form. A fine sales annual was published.

In 1932, the country was in the bottom of the depression, but in spite of that, Country Life increased its total of business in force by $3,560,000. With many farmers in deep financial trouble, there was an understandable lapse rate of 12 per cent, up from eight per cent in 1931. (These figures were much below the average for industry.) Total assets rose to $1,824,778.90. Recognizing the problems incident to the depression, the Company started selling a new term policy (participating) which could be carried to age 65. The following year, 1933, was another tough one, but business in force increased some $7 million, to a total of $54 million. Only one other company in the United States made a larger percentage gain. Rate of lapse dropped to below eight per cent.

The next few years saw steady and solid gains. Dr. John E. Boland, medical director, was making history in careful underwriting. Fieldmen Dave Mieher, Bernie Mosier, and Clarence Ramler were rendering yeomen service, as were Actuary Howard Reeder and Office Manager John Weaver. Manager Williams was at the height of his career. He was known to have made 200 speeches a year at Farm Bureau meetings. By 1936, the last full year under the management of Williams before he left the company, Country Life had more than $100 million of insurance in force, and its net worth exceeded $5 million. The previous year's business had been topped by nearly 37 per cent. This tremendous increase put a severe responsibility on all departments. Office space had to be enlarged by one-third.

Many of his associates regretted Williams' leaving. He went on to help build up Farm Bureau insurance companies in Indiana and Iowa, and later became an insurance consultant. In 1961, a quarter century after leaving, he came out of semi-retirement to deliver the principal address at the Annual Roundup Convention of Country Life. He still retained his old magic as an orator.

At the end of its tenth year, Country Life had $125 million of insurance in force. Never before had an insurance company built that much insurance business in one state in ten years. Assets had grown from $121,000 in 1929 to $8.5 million, nearly one-half million dollars more than required by law.

Starting in 1939, Country Life made enormous strides. In fact, for the next 23 years, each year's production exceeded that of the previous year in every year except five. Insurance in force went from $125,154,425 in 1938 to $138,298,599 in 1939, to $153,510,105 in 1940, to $166,341,293 in 1941, the year that World War II began.

The war years showed steady increases, and in 1946 came the greatest year in history, when production that year rose an incredible 39.4 per cent above the previous year. Country Life agents that year sold 14,701 policies for a total of $43,499,746!

In 1952, insurance in force exceeded half a billion dollars, and by 1961, it had reached $994,681,169. It passed the billion-dollar mark in 1962.

The stock dividend record over the years is equally impressive.

The first dividend in 1930, amounted to $20,000. By 1940, it was $108,000; ten years later, it was $310,000; and in 1960, it reached $495,000.

Dividends to policyholders rose from $38,804.50 in 1931 to $271,993.36 in 1941; to $995,849.94 in 1951; and to $3,830,954.13 in 1961. In thirty years, total dividends to policyholders amounted to $29,653,585.70. In that year, there were 327,700 policies in force.

Admitted assets of the Company rose rapidly from $121,000 in 1928 to $1,195,586.25 in 1931; to $15,349,031.49 in 1941; to $71,162,538.02 in 1951; and to $218,681,434.84 in 1961.

One of the big reasons for the popularity of Country Life Insurance has been the practice of fitting the policy to the needs of farmers. For example, in 1940, a new Home and Family Protector policy was introduced. This policy was designed to cover mortgage or other indebtedness, or to provide maximum protection for a limited time. Sold in units of $5,000 at low premium cost, the face of the policy is reduced each year as indebtedness is reduced. The wide acceptance of this policy has proved beyond doubt that it filled a real need for farm people.

In 1941, accident and health policies were offered for the first time. The amount of such insurance sold in 1941 was only $23,192.23; but ten years later it had risen to $272,264.55, and to $2,614,977.90 in 1961. Obviously, this policy also met a real need.

A big factor in keeping costs down has been the care used in medical examinations. Picking a year at random, we find that in 1940, a quarter of the death claims were in the cardio-vascular-renal group which is notably lower than we find in the experience of other companies. Examining physicians have been alert in detecting early symptoms in those applying for policies.

Looking at Country Life today, one sees little technical difference between it and any other great life insurance company. Its agents have a high degree of professional skill, its standards of underwriting are high, its investments are properly diversified. It has competent management. Competition has been an important factor in keeping the organization on its toes, from top to bottom.

Country Life could not long survive today with an agency force such as it had in its early years. The County Farm Bureaus were acting as general agents. Local agents were hired by the Farm Bureau, and they were largely part-time agents. Some farmed in the summer and sold insurance in the off seasons. The Illinois law (adopted in 1935) requiring the licensing of all insurance agents put an end to that. It was time for a change, anyway, and Country Life, along with the other IAA affiliated insurance companies, went to work immediately to strengthen the agency force. Every encouragement was given to the man with talent. Only career men were wanted. Beginners were trained by more experienced men. All of this took time, and it was not until 1946 that all part-time agents were eliminated. The results speak for themselves. The agency force was cut more than half to about 350 full-time agents. A big step was taken when specific territory was staked out for each agent, (for non-life business), taking care that each territory had enough potential business to make the job rewarding.

These changes contributed much to the morale of the agency force. Every agent had the advantage that goes with a full line of insurance. Every insurance need, from life insurance to employers' liability and crop insurance, could be met in IAA companies, all handled by one man in the area. There has been further subdivision of territories since 1946, and the agency force numbered about 525 in 1962, including 95 agency managers who supervise the work of all agents in their respective territories.

The stock setup of Country Life is complex. At the time Country Life was organized, it was inadvisable for the IAA to own shares in an insurance company, therefore a corporation, the Illinois Agricultural Holding Company was created to own all shares in Country Life, but with the IAA owning stock in the Holding Company as follows: 6,000 shares of common stock and 600 shares of second preferred, 7 per cent cumulative. The only other stock outstanding consists of 2,000 shares of first preferred, 7 per cent cumulative, which was sold to Farm Bureaus and members at the start, plus a few qualifying shares.

All regular policy dividends are paid directly by Country Life to policyholders. All dividends on capital stock go to the Illinois Agricultural Holding Company, which in turn distributes them to the owners of the common and preferred stock, namely, as indicated above, the IAA itself and Farm Bureaus and members owning the preferred stock. "Charter policy" dividends go to holders of charter policies. Farm Bureau "differential dividends" are also paid to Farm Bureau members having Country Life life policies two or more years old. Dividends to charter policyholders are sufficient now to pay each year's policy premium.

In any insurance company, and particularly in a life insurance company, the rate of return on assets is a most important consideration. Country Life, on December 31, 1947, had more than $35 million invested in bonds, roughly half of it in government issues, and the balance in state, municipal, railroad, public utility, and industrial bonds. If average yield of such investments could be raised one per cent, it would mean increased income of $350,000 a year.

Starting in 1948, a number of changes in investment policy were made which have since resulted in increasing yields to a significant degree. For example, about that time, yields on treasury bills rose substantially. Since such bills are the equivalent of cash, a policy of "close investment" of cash was adopted, which put more money to work. That policy continues today, with greater or less emphasis, depending on conditions.

Investment committees also departed from traditional policy by beginning to buy mortgages on a conservative basis. Techniques were changed too in the buying of industrial bonds. In the past, it had been general practice for a bond house to buy an issue of bonds by a big corporation, and assume the responsibility of selling it to the public. Now, insurance companies began buying bonds direct from industrial corporations, thus saving the expense of underwriting, which is often considerable.

Another practice developed over the years has been "forward commitment" of funds. A life insurance company knows pretty accurately just about how much money it will have to invest for at least a year ahead. Whenever an exceptionally attractive bond issue was announced for some months ahead, Country Life could, and often did subscribe to it in advance, thus making sure of getting a sound issue at better terms than would have been otherwise available.

Another rewarding practice which soon came into general use is called "lease-back." Under this plan, an insurance company will buy a building erected by a big corporation, then lease it back to the same corporation. Many of the biggest corporations welcome this practice, since it frees their own funds for other uses, such as expansion of the business, and also because it carries with it some tax advantages. It's good for the insurance companies, too, since in this way they can realize a higher return than can usually be realized from government or corporate bonds.

All practices described above have helped to lift average return on investments by Country Life without jeopardizing in any way the first principle of investing, which is safety of principal from below three per cent in pre-war days, to more than four per cent in recent years. Research into better ways of investing money goes on continuously. There is an ebb and flow in the money market to which investment policies must be adjusted. Thus, investment policies are kept flexible to meet changing conditions.

To indicate how Country Life investments have been diversified, in 1947, its investment portfolio contained over $35 million in bonds, and some $2 million in FHA secured mortgages. In 1961, it contained well over $93 million in bonds, but it also contained over $69 million in mortgages, over $11 million in real estate, transportation equipment, and trust certificates, and over $9 million in stocks (at market value). The entire business of insurance-company investment had changed sharply over the years, and Country Life had modified its policies to keep up with the changes, as practically all life insurance companies did. Country Life, in fact, was in the vanguard among the insurance companies in recognizing changes that required new approaches to investment problems.

Farm Bureau members regard Country Life as one of the greatest achievements of the IAA. Here is an insurance company which started out in 1929 when the IAA, county Farm Bureaus, and members raised $125,000 for the purpose, which has grown in a third of a century to one of the leading life insurance companies in the United States. It is owned by farmers and controlled by the IAA itself. Its board of directors is identical with that of the IAA board, and the IAA president is always elected to the presidency of Country Life. Country Life now has assets valued at well above $200 million. No money, beyond the original $125,000.00 except from earnings, has been put into it. How that nest egg grew!

It goes without saying that Country Life has been well managed. Williams gave it a tremendous shove at the start. When he left, Howard Reeder as manager of the home office, and Dave C. Mieher as sales manager, maintained and enhanced the momentum until Reeder resigned. Then Mieher became manager, and continued until he left late in 1946, to become manager of the new Southern Farm Bureau Life Insurance Company in Jackson, Mississippi. He was succeeded by A. E. Richardson, who had made a spectacular success of the Illinois Agricultural Mutual Insurance Company during the previous 19 years, as described in the preceding chapter.

Richardson served until February 1953, when he reached retirement age. He went right to work again, after he was asked to do a special job for the American Farm Bureau Federation for a few years until his final retirement. He died in Bloomington on August 21, 1962. He was succeeded by his assistant, Duane Kuntz, who served through 1954, when he was succeeded by Leonard L. Fuchs who had started his Farm Bureau career only nine years before as farm adviser in Pike county. Fuchs had the honor of managing the company when insurance in force rose well above the $1 billion mark.

Following World War II, and particularly after 1950, Country Life officials sensed a growing interest among farmers in the role of life insurance in estate planning. This was due to the huge increase in land values, plus the wartime prosperity that farmers enjoyed. Thousands found themselves growing old, with much bigger estates than they had ever contemplated, and faced with the problem of distributing their property equitably to heirs. They were beginning to realize that life insurance could be put to good use, not only to provide cash to pay inheritance and other taxes, but to permit more satisfactory division of the estate among heirs. Interest in this field grew to such an extent that Country Life has added to its staff a full-time attorney to point up the value of life insurance in estate planning. This service is expected to greatly enhance the value of Country Life service to policyholders.

Enormous changes have taken place in economic and social conditions in agriculture since Country Life was born in 1929. Farm population has shrunk dramatically as farms have become larger, the opportunities to become farm owners have dwindled, more people live in the country while holding jobs in town. We are well on the way to wiping out city-country barriers. All this has affected the life insurance business. As farm insurance prospects have become scarcer, agents more and more sell to non-farmers. But agents are never permitted to forget that their first duty is to the 400 or so Farm Bureau members and their families in their respective territories. The farm prospect still has a slightly greater life expectancy than the non-farmer, hence the agent prizes the farm prospect. He is equipped to supply all of the member's insurance needs, and his effectiveness is measured by the degree to which he fulfills this great responsibility. As you study the history of this great enterprise, you get the feeling that to Farm Bureau members Country Life will never be just another insurance company. It will be the Farm Bureau members' own company, a commercial enterprise which they consider a living monument to organized agriculture.

SUMMARY

Thus, as we conclude this phase of our story on the development and tremendous growth of the insurance companies within Farm Bureau in Illinois, it seems fitting to summarize these vast accomplishments. Let's take a current look at these companies as they stand at the end of 1962.

Country Mutual Insurance Company, which is now a complete multiple-line property and casualty insurance company, has total assets of $65,750,000. Its policyholders' surplus account of $36,-260,000 make it one of the most financially stable companies of its type in the country.

Country Life Insurance Company, with its broad scope of life and health coverages, has total assets of $239,190,000. It is also one of the nation's strongest companies financially with $1,057,-000,000 of life insurance in force.

Together, these companies under the control of Farm Bureau and dedicated to preserve the financial security of the Farm Bureau families, have accumulated assets of more than $300,000,000. Few institutions of any kind serving only downstate Illinois equal this in size and breadth of activities.

It had been the belief of IAA officials for some time that because of the increasing scope of the companies' operations, and because of their coordinated activities in serving the same group of people through one combined agency force, that a better-coordinated management team should be established. Therefore, on June 26, 1962, IAA President William J. Kuhfuss announced a change in the top management organization of the companies.

Darrell L. Achenbach, vice president and general manager of Country Mutual was named executive vice president of both Country Life and Country Mutual; Walter H. Land, controller of Country Mutual, succeeded Achenbach as vice president and general manager; Leonard L. Fuchs continues as vice president and general manager of Country Life.

At the end of the year, Robert G. Holmes was named director of insurance marketing. This new function in the companies was established to coordinate the sales, advertising, public relations and research areas for the Country Companies.

Country Life is a financial leader among the Farm Bureau type insurance companies in the United States. When Country Life offered its new health insurance program it became the first of these companies to enter into such an extensive health insurance program. The Idaho Farm Bureau Federation, recognizing the quality of the policies provided by Country Life, requested that these policies be made available to Idaho Farm Bureau members. Arrangements were completed during the summer of 1962 and training programs were held during the latter part of that year for these policies to be introduced and sales to begin on January 1, 1963. The contracts, Hospital-Surgical-Medical, Medical Catastrophe, Disability Income and Personal Accident were offered to members of the Idaho Farm Bureau Federation and sales were handled through the Farm Bureau insurance agents of that state.

It seems logical to assume that the country insurance companies will continue their dynamic growth and service with a rapidly changing and diversified agriculture. Country Mutual is just beginning a new era in providing commercial coverages and workmen's compensation insurance for members. Country Life in the past two years has greatly expanded health insurance services through hospital-surgical-medical policies, medical catastrophe and disability income protection. Group term life insurance for regular Farm Bureau members has just been authorized.

These companies rank high today among the leading insurance companies of the nation and have far more than justified their investment and meager beginnings. An even greater future is surely in store for them.

Chapter 24

"FS"

FS Services, Inc., the farm supply cooperative serving rural Illinois and Iowa stands today as a business giant—one of the top 500 corporations in the United States. Business volume in 1963 topped $109 million.

Illinois Farm Supply Company was born of the same post World War I age which brought in the tractor. Need for good lubricants and dependable petroleum fuels prompted farmers to seek means of improving the sources of supplies.

First in Hancock county (1923) and then in several others, farmers' supply companies were organized. They bought supplies wherever they could get them and resold to farmers.

The business atmosphere into which these cooperatives were born was one in which profit margins on petroleum products were wide. In the free and easy days of 1927-29, credit policies were loose, to say the least, and it was so easy to make a profit that all business practices were somewhat lax.

This general attitude on the part of most business created a void in which the cooperatives found fertile ground for growth. The ten Farm Supply companies which were operating by 1926 had shown that farmers can work together in cooperative supply companies.

Other counties wanted to know more, and the demand for action had become so great, that the IAA called a series of conferences in Henry, Springfield, Centralia, Champaign, Rockford, and Galesburg to discuss the matter. As a result, the IAA legal department drew up a model set of articles of incorporation which met requirements of the Illinois cooperative law.

Meanwhile, in the summer of 1926, the IAA sent John R. Bent to Minnesota to study three cooperative petroleum ventures at Albert Lea, Owatonna, and Cottonwood. His report, part of which was published in the IAA RECORD, fired the imaginations of those who had been considering such projects in their own counties. Bent reported, in part, as follows:

"Minnesota has 40 cooperative distributive stations in operation, most of which are of recent origin. But the older companies have been paying almost unheard of dividends on their investments. The Cottonwood, Owatonna, and Freeborn county companies have made a pronounced success of their operations in both service and savings. Their earnings are almost too good to be true."

Bent went on to report that one of the companies had net profits in the month of July, before taxes, insurance, and depreciation, of more than $4,300, and another of more than $4,500. This was exciting news for Illinois farmers who had been paying high prices for tractor fuel and oil which was not always of good quality.

A word of caution was injected into the report in the following:

"The chief reason for the outstanding success of these companies is the splendid way in which the Danish, Norwegian, and German farmers of those sections cooperate in patronizing their own companies. Then, too, the companies got into the field early when there was little competition. Their profits may decrease somewhat as more competition develops."

The IAA itself, reflecting the conservative attitude of President Earl C. Smith, George Metzger, and Robert A. Cowles, made the following announcement:

"The Illinois Agricultural Association is prepared to offer complete service and advice to counties interested in the formation of such companies. A detailed summary of the experiences of the Minnesota companies with facts and figures about their operations is being prepared for the benefit of the companies organized in Illinois.

"The IAA is cautioning its members to be sure the local people are ready to support the cooperative venture before launching their organization. An aggressive and active board of directors and manager are essential to the success of such companies. The oil co-op is being looked upon as one of the greatest opportunities ever offered for farmers to save money. Minnesota, apparently, is more successful with its cooperative ventures than other states, largely because its Northern European population thinks in terms of cooperation."

It was well that some restraining words were uttered in those days; otherwise enthusiasm might have gotten out of hand. Even as it was, in spite of all precautions, some Farm Bureau companies did get into financial difficulties. All during the fall and winter, Farm Bureau meetings all over the state buzzed with talk of the easy way to cut production expenses through cooperative buying of petroleum products. By the end of the year, it was clear that IAA officials would have to set up a wholesale business to supply the county companies already in operation.

On March 7, 1927, the Illinois Farm Supply Company was chartered under the State of Illinois Cooperative Marketing Act of 1923. The incorporators were: M. G. Van Buskirk, B. F. Mitchel, John M. Winkleblack, George L. Stanford, Harry W. Watts, H. T. Marshall, George H. Rudy, George F. Tullock, L. F. Boyle, V. Vaniman, and R. A. Cowles.

Van Buskirk and Tullock became president and vice president. Directors were A. R. Wright, Ernest D. Lawrence, M. G. Lambert, W. A. Dennis, Lloyd R. Marchant, Harry Jewell, and Sam Sorrels.

George R. Wicker, IAA director of business service, was appointed manager.

One of the first things done after incorporation was to hire two competent petroleum engineers to assist in drawing up a set of specifications for gasoline, kerosene, lubricating oils, and greases, which became the basis for all purchases. The fact that to this day, FS has never deviated from its policy of rigid quality control, has been one of the big reasons for its spectacular success.

Immediate service began to Marshall-Putnam Oil Company, Knox County Oil Company, Ford County Service Company, McLean County Service Company, Edgar County Farm Supply Company, Coles County Supply Company, Menard County Farmers Supply Company, Montgomery County Farmers Oil Company, and the De Kalb County Agricultural Association. All of these had bought stock in the Farm Supply Company. The first county company to be organized (in 1923), the Farm Bureau Supply Company in Hancock county, had not yet bought stock in Farm Supply, but it received service, along with the Warren-Henderson Oil Company; Cass Farmers Oil Company; Farm Bureau Supply Company, Burlington, Iowa; and Farmers Exchange of Stockton, Illinois. During its first six months of business, Farm Supply sold more than a million gallons of fuel and its total business amounted to $155,906.92.

Capital was provided by requiring each member company to subscribe to both common and preferred stock to the extent of 10 per cent of its own capital stock. The preferred stock bore a fixed rate of return, and the common stock entitled the local company to share in the net earnings. A small amount of cash was required as a down payment, and Farm Supply accepted notes for the balance, most of which were paid off from earnings of the local company. Thus, an operation which was to earn millions in later years was launched with a very small amount of capital in the form of cash.

Early in 1929, manager George R. Wicker left the IAA to undertake other work, and Lloyd R. Marchant, farm adviser at Galesburg, who had played a leading role in organizing the Knox

Early Edgar County Farm Supply Company equipment and facility

County Oil Company, became manager. Marchant was a tireless worker and a shrewd bargainer. He was to stay for 12 years and to see Farm Supply grow from a membership of 16 county companies in 1929, to 64 in 1941. He was to make a major contribution to the growth and prosperity of the company.

As the thirties opened, Illinois Farm Supply listed 38 member companies. The casual observer might conclude that such growth in just three years represented hasty action by the county Farm Bureaus, but that was not the case. County leaders everywhere had been considering the matter for years and in most cases, the decision to organize a company was the result of mature deliberation.

From the beginning, IAA and Farm Supply officials insisted on clean-cut business practices, top-grade service, and enforceable contracts between Farm Supply and member companies. There was to be no price cutting and no buying of supplies by member companies except from Farm Supply. Similarly, Farm Supply agreed to sell to no other company in the territory except the member company. There were to be no loose credit practices. Difficulties loomed when the banks began to fail in the early thirties, but Illinois Farm Supply and most of the member companies came through the depression with gratifyingly small losses.

What had begun as a brokerage business moved by transition into the trading field and the kind of products handled began to broaden. Solidly established as a distributor of petroleum products, Illinois Farm Supply added such items as fly spray, stock dip, sulphurized mange oil, wood preserver, cod liver oil, automobile and truck tires, alcohol, glycerine, and chemical weed killers to its product list.

In 1931, two men came upon the Illinois Farm Supply scene —two men who were to have profound effect on the company through the years. The first of these was Fred E. Herndon who succeeded to the Farm Supply board presidency. Van Buskirk, the company's first president, served only until 1928, and was succeeded by the late Ernest D. Lawrence, a notably successful farmer in McLean county. Lawrence served three years until Herndon was elected.

Fred E. Herndon grew up on a farm in McDonough county, played outfield on the Macomb baseball team for many years as a young man. When he started farming for himself, he liked to keep records of his business. As a member of a threshing ring, he worked out an ingenious system of keeping records of hours spent by both men and teams, so that at the end of the season settlements between members could be made with a minimum of difficulty.

Always interested in community and cooperative affairs, he joined Farm Bureau early, and served as president in McDonough county from 1929 to 1938. He watched a number of Farmers' Alliance stores in the area go into business and fail. He watched the evangelistic campaign of Aaron Shapiro on behalf of farmer cooperatives. He studied a number of crusades to bring cooperative enterprise to the service of agriculture, and as a result he formed some firm convictions on the subject.

He decided that it was utter folly to establish a cooperative unless: 1) there was sufficient volume in sight to insure economical operation; 2) members had real desire and loyalty; 3) there was sufficient capital; and 4) there was competent management.

As a result of his activities in livestock marketing, and in Farm Bureau affairs generally, Herndon became quite well-known over the state as a man with sound ideas and the courage and ability to defend them.

Farm Supply policies and sound business practices were a reflection, pretty largely, of the ideas of IAA President Earl C. Smith and his trusted advisers; namely, Robert A. Cowles; Donald Kirkpatrick, the second Farm Supply manager; Lloyd Marchant; and George E. Metzger. All of these men, as well as the board of directors, had confidence in Herndon as a thoroughly capable and dependable man. He fitted admirably into the pattern of the IAA structure. The almost unparalleled success that Farm Supply was to attain in later years was primarily the result of

Fred E. Herndon

team effort. The fact that Fred E. Herndon did a lot to encourage this sort of effort is to his everlasting credit.

The other half of this team effort is a man who went to work for the Illinois Farm Supply system in 1931—the year Herndon became president. He is C. H. Becker, now executive vice president and general manager of FS Services, Inc.

Becker entered the Farm Supply picture as manager of the Farm Supply member company in Shelbyville. Later he went to Whiteside county where he attracted the attention of Farm Supply executives who brought him to the home office in 1935. In six years, Becker succeeded Marchant as manager.

Becker came from a Tazewell county farm. He attended Illinois State Normal University and took his first job as a Dairy Herd Improvement Association tester. Following that job, he joined Union Oil Company in California and spent three years in the company's marketing division gaining experience which was to stand him in good stead when he returned to Illinois.

Coming up through the ranks as he did, Becker learned the Farm Supply business thoroughly. In his years as manager, earnings have increased twelvefold and the future promises even greater accomplishments.

Known in his company and in his general professional field as a recruiter and builder of men, he and Herndon worked together to build a management team at Farm Supply second to none in the nation. As Farm Supply began to take on the complexion of "big business," Becker introduced the methods which would see his company continue to pace the field of farmer cooperatives.

The recipient of many awards, Becker holds the respect of other men in his field and has served in high posts in many business and cooperative associations.

The most important step that Farm Supply took in 1931 was the introduction of soybean oil paint, pretty much on an experimental basis. No paint manufacturer had heretofore used soybean oil as an ingredient of paint. At the insistence of W. L. Burlison, head of the Agronomy Department at the University of Illinois, the University had proved that refined soybean oil

C. H. Becker

was indeed suitable for use in paint. The Illinois Farm Supply Company, aware that the soybean was becoming a major crop in sections of Illinois, finally made a deal with a division of the Glidden Company to manufacture such a paint for distribution through Farm Supply. Glen W. Bunting of Farm Supply, a bundle of imagination and energy, was a key man in working this project which was to have such happy consequences. Farmers began to buy the soybean oil paint—some 3,000 gallons the first year. Ten years later, Farm Supply was to sell 300,000 gallons in one year.

The venture into soybean oil paint was carefully planned. The IAA, like all other farm agencies, was searching for new industrial uses for farm products. It was certain that farmers would buy soybean oil paint in order to enlarge the market for one of their own crops, once they were convinced that it was good paint. Farm Supply and IAA officials, after intense study of experimental results, had made up their minds that the soybean had great possibilities, not only as a source of oil, but also as a source of protein concentrate for livestock feed, and they began to promote it with vigor. Illinois farmers needed another cash crop, because the market for oats had fallen off badly as the horse population declined. Events were to prove that confidence in the soybean was not misplaced, for today it has become second only to corn among the cash crops grown in Illinois, accounting for 16.6 per cent of the farm income, fully three times as much as income from wheat, and three-fourths as much as income from hogs. For Illinois farmers, it has become truly a "wonder crop."

In 1933, Farm Supply distributed more than 40 million gallons of petroleum products, worth more than $3 million. In those days, there was much talk of whipping the corn surplus problem by making alcohol out of corn, then blending the alcohol with gasoline (10 per cent alcohol) for use in cars and tractors. Congress seriously considered making such a blend compulsory, but gave up the idea. Farm Supply, alert to the situation, prepared for the future by putting a blend on the market at a premium of three cents a gallon. It was soon demonstrated that farmers would not pay the premium.

Steady progress was made during these years, in spite of depressed conditions. In 1934, "the year of the chinch bug," Farm Supply distributed more than 500,000 gallons of chinch bug oil, some 75 per cent of all that was used in the state.

In 1936, Farm Supply began to handle feed, fertilizer, and fencing in volume. Cooperative livestock marketing associations and farmers' elevators had been looking for a source of supply for these products but when it was finally provided, experience was to prove that this move was a mistake. A livestock marketing association is not the proper outlet for products that must be handled in volume in a community. The business demands a real merchandiser to keep volume up.

Another drawback was that the farm advisers, taking their cue from the University of Illinois, were generally against commercial feeds. In the mid-forties, this situation was changed rather quickly as a result of Farm Supply setting up a quality-control committee consisting of representatives of IAA, FS, and the Farm Advisers' Association. This committee met regularly, and sought the counsel of research men at the University.

It was soon apparent that the results of new research in animal nutrition, plus new conditions in the feed industry itself were certain to open up new opportunities for the business. With new ingredients containing important growth factors available, with new mixing techniques in practice, and with competitive conditions forcing manufacturers to put out good feeds or go broke, it was easy to see that commercial feeds were to assume new importance in farm feeding operations. Farm advisers were quick to sense the trend, and they modified their previous position which had been based on conditions that no longer existed. This about-face by Extension forces was a big factor in the sensational advance of the feed business in the years to come.

In 1936, a step of far-reaching importance was taken when Farm Supply entered into an agreement with the Wabash Valley Service Company, a member company, for the joint operation of a marine terminal at Shawneetown with the storage capacity of 300,000 gallons. Barges carried supplies to the terminal, from which tank trucks completed the journey to member companies.

It was the beginning of a great era in waterway transportation.

Enormous savings in transportation costs have been achieved by moving bulk shipments in river barges. Morris Crandall, manager of the Wabash Valley Supply Company, was really responsible for the marine venture which has proved so profitable. He convinced his board members that they could move their gasoline to Shawneetown by barge more cheaply than by railroad tank car. The board of directors agreed that the plan was worth a try. They believed in it so strongly that after Farm Supply turned down their request for help in building a marine terminal, they sold $14,000 worth of stock in their own company and built it themselves. Farm Supply financed the inventories for them, however.

They unloaded their first barge load of gasoline on July 4, 1937, and within a year the project was an assured success. It survived a disastrous flood in 1938, and in 1939, Farm Supply took it over so that the advantages of water transportation could be extended to more Farm Bureau members. Actual savings were not impressive, but it was obvious that if the bulk of fuel handled by Farm Supply could be by barge to terminals on the Illinois and Mississippi Rivers, costs would be dramatically reduced.

Another milestone of progress was established in 1939, when a new marine terminal was built at Kingston Mines on the Illinois River near Peoria, with storage capacity of 1.5 million gallons. Over 5 million gallons of gasoline flowed through this terminal in a three-month period. Huge savings in transportation costs were realized. More than half of all gasoline sold went through the Shawneetown and Kingston Mines terminals.

In 1940, the importance of water transportation was indicated when Farm Supply put into service two new all-steel barges which cost about $45,000. Volume of petroleum products handled topped 100 million gallons.

A look at Farm Supply operations in 1940 is appropriate at this point. The surplus account stood at more than $450,000. Blue Seal tires were introduced. Sales of feed, fertilizer, fencing, and other steel products had grown to amount to some 10 per cent of the business. More than 10,000 tons of feed concentrates were sold during the year. Sixty county service companies and 78 other farm cooperatives were being supplied. Every indication was that Farm Supply "had it made," but nobody could foresee the extreme difficulties that the ensuing war years were to bring —crises that could have meant ruin if the right decisions had not been made. Neither could the vastly enlarged opportunities be anticipated.

Business was growing so fast that in 1941 it was necessary to increase gasoline storage at Kingston Mines to 4 million gallons, at Shawneetown to a million gallons. Two new barges were bought, and work started on a diesel-powered towboat with 800 horsepower, the *Blue Seal*. Water transport and the leverage it provided were slashing costs by at least a million dollars a year. The war in Europe was having its effect on the U.S.A. For the first time in its history, Farm Supply had difficulty in getting supplies. Farmers were asked to expand production. Demand for petroleum products, feed and fertilizer would be bigger next year.

In 1942, the first full year of war, fertilizer sales jumped 34 per cent, and feed sales 60 per cent. Restrictions of many kinds were imposed on production and on transportation facilities. The new towboat, *Blue Seal,* was a godsend. Tire recapping facilities were installed at Kingston Mines to prolong the life of the 4,000 tires on Farm Supply and member company trucks. Rationing of critical materials created nightmares for harassed executives. Anything that could be produced found eager buyers. Member service companies and their employees collected 1,150 tons of scrap rubber for the war effort. Business boiled. Net worth of Farm Supply jumped to well over $1 million.

Manpower was being drained away by the Armed Forces. Fifteen out of 52 office workers left for other jobs. Red tape, rationing, allocations, job freezes, restrictions without end—all these drove men in responsible positions to near distraction. Work on Sundays became routine for executives. Manager Becker had to go to Washington at least once every two weeks to clear up matters with government officials. Even though Farm Supply was in the "essential" class of businesses, sometimes it was like pulling teeth to get official rulings on critical problems. You couldn't rely on your own interpretation of a new order—you had to get an official interpretation.

It was a crushing blow when suppliers, as Becker puts it, "began to walk out on us." To meet this situation in feed, Farm Supply joined with other cooperatives to establish the Farm Bureau Milling Company at Hammond, Indiana. Farm Supply also leased the old Badenoch Mill in Chicago. The latter facility produced 14,000 tons of feed in 1943. The situation was almost as bad in petroleum supplies. It became apparent that Farm Supply would be forced to go into oil refining, hazardous though it might be, in order to be sure of supplies.

In 1944, Farm Supply and several other cooperatives set up Cooperative Plant Foods, Inc., with a plant at Hartsdale, Indiana, not far from Chicago, to manufacture mixed fertilizers. A trend toward greater use of mixed goods, superphosphate, triple superphosphate, and muriate of potash was apparent. The feed shortage got worse. Volume of feed sold dropped from some 50,000 tons in 1943, to less than 40,000 tons in 1944. An abandoned mill in Benton was bought and equipped, but it didn't come on stream until 1945.

The end of the war in 1945 found Farm Supply prosperous beyond the dreams of the founders. Net worth was close to $2 million. During the year, patronage refunds of more than $1 million had been returned to member companies. The member companies were correspondingly prosperous, for they returned to individual farmer members more than $2 million in patronage refunds. When one considers that total investment of farmer members in the county companies was only slightly over $2 million, one can begin to appreciate why farmers have such a high regard for the supply business.

The war had given business such an impetus that the momentum carried over with such force that some shortages actually became worse at the war's end. Costs rose rapidly. The need for more capital to make long-deferred improvements was pressing. In 1946, Farm Supply retained $273,584.01 out of earnings, and raised another $350,000 through the sale of additional stock.

Another spectacular achievement was the sale of 111,118 tons of plant food (including 68,648 tons of raw rock phosphate), compared with only 36,709 in 1945. Farm Supply, along with other cooperatives, had set up the Central Farmers Fertilizer Company which began centralized purchasing of raw materials, and which in the late fifties built a plant in Idaho to manufacture triple superphosphate, the latter by a new and untried electrical process.

In 1947 petroleum gallonage increased from 150 million to 170 million; fertilizer tonnage from 111,000 tons to 179,000 tons (raw rock again included); feed from 43,000 to 60,000 tons. Earnings exceeded $2 million. But serious problems loomed ahead. Petroleum supplies were so hard to get that at times Farm Supply had to pay more for gasoline than it could sell it for. The big refiners could sell all they could produce in the general market. Why bother with the farm market? Farm Supply had to allocate gasoline among its customers. Some suppliers refused to renew contracts for 1948. Extraordinary steps had to be taken.

Early in February, 1948, negotiations for purchase of the Pana Refining Company and the Loudon Pipeline Company began. The Pana facilities could produce 35 million gallons of refined products annually, but this amount, added to the amount under contract with other suppliers, still left Farm Supply at least 35 million gallons short of minimum requirements. After much soul-searching, Farm Supply directors finally approved of a risky venture, the purchase, along with two other cooperatives, of the Premier Oil Refining Company of Texas, owner of five refineries and some 600 miles of crude oil pipelines. As it turned out, this was a losing venture because the high price of gasoline had encouraged forced-draft production, and within a year suppliers who had summarily rejected pleas for some of their production now came around with offers of abundant supplies. The Pana plant paid its way from the start, and was a profitable operation until its closing in 1962. Premier was sold at a loss in 1956, but the loss was cheerfully accepted, since it provided badly needed supplies during a very critical period.

The feed business was booming. Early in 1948, construction was started on a new mill at Mendota to replace the leased Chicago mill. Capacity was rated at 36,000 tons annually. Some 86,766 tons of feed were sold in 1948, along with 209,000 tons of plant food, mostly raw rock phosphate. Construction was begun on a new fertilizer plant at East St. Louis, with a yearly capacity of 60,000 tons. In the same year, a new, much larger towboat with an integrated tow of barges, the 2400 horsepower *Illini*, was purchased.

Expansion costs a lot of money. Prior to 1947, the company had never borrowed money, but it was necessary in that year. That experience led to an issue of cumulative preferred stock in the amount of $3.5 million. In addition, other stock was made available to member companies to the amount of $1.5 million to be taken up during the following three years. To finance the growing capital needs of the member companies, Farm Supply urged a stock-selling campaign to encourage every patron to become a stockholder in the local company. It should be noted here that in 1948, Farm Supply, its affiliates and member companies paid nearly $1 million in federal income taxes.

The ensuing years were years of steady progress. Facilities were expanded and improved in all fields. Earnings rose. New capital was raised through preferred stock and debentures, and heavy additions made to the surplus account. In 1951, the 25th year of operation was celebrated.

Managing a business of the size of Farm Supply is an awesome responsibility. Changing conditions require continuous evaluation. There are plenty of opportunities to take a wrong turn along the way. Mushrooming growth carried plenty of hazards. Farm Supply management has been most diligent in studying all phases of a problem prior to making a decision. At times, beginning in 1947, professional management consultants have been employed to study specific problems and report objectively.

Aerial view of the Farm Supply "Illini" with barges loaded with 2,700,000 gallons of fuel.

Such consultants must be competent in the highest degree, with a high order of integrity, if they are to be of any value. Experience has demonstrated that money invested in such services can yield big returns.

For example, during and immediately after World War II, one of the most frustrating problems confronting Farm Supply was the big turnover in staff. Many key staff men had acquired invaluable experience in distributing farm supplies to farmers. They had acquired a know-how that was fairly rare. Consequently, other distributors were seeking them out and offering them tempting jobs with extensive fringe benefits such as liberal retirement benefits. With cost of living going up much faster than salary, many a man found it hard to resist the lure of greater opportunity elsewhere.

Becker, backed by Herndon, recommended to the board of directors that a thorough analysis of the situation be made. It revealed the plain fact that Farm Supply was far behind competing institutions in rewarding its staff men, and would surely lose a substantial number of them if current policies were continued. It also indicated that it would cost more to train replacements than it would have cost to pay experienced men adequate salaries. It was further pointed out that it was important to give proper incentives to younger men who were on the way up, so that replacements would always be available in the organization to replace men in the top echelon who might be lost in the normal course of events.

These conclusions made a lot of sense to the Farm Supply board members. To make a long story short, a program embodying most of the recommendations of management consultants was inaugurated by Becker and his top staff. This program has developed over the years to a stage at which it is fair to report that any competent young man starting out with Farm Supply can look forward confidently to a future just as bright and just as rewarding as he could expect in any comparable organization. A very fine retirement program was adopted. It has been a big factor in assembling a staff that is exceptionally talented, deeply imbued with team spirit and a degree of morale and enthusiasm that is outstanding.

In 1947, Farm Supply, with the approval of the member companies, started the practice of paying a small portion of patronage dividends in preferred stock. This practice met with general approval. In 1959, a massive distribution of preferred stock was made. The amount was $2,074,800. At the same time, $3,112,321 was returned in cash. The next year, $900,000 of patronage refunds was in the form of preferred stock, and in 1961, the amount was $1,150,000. This method is now the principal way of raising additional capital and has proved adequate to meet all except extraordinary needs. To get an idea of the enormous growth, consider the fact that in 1941, total investment in Farm Supply stock by member companies was $251,703, and 20 years later it was $17,243,664!

The 1950's were years of remarkable development. One of the milestones of progress was the opening of a new feed mill in Springfield in 1957. Built after years of planning, its design was as modern as technical skill could make it. It was highly automated. One man, seated before a glass-enclosed electronic panel, controlled most of the operations. Capacity was 200 tons of feed in eight hours.

Rapidly growing demands for gasoline and burner fuel products in the early fifties coupled with strong competitive influences brought about the expansion of facilities at Kingston Mines Terminal. Begun in 1939, the 1950 expansion brought the Illinois River point up to a level where it could store 17.5 million gallons of fuels.

New terminal facilities were built at Albany and Norris City. The large terminal storage provided great flexibility and made it possible to meet peak demand requirements of farmers. By the maximum use of barge transportation literally millions of dollars have been saved for Illinois farmers. Today, about one-half of all of the petroleum products distributed in Illinois move through the Kingston Mine Terminal.

Also, in the late fifties came Farm Supply's first venture into

Highly automated Springfield feed mill

the use of the big cross-county pipelines as a source of supply for petroleum fuels.

The "Big Inch," built for the purpose of moving natural gas from the great Southwest to the Eastern Seaboard during World War II, was converted to liquid fuel use. It became possible for Farm Supply to build a terminal on the pipeline at Norris City in southeastern Illinois. With the opening of the Norris City terminal, this entire area could be served at a considerable saving in transportation costs.

Cost consciousness, always a Farm Supply watchword, also brought about a virtual revolution in the plant food operations. Until the 1950's, farmers bought fertilizer in established formulas such as 12-12-12 or 5-20-10. But as the use of soil testing became more and more important in determining the plant food needs, it became obvious that these rather "patent" formulas were no longer sufficient.

This development meant that plant food dealers were faced with handling hundreds of formulas in order to give the customer what he needed or that the dealer would carry ingredients in stock and would blend bulk fertilizer to specific prescription. This latter route became obviously beneficial and many Farm Supply member companies invested in bulk blending equipment, which proved to be wise in that it provided better service to farmers at a a lower cost.

So today, farmers can apply nitrogen, phosphorus, and potash to their fields in the exact proportions demanded by soil test analysis.

In this period of great change in the fifties, the need for a new trademark became evident. Illinois Farm Supply was using a modified version of the IAA trademark and slogan "For better farming." In addition to this emblem and slogan, some 26 different trade names were used on various Illinois Farm Supply packages. The need for uniformity and the design of a striking symbol became evident. Raymond Loewy Associates was hired to design a new trademark. After a year of study and work the new "FS" house flag was unveiled.

It has now become a well-known symbol across Illinois and Iowa and the red and black initials in the red parallelogram rolls on hundreds of pieces of FS rolling stock and member company trucks.

In 1958, sales of feed jumped 16.2 per cent over 1957, and earnings soared, reflecting greater efficiency in distribution, due partly to the strategic location of the Springfield mill, together with improved efficiency in manufacturing. Changes in the commercial feed industry were coming with rocket speed. A manufacturer had to be fast on his feet to keep up with them. This put a tremendous responsibility on management, and a new premium on research.

The old practice of waiting until research projects were completed in public institutions was totally inadequate to the need. Furthermore, the university experiment stations necessarily confined their operations pretty largely to basic research, the discovery of fundamental principles in animal nutrition. What was sorely needed now was applied research on specific problems confronting the feed manufacturer. Other cooperatives faced the same problems. Extended discussion among them led to a decision, in 1958, to establish a research farm near Lexington, Illinois, owned by Farm Supply but serving eleven other cooperatives as well. Work got under way quickly, and was in full swing in 1959. The operation at Lexington involved experiments on 120 head of feeder cattle, and 1,600 head of swine from birth to market. Tests on such a large scale carry much greater significance than tests on just a few under what might be termed "laboratory" conditions.

As the fifties closed, another transformation in the business practices of the Farm Supply member companies became increasingly obvious. Most of these companies had been founded as distributors of petroleum products. Gradually, the move was made into the feed and plant food distribution lines, but the real impact of this diversification came just before 1960 with the emergence of several large member companies with a multi-line operation.

With the advent of bulk blending, many companies had become a sort of on-the-spot manufacturer, buying ingredients from Illinois Farm Supply and blending them to order for each patron. Needs of farmers for custom application of these plant foods prompted some of the member companies to enter this field of service with the resultant benefit to the farmers they served. Liquid ammonia became more and more important, and the major move into liquid ammonia distribution came about, setting the stage a few years later for a decision to enter the liquid ammonia production field.

Some of the member companies bought grinding and mixing equipment, increasing their ability to provide custom service to the farmer-patron. Also, LP gas took on significance as a fuel and many companies began handling it.

The entire movement has resulted in the growth of real farm production suppy centers where the patron can make one stop for his feed, plant food, steel products, paint, insecticide, and many other supply needs. Not only did this increase the volume of these diversified companies but, and this is more important, it provided better service to farmers whose time was becoming more and more valuable as the demands on it increased.

In 1959, after 28 years as president of Farm Supply, Fred E. Herndon retired. In recognition of his great contribution to Farm Bureau and Farm Supply, the latter established in his honor the Fred E. Herndon Scholarship, to be awarded to some student interested in agricultural business or research.

Herndon's successor was Melvin E. Sims of Adams county, only 39 at the time, who, with his brother Dean, was farming some 800 acres of land. A graduate of the Universty of Illinois in 1941, he served in World War II as an artillery captain. In 1946, he was elected treasurer and director of the Adams County Service Company, 10 years later was named a director of Farm Supply, and a year after that was named vice president. A quiet, soft-spoken man, his gift for leadership is of the unobtrusive kind, but it is quickly recognized by those who associate with him. Significant to the growth of closer ties between Illinois Farm Supply and its member companies was a program of management training, placement, transfer, promotion and development.

Programs were instituted which worked to improve the abilities of men in the field and in the home office so that they could, with good skill, manage these growing, changing companies in a faster paced agricultural market.

Leader in the development of the management training and development program was W. B. Peterson. Peterson joined the Illinois Farm Supply organization in December, 1932.

As manager of the Kankakee County Service Company, he became unhappy with the sales program of the state company and wrote of his dissatisfaction to Manager Marchant. Discussions ensued and in November, 1934, Peterson was hired by Marchant to improve the sales programs of Illinois Farm Supply. Thereafter his responsibilities included: sales programs, organization of distribution, organizing and reorganizing member companies, supervision of field services and management services to member companies.

Early in his career, Peterson developed the manpower recruiting, training, and development programs which were the prototype of the programs still followed by Farm Supply. Personnel policies were developed; improved product information was made available to county service companies.

After World War II, the source of member company managers and other specialized people was depleted and new manpower sources needed to be developed. So a college recruiting program was launched.

Through Peterson's urging, IFS helped pioneer the management training institutes for cooperatives.

In 1952, Peterson was assistant general manager of IFS. In March of that year, Peterson was invited to assume a dual role with the IAA as secretary of marketing for the Illinois Agricultural Association and as secretary of the Illinois Agricultural Service Company which provides management counseling services to IAA affiliates that have contracts with the "Service Company."

For more than 30 years, Peterson has played a leading role in the growth and development of both the affiliated companies and the general farm organization itself.

One of the continuing problems faced by Farm Supply when

W. B. Peterson

Sims took over, was the problem of Central Farmers Fertilizer Company in which Farm Supply in 1960 had an 11 per cent interest, representing an investment of $1,548,734. The centralized purchasing and investments in nitrogen production had done very well; but heavy losses had been sustained in producing phosphorus at the Idaho plant. Progress had been slow, and at times quite discouraging. Central Farmers earned over $3 million annually on nitrogen, potash, and purchased phosphates, but its losses on the Idaho plant had kept the operation from becoming profitable. In July, 1964, the Idaho plant was sold, thereby opening the way for a stock reorganization, the flow of earnings to member companies, and the development of its business on a sound basis.

In the fertilizer field also, a project long contemplated became a reality in early 1962 when Central Nitrogen, Inc., was chartered to manufacture ammonia for fertilizers. Ownership is vested in Farm Supply, 50 per cent; Indiana Farm Bureau Cooperative Association, 32 per cent; Ohio's Farm Bureau Cooperative Association, 18 per cent; and Central Farmers Fertilizer Company, Chicago, which will perform certain marketing functions and plans to become a part-owner eventually.

The plant, located five miles north of Terre Haute, Indiana, cost some $20 million, and has a capacity of 350 tons of ammonia a day. Operations began in the late fall of 1963. The first few months of operation created earnings of in excess of a million dollars. The budget for 1965 anticipates earnings of $3.5 million. It provides an economical and assured source of nitrogen. It represents the final step in making Farm Supply fertilizer operations fully integrated, from production of the basic materials to final delivery to the farm, with Central Fertilizer Company supplying the phosphorus and potash, and Central Nitrogen, Inc., supplying the nitrogen. Farm Supply is in a highly advantageous position in the fertilizer business. It is now the largest distributor of fertilizer to farmers in Illinois.

Close on the heels of the announcement of the fertilizer

project came news that Illinois Farm Supply Company planned to merge with its counterpart in Iowa, the Farm Service Company of Iowa, to form FS Services, Inc. Study of the feasibility of the step had gone on for some months, and the member companies were asked to give their approval.

This move was entirely logical, and it is in line with the trend toward bigger business units in all lines, from banking to baby foods. Greater volume offers greater opportunity for more economical operation in many businesses. Farm Supply was three times as large as its Iowa counterpart, and it would seem, on superficial examination, that Iowa stood to gain more from the merger than did Illinois.

However, the Iowa company had one asset that is of outstanding value to FS—a substantial interest in an oil refinery and pipeline. The Iowa company had a 20 per cent interest, worth $7 million, in the National Cooperative Refining Association at McPherson, Kansas, which has its own pipeline to Council Bluffs, Iowa, where it joins the Great Lakes Pipeline System. The present capacity of the refinery is 32,000 barrels daily, ample to meet the needs of all five stockholders, all cooperative organizations; namely, Consumers Cooperative Association of Kansas City, Farmers Union Central Exchange of St. Paul, Farmers Union State Exchange of Omaha, and Midland Cooperatives, Inc., of Minneapolis, Minnesota.

With a relatively small investment, capacity can be increased to 40,000 barrels. With this source of supply now in hand, Farm Supply has announced the closing of its refinery at Pana, which for 15 years had served Farm Supply so effectively.

In the opinion of most Farm Bureau observers, the merger opens the way to notable further developments in the field of furnishing basic supplies to farmers in both states. The merged unit will be in better position to meet competition, it will provide additional savings through elimination of duplicate overhead cost, greater flexibility in procurement and wholesale distribution of supplies. It is confidently expected that farmer members will be assured of improved service at reduced cost.

FS officials are notably "volume-conscious." They know from past experience that many cost-cutting plans or devices can be employed only in large-scale operations. Just as it is profitable to a farmer to use a four-bottom plow only when it can be used on a large acreage, so in business there are many machines that cost too much for use in small enterprises.

Marine terminals were built and over the years savings have run into the millions. The volume handled by one towboat is simply fantastic. For example, the *Blue Seal,* first Farm Supply towboat which went into operation in late 1941, was kept on a 24-hour schedule seven days a week all through the war year of 1943. In that year it moved a total of 51 million ton miles. It moved the bulk of more than 117 million gallons of refined products handled by Farm Supply that year. You must realize that one modern tow now carries the equivalent of three trainloads of tank cars before you can even believe these figures. Only then can you grasp the enormous economies made possible by water transportation.

On land, FS has won fame for the efficiency it has attained in moving things by trailer truck. Every tractor owned can be attached to any trailer. Diversity of products handled permits many a shortcut. For example, a tractor may haul a load of feed from Springfield to East St. Louis and bring back a load of fertilizer from the East St. Louis plant. Operations are planned ahead so that whenever a tractor starts a trip, it carries a full load. Tractors are operated generally on a round-the-clock basis. Size of the truck operation is indicated by the fact that 38 huge tractors were bought in one deal a few years ago. All of them moved from the factory in one spectacular convoy.

Every tractor is overhauled at regular intervals in the FS maintenance garage. A tractor is expected to deliver efficient performance for 500,000 miles. Records on truck performance are so meticulously kept as to attract nation-wide attention. Tractor manufacturers have been known to turn over to FS a tractor with a new type of transmission or other new feature, with the injunction: "Wear it out, and send us the record it makes."

The situation has changed drastically in recent years in the transport of oil. The pipeline is now a big factor, but still more than half of the gasoline distributed by FS is carried in barges. The economy achieved through pipeline and barge, over the old method of railroad tank car transport can be fully appreciated when you realize that no distributor, no matter how efficient, could stay in business today at present prices if he had to pay transportation charges equal to tank car rates.

The most modern business practices have been utilized to promote the business of FS. You can't drive very far in any part of downstate Illinois without being aware of this business institution. You will see the FS emblem anywhere you go—on trucks, on billboards, on buildings housing all sorts of FS activities. The symbol also jumps at you from the advertising pages of daily and weekly newspapers and farm papers. The member companies in the counties make effective use of the emblem in all of their activities. Within months after the change, however, it was apparent that the adoption of the new symbol had been a master stroke in promotion. It had caught on instantly with Farm Bureau members, and aroused the curiosity of the general public. Today there is an awareness of FS everywhere never before equalled. The value of the symbol is incalculable. It is one of the greatest assets of the organization.

A quick and far from comprehensive appraisal of FS Services, Inc., as of 1962 seems in order. Here is a business organization only 35 years old that distributes annually farm supplies worth $100 million at wholesale value. In attaining such impressive stature, it might be said that this farmer-owned corporation has exploited to the fullest extent two principles which are accepted as fundamentals in today's business world: integrated operation and big volume. The principle of integrated operation is best illustrated perhaps in the fertilizer business. FS brings phosphorus, potassium and nitrogen from its own mines or plants to its own processing or blending plants, moves it to member companies which distribute it directly to Farm Bureau members, and in some cases actually spread it on the field. It is fully recognized that any business unit which reaches for total integration is thereby incurring greater risks. Such calculated risks are taken in the belief that improved efficiency will result.

In making the decision to build a nitrogen-producing plant near Terre Haute, Indiana, in cooperation with Ohio and Indiana Farm Bureau cooperatives, FS officials were convinced that no undue risks were involved. The sensational increase in the use of nitrogen by farmers since the war is not considered to be a flash-in-the-pan, but rather a firm movement, which will continue permanently and expand still further. Thus, millions are being invested in complete confidence of success.

In other cases, admittedly shaky ventures were undertaken because of seeming necessity. The purchase of the Premier Oil Company was a good example. It seemed absolutely necessary at the time to insure the continuity of supplies of petroleum products. It turned out badly, but FS was prepared for that. The main thing is that through this action, supplies were assured, the big FS objective. Some experience has been gained in owning or leasing of oil wells, and that experience indicates that this is one phase of the oil business which may well be left to others. However, minds are not closed on the subject.

On the subject of volume, reference should be made to the recent merger of the Iowa and Illinois companies as the most conspicuous example in FS history of striving for greater efficiency in distribution through increased volume and reduced duplication of facilities, personnel and effort.

However, after giving fair weight to following sound business practices in this epic of business success, the observer is impressed with the possibility that another factor is equally important. That factor might be called the integrity of those who make FS policies. The overriding aim of FS is, simply expressed, to make farming more profitable for Farm Bureau members. In fertilizers, for example, the big objective has not been to attain volume, but rather to make sure that fertilizers carrying the proper ingredients for the soil on each man's farm are made available. When this has been done, volume will come, inevitably. Every effort has been made to encourage each man to have his soil tested so that he can buy fertilizers intelligently, and so make his farming operations more profitable and maintain the fertility of the soil.

Similar policies have been followed in the feed business, which has enjoyed spectacular success. The aim has been to utilize the very best information available on how to make a pound of beef or pork most economically—not on how to concoct a feed that will show the greatest profit to the company supplying it. Nor is this principle confined only to FS among the IAA affiliates. We find it also in the insurance companies, striving at all times to sell insurance best suited to the needs of the member. The same principle pervades the policies of all IAA affiliates, and it goes far to explain the advantages of a setup of this kind, in which farmers themselves give direction and force to policies adopted.

President Melvin E. Sims stated the situation very well in his first address at the annual meeting of FS Services, Inc., when he said:

"I subscribe without reservation, to the belief that an agricultural cooperative attains its greatest strength and makes its greatest contribution when affiliated with a strong farm organization. I would hope that the advantage would be reciprocal. In the states we serve, Farm Bureau is unquestionably the strongest farm membership organization. Our patrons are composed of the same group, our aims and objectives are compatible, the two organizations complement each other. There may be specific situations which might cause either party to question this belief— this even happens in matrimony. In the main, however, this close affiliation is one of the pillars of our combined strength."

The attractive future which looms ahead was described by General Manager Chester H. Becker in his 1962 annual report. He wrote:

"We should now be prepared to go forward. We have an excellent foundation; the finest kind of product lines, suited to our members' needs; a tried and tested system; experienced boards and management throughout the system; sound resources in terms of capital and people. The potential for increased savings and earnings, as compared to our separate operations, now appears greater than we originally estimated it to be.

"Our purpose now is to capitalize on our opportunities; to use every resource at our command to gain renewed support and enthusiasm from Farm Bureau membership in Iowa and Illinois. This we propose to do."

The above optimistic appraisal was amply borne out, for at the end of the first fiscal year of combined operations, August 21, 1963, Becker was able to report that earnings of FS Services, Inc., amounted to well over $8 million, or 25 per cent more than the combined earnings of the two companies operating separately in the previous year. Results made possible by the merger exceeded expectations by a wide margin, and offered the prospects of still greater things to come.

Earnings before Distribution & Taxes
Illinois Farm Supply Co. *FS Services, Inc.
1930-1963 Organized 1927

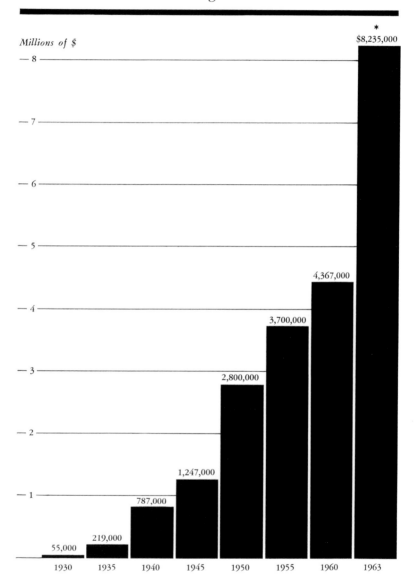

*
$8,235,000

Millions of $

4,367,000

3,700,000

2,800,000

1,247,000

787,000

219,000

55,000

1930   1935   1940   1945   1950   1955   1960   1963

Assets
Illinois Farm Supply Co. *FS Services, Inc.
1930-1963 Organized 1927

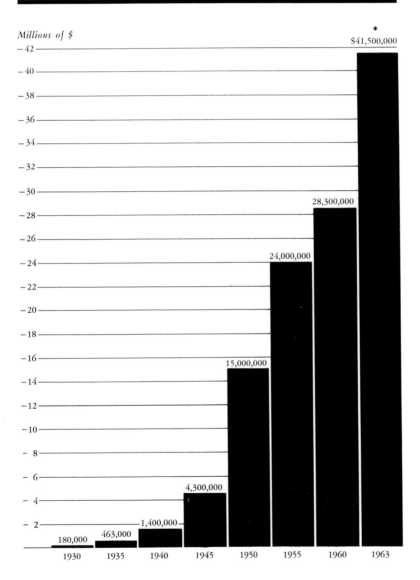

Millions of $

*
$41,500,000

28,300,000

24,000,000

15,000,000

4,300,000

1,400,000

463,000

180,000

1930 1935 1940 1945 1950 1955 1960 1963

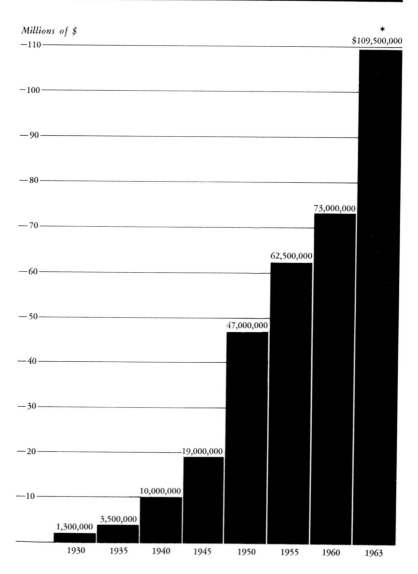

Sales

Illinois Farm Supply Co.   * FS Services, Inc.
1930-1963 Organized 1927

Millions of $

*
$109,500,000

—110

—100

—90

—80

73,000,000

—70

62,500,000

—60

—50

47,000,000

—40

—30

—20 —————19,000,000

10,000,000

—10

3,500,000

1,300,000

1930   1935   1940   1945   1950   1955   1960   1963

Chapter 25

Sports and Recreation

From the earliest days of Farm Bureau, the county organizations held annual picnics for members. There was always speaking and music, often band music, horseshoe pitching contests, baseball or softball, and other events. When the county organizations federated to form the IAA, it was natural that a state-wide picnic be staged. In 1920, President Harvey Sconce entertained a huge crowd at his estate in Vermilion county. In 1921, the picnic was held at Assembly Park on the Rock River at Dixon, with 10,000 in attendance. Three bands furnished music practically all day, a program of athletic events, such as tug-of-war, horseshoe pitching, and footraces, was staged. William G. Eckhardt of De Kalb county, and Mrs. Charles W. Sewell of Otterbein, Indiana, were the main speakers. Howard Leonard, IAA president, spoke briefly.

Naturally, the bulk of the crowd arrived in automobiles, but railroads were still an important means of passenger transportation, as indicated by the fact that Leland S. Griffith, farm adviser in Lee county, had arranged with the railroads to grant half-fare rates from anywhere in the state to the picnic site.

Rains and muddy roads held the attendance down to 6,000 at the next year's picnic in Olney. At this picnic, the big athletic event was the horseshoe pitching contest. For the third consecutive year, the De Witt team of Joe Heskett and Ed Torbert won the championship over 13 other teams.

Early in 1924, in response to demand from several counties, the Illinois Farm Bureau Baseball League was organized to provide formal competition among the county teams. George E. Metzger was the first secretary-treasurer and manager. The Marshall-Putnam team won the playoff game at the IAA picnic held at Lincoln that year by defeating the Morgan county team, 6 to 0. Attendance at the picnic was 12,000.

At the 1925 picnic in Taylorville some 25,000 people showed up. Baseball had become a feature and Farm Bureau teams from Henderson and Tazewell counties fought it out for the state championship with Tazewell winning by a score of 8 to 6. The centerfielder on the Henderson team was Otto Steffey, who was to become president of the IAA many years later. Champion horseshoe pitchers were Walter and Harry Torbert of De Witt county, sons of Ed Torbert, a member of the champion team in 1920, 1921, and 1922.

In 1926, the Marshall-Putnam team beat Henderson county for the state championship by a score of 12 to 2. Otto Steffey was still centerfielder for the Henderson county team. Marshall-Putnam won again in 1927, beating the Logan county team by a score of 12 to 3 at Mooseheart, where the picnic was held. An automobile driving and parking contest was a new feature on the picnic program. It was sponsored by the Illinois Agricultural Mutual Insurance Company.

By 1928, Farm Bureau picnics in congressional districts had replaced the state-wide picnic, and the baseball teams played their regular schedule without regard to picnics. In the final playoff game that year, the Tazewell county team won the championship for the second time, beating Lawrence county by a score of 6 to 4. Twenty-two teams were now members of the league. In 1929, the

McLean county team won the state championship. The Mc-Donough county team won the flag in 1930. Thirty one teams competed. Livingston county won in 1931, defeating Knox county in the final game.

The Farm Bureau baseball league developed rapidly over the years with George Thiem, IAA director of information, in charge. In 1936, before the annual meeting of league representatives, someone had suggested that a softball division be established. Clifford V. Gregory, who had originated the Prairie Farmer corn husking contests, was deeply interested. He suggested that it might be a good thing to establish a field day for farmers, with athletic contests of all kinds on the program. He promised the full co-operation of Prairie Farmer and WLS.

When representatives of some twenty counties met at Peoria, the idea won unanimous approval. Ebb Harris, president of the league, appointed a committee, consisting of Alvin O. Eckert, Otto Steffey, and Albert Hayes, all IAA directors, to outline a plan and present it to the next meeting of the IAA directors. The upshot of it was that the IAA board, not without some misgivings, directed George Thiem to organize and stage the first annual Sports Festival, and provided a budget of $1,500 which was later raised to $1,600. On June 20, Roy P. Johnson, athletic coach at Mahomet High School, was hired to visit county Farm Bureaus and get definite entries for a track meet, tug-of-war, horseshoe tournament, and other events.

When University of Illinois officials were approached, they quickly agreed to permit the festival to be held on University playing fields and to give every possible help during the event. The Champaign County Farm Bureau, under the leadership of Farm Adviser J. Edward Harris, went to work on local arrange-ments.

When the Festival was held, on September 4 and 5, no less than 30,000 people turned out to see more than 2,000 contestants go through their paces. It was a spectacular success. There were 70 softball teams, 8 relay teams, 5 baseball teams, 12 tug-of-war teams, and many entries in contests covering horseshoe pitching, horse pulling, rolling-pin throwing, square dancing, hog calling, folk dancing, novelty bands, and even checker playing. There were three Farm Bureau bands to furnish music. Radio Station WLS sent entertainers. When the event was over, everyone was worn out, but there was no doubt in anyone's mind that the Sports Festival had made a big place for itself in the category of worthwhile Farm Bureau activities.

In addition, it is quite likely that many of the thousands of young people who became familiar with the facilities of a great university for the first time were inspired to go to college as a result of their experience at the Festival.

Experience gained in 1936 helped a lot in planning and staging the second festival in 1937. Frank Gingrich, who had been appointed director of young people's activities in 1936, and C. M. Seagraves, director of farm safety activities, were in charge. Trap shooting and swimming events were added to the program. Added interest all over the state was reflected with more entries and tighter competition. Each year thereafter, the event was run more expeditiously. The 1939 Festival opened on September 1, the day that news of the outbreak of World War II was flashed to this country. Some 3,500 people, old and young, from 80 counties, competed in the various events. More than 20,000 spectators were on hand.

By 1941, the Festival had become established as one of the important Farm Bureau events of the year. Members had backed it enthusiastically. It seemed to fill a need in every community. Earl C. Smith, in a foreword to the 1941 Festival rulebook, wrote as follows:

"The future success of organized agriculture will depend, in large measure, upon the ability of young people who will be its leaders to learn how to be considerate of others, proud of success, equally graceful in winning or in losing. Because it is teaching these things, the Illinois Farm Sports Festival has become a major agricultural event."

The Festival was canceled for the four war years, but in 1946 it was back, bigger than ever. It continued to attract around 20,000 visitors until 1950, when attendance dropped to some 5,000. There have been no huge crowds of spectators since that time, due to fundamental changes in the setup. Baseball, basketball, trapshooting, and bowling finals are not held at the festival. Bowling and basketball are winter sports, hence the tournaments are held in March, and the finals early in April. Softball competition is by counties and districts, but the finals are still a part of the Festival program. Golf was abandoned in 1949 because of lack of interest, but it was restored for 1962. The entire program has been decentralized, with emphasis on wide participation in the community. More people are participating than ever before, and that is the big objective. Festival crowds now are made up largely of those taking part, along with members of their families.

The music and folk dancing features were quite popular at first, but as crowds became smaller at the Festival, and also because square dancing and similar features are not really hot-weather events, this program, called the Music and Folk Festival, was staged as part of the Farm and Home Week program at the University of Illinois, which is held in February. This arrangement continued for several years, but was finally dropped.

The baseball league flourished for many years, but after the 1951 season in which only five teams were entered in the competition, it was disbanded. Thus, the sport which led to the establishment of the Sports Festival is no longer a part of it.

Other changes have been made through the years. The horse pulling contest was dropped many years ago, as was the hog calling contest. Croquet and shuffleboard continued to attract entries. An added feature in recent years has been the Talent Find contest. The finale of this competition is held at the IAA annual meeting, but elimination contests are held at the Festival. The purpose is to encourage the development of talent—dramatic, musical, vocal, dancing, and so on. This is a major feature of the entire program, and many acts of real merit have been staged.

Roy P. Johnson, who helped organize and run the first Festival in 1936, and who was employed in 1946 by the IAA as director of special services, took over the management in that year. He was farm adviser at De Kalb, after service in the Army. In 1951, he returned to active army service. Roy Will, who had been assistant farm adviser in De Kalb county, succeeded him and has carried on to the present time (1963).

Chapter 26

Moving Things

When President Howard Leonard addressed the IAA annual meeting on January 13, 1920, he mentioned a few major problems facing Illinois farmers. One of them was the "zone system" of shipping livestock to the Chicago market. Under this system, farmers living within 300 miles of Chicago were required to ship their livestock for arrival only on Tuesdays and Thursdays. According to President Leonard, this system resulted in market gluts, and consequently lower prices on those days. He said that the system must be changed.

Lee J. Quasey had been hired only a few months before to handle claims by farmers against railroads for livestock crippled enroute or killed on railroad right-of-way, for freight overcharges, etc., as well as to look after the Farm Bureau wool pool which amounted to nearly a half million pounds in 1919. The point is that moving products from farmer to consumer, and moving equipment from manufacturer to farmer, were vitally important to farmers, and they put their organization to work in this field from the very beginning. Heavy tonnage is involved in shipments of limestone, fertilizers, livestock, farm machinery, grain, and such products as potatoes. Since the farmer pays the freight both ways, rates were then, and are now of great consequence to him. It's easy to understand how the original claims department grew quickly into the transportation department and became a beehive of activity. Many years later, with the advent of the Illinois Farm Supply Company and its member companies over the entire state, responsibilities of the department increased by geometric progression, until today, with these agencies handling trainloads of supplies by rail, barge and truck, transportation charges run into the millions.

In 1921, Quasey reported that during the previous year his department had recovered more than $6,000 for members for loss or damage, overcharges, and the like. In 1921, the claims and service department really hit paydirt when it secured reductions in freight charges on limestone, saving more than $30,000 for Illinois farmers. Continual study was made of the complicated rate structure, in order to be able to advise farmers. Quasey was studying law, and was later admitted to the bar, but he was not a rate man, and he needed a rate man. Hence, Guy W. Baxter, an employee of the Illinois Central Railroad, was hired for this work. He was a rate specialist, and moreover he was a Registered Practitioner, licensed to appear before the Interstate Commerce Commission. He made many such appearances during his IAA career which extended over 37 years. He was to succeed Quasey as head of the department in 1933 when the latter resigned to engage in the practice of law. He and Quasey teamed up very effectively from 1922 to 1933.

Much of the work involved such matters as icing of cars of perishables in summer and heating them in winter, proper bedding of livestock cars, condition of holding pens at railroad stations, stock scale sites, minimum weights on mixed shipments, and so on. Overcharges were troublesome, involving the application of improper rates to shipments. Most of them were the result of human errors on the part of freight agents, and hence were quickly settled. Amounts of money involved were usually small, in some cases, trivial, but members highly appreciated this service. One example was a case involving two routes by which milk and cream could be shipped from Algonquin, Illinois, to Chicago. Railroads had been using a rate based on the longer route. The IAA presented the facts to the railroads, which granted a lower rate, saving milk and cream shippers from that station $45 a day. In 1924, the ICC proposed a rate increase of some four cents a hundred on fruits and vegetables from Illinois points to Chicago, but the IAA transportation and claims department succeeded in holding the increase to a maximum of one-and-one-half cents. Work on claims increased to such an extent that in 1926, no less than 1,359 were handled, and more than $28,000 collected for members. Other matters were demanding attention, such as the electric high tension line right-of-way problem, scheduled rates for rural light and power, the construction of rural electric lines, telephone rates, standards of service, and pipeline rights-of-way. With the advent of the Illinois Farm Supply Company in 1927, came a heavy increase in traffic problems which was to continue until, in 1962, administration of the entire department was transferred to FS Services, Inc., the new name of the merged Illinois Farm Supply Company and its Iowa counterpart, the Farm Bureau Service Company of Iowa. The department continues to serve the IAA and county Farm Bureaus.

The years of the great depression brought increased work in the department. Railroads had allowed fences to deteriorate, creating more damage cases when livestock wandered onto railroad property. Freight rates seemed unduly high in relation to price of products, hence farmers were demanding lower rates. In 1934, Baxter, now heading up the work, succeeded in getting a reduction of $108 a car on soybeans shipped from Illinois to eastern seaboard territory, and a reduction in the rate on pears shipped from Illinois to western points, amounting to $30 a car. Baxter and Donald Kirkpatrick, general counsel, fought vigorously against the efforts of railroads to secure a nation-wide general increase in freight rates.

About this time, the continuing shift of freight from rail to truck was creating problems. In some cases, railroads proposed to abandon branch lines as unprofitable, and in others to close small stations. The IAA sought to protect the farmers' interests in all such cases.

Rate controversies are always with us. In 1938, for example, railroads filed application for increases amounting to $30 a car on livestock stocker and feeder rates from western points to some 135 Illinois towns. Old rates were restored, under certain restrictions, only after strong protests by IAA.

Freight rate cases have been a continuing concern of the department. To list them all is impossible. A typical case developed with the coming of barge transportation via the Illinois, Mississippi, and Ohio Rivers. Farmers within 30 miles of barge docks enjoyed much lower rates on grain or other commodities exported than did those in other areas. At the instance of the IAA and other interested parties, the ICC in 1940 ordered the lower rates applied on such shipments from all parts of the state. The importance of freight rates to livestock feeders was brought out in a case in 1941, in which an Illinois cattle feeder was overcharged $529 on a shipment of feeders from the West. Protest from IAA brought a prompt refund to the farmer.

As the use of phosphatic materials for fertilizer expanded, it became necessary to buy much of the material from Florida deposits. Under existing rates in 1945, shipments from Florida to Illinois points except Chicago were prohibitive. Baxter made a plea to the Southern Freight Association at Atlanta which resulted in a saving of $65,000 to Farm Supply Company on shipments from April to October.

In 1947, the burden borne by the transportation department had grown so great that Robert L. Graves, a young man from the rate department of the Illinois Central Railroad, was brought in as assistant to Baxter. The fast-growing business of the Illinois Farm Supply Company created a great deal of work, particularly with respect to supplying information needed to make the right decisions as to location of new plants, terminals, and distribution points. Graves had won his certificate as Registered Practitioner, hence was well equipped to help Baxter in his many responsibilities. (He was later to succeed Baxter as director of the department.) In 1947, also, a case that had been simmering for years was finally resolved. As barge traffic on the Illinois River increased, common carriers had denied barge-shipped grain destined for the East via Chicago the same rates as applied to shipments arriving in Chicago by rail or lake boats. The ICC finally decided in favor of the barge shippers. It was of vital importance to farmers whose grain was loaded on barges at the river houses.

The amount of money involved in proper routing of shipments is well illustrated in the case of shipping phosphate from Florida. By shipping from Florida mine to Port Tampa, loading there on a deep-water barge for New Orleans, and reloading there on a river barge for the FS fertilizer plant at East St. Louis, a saving of 58 cents a ton, or $1,200 per barge, under all-rail rates was realized.

The department was constantly extending its service to the member companies of Farm Supply, even to auditing all of their freight bills. In 1949, another man was added to the staff to assist in this work. Substantial recoveries of overcharges were made.

During the early post-war years, a great deal of time was devoted to helping farmers fight against increasing telephone rates. Many of the increases were justified, or partly so, because of inflation. Nevertheless the department was quite effective in holding increases to reasonable levels.

The tremendous increase in business enjoyed by the affiliated companies, and particularly by the Illinois Farm Supply Company, kept the department busier than ever. In 1952 more than $44,000 in claims was collected. Telephone rate cases were still numerous, and the department was called upon to help farm groups in organizing telephone cooperatives in areas where other companies were not rendering service. Such groups could obtain loans from the Rural Electrification Administration.

The building of toll roads and new roads in the interstate highway system in the late 1950's brought a flood of calls for help from members whose interests were affected. Because of long experience in such matters, members of the department were in a position to render invaluable help in securing adequate remuneration for land sold, as well as compensation for hardship created when a farm was cut in two, for instance. Similar problems faced farmers whose land was crossed by high-voltage electric lines and gas or oil pipelines. Settlements entirely satisfactory to landowners have usually been made.

In 1958, the department filed claims for overcharges on rock phosphate shipped from Florida. Refunds to Farm Supply member companies on this deal eventually reached about $68,000. This incident demonstrates the importance of meticulous checking of all freight charges. The entire rate structure is so intricate that errors are bound to be made by common carrier personnel, and by the same token only an expert on rates is likely to detect the error. The department maintains one of the most complete libraries in the country on rates, and experienced employees are able to ferret out mistakes with astonishing accuracy.

On February 1, 1960, Guy W. Baxter retired after more than 37 years of service. Robert L. Graves succeeded him and still runs the show with the help of Anthony Skul, Rogers P. Freedlund, and John W. Rice, former traffic man with the Iowa Farm Bureau Service Company. In 1961, the department handled one of the biggest jobs in its history when it made all arrangements for moving the office equipment of IAA and its affiliates from Chicago to the new IAA building in Bloomington, together with household goods of some 275 employees. The move was made with amazing speed and a minimum of disturbance to office routine and service rendered. Total weight of material moved was 3,439,967 pounds. Of 346 shipments, 275 were household goods of the families moved, and 71 were shipments of office equipment. Total cost of the move was $207,581. There were practically no damage claims. A move of this magnitude can be carried out with speed and precision only through careful planning long in advance. In this case, planning was begun a year ahead of the move, and the big reason why everything meshed into smooth performance was that it was planned that way with meticulous care.

After 42 years of service, members of the staff can look back with satisfaction to innumerable cases in which the department has been able to render invaluable service to county Farm Bureaus and to individual members who needed help in a field in which expert counsel was essential. The value of the service rendered is not to be measured by the number or amount of claims collected, since this is really only a small segment of the field in which the department operates. Nevertheless, it is interesting to note that during its existence this department has collected on behalf of its clients the sum of $921,740.61.

As early as 1922, the IAA was working on the problem of extending electric service to rural areas, where only one per cent of the farms enjoyed such service. (Some had individual lighting plants, and some had gas lights supplied by so-called "carbide" plants.) In its report for 1922, the legal department of the IAA reports its activities on rural electrification as follows: "Numerous hearings have been held before the Interstate Commerce Commission and temporary rates have been fixed covering some ten counties traversed by the various power lines in the state. The old regulation written by the former Public Utilities Commission was rescinded and a new set of regulations, covering the entire subject, is about completed and will be presented shortly to the Commerce Commission for consideration."

On March 8, 1923, the American Farm Bureau Federation met with representatives of the National Electric Light Association, the USDA, and the American Society of Agricultural Engineers to discuss the problem of extending electric service to farmers. Out of this meeting came the creation of a national organization called the Committee on the Relation of Electricity to Agriculture. Its job was to further the cause of rural electrification.

Some two years later, the Illinois State Electric Association supplied funds to build an experimental rural line in Champaign county for a study by the Illinois Agricultural Experiment Station. Records were kept on eight farms for 32 consecutive months. These records proved conclusively that farmers did not use enough electricity to justify building lines conforming to minimum standards required by the Illinois Commerce Commission. Accordingly, the ICC revised standards to permit building of cheaper lines ($450 per customer mile). These changes resulted in some progress, and by 1929 we find that 18,317 Illinois farms were electrified, and by 1935, the number had risen to 28,000.

Then, in 1935, the Norris-Rayburn Bill creating the Rural Electrification Administration was passed by Congress, with the backing of all farm organizations. From then on, giant strides were made. The public utilities began frantically to "sew up" the best populated areas before REA cooperatives could build lines. On numerous occasions IAA representatives appeared before the ICC to defend the cooperatives against such encroachments. IAA offered its services to all county Farm Bureaus to make surveys to determine the potential business of each area. Using the information gained by these surveys, farmers in the county could bargain with the public utility involved on matters such as price, minimum use, and so on. The IAA engaged in no "war" on public utilities. If the utilities offered to supply current at reasonable rates, the farmers affected were advised to accept public utility service; if not, then an REA cooperative should be formed. In 1936, Paul E. Mathias, corporate secretary of the IAA stated flatly: "Electric Service should be brought to every farm which desires a cooperative to furnish electric service, with funds to be obtained from the Rural Electrification Administration, wherever such a cooperative is feasible and practical." He added: "Farmers are entitled to electric service on a fair basis. Where the public utilities are ready to furnish service on this fair basis the Association desires to cooperate with them. Where service on this basis is not available the Association will assist farmers to organize and secure this service for themselves."

Through 1936, rural electrification matters were handled by Guy W. Baxter of the transportation department, but the work had grown to such an extent that additional expert help was necessary. Upon the recommendation of John M. Carmody, REA administrator, Colonel Charles W. Sass, assistant chief engineer of the REA, was hired by IAA as engineering consultant. The

IAA also set up a state-wide management cooperative to furnish engineering, management, and other expert services to REA co-operatives in Illinois. It was incorporated under the Agricultural Cooperative Act.

Before Colonel Sass started his work, the Menard County Rural Electrification Cooperative, the first project of its kind sponsored by Farm Bureau, held its pole-setting ceremony on February 26, 1937. K. T. Smith, IAA director, represented the IAA. A similar celebration was held on April 9, 1937, by the Wayne-White County Electric Cooperative. President Earl C. Smith of the IAA was the principal speaker. In June, Earl C. Smith, and Oscar Meier of the REA were the principal speakers when the Illinois Rural Electric Company set its first pole. Meanwhile, the first 1,000-mile REA project in the United States got under way in Iroquois, Ford, Livingston, and Vermilion counties. IAA men, particularly Paul E. Mathias and Guy W. Baxter, had spent a great deal of time on legal matters and field work in helping this project to get an early allotment of federal funds.

Colonel Sass devoted a lot of time to dealing with public utilities which wanted to furnish electricity for the REA groups. He worked out a contract with the Central Illinois Public Service Company for both the Eastern Illinois Power Cooperative and the Wayne-White County Electric Cooperative. The first contract with the Public Service Company of Northern Illinois was signed in Livingston county. The wholesale rate agreed to by the CIPS Co. was 1.2 cents per kilowatt hour, the lowest offered to any REA cooperative in the United States.

Late in 1937, the Rural Electrification Administration decided to furnish technical assistance to REA cooperatives direct from Washington, and Colonel Sass returned to his old job. The Illinois Agricultural Electric Company was later dissolved, but the IAA continued to foster rural electrification through both REA co-operatives and the public utility companies. By 1939, the Public Service Company of Northern Illinois had extended service to about 75 per cent of the farms in its territory. By 1940, the records show that the utility companies were serving 94,600 farms, while REA cooperatives were serving 29,800. In 15 years, the number of electrified farms had tripled!

There was a lull in construction during the war, but it zoomed again at the end of the war, when most of the activity was by the REA. The utilities serving northern Illinois already were serving about 90 per cent of the farmers in their areas, hence had little room for expansion. By the end of 1947, about 154,000 farms had been electrified, and the IAA was receiving very few requests for help in this field.

By this time, REA advocates were demanding federal money for building generating plants and transmission lines in Illinois. Charles B. Shuman, IAA president, made arrangements for top-level utility people and REA representatives to get together for negotiations. The result was that a number of REA groups bought their power from the utilities at new low rates, as low as nine mills per kilowatt hour. This did not quiet the clamor, however. In 1952, delegates to the IAA convention re-stated their position on the question in a resolution which reads, in part as follows: "In the event the cooperative companies are unable to obtain their power at a fair cost or if the generating or distributing capacity of their supplier is inadequate to meet their reasonably anticipated needs, the Association will support construction of cooperative generating plants and transmission lines. Funds for loans for such facilities should be made available. However, the loans should be made and such facilities constructed only when necessary to secure an adequate supply and distribution of power at reasonable rates and when the operation of such facilities appears to be economically sound and feasible."

The IAA position is still substantially the same as that outlined above. By the end of 1957, Illinois farms were about 98 per cent electrified, or had service available. The job appeared to be about complete, but knotty problems still arise. For example, many areas that were once distinctly rural are now suburban, and some even industrial. This situation leads to arguments between public utilities and REA cooperatives. If rural territory is annexed by a town or city, should it be served by the public utility serving the city, or by the REA cooperative which had been serving the farmers? IAA convention delegates stated their position in a resolution adopted at the 1962 convention. That part of the resolution dealing with this problem reads as follows: "To require the rural electric cooperative to discontinue service and to withdraw from these disputed areas, entered and developed by them in good faith, would impair the territorial integrity of the cooperatives and deprive them of revenue rightfully gained.

"We therefore direct the Illinois Agricultural Association to support legislation properly designed to protect the territorial integrity of rural electric cooperatives."

The position taken is crystal-clear. But more important issues have arisen: public power and the subsidy which the federal government grants REA projects through two-per cent loans. IAA President William J. Kuhfuss discussed these issues clearly and forcefully when he addressed the annual meeting of the Association of Illinois Electric Cooperatives on September 8, 1960, at Springfield. He said, in part: "The concern of farmers and the concern of most REA members is that of receiving good electric service at a reasonable rate. A few leaders in REA have seen fit to try to change the objectives and the purposes of REA and they seem to believe it their responsibility to fight for every public power project that comes before Congress . . . I do not feel that the purposes nor the aims of REA need to be changed. The Farm Bureau would like to see REA as a free enterprise cooperative, managed, owned and operated at the direction of farmers, and not to become a government-supported, subsidized public utility . . . I feel that it was not the intent nor the purpose of REA to operate as a general farm organization. I am opposed to a check-off being assessed to all REA patrons without consent to promote and, in many areas of legislation, to sponsor a lobbying service for farmers. I doubt that many farmers signed up with REA to get representation on legislation in fields unrelated to REA service. I also do not feel it is right that REA should be used as a vehicle for insurance or any other service other than that service of providing electricity and telephones to farmers, as was originally intended. These changes that have been made in the purpose, aims and attitudes of REA, in my opinion, have been at the direction of a few people and not at the direction of the farmers and patrons of REA.

"REA, at the start, had a justification to be under the arm of government. We needed government financing and had it not been so, the great improvement in American agriculture would have been stifled for many years. A two per cent interest rate was fair and realistic in the 1930's. We can be criticized if we insist that a two per cent interest rate is fair and reasonable on *new* loans today. The fact that some of your cooperatives are now purchasing the two-per cent government bonds, with surplus funds, is evidence that they recognize this fact . . ."

The issue discussed above—or rather two parts of one big issue—is not yet resolved, and is not likely to be decided quickly. There is a lot riding on how it is finally resolved—and the ultimate decision will be of great consequence, not only to farmers, but to every citizen.

Chapter 27

Cooperative Auditing

There were compelling reasons for the IAA to set up an auditing service. Since professional auditing companies must earn a profit, it was obvious that a cooperative auditing company could save money for its members by rendering service at cost. Further-more, laws under which cooperatives operate are rather complex, and auditors working only with cooperatives quickly develop into specialists in handling this type of accounting.

George R. Wicker, first manager of the Association, had had long experience with cooperatives. He hired and trained men who became specialists who could perform efficiently. In addition, his auditors soon acquired considerable knowledge of agriculture in general, which was helpful to them in dealing with and advising their member-clients, most of which in those days were farmers' elevators and county Farm Bureaus. Before the end of 1924, the Association had enrolled 112 member-clients, each for a three-year period. Fees were to be based on time and expense necessary for each audit, plus 10 per cent to go into a reserve fund.

In 1925, membership jumped from 112 to 185, and 189 audits were completed. Branch offices were opened in Springfield, Galesburg, and Champaign. The 1924 audits had required extra work because existing accounting procedures had to be changed in numerous cases. In 1925, so much less work of this kind was necessary that average fees were reduced some 20 per cent, a circumstance that did much to enhance the prestige of the association.

Wicker was much more than an accountant. His deep interest in, and knowledge of the cooperative movement enabled him to advise member-clients on how to qualify for income-tax exemption, as well as on many other aspects of cooperative laws. In fact, he headed a business service department of the IAA which undertook to provide counsel to county Farm Bureaus on business problems. He expanded the work of the Association to include development of uniform systems of accounting, income-tax work, reports for commercial agencies, inventories, appraisals, statistics, trade surveys, and even collections. All such services were available on a fee basis.

In 1926, a study of 65 farmers' elevator companies revealed weaknesses such as lax credit policies, unduly high operating costs, and various inefficiencies in a number of cooperatives. In a few cases, speculative grain operations resulted in heavy losses. Managers were advised of more economical methods, and warned that speculation should be shunned as a plague. If adequate insurance was not being carried, the manager was so advised. Members of cooperatives appreciated such service. Member clients increased from 185 to 212, and 273 audits were made. Average costs again went down.

By 1927, most member-clients renewed their three-year contracts, and others joined, lifting the number to 227. It was highly gratifying to Wicker and to IAA officials that great improvements had been brought about in the operating procedures of many cooperatives in three years. Wicker was also managing a new IAA business venture, the Illinois Farm Supply Company, which began business in March, 1927. It was arranged that each county member of "FS" must agree to use the IAA auditing service. This precaution did a great deal to safeguard these new county companies.

In 1928, the last year that Wicker managed the Association, he summarized the reasons why cooperatives failed, listing them in the order of their importance as follows: insufficient capital, inefficient management, indifferent administration.

In 1929, Wicker resigned to go into other work, and Fred E. Ringham, his assistant, succeeded him. The 265 audits made in 1929 disclosed the facts that the 233 member-clients had assets of over $15 million, and gross business amounting to more than $100 million.

In 1930, probably because tightening business conditions were forcing managers and boards of directors to take a sharper look at the financial condition of their institutions, 54 new member-clients joined the Association, and 303 audits were completed.

In 1931, the Association was reincorporated under the Illinois Cooperative Act of 1923, as a cooperative with capital stock, and was renamed the Illinois Agricultural Auditing Association.

In 1933, new burdens were placed on accountants by the advent of the first Illinois retailers' occupational tax and new federal taxes imposed by the National Industrial Recovery Act, later known as NRA. In 1934, a new record was made when 401 audits were completed.

By 1936, new developments in federal taxation had created so many more accounting problems that a lawyer and income-tax specialist, Clarence C. Chapelle, was added to the staff to counsel with member-clients on such problems. During that year, it was necessary to defend the interests of member-clients at 33 official hearings conducted by income-tax officials. With some $16,000 in taxes involved, settlements were reached by the end of the year, saving nearly $10,000 for member-clients, and with several cases still pending. The soundness of accounting methods employed was clearly vindicated.

The scope of the work of the Association was illustrated in the fact that during 1936, applications for exemption from income and capital stock taxes were filed on behalf of 35 agricultural cooperative associations. In 23 cases, exemption was granted, and in only three cases was exemption denied. As a result of the exemptions granted, claims for refunds on taxes previously paid brought refunds amounting to more than $4,000. In work of this kind, the Association was rendering service to cooperatives that was extremely valuable, service that few professional auditing companies could have rendered so effectively.

At the end of 1937, Fred E. Ringham resigned to accept a position with the St. Louis Bank for Cooperatives, and Clifford E. Strand came in as manager.

In 1938, the Association had to defend the interests of member-clients against Illinois revenue officials who had tried to impose occupational retailer taxes (sales taxes) on items that were really exempt under the law. In these actions, the Association was able to save some $10,000 for member-clients. Cases involving income-tax exemption were numerous too. One case was carried to the U.S. Board of Tax Appeals, which rendered a favorable verdict, saving the member-client about $3,000. Expert knowledge in this subject on the part of Association officials was paying off. Amount of money involved was not great, but precedents important to all co-ops were being set.

The Association was now twelve years old, and firmly established. It had come through the depression in good shape. John L. Baker, who retired from his position as field supervisor after 36 years of service, has called attention to an interesting fact with respect to farmers' elevators. He observes that most of the failures took place before the great depression. It was in the boom times of the late twenties that elevators got into trouble, times when a manager could get by with lax business methods. Then, when the boom ended, the manager was in for real trouble. The weak farmers' elevators were pretty well weeded out following 1929.

In Baker's opinion, many more elevators would have failed during this period were it not for the fact that directors of a goodly number of them had sensed difficulties ahead and had sought expert counsel after unfortunate experiences in the early years of their existence. It was too often true that such elevator companies started off without competent management, with poor accounting methods, lax credit policies, and dangerous fiscal policies. In many cases, a farmer, or the son of a farmer was hired as manager when he had practically no business experience. Some learned quickly, but many soon found themselves in trouble.

During the early years of its existence, the Association rendered a counseling service to companies asking for it. They followed the practice of making comparisons between elevators to show just why one business was prospering while another similarly situated was in trouble. Some board members took it as a personal affront when the truth about their business was revealed to them. When an elevator was in trouble because of years of poor business management, the first audits were costly affairs, for obvious reasons. Often boards had hired the manager because they could get him at a low salary, and they were outraged when they found out what expert auditing and counseling was going to cost them. Some member-clients pulled out of the association as a result. But those that faced the situation realistically made the necessary reforms and profited thereby.

It is probably true that most farmers who became stockholders in either cooperatives or stock companies in the early days did so with no proper comprehension of the hazards to be encountered in running the business. Many inexperienced men who became managers had only hazy ideas about the function of "hedging," which is common in the conduct of the business. Some such began to speculate in the name of the business and also on their own, with disastrous results. Some would lose money, and then try to recoup by taking greater risks, which led to greater disasters. Generally, in such cases, boards of directors were really at fault. Too many of them left all decisions to the manager, and seldom checked up on him. Invariably, trouble followed. In some cases, managers were actually dishonest, but incompetence was the usual cause of trouble.

In spite of the difficulties and disasters that have attended the cooperative movement in grain marketing, John L. Baker, after 36 years of intimate experience with it, believes that a true cooperative is the most satisfactory agency for handling grain in a community. It is better than a farmer-owned stock company, because all members share in the profits, if any. It also follows that the risk is equally shared.

On the record, it is apparent that the Association played a big part in bringing about improved practices in the businesses they audited. The counseling service rendered became very popular, which is evidence enough of its value. As the Illinois Farm Supply Company and the Illinois Grain Corporation grew, both companies began to furnish counseling service to their member companies, which relieved Illinois Agricultural Auditing Association of this responsibility. The Association now provides audit service to about half of the farmers' elevator companies in Illinois.

There is a widespread opinion that an audit report is a guarantee as to the facts set forth therein. This is definitely not true. A definition of an audit suggested by the American Institute of Certified Public Accountants indicates that an audit is rather the statement of an *opinion* rather than of fact: "An examination intended to serve as a basis for an expression of opinion regarding the fairness, consistency, and conformity with accepted accounting principles, of statements prepared by a corporation or other entity for submission to the public or to other interested parties."

Nevertheless, audits generally do reveal enough as to the facts concerning the business and its accounting procedures to permit appraisal of the alleged facts set forth in the accounts audited. As a matter of fact, in a small portion of the audits made each year, there is evidence of irregularities, including downright dishonesty on the part of manager or other employee. It is also true that not all irregularities are discovered. It is still possible for dishonest practices to continue for years before being discovered. This is true for businesses as firmly regulated as banks, and savings and loan associations; hence it is not surprising to find it true for farmer cooperatives. General Manager T. Melvin Holt of the Association says that it is simply impossible for an auditor to detect *all* dishonest practices. To uncover every one would require verification of so many transactions and records that the cost would be prohibitive. There are clever ways of covering up that will be successful for years, as bankers so well know. Holt agrees that so long as people are human, subject to all the weaknesses of our imperfect natures, there will be dishonest practices.

Without any question, accounting methods as well as business management of cooperatives have greatly improved over the years. With more skilled managers on the job, we get better performance than we did 30 years ago. Better management is one of the essentials to success nowadays, if for no other reason, because margins are generally lower than in the early days.

There must necessarily be more emphasis on volume today, according to Holt. He says that an elevator which could "get by" fairly well in a small community 30 years ago often finds it impossible to operate successfully today without finding some way to increase its business. There is an increasing number of county farm supply companies which absorb a local elevator, whether cooperative or not, and are able to run it as a part of the supply business quite successfully, when there is insufficient volume to support it as an independent business entity. As in all other businesses, the trend is toward bigger business units which make possible economies in overhead and other costs.

The Association itself has its own problems. One of the difficulties since the beginning has been the seasonal nature of the work, due to the fact that most member-clients operate with their fiscal year ending late in the year. Part-time auditors were needed during rush seasons, while the regular staff had a hard time keeping busy during May, June, and July. The problem has never been completely solved, but the situation was relieved in 1940, when member-clients agreed to cooperate by permitting auditors to come in during slack periods to do some preliminary work which otherwise would have to be done during the busy season. Branch offices were opened in Bloomington, Oregon, and Mount Vernon to improve service and efficiency. Thereafter, the work load was distributed more evenly throughout the year, with great accruing advantages.

The war years were years of great strain, what with experienced staff people leaving for military service with no replacements in sight, restrictions on purchase of equipment, increased demand for service—in short, the whole array of dislocations caused by war. (The time came when it was almost impossible to rent a typewriter, much less buy one.) Somehow, however, the work was turned out, and by war's end the Association had more member-clients than ever before, and was making more audits. In 1945, two key men were lost when Clarence C. Chapelle became controller, and Jay T. Nelson, chief accountant, for the IAA. By 1946, it was necessary to open a branch office in Peoria to take care of increasing business. In that year, 497 audits were completed. By 1948, there were 27 field auditors at work.

During the next few years, every effort was made to increase efficiency. Gradually, new districts were formed, with a field auditor living close enough to his work to enable him to return every night to his home.

By 1955, there were 14 districts, with one or two auditors living in each. This arrangement was quite helpful. Only 21 field auditors were employed, and 527 audits were completed for 500 member-clients. Furthermore, extra help employed was the smallest in many years. The staff had become stabilized too, about one-fourth of them having been with the Association for ten years or more. New office equipment enhanced the efficiency of office workers. Number of members remained stable. In his annual report for 1956, Manager Strand reported with pride that 56 of the first 110 member-clients were still using the service.

It is interesting to note that of 346 income tax returns prepared for member-clients in 1959, only 60 were for tax-exempt cooperatives. Total income-tax liability of the cooperatives audited was in excess of $1 million.

In 1960, Clifford E. Strand died after a lengthy illness, and T. Melvin Holt, Director of the School of Accounting of LaSalle Extension University, Chicago, succeeded him as general manager, after a few months during which the veteran field supervisor, John L. Baker, served as acting manager. Holt had had experience with cooperative enterprises in Oregon, where his father had been manager of such enterprises for many years. He earned his master's degree at the University of Oregon. Subject of his thesis was: "Oregon Cooperatives and Taxation."

In 1961, the Association moved its main office to the new building in Bloomington. The central location is a great advantage. A man can travel from Bloomington to almost any of the field offices, transact his business, and return the same day, as a rule. It's a great help to the offices in the southern part of the state to have the home office so much closer than it was in Chicago. Average distance of district offices from Chicago was 163 miles—from Bloomington, it is only 102 miles.

The Association is believed to be the largest of its kind in this country. Business transacted by its member-clients runs to around $350,000,000 annually. No effort is made to extend its operations beyond the field of farm cooperatives. It was set up to provide a specialized auditing service to farmer cooperatives, at cost, and for nearly 40 years it has carried out its mission most capably and efficiently. It has always upheld the high standards of auditing and the rules of professional conduct adopted by the American Institute of Certified Public Accountants. The fine service rendered has been a great asset to the farm cooperative movement in Illinois.

Chapter 28

Illinois
Fruit Growers' Exchange

The Illinois Fruit Growers' Exchange, founded at Centralia in July, 1921, was one of the first commercial ventures of the Farm Bureau in Illinois, as simply a sales agency for a few scattered cooperatives. All of the cooperatives except the Calhoun County Apple Exchange have disappeared, and now the exchange is a direct-membership organization of growers, plus the one remaining cooperative.

In the beginning, the fruit growers were generally small growers, with fruit just a sideline to their other farming activities. As time went on, the small growers either went out of business or enlarged their operations, and now the grower members are all "large" operators, with fruit production their main concern.

As individual businesses were expanded, demand naturally arose for cooperative purchasing of supplies. The business increased to such an extent that in 1935 a supply division was set up to furnish all necessary supplies, including spray machines, spray materials, packages, picking bags, pruning equipment, fertilizers, tray packs, and miscellaneous items including caps for pickers. This business now grosses in excess of half a million dollars annually. One of the spray rigs sells for $7,000.

In 1934, the Exchange moved to Carbondale, where the city turned over to it a building which it had on its hands. This building housed all Exchange activities until 1946, when it built its own storage facility. Eleven years later, quick-freezing equipment was installed. This has proved quite profitable.

Cool storage capacity is now 40,000 bushels. Peach sales each year will run from 75,000 to 135,000 bushels, and apple sales from 350,000 to 475,000 bushels. Apple production is expanding in the area, while peaches are losing ground.

The Exchange does no grading or packing, because each member has a business big enough to justify investment in packing machinery, and federal inspectors supervise the grading. Washing and sorting machines are standard equipment for most growers, and hydro-coolers to prepare apples for cool storage are coming into use.

Today's growers know that they will soon be out of business unless they change their practices to keep up with fast-changing conditions in the industry. The Exchange is a convenient clearing house for swapping ideas and experiences. You must be up on your toes at all times to keep up with changing consumer preferences. For example, The Arnold Brothers of Carbondale were the first to pack apples in consumer bags (1948). Most of the apples now sold are packed in cartons, trays, and "poly" bags. They have also developed and patented a fruit-sizer designed for the grower who has only a medium-size operation.

E. D. McGuire and his son Dan at Makanda use a good deal of homemade equipment, and they have developed a well-cushioned box for tree-ripened peaches that enables consumers to enjoy fruit that has been picked at just the right stage of maturity. The McGuires feel that growers simply must get their fruit to the consumer in practically perfect condition to enable the industry to survive and prosper. Nobody likes a peach that was picked before fully ripe so that it could withstand the rigors of shipping.

The Exchange keeps in close touch with horticulturists at the University of Illinois, so that up-to-date information on technical problems is always available. The insecticide or pesticide to use under existing conditions is a problem that experts are often helpful in solving, and the spray schedule is all-important. It is in constant contact with the chemical companies also, which is a big help.

The biggest factor in the entire deal, as far as members are concerned, is that they have their own selling agency. They can come in at any time and look at the records. Before the Exchange was established, growers were inclined to believe that they were more or less at the mercy of the commission men. With their own agency, staffed by men they have themselves selected, they learn the ins and outs of the business. They make the policies under which the Exchange operates. Marketing problems that were puzzling indeed to growers before they organized, were quickly clarified once the Exchange got under way. After they got into the business themselves, they at least were able to size up their problems with greater insight.

The many, many details incident to selling are looked after by the Exchange, to the great relief of the member. Matters involving transportation, credit, billing, and so on are much more easily handled by the organization than by the member, and the member appreciates it.

The records of the Exchange reflect many changes that have taken place in the fruit business during the past 40 years. For example, in 1934, no less than 110 carloads of pears were handled, while today the pear business has practically disappeared. Other areas, better suited to pear production, have taken the business away. Strawberry production has also gone. In 1933, the Exchange marketed some 20,000 cases, but today none are handled.

At various times, many projects have been tried out with no lasting results. In 1928, the IAA sponsored shipping peaches from the producing areas in carlots to Farm Bureaus in other counties, figuring that Farm Bureau members would be glad to patronize their fellow Farm Bureau members in the peach-growing counties; but the plan just didn't work out well. On another occasion, an attempt was made to encourage growers to set up roadside markets of their own, and some were set up on an experimental basis, but results were not too encouraging. And numerous attempts to get vegetable growers to form local cooperatives were made, with indifferent results.

At one time, the tomato business looked promising, so promising that grading and packing machinery was installed. In 1948, well over 20,000 cases of tomatoes were sold, and about as many up to 1951; but the business dropped off suddenly in 1952, and has never come back to any great extent.

The fruit business is truly risky. Rare is the year when a late spring freeze, a drouth or other disaster does not occur. Growers must accept these conditions as part of the business. Peach growers are resigned to the fact that at least one year in seven will be a year of no profit or maybe a loss. Any disaster puts a severe strain on the Exchange, and the management must be prepared to take steps to offset the loss. In 1955, the apple crop was ruined by a late frost. This emergency was met by buying apples from Virginia and Michigan and merchandising them in order to supply regular customers, minimize losses, and keep personnel employed. This is the sort of thing that keeps management on its toes, and the board of directors alert. The business is a fast-moving one in which only the quick are likely to survive.

Emergencies in this business can come with no warning. As an illustration, on VJ Day, when Lawrence L. Colvis was manager, peach picking was at its high point. A national holiday was proclaimed. The Exchange found itself with 64 carloads of peaches on hand, but unable to call by telephone a single customer, because all offices were closed. Here was a real emergency, and a quick decision had to be made. The refrigerator cars were loaded and started east, unsold. To make matters worse, a second national holiday was proclaimed for the following day. More peaches were ready and had to be picked. They were picked and put into refrigerator cars (67 this time), and started east. The next day, telephone wires buzzed with messages to eastern outlets, and the shipments were sold, without loss. In fact, sales were made readily at good prices, because the cars were well on their way at the time of sale, and those on the receiving end were delighted to get the peaches much sooner than they had expected to. Here was a situation in which fast and decisive action had to be taken, along with some risk, to avoid a great loss. The Exchange was able to meet the situation. It is at times like this that members appreciate the value of membership in the Exchange. What could a grower have done on his own in such a situation?

There simply are no fixed routines in the business of selling fruits. Ordinarily there is an interval after the peach crop has been sold in Arkansas, Georgia, South Carolina, and some other states, before Illinois peaches are ready. But in some seasons, the southern crop is late, and is still moving into market outlets when Illinois growers must begin picking. The Exchange is in close touch with day-to-day events, and is thus able to advise the member. It is situations such as these that cement the bond between grower and the selling agency. These are some of the reasons why the Exchange has survived for over 40 years, and why many members will tell you that they would not care to be in the fruit business if they didn't have it to sell their products for them.

It goes without saying also that the Exchange has had to render top-grade service to survive. Take the matter of machinery and orchard supplies. When the decision was made to enter this business, it was agreed that service equal to any other available must be supplied. It was agreed that repair service and an adequate supply of spare parts would be absolutely necessary. Reflecting this policy, the inventory of spare parts for sprayers today is one of the largest carried by any agency in the Midwest. The member can bring his equipment to the Exchange during the winter for overhauling, secure in the knowledge that his machine will be put back in shape and ready for another season's work when the time comes. Unquestionably, the high standards adhered to in this service have contributed greatly to the confidence of the member in his organization.

The Exchange demands that members discharge their responsibilities to their organization. There are times when attractive offers from outside are made for fruits produced by members. There have been times when such offers have been made deliberately for the purpose of luring the member away from his organization. To meet such situations, the member is asked to call the Exchange on such occasions, and if the price is higher than the agency can hope to get, the member is told to go ahead and make the sale; but the sale is considered as made by the Exchange, and the usual brokerage is paid by the member. With such arrangements in effect, buyers who hope to harass the Exchange soon get discouraged. They can't go on springing prices for very long.

Maybe one of the secrets of success of the organization is revealed in the 1922 report of Charles E. Durst, who was in charge of fruit and vegetable marketing for the IAA. The Exchange had been organized a year before, but the 1922 report covered the first full year's operations. Mr. Durst reported, in part, as follows:

"Previous to the past season, Illinois fruits were shipped largely to Chicago. Because of the large crop, the Chicago market was flooded most of the season with poorly graded products shipped by unorganized growers, and as a result prices ranged low. The exchange, in seeking the best markets possible for its members, distributed about 900 cars of products in 115 markets in 24 states . . .

"The standardization methods of the Exchange deserve particular mention. A number of local associations constructed packing houses in which modern sizing machinery was installed. The packing is done better and cheaper in such plants than by the average individual grower. Locals which had no packing houses installed inspection service at the receiving station. All standardization was in charge of the Exchange.

"As a result of the splendid spirit of cooperation on the part of members and local officers, the Exchange shipped a very fine quality of products. A number of buyers stated that the quality of Exchange products was the best shipped out of Illinois this season. Many favorable reports were received from the markets. The best grade of products was marketed under the Illini brand, which has been adopted by the Exchange."

Emphasis in those days was on organizing local associations, although membership in the Exchange was on an individual basis —with $5 annual dues, plus a note for $100 to guarantee working capital. One thousand members were signed up, and local units were set up in eight counties. Business covered a wide range of commodities, not only apples and peaches. In 1923, asparagus, cherries, cabbage, pears, potatoes, strawberries, tomatoes, and can fruits were marketed. In Alexander and Union counties, an alfalfa and truck growers' association was launched, a produce growers' association in Peoria, and an onion set association in Cook county, where some 85 per cent of all onion sets were produced. In addition the Exchange bought for Farm Bureau members in 54 counties no less than 201 cars of potatoes. As of today, as I have indicated, the business is pretty much apples and peaches, plus the quick-freezing business which has proved quite profitable.

The Exchange has probably been fortunate in its leadership, as well as in management. On the management side, following Durst, the names of A. B. Leeper, Harry W. Day, and Lawrence L. Colvis (who started September 15, 1941) stand out. The present manager, Matt Zilinskas, son of a coal miner in southern Illinois, worked on fruit farms during summer vacations, studied business administration in college, worked for a spray chemical company, and succeeded Harold Kaeser who had taken over for Colvis in 1952 when the latter left to manage the Illinois Livestock Marketing Association.

Among the officers and directors, a lot of names stand out, including Alvin O. Eckert and his son Cornell, Talmage Defrees, E. D. McGuire, Logan N. Colp, Harold E. Hartley, Dr. L. A. Floyd, William E. Sauer, and a number of others. Over the years, directors, all familiar with fruit grower problems through years of experience, have been quick to modify policies and practices to meet changing conditions, and have kept the Exchange on a steady course. It is the smallest organization among the IAA affiliates, but for the few members it means everything to their business. It has stood the test of time. It is a bright star, though small, in the firmament of IAA affiliates.

Chapter 29

Selling Grain

Since Illinois produces one-sixth of the U.S. corn crop, and one-tenth of the oats, and since Chicago ranks second only to Minneapolis as a grain market, it was entirely natural that the young Farm Bureau organization should turn to cooperative grain marketing for its members in the early twenties.

In previous chapters I have discussed that abortive enterprise, the U.S. Grain Growers, along with the failure of another attempt to form a huge grain marketing organization to be called the Grain Marketing Company.

In 1925, Chester C. Davis was hired to set up a grain marketing system, but he left soon to lead the Farm Bureau forces in Washington in the McNary-Haugen battle for surplus-control legislation. During his short stay with the IAA, Davis had actually brought about the incorporation of the National Farmers' Elevator Grain Company, and a subsidiary called the Rural Grain Company to handle grain on the Chicago market. When Davis resigned, the plan fell through, and in 1927 grain marketing activities were at a standstill.

It was not until October 1, 1928 that activities were resumed, this time under Harrison Fahrnkopf as director of grain marketing. Throughout 1929, work was confined to educational activities, plus organizing the Soybean Marketing Association (described in a previous chapter). In that same year, of course, came the Agricultural Marketing Act and the Federal Farm Board, and later the Farmers' National Grain Corporation, which was to act as the national sales agency for local or regional cooperatives.

The IAA immediately went to work and organized a statewide grain marketing agency, the Illinois Grain Corporation, which received its charter on February 17, 1930. Sale of stock was limited to *bona fide* cooperatives and to individual producers. Producers only could be named directors. Control was kept in Farm Bureau hands through the issue of "B" stock. This device, used in many IAA cooperatives, was later to become the focal point of serious disagreement, as will be seen later. A subsidiary, the Midwest Grain Corporation, was to handle actual sales, through memberships in the grain exchanges of Chicago, Peoria, and St. Louis. By December 31, 1930, forty-two farmer-owned elevator companies had tentatively agreed to go along, and Farm Bureau members began to think that at long last they had a grain marketing facility that would really work. Why not? The national administration was solidly back of cooperative marketing, and the Farm Board had at its disposal $500 million to use at its discretion to encourage co-op efforts and to stabilize farm prices.

From January to September, 1931, some 6 million bushels of grain had been sold through Midwest Grain Corporation. By that date, it was decided that there was no need for a sales agency, and that grain could move directly from Illinois Grain Corporation to Farmers' National. Midwest Grain Corporation was dissolved; and the manager, C. P. Cummins, became manager of Illinois Grain. Harrison Fahrnkopf remained as director of IAA grain marketing activities.

By 1932, membership in Illinois Grain had grown to 111 farmer-owned elevators, and about 14,500,000 bushels of grain were sold through Farmers' National. Net income before patronage dividends was reported as $39,262.04. The following year, membership grew to 149, but volume of grain handled increased only slightly, to 15,040,135 bushels, and net profits amounted to $25,160.72. In November, Mr. Cummins resigned, and Mr. Fahrnkopf became manager.

Membership grew to 175 in 1934, and volume of grain handled stood at 13,415,262 bushels. Farmers' National had grown to be the biggest grain marketing agency in the United States. In 1934, it built facilities at Peoria and Morris to handle barge shipments on the Illinois River. Farm Bureau officials believed that now they had available to farmers a complete grain marketing system, with their grain handled by their own agency.

Things went along pretty well until 1937, when it became apparent that Farmers' National Grain Corporation was washed up. This would leave Illinois Grain without a sales agency. Plans were made to meet the emergency, and early in 1938, Illinois Grain was reorganized. It took out memberships in the Chicago, Peoria, and St. Louis grain exchanges, and leased river elevators at Havana and Morris. Arthur E. Burwash of Champaign county was named president. Membership had dropped to 107 farmer-owned elevators and 44 Farm Bureaus. Frank Haines was named manager, and continued as manager until February 1947, when Howard McWard succeeded him.

In 1940, Harrison Fahrnkopf resigned as director of grain marketing and moved to his farm in Piatt county. The leased elevator at Morris was bought outright from the Farm Credit Administration, which had taken over the assets of the Farmers' National Grain Corporation in 1933. Illinois Grain many years ago signed a reciprocal agreement with Indiana Farm Bureau Cooperative Association, Inc., under which grain grown in Illinois but sold through the Indiana group is treated as member grain and earns the same patronage refund as Indiana grain. This arrangement has proved mutually satisfactory, and as these words are written the patronage refunds on grain shipped to the Indiana cooperative have amounted to several hundred thousand dollars.

In 1944, the Farmers' Grain Dealers Association of Iowa became a member of Illinois Grain and is a member today. Volume of Iowa business has never been large, but the arrangement seems to be mutually satisfactory.

The years up to the outbreak of the war in 1941 were uneventful, with IGC handling around 13 million bushels of grain annually. It was operating only as a commission and brokerage agency for its members, and officials believed that eventually they would have to go into merchandising, but the advent of the war made this step inadvisable at the time. Substantial additions were made to the surplus account, against the day when a terminal elevator would be established.

By 1944, IGC was handling 17 million bushels of grain, its surplus had grown enough to warrant paying patronage dividends for the first time. (Dividends of the preferred stock had been paid regularly.) It was decided to surrender exemption from income-tax payments which it had held. It was in sound condition. In 1945, volume rose to a new high of 25,000,000 bushels, and cash patronage dividends of $173,488.92 were paid.

In his report for 1947, Manager Frank Haines wrote: "The imposition of ceilings on grain and soybeans and the necessary regulations in connection therewith has made the last year the most difficult experienced by the grain trade." Nevertheless, it was decided that the time had come to go into grain merchandising, and the Illinois Grain Terminals Company was organized for the purpose of buying, storing, conditioning, mixing, blending, and reselling grain after it reaches the terminal market. It would use the services of IGC as a selling agency when the time came to sell. A lot of time was needed to sell stock in the new company, and it was not until June 1, 1949, that the first shipment of grain moved into the terminal elevator, the old Irondale structure with a capacity of 2.5 million bushels. The shipment came by barge from the Prairie Grain Company of Lacon. The day was considered to be a red-letter day for Illinois grain growers.

In 1949 also, the Illinois Grain Corporation undertook a new venture by setting up a supply division called Farmelco to furnish supplies, such as livestock and poultry feeds, seeds, fertilizers, steel products, and miscellaneous items to their member elevators. This service never proved profitable, and it was finally discontinued in 1961.

By 1950, IAA officials believed that Farm Bureau was on the way to real progress in grain marketing. The Havana River Grain Company, organized in 1947, was contributing a big volume of business, as was the Morris facility. In 1950, Illinois Grain Company volume rose to a new high of 32,661,372 bushels, and the Grain Terminals Company in its first full year of operation handled 7,964,373 bushels. During the year, it had bought the Morris facility. IGC paid patronage dividends of $264,269.29. Income taxes amounted to $16,721.34. Dollar volume of business was about $47 million.

But trouble was brewing. Dissension within the ranks looked ominous. It finally came to a head at the IGC annual meeting in St. Louis. The issue was "B" stock control. The dissident group felt that IGC should be controlled by its members, principally the local farmer elevator companies. As holder of the "B" stock, the IAA could vote in election of officers and in determining policies. After a long argument, the meeting adjourned far after midnight, with the IAA firmly in control. Not long after this, the dissident group centered in the cash grain area of east central Illinois, organized another grain company which is still in business. This development was unfortunate because it meant duplication of facilities, and further because it gave ammunition to those who belittle cooperative efforts, and who still maintain that "farmers won't stick together." However, there is no indication that Farm Bureau members generally want to eliminate the "B" stock control of IAA affiliates by Farm Bureau itself. Generally, they seem to feel that it is a wholesome thing for the parent organization to have at least that much control over the policies of its own affiliates.

Both IGC and IGT were steadily improving their facilities for greater efficiency and economy. In 1950, IGT had bought five new barges with a capacity of 40,000 bushels each to handle the increasing river traffic. As a result of an intensive membership drive by IAA, by the end of the year IGT was serving 93 member agencies. By 1951, IGT was operating in the black as a result of increasing volume to more than 11 million bushels. Fred J. Watts, Jr., who had started as a very young man in a local elevator and learned the business, was brought in as manager. (He was later to become manager of IGC, and to remain until 1962.)

There was more trouble ahead. Margins in the grain business had been steadily reduced, partly at least because of the additional competition of the cooperative agencies, and a bad year such as 1952 made tough going for everybody. Wet grain and poor quality of kernel were the main difficulties in 1952. An intensive study of the possibilities of achieving greater efficiency through merging Illinois Grain and Illinois Grain Terminals was made, and the evidence seemed to indicate that the merger should be made. The issue simmered until June 8, 1953, when a special meeting of Illinois Grain shareholders was held at Springfield. The dissident group, consisting of 21 elevator companies which had caused trouble in 1951, was adamant, and, by the time the meeting was held, had filed suit in the Champaign County Circuit Court to void the "B" stock held by the IAA. The meeting was a stormy one, and in an attempt to pour oil on the troubled waters, IAA officials offered to vote the "B" stock in favor of the merger, provided the majority of holders of preferred stock ("A" stock) voted that way, and to refrain from voting at all if the majority were against the merger. Attorneys for the dissidents refused the offer. The result was that the issue continued to simmer until the court case was settled.

Illinois Grain Terminals was on shaky ground, in the red, in fact. Shareholders met November 10 in Peoria and approved a plan to recapitalize, under which one share of "A" stock with a par value of $100, would be exchanged for a new share with a par value of $25 and a debenture note for $75, to be repaid in 20 years. Dividends on "A" stock were reduced from 6 per cent cumulative to 4 per cent non-cumulative. The company came through the year with a good financial showing. The shoals on which it might have foundered were avoided. Mr. J. O. McClintock, who had just finished a 5-year term as executive vice president of the Chicago Board of Trade, became a vice president of Terminals on January 1. He was in charge of merchandising, and his astute merchandising skills were credited in large part for the improved financial results during the year. The reduction in interest charges through recapitalization had a very wholesome effect in 1954, and another good year was recorded. The troublesome matter of the dissident members was finally settled without going through the courts. Stock owned by the dissidents was bought back by the Corporation, and the owners immediately set up a new cooperative and hired Harrison Fahrnkopf to run it. Such developments are bad for the cooperative movement, but they probably will continue to occur. Men of great integrity will continue to differ with other men of integrity in all lines of business, and cooperative business is no exception.

The long-awaited integration of IGC and IGT came about in 1955. In March, IGC shareholders voted almost unanimously for the merger, and on April 6, shareholders of IGT voted practically unanimously in favor. The merger became effective on June 6. Terminals bought the stock of IGC and adopted its name after taking complex legal steps required by law.

Facilities of the merged companies included the Irondale terminal elevator and sub-terminal elevators at Morris, Hennepin, Lacon, and Havana, and member elevator companies numbered about 177. It looked like a good set-up. Otto Steffey, who had succeeded Charles B. Shuman as IAA president, congratulated officials of both organizations for taking this vital step, and he added: "We shall have some transitional problems . . . but we hope that before long, Illinois Grain Corporation may be one of the leading regional grain cooperatives in the entire country."

The new IGC moved ahead quickly. It made arrangements to lease a new 6.5 million bushel terminal elevator to be built by the Chicago Regional Port Authority, and completed a new 160,000 bushel elevator at Tampa, Florida, to serve as an outlet for Illinois grain in that rapidly growing market. Fred J. Watts, Jr., was named vice president and general manager, and Howard

369

McWard assistant general manager and vice president. J. O. McClintock was named vice president in charge of grain marketing. Louis Hertel of St. Clair county was elected president.

Financially, the Corporation did well in 1955, and much better in 1956, the first full year of operation after the merger. New problems had to be faced almost constantly in this fast-moving business. In the annual report of the manager, we find the statement: "During the year grain operations were probably as near to normal as they can be in this era of government domination of the general agricultural economy and the grain trade." And further: "During much of the fiscal year corn business, particularly in the export field, was almost completely dominated by Commodity Credit Corporation." One begins to wonder about a situation when farm cooperatives, which have been encouraged by the federal government, begin to complain about government interference in the business of cooperatives. You wonder if eventually the government won't completely dominate grain marketing, with all business done at fixed prices and fixed margins.

By 1957, the new elevator, called the Gateway Elevator, came into use. The old Irondale facility was sold. Additional grain silos were built at Morris and Dallas City, giving IGC total elevator capacity of 7,750,000 bushels. During fiscal 1958, no less than 42 million bushels of grain were handled. The next year, volume increased to 52 million bushels. Still IGC was not doing the job that its management wanted it to do. In fact, it was implied several times in official reports that the Corporation needed double the facilities available for the kind of job that should be done. The handwriting was plain on the wall. Small companies were being forced out of business. The big, integrated business seemed to be the only kind that could survive in such times. The premium was on skilled merchandising. IGC joined other cooperatives to form the Producers' Export Company to push foreign sales.

By 1961, one badly needed facility was completed at Naples, to add 300,000 bushels of elevator space. Another project, long contemplated, that of building an elevator on the Chain-of-Rocks canal to handle business in the St. Louis area, was pushed ahead, but was still far from realization.

In 1961, well over 53 million bushels of grain were handled; but it was a situation, too familiar in these times, which might be summed up tersely in four words: "Volume up; profits down." The Corporation was actually losing money. The time had arrived when painful adjustments had to be made. The board of directors faced the situation realistically; made the changes that seemed to be necessary; and reiterated its conviction that the grain marketing problems *can* be solved.

The first step in tightening up the operations of the Illinois Grain Company was taken when Merrill D. Guild, who retired on April 30 from long service to the grain division of the Indiana Farm Bureau Cooperative Association, which has been notably successful, was made general manager. He had back of him 24 years of experience in the cooperative marketing of grain. The son of a farmer and a country grain elevator operator, he practically grew up in the grain business.

The annual report of the corporation for the year ending May 31, 1963 was most encouraging. During the previous fiscal year, 54 million bushels of grain were handled, and the net loss on the year's operations was $26,564.00. At the end of the 1962-63 fiscal year, after ten months under the new management, volume handled rose to 76 million bushels, and earnings before deductions for patronage refunds and income taxes amounted to $307,067. This remarkable change in only one year indicates as nothing else can the possibilities of the business. Everett E. Glasgow, president of Illinois Grain, is now confident the crisis that confronted the company has been safely passed, and a new era of improved grain marketing service lies ahead. On August 1, Loren Daily, who had been assistant general manager, was promoted to general manager, and Mr. Guild was advanced to the position of executive vice president.

Chapter 30

Selling Milk

Arthur D. Lynch succeeded Professor Chris Larsen as director of dairy marketing in 1922. He energetically carried on the projects already started, principally in the field of bargaining associations for producers of whole milk and butterfat, and he did considerable work with small, farmer-owned cheese factories in the northern part of the state, and with farmer-owned creameries and milk-distributing plants.

Since some three-fourths of the dairy production in Illinois was sold as whole milk, a lot of work was done helping farmers in the big city milksheds to organize bargaining associations. The first to get into operation was at Peoria in 1926, when the Illinois Milk Producers Association secured dealer recognition amicably. It has continued to render service in that market to this day.

After years of bitter controversy, the Pure Milk Association in the Chicago milkshed won recognition from the milk distributors in 1929. Membership was above 8,000 at the time, and as it proved its effectiveness, it came to include some 80 per cent of the producers in the area. Soon after the first Agricultural Adjustment Act of 1933 was signed by President Roosevelt, the Pure

Milk Association applied for a license and marketing agreement. Although there was never full compliance on the part of the milk dealers, the license remained in existence until the AAA was declared unconstitutional by the courts. From that time until late 1939, there was no government regulation in the Chicago market at which time the federal milk marketing order was issued which is still in effect. By the terms of this order, the USDA establishes minimum producer prices on milk.

In the St. Louis area, the Sanitary Milk Producers, sponsored and largely financed by the IAA, was organized over bitter dealer opposition. In 1929, it had 3,300 members, and success was assured. In 1930, Lynch resigned his IAA position to become manager of the St. Louis cooperative. He left with the satisfaction of knowing that the two big milksheds in Illinois were well organized. Also, the Illinois Milk Producers Association at Peoria, with Wilfred Shaw as manager, was a conspicuous success; as was the McLean County Milk Producers Association at Bloomington, under Forrest C. Fairchild. The Champaign County Milk Producers was marketing more than 80 per cent of the milk used in Champaign and Urbana. Dairymen whose product went to condensaries were dissatisfied with conditions, and were starting to organize.

Lynch became manager at St. Louis in time to go through the hardest fight in the history of Sanitary Milk Producers. Members scorned the contract offered by the Pevely Dairy Company, the biggest St. Louis distributor, and Sanitary finally called a milk strike. Sanitary officials called on members to come to St. Louis to tell their story to consumers. Members responded wholeheartedly. When they arrived, each day, they were taken to residential areas to make house-to-house calls to tell the facts regarding the controversy directly to housewives. This plan proved highly successful, and soon the producers had a lot of consumers on their side. Many distributors signed contracts acceptable to producers, and the strike ended. Pevely, however, still held out, and did not come to terms until 1933. It was a rough experience, but it did a lot to strengthen the morale of the producers. and from that time on, things went better. At that time, the president of the cooperative was the late Ed W. Tiedeman, who later managed a big dairy cooperative in Wisconsin, headed for a time the dairy section of the USDA, and still later did work in the dairy field for the American Farm Bureau Federation.

There were other battles between producer and distributor. In the Moline-East Moline-Rock Island-Davenport area, producers organized the Quality Milk Association, but distributors refused to recognize the Association as bargaining agent. The producers bought a creamery, and for 60 days separated the cream and made butter. Then, the Sturtevant Ice Cream Company, which was in sympathy with the producers, started distributing for the producers, and farmers came to town to solicit business among consumers on behalf of Sturtevant, who was offering consumers a real bargain. This brought the distributors into line (all but one) and they signed a contract.

In Bloomington, members of the McLean County Milk Producers, aware that 75 per cent of their milk was surplus above whole-milk needs, organized the Farmers Creamery Company, built a butter-making plant, and handled their own surplus so that they would be in a better bargaining situation with respect to milk distributors.

In 1933, milk producers around Danville, with IAA help, organized the Danville Milk Producers Association, but distributors refused to recognize the Association, and refused to buy milk produced by leaders of the movement. The Association retaliated by leasing an old, inoperative plant which had been the Blue Banner Dairy, and started retail delivery, adding a new gimmick by setting up cash-and-carry dairy depots which attracted a lot of business.

In Peoria, the Peoria Milk Producers (formerly the Illinois Milk Producers Association), as the outcome of a strike by producers against dealer discrimination against members of the Association, organized the Peoria Producers Dairy, bought a plant, and soon had to buy another to handle the increasing business in bottle milk and ice cream mix.

375

In the Quad-Cities area, when a full-scale milk price war broke out, the Quality Milk Association called in officials of the Agricultural Adjustment Administration for an investigation. As a result, the area obtained a Milk Marketing Order, with a market administrator to handle the program. Uniform producer prices were established, and the war ended.

By 1935, farmer-owned milk distributing plants were in operation in Quincy, Springfield, Peoria, Danville, and Harrisburg. In August of that year, Wilfred Shaw, at the invitation of IAA President Earl C. Smith, left his job as manager of the Peoria Milk Producers and Prairie Farms Creamery (Peoria) to become director of milk marketing for the IAA. He helped to organize more bargaining associations and bottle milk plants, and by 1941, the Illinois Milk Producers Association, a federation of milk cooperatives, had a membership of 17 bargaining associations (including those at Chicago and St. Louis), and six distributing associations. Volume of milk handled rose to 1,938,571,684 pounds, worth $38,300,977.06.

The war years were years of feverish activity. Priority was given to production of cheese and evaporated milk. In 1942, cheese output in Illinois went up 38 per cent over 1941, and volume of evaporated milk increased 24 per cent. This put a severe strain on dairy plants, not only in securing equipment, but also in meeting specifications for the products. Some cheese plants could not meet specifications.

During these war years, the dairy industry faced rationing, controlled prices, and restriction on truck mileage on delivering milk. The Office of Price Administration had fixed milk prices at unrealistic levels and a system of subsidies was arranged to reimburse producers who could not produce milk at a profit so it could be sold at the ceilings which had been established.

At the end of the war, price ceilings were maintained until June 30, 1946. Prices then advanced, but returns to farmers were not materially increased, since feed subsidies were discontinued. On June 15, Wilfred Shaw left the IAA to become the first director of the dairy department created by the American Farm Bureau

Federation. Emery E. Houghtby succeeded him, to be followed by Judson Mason, who served until 1957. Milk prices rose to the highest on record in the fall of 1946. In 1947, value of milk marketed through the Illinois Cooperatives rose to an all-time high of $97,569,761.28.

In 1944, in response to the needs of members, the Illinois Milk Producers Supply Company was organized, with Wilfred Shaw as manager, to purchase equipment and supplies for the cooperatives. In 1945, its sales totaled $43,631.03. However, a huge program of rebuilding was undertaken by member cooperatives, and sales soared. In 1948, sales amounted to $617,870.41. Annual sales later rose to more than $1,000,000; but 10 years later, due to mergers among cooperatives and changes in buying practices, business had declined to such an extent that the company was liquidated.

Sweeping changes in the entire dairy manufacturing and distribution field, including mergers of cooperatives, have been reflected in the operations of the Illinois Milk Producers Association. Bargaining power of producers and their local cooperatives has been greatly reduced since the war by mergers and concentration of sales in large units. Chain stores and supermarkets have had a heavy impact on the business. Membership in IMPA shrunk to 13 associations, compared to 23 through the war years. Work of the Association now consists largely of keeping tab on legislation affecting dairy farmers and the dairy business, supporting dairy promotion plans, keeping a watchful eye on developments in the field of federal marketing orders, and doing everything possible to coordinate activities of member associations. The affairs of the Association for the past 12 years have been supervised by a secretary-treasurer named by the board of directors. In recent years the dairy marketing economist of the IAA, Mr. L. K. Wallace, has served in that capacity.

The big bargaining associations, and all going strong, are the Pure Milk Association, Chicago; the Sanitary Milk Producers Association, St. Louis; the Mississippi Valley Milk Producers Association in the Quad-Cities area; the Peoria Milk Producers; and the Midwest Dairymens Association at Rockford.

Chapter 31

Selling Butterfat

In his report for 1927, Frank A. Gougler, who was in charge of produce marketing for the IAA, pointed out that, "poultry, eggs and cream are at present marketed in a less efficient manner than perhaps any other farm commodity." Mr. Gougler stated further: "The present system of marketing places a premium on carelessness and hinders tremendously the development of the industry." It was the responsibility of the farmers' organization, he implied, to develop a plan under which cream and eggs particularly, could be sold on a graded basis, so that the man who produced top-quality products could be rewarded.

Gougler had investigated cooperative activities in Minnesota and California which seemed to be making excellent progress. He reported: "Producers from those states are rewarded for special effort in producing a quality product. The produce from Illinois comes directly into competition on our terminal markets with the high quality product from these other states, and unless we improve our quality in a like manner we must be satisfied with lower prices for our produce."

Farm Bureau members were deeply interested. As early as 1924, a bargaining association had been organized at Paxton, and by 1927 there were 11 such associations in operation. Cream was sold by the association, on tests made by the association managers. Object of the associations was to increase bargaining power through greater volume, and to improve quality. Some of the associations handled as much as 75,000 pounds of butterfat annually, with handling charges to the farmer of less than 3 cents a pound, while small private cream station charges ranged up to 5 cents. With Illinois butterfat production amounting to 62,544,000 pounds in 1926, it was apparent that great savings could be made if farmers pooled their efforts. There were 4,000 private cream stations operating in Illinois, and Gougler estimated that 500 farmer-owned stations could handle all of the business, provided only that farmers would get together on the project. It was an exciting prospect, particularly in view of the fact that some of the larger associations were keeping their handling costs below two cents a pound.

The work was pushed vigorously in 1928, and by the end of the year there were 28 bargaining associations in operation, handling well over 2,000,000 pounds of butterfat. Some of them were handling eggs and poultry, in addition to butterfat. Volume practically doubled in 1929, and Farm Bureau members became so enthusiastic that it was an easy matter to get approval for the creation of the Illinois Produce Marketing Association on November 6, 1929, at a state-wide meeting in Decatur. The stock setup followed the pattern which had become standard for IAA cooperatives: 30,000 shares of Class "A" preferred stock at $25 a share to provide working capital; 75,000 shares of common stock (no par value) to be issued to member associations, and 150,000 class "B" preferred (no par value) to the IAA to insure Farm Bureau control. No stock was to be sold until 15 counties had joined the state association, and the state association was to be financed by a one-per cent deduction from gross sales. By the end of the next year, 1930, 31 of the 37 local associations then operating had joined the state association, and volume rose to nearly

5 million pounds. Thirty creameries contracted to buy the pooled butterfat.

The next year was a tough one. In addition to the usual difficulties of a new organization the Association had to face, during the period of June 1, 1930, to March 31, 1931, the price of butter fell from around 40 cents a pound, to 21 cents. The Association had 49 county produce associations as members, and gross sales amounted to $722,905.00.

Continued difficulties with butterfat buyers throughout 1932 resulted in another step which was bound to be taken, sooner or later. The Association was reorganized, in January, 1933, to become the Illinois Producers Creameries, a sales organization for its members. Butter-making plants built by local capital or plants already in operation were taken in as members in Bloomington, Peoria, and Davenport. Additional plants were planned and promoted for Champaign, Olney, Mt. Sterling, and Carbondale. John B. Countiss, director of dairy marketing for the IAA, was named as manager and also acted as sales manager of Illinois Producers Creameries. Before the year ended, "Prairie Farms" butter was being sold to some 500 stores, restaurants, and hotels, and was becoming quite popular. Quality standards were strictly adhered to, under a federal butter grader's supervision.

In 1934, creameries were started at Champaign and Olney, and in 1935, plants came "on stream" at Carbondale, Galesburg, and Mt. Sterling. Volume of butter produced rose to 6,106,929 pounds. In 1936, a premium of one cent a pound was announced for grade "A" cream, as an inducement to the producer to take better care of his cream at home (during certain seasons, two cents). A central cutting and packaging plant was established in Chicago to serve all member creameries. Almost from the beginning, creamery supplies were bought cooperatively. This business amounted to more than $60,000 in 1936. A new Producers creamery was opened at Carlinville in 1937.

Producers Creameries were going great guns by 1941 when volume went up to 7,346,721 pounds of butter. Constant emphasis on quality had increased the production of 92-score butter. The brand name "Prairie Farms" was well established. World War II brought many problems. War demand was not so much for butter as for dried milk and cheese. The creameries at Galesburg, Mt. Carmel, Olney, and Mt. Sterling all installed roll dryers, which meant that the creameries would have to buy considerable whole milk, and less cream. The Moline plant, the Quality Milk Association (which had been moved there from Davenport), put in cheese-making equipment.

In 1943, 6,452,743 pounds of butter were churned, 1,348,040 pounds of powdered milk, and 202,170 pounds of cheese were produced. A good share of all these products had to be set aside for government use. This year marked the beginning of a fundamental change in the manufacturing business. Once farmers got started selling whole milk, few of them wanted to go back to selling cream. In 1944, production figures were: butter, 6,722,453; milk powder, 2,577,083; and cheese, 233,740 pounds. It was a very prosperous year. No salesmen were needed. It was a case of rationing the regular butter customers, while half the production went to war purposes. In 1945, production of milk powder went up 47.12 per cent, and that of cheese, 147 per cent. Profits nearly doubled. Farmer owners had more than $1,000,000 invested in their manufacturing facilities.

On June 28, 1945, the name of the cooperative was changed to Prairie Farms Creameries, with John B. Countiss who had been manager since 1943, continuing in charge. Frank Gougler had been named manager of the Illinois Cooperative Locker Service which had been set up in 1940. Countiss remained as general manager of Prairie Farms until 1946, when he resigned to accept a position with a hybrid seed corn company. He was succeeded by David H. Henry, who served for more than a year, after which Forrest C. Fairchild, who had managed the Prairie Farms plant at Bloomington for many years, took over.

By this time, it was apparent to everybody that the dairy industry was undergoing a basic change. In 1947, for example, Prairie Farms sold 7,672,325 pounds of butter, for a new record, but it also produced 5,068,142 pounds of powdered milk. Instead of separating the cream from the milk at the farm, producers were now selling whole milk. (The Federal Government was buying huge quantities of powdered milk in order to maintain the price support level.) Furthermore, the price support of butter was so high that people were turning more and more to butter substitutes. Also, demand for cream for ice cream mix was increasing. On top of all this, producers in the big city milksheds were operating under federal milk marketing agreements and orders and producing huge surpluses which had to be converted to other than whole-milk uses. All of these factors confronted the cooperative creameries which had rendered such great service to Illinois farmers for so many years. Officials of the Bloomington unit of Prairie Farms took a realistic view of the situation and met it by merging their unit with the McLean County Milk Producers Association to form the Prairie Farms Creamery of Bloomington. It was an economy move, as both plants were almost entirely on a whole milk basis, and there was no good reason for continued duplication of effort. Both organizations had the same management for years, anyway.

In 1950, Prairie Farms sold $17,095,063.83 worth of dairy products for some 20,000 farmers. Of the 15,735,638 pounds of butterfat received from farmers, only 3,577,638 came is an farm-separated cream. The milk and cream received was sold in the form of bottled milk, cream, fluid by products, cottage cheese, ice cream, ice cream mix, dried milk, cheddar cheese, condensed buttermilk, butter, and other products. The member companies, originally set up mainly to convert cream into buttter, had been forced to increase investments by huge amounts to enlarge plants and buy equipment needed to manufacture products other than butter. By 1950, member companies had more than $3 million invested, with costs going up rapidly. All were faced with a real cost-price squeeze.

In spite of the recognized hazards, a new plant was built at Carlyle in 1950, and it began receiving whole milk for the St. Louis district. It had no manufacturing facilities, but did distribute fluid milk, ice cream, cottage cheese, and butter processed by

Prairie Farms Creamery at Carlinville. It never had enough volume to operate efficiently, and was taken over by the Carlinville creamery on lease within a few years.

By 1955, it was evident that only dairy plants with a huge volume of business could carry on under the changed conditions. In 1955, Danville Producers Dairy bought Prairie Farms Creamery of Champaign. A little later, operations at Carlinville, Carbondale, Olney, and Carlyle were consolidated under the name Prairie Farms of Southern Illinois. Prairie Farms of Bloomington bought Prairie Farms of Henry, and then sold out its entire business to Pure Milk Association of Chicago. Quality Milk Association of Moline bought Prairie Farms of Mt. Carroll and resigned its membership in the state association. Prairie Farms of Galesburg gave up entirely and leased its facilities to Sugar Creek Creameries. Prairie Farms Creameries became a non-operating company on January 1, 1958, with its responsibilities limited to control of the "Prairie Farms" trademark, quality standards, and matters of mutual interest among the remaining members—Prairie Farms of Southern Illinois, Prairie Farms of Western Illinois, Danville Producers Dairy, and Pure Milk Association (Bloomington).

The small dairy had become a victim of changing times, changing food habits, government price-fixing, lack of volume (in some cases), and even poor business judgment in a few cases. The setup was simply inadequate to cope with modern conditions, and changes had to be made. Facilities at eight locations are still farmer-owned, since the original stockholders exchanged their stock for stock in the larger units; but in cases where creameries ceased to operate or were sold to non-farm interests, considerable losses to stockholders were incurred. Again it had been demonstrated that in any business, cooperative or corporate, alert and progressive management is all-important. It is possible that, generally speaking, a cooperative is likely to be reluctant to make the changes necessary to keep up with changing conditions. Once again, too, experience has proved that in today's fast-moving and rapidly-changing business world there is small place for the outfits that are slow in coming to a decision on matters of policy. Those that refuse to face realities find themselves far back in the procession.

Following the current trend toward consolidation for greater volume, the three Producers companies in Carlinville, Mt. Sterling, and Danville were merged on February 28, 1962 to form Prairie Farms Dairy, Inc., as an IAA affiliate with headquarters at Springfield. The new company has annual gross sales of more than $18 million, and a net worth of about $4.5 million. It serves more than 2,000 dairy farmers in the southern half of Illinois.

The well-meant efforts of government agencies to fix farm prices have disrupted normal patterns in production and marketing to a degree not realized by most people. Through marketing orders, government has raised prices to producers in the city milk sheds. These prices have led to over-production, hence surpluses of whole milk have to be diverted to other uses. This has resulted in rough competition with producers outside the milk sheds for markets for ice cream mix, cottage cheese, milk powder, and other products. With prices for most of these products supported by government, surpluses could be sold to government agencies which use them for school lunches, foreign aid, barter deals with other governments, and so on. So, we have the curious situation of U.S. citizens reducing their consumption of butter because of high prices, while government buys it to give away or sell it at great loss. The whole business thus rests on a wholly artificial underpinning. How long such a situation can endure is anybody's guess; but one thing is certain, and that is that sooner or later, if we continue on the present course, every farmer will be licensed, so to speak, to produce his own limited share of farm commodities.

Of all the business ventures attempted by Farm Bureau, the cooperative marketing of eggs was probably the most unrewarding, the most baffling, the most frustrating. In the first place, egg production in the early days was a minor adjunct to the farm business, and little thought or energy was put into it, as a rule. Flocks were small, which meant that it was impractical to take eggs to market while they were in top condition. There were no good storage facilities on most farms, hence eggs deteriorated quickly. Few farm products went to market in worse condition than eggs.

When Frank A. Gougler was in charge of produce marketing for the IAA, he worked long and hard to develop more efficient marketing practices, and in a number of counties, Farm Bureaus sponsored marketing projects. The various Producers creameries became interested, and in late 1936, the Producers Creamery at Olney made elaborate preparations to market eggs for members in large enough volume to achieve substantial savings in handling charges and to warrant paying for eggs on a grade basis.

Frank Gougler had the problems well-analyzed. He knew the pitfalls ahead, and he realized fully that real money could be returned to producers only if they produced eggs of highest quality. In the counties to be served, some 1,800 carloads of eggs were produced annually. If, through closer attention to quality standards, the average price could be raised five cents a dozen, it would result in increased returns of a million dollars. Studies had revealed that only 40 per cent of the eggs then being marketed graded "extra," 40 per cent as "standard," 19 per cent as "trades," and 1 per cent "checks and cracks." Frank hoped that once the project was under way, members would improve quality to the point that 60 per cent of the product would be top grade.

On paper, it looked like an attractive proposition, and a feasible one, but it just didn't work out. During the months of March and July, volume was disappointing, and a check revealed that only 12.4 per cent of the eggs received graded "extra." So disappointing was the experience, that it was decided that in the future eggs would be marketed only for producers who would meet rather rigid requirements. Producers would have to become, in effect, professional poultrymen. This program apparently never got off the ground, since it isn't even mentioned in the annual report of the produce marketing department for 1938.

The IAA was not the first farm organization to stub its toe on this problem. Farm Bureaus in many states had lost heavily on similar ventures. During the days of depression, a great deal of federal money was loaned to egg marketing cooperatives, but few indeed were successful. Those which did succeed were invariably those in which membership was largely among poultrymen with large flocks, producing eggs of highest quality. Vexatious marketing problems caused countless farmers to get rid of their poultry flocks. It's quite likely today that the average cornbelt farmer can buy his poultry and eggs more cheaply than he can produce them himself. The situation reminds one of the disappearance of the apple orchard on farms. One cannot afford to maintain an orchard for family use today. These developments are a part of the trend toward specialization and big units of production. It is only the turkey grower with a big flock who can make money out of turkeys. Therefore, we might say that the problem of egg marketing has not been licked, but it has been eliminated by developments in the industry itself.

One of the cooperative projects undertaken by the IAA produce marketing department was the Illinois Locker Association, first organized in 1940 as the Illinois Cooperative Locker Service. It failed to fulfill the bright prospect that loomed for the frozen food industry twenty years ago.

Locker service was very much in demand during World War II. About 40 cooperative local associations, operating 104 plants, were members of the state association. But as costs increased after the war, revenues failed to increase in proportion, and it was soon apparent that many were headed for trouble.

Most locker plants never did charge enough for services, and if they had, it is unlikely that they could have survived anyway, because freezer compartments in the home refrigerator began to replace the rented locker. The handwriting was plain on the wall. The Association continued to be fairly active until 1956, but within two years it became inactive, and remains today simply to provide group insurance to members.

Chapter 32

Maintaining Animal Health

When the Farm Bureau movement was young in Illinois, one of the big problems of hog producers was hog cholera. Immunization was a new thing in those days, and veterinarians who were experienced in administering serum and virus were few and far between. A number of farm advisers had learned the technique at the University, and they undertook to teach farmers how to do the job themselves.

The first venture into cooperative buying of serum and virus of which we have any record was undertaken by the Hancock County Soil Improvement Association on May 22, 1915, less than a year after it was organized. The association bought serum that year, and farmers vaccinated their own hogs. When J. H. Lloyd became farm adviser early in 1916, he made hog vaccination a major project. He vaccinated thousands of hogs himself, and trained hundreds of farmers to do it themselves.

Other farm advisers were active too. For example, the farm adviser's report in Rock Island county filed November 30, 1919, records the following:

"Work in diagnosing and recommendations for treatment of hog diseases along with the work of giving instructions to Farm Bureau members in how to properly vaccinate their own hogs for Hog Cholera has taken more than half the time of one man since July 1st." Number of hogs vaccinated was listed as 4,013.

By 1924, Farm Bureau members were clamoring for a method of pooling the serum business of the various counties through the IAA. IAA officials responded by setting up the Illinois Farm Bureau Serum Association, which received its charter on March 21, 1924. Forty-six county Farm Bureaus joined. Four others which were in the business stayed outside, but the project was a success from the start, and by 1930, membership had risen to 71 county Farm Bureaus, which used more than 30 million cc. of serum and virus. The Farm Bureaus appreciated the advantages of a state-wide organization, not only because of the added bargaining power due to volume purchases, but also because of the higher quality standards that could be enforced by the state organization. Directors of the organization the first year were: R. A. Norrish of Morrison, L. F. Boyle of Hennepin, O. B. Goble of Charleston, J. H. Lloyd of Carthage, Sam Sorrells of Raymond, J. W. Gillespie of Lawrenceville, and C. A. Stewart of the IAA.

As vaccination of hogs became common practice, veterinarians began to complain about farmer vaccination. Many contended that it was dangerous to have untrained farmers handling serum and virus, and quite a campaign was carried on to get a law on the statute books limiting the practice of vaccination to qualified veterinarians. The subject became a hot issue, but such a law was never enacted, and eventually good feeling was restored between the veterinarians and Farm Bureau.

The value of a state-wide organization was demonstrated in 1926, when severe outbreaks of cholera caused demand for serum and virus to skyrocket. In this emergency, the same suppliers stood by the IFBSA, honoring its orders at the regular price, when they could have sold to others at greatly enhanced prices.

In 1931, volume went up to a new record, 49,321,245 cc. of serum and virus, enough to immunize 1.5 million hogs. It was estimated that the saving through quantity purchases was at least 20 cents per hundred cc., therefore Illinois farmers may have saved as much as $100,000 in one year on this deal. Ray E. Miller was managing the Association, as part of his job as director of livestock marketing.

On April 13, 1931, the Association took another step forward by reincorporating under the Illinois Agricultural Cooperative Act, to give it all the rights and privileges of a true cooperative. By 1932, the financial condition of the Association was so good that it cut the commission charged to county members by one-half.

The financial experience of the Association was steadily good. In 1934, even though volume declined from 39,528,075 cc. in 1933 to 28,727,153 cc. it was able to declare a patronage refund of 10 cents per 100 cc. of serum and virus, as well as a cash dividend of 5 per cent on outstanding preferred stock. In 1934, the old method of the IFBSA acting merely as a broker for the county members in the purchase of serum and virus, was dropped in favor of a merchandising plan under which the Association charged just about the same prices as competitors, and distributed the savings in the form of patronage refunds as well as adding to the surplus fund. The Association was one of the biggest distributors of hog cholera serum and virus in the United States.

The matter of proper prices for serum and virus was always troublesome until 1935, when the original Agricultural Adjustment Act was amended to provide for a marketing order and agreement under which uniform prices could be maintained. Even after that, disputes arose, and one was carried to the office of the Secretary of Agriculture, who sided with the farmers, and the matter was settled.

The Association tangled with the veterinarians again in 1937 and 1938 during the outbreak of encephalitis in horses. The Association believed that the veterinarians were overcharging farmers for immunizing, and when veterinarians were adamant on the issue, undertook to supply the serum to the county Farm Bureaus. It was able to effect big savings, but did not get into effective operation until the epidemic had spent itself.

At various times, the question of the Association entering the business of manufacturing serum and virus has been considered, but the decision has always been negative, and prospects at this writing are that such a step will not be taken as long as the products can be bought at reasonable prices. There is enough competition in the business to keep prices in line.

Until the war broke out in 1941, the Association ran along on an even keel, paying patronage refunds ranging from $30,000 to around $80,000 a year. It never faced a really serious financial situation, due to low overhead and a very efficient system of distribution. (Sam Russell managed the business as part of his duties as director of livestock marketing.) The war brought its difficulties due to shortage of supplies, narrowed margins, and the dislocations due to war. However, the Association was able to render satisfactory service to members, on the whole. A small price increase had to be made in 1941, but it seemed trifling because the price of hogs had risen substantially. In 1942, business was so good that patronage refunds of more than $100,000 were declared.

In 1948, the Association, in response to demands of members, started handling biologics, pharmaceuticals, and instruments. Sale of these items amounted to more than $6,000. Also, it began paying federal income taxes, having given up its exemption as a farm cooperative. The tax in 1948 amounted to $2,862.06. Patronage refunds amounting to $92,579.59 were paid, bringing the total paid to members since 1933 to more than one million dollars. A forward step was taken by appointing eight veterinarians in different parts of the state to look into cases in which trouble arose after vaccination. Relatively little trouble was experienced, and in most cases it was established that the hogs were not in top condition at time of vaccination. In 1947, Cecil Musser, former fieldman in livestock marketing, was named manager on a full-time basis. Russell V. McKee of Marshall county was president.

In 1950, Sam Russell returned as manager on a part-time basis, Cecil Musser having become director of grain marketing. Sales of biologics and pharmaceuticals increased substantially. The year saw another innovation, that of using a new hog cholera vaccine, Crystal Violet, a vaccine which, unlike the live virus, does not actually infect the animal with cholera. It was used on several thousand hogs, under careful supervision. During the year, seven district meetings were held throughout the state, with speakers on technical subjects to discuss new developments in veterinary medicine, livestock sanitation, and other matters of interest. The Association made a grant in 1949 to the University of Illinois for research in swine diseases, with particular reference to brucellosis.

In 1953, the Association began using Tru-Vac, a modified-virus which contains no disease-producing bacteria, gives quick protection, requires no change in feeding practices, and which may be used on pigs as young as five weeks. This vaccine has proved highly successful, and now has entirely superseded live vaccine. Crystal Violet vaccine is still used to some extent.

The year 1954 was a year of many developments. A field representative, M. R. Johnson, was employed to work with the county members, to look into complaints and misunderstandings —in short, to keep members in closer touch with the Association. First steps taken were to add to the number of distribution outlets for greater convenience to the patron, secure a qualified person in each county to be responsible for distribution, and to intensify the program of information and advertising. Having a fieldman on the staff helped a lot in bringing about these changes. By this time, 80 per cent of the members were using Tru-Vac, 15 per cent serum and virus, and 5 per cent were using Crystal Violet. Trouble cases following vaccination were almost eliminated. The modified-virus had made good in a big way. Patronage refunds amounted to $98,480.70.

By 1955, sales of biologics, pharmaceuticals, and instruments had risen from $6,000 in 1948 to nearly $100,000. A new bacterin to treat erysipelas in hogs and turkeys was rapidly replacing the old treatment by serum and culture. Erysipelas at that time was second only to cholera as a killer of swine. Field work was stepped up. Some 20 county-wide animal health meetings were held, and

376 people attended meetings for leaders in the various districts. The Association was in high gear now, and its prestige was steadily growing. The emphasis now was on prevention of disease through sanitary measures, and on keeping farmers fully informed of developments.

Sam Russell retired in 1957, and M. R. Johnson succeeded him. Howard J. Struck and Floyd Evans were taking care of the field work. Bill Crews was added in 1961. This year was a banner year. No less than $149,748.53 was returned to members as patronage refunds. This brought the total amount returned to members in 30 years to $2,420,150.27. (No patronage refunds had been paid in the early years.)

The IAA could look back with satisfaction. All counties in the state were being served. A very real need had been met by making a quality product readily available at a reasonable price. Here was an affiliate that farmers never put any money into that had returned to their county organizations more than two million dollars. The common and preferred stock which the local organizations hold was paid for by refunds. The IAA had provided the small investment required to get the project off the ground.

The educational work carried on had been immensely rewarding in terms of better sanitation on farms, better treatment when disease threatened, and certainly better feeding and care of farm animals. For some six years the work of the Animal Health Advisory Committee, made up of representatives of the IAA, the Illinois Agricultural Service Company, the Farm Advisers' Association, the Serum Association, and the College of Veterinary Medicine at the University of Illinois, has functioned with increasing effectiveness with respect to procedures and policy concerning product recommendations.

Here is an organization which has never had a serious setback, which has paid substantial refunds, which has supplied competition to keep prices in line, and which has contributed heavily to more enlightened methods of livestock care and management.

Chapter 33

Public Education

In 1941, the state legislature passed a law providing for school surveys to be made by committees chosen by town and country school boards in 17 counties. John C. Watson, retired head of the IAA department of taxation, was now working as an IAA consultant on schools and taxation. He and Allen D. Manvel, who was director of research and taxation, teamed up to provide help in the way of statistics and other basic information needed in any county under survey. Later, when Manvel left the IAA, Lawrence H. Simerl helped in this work.

The school survey law was the signal for farmers to go into action. The fact that the legislature had ordered surveys convinced farm people that the school situation had reached the point where some action was going to be taken, and that they had better see to it that they had a voice in the plans. They feared, with good reason, that if they did not help write the coming legislation, farm interests were likely to suffer. In some communities, they had already been the victims of "land-grabbing" tactics, when city districts had annexed farm land with high assessed valuations. Farm land of low assessed valuation, on the contrary, was often left out of new districts, even though it was close to the school. The school taxes paid on such property were far out of line with the benefits received, largely because farm property was usually assessed higher, in relation to real value, than was city property. Also, personal property on farms, which was usually clearly visible, was being taxed, while intangibles in town were not taxed at all in many cases.

President Earl C. Smith, who always had his ear close to the ground in such matters, knew that the membership was now ready to support a real effort to do something about the public schools. He alerted the staff, particularly the economists, information men, and organization men to the importance of the issue, and mapped out procedures for the coming years. Reports of the results of surveys in the 17 counties under study were given critical examination. It so happened that one of the schools that had stood out in the survey was in Pulaski county. The principal was Charles S. Mayfield, a young man who had recently earned his master's degree at Oberlin College. Smith decided that this young principal had a deep understanding of the problems involved, and that he was the man who could be most helpful to the IAA as it developed policies on public education. Accordingly, he joined the IAA staff as adviser on school affairs on June 1, 1942, and remained until he joined the navy. He resumed his Farm Bureau career after the war, and on June 1, 1962, he succeeded Wilfred Shaw as IAA secretary. This incident is recorded to indicate Smith's deep commitment to resolute action on the education front. What Smith feared, above all else, was that action at Springfield could easily result in loss of local control of school policies. Even though problems incident to the war took high precedence, he went all out in planning to meet the issues on public education.

From the beginning, the IAA had been concerned with the problems of rural education, but it was not until the late 1930's that it began to give them major attention. By that time it was apparent that country schools faced a crisis. Thousands of little school districts had lost so much population as a result of smaller families and the rapid mechanization of farm operations that it was obviously impractical to keep the schools open. Many had already closed, and the few remaining pupils sent to school in other districts. Schools that were still operating found that per-pupil costs were too high, and teachers hard to get for the salaries that taxpayers could afford to pay. The jobs were often unattractive to teachers too. Many of the best teachers tended to go to bigger schools, where salaries and opportunities for advancement were much greater.

Proposals providing for state-wide consolidation of school districts had been presented to the state legislature, but the IAA had considered them unacceptable, primarily because of mandatory features. The IAA stood firmly for local control, and as firmly against any plans that made consolidation compulsory. It was reasoned that the local people must take the initiative and that action must come from the people involved, not from higher up.

Thus the issue simmered until the early 1940's. By that time, 1,606 of the 9,680 one-room country schools had been closed for lack of pupils, and many of the others had less than half the enrollment they had had 40 years before. Clearly, the time had come for the IAA to act. In March, 1943, the IAA board of directors authorized the appointment of a state-wide committee to make an exhaustive study of the problems, and to make recommendations as to policies that should be pursued to bring about needed improvements in our schools. Earl C. Smith, IAA president, appointed the committee, thirty in number, of whom five were women. Many were school-board members, or had had teaching experience. K. Taliaferro Smith of Greenfield, IAA board member and chairman of the public relations committee, who had long represented the IAA at Springfield in legislative matters, was made chairman. The committee began work in August, heard testimony from leaders in education, encouraged county Farm Bureaus to appoint school committees, and made arrangements for a conference on school problems at the annual IAA convention in November. The intense interest shown at the conference convinced the committee members that farm people were deeply concerned with the future of rural education, and they renewed their activities with increased vigor. By January, 1944, they made a preliminary report, and in November their complete report of the results of their deliberations was published in printed form. It was an eye-opener. Well over 15,000 copies were distributed, many of them to school officials and teachers in other states. In Illinois, at least, it made history.

The report showed unmistakably that rural education in Illinois was indeed in a deplorable state. Nearly three-quarters of the one-room school districts had less than 15 pupils, 44 per cent had less than 10, and 11 per cent had less than 5. Only about one in four districts had an average of two or more pupils per grade. From 1880 to 1942, enrollment in one-room country schools had dropped 69 per cent! The inefficiency and the high cost of operation of little schools was clearly shown. The report recommended a thorough overhauling of the entire educational structure, with districts consolidated into larger units, instruction upgraded, facilities improved, transportation furnished, and the burden of taxation equitably distributed.

In the course of its studies, the Committee had taken a look at a highly successful school at Buffalo, Illinois, the product of the consolidation of three original high school districts. John K. Cox was the principal. His experience, and his grasp of the problems of rural education so impressed members of the committee, that he was recommended to the IAA as the man to head up its education activities. He was hired, and went to work on June 1, 1944. From then on, things moved ahead with remarkable speed. With the cooperation of many interested educational leaders and the Illinois School Boards' Association, a bill was whipped up to introduce in the 1945 session of the legislature. School problems were aired in the columns of the IAA RECORD, and discussed in Farm Bureau meetings all over the state.

Members of the legislature in 1945 accepted the bill, and it was signed by Governor Dwight H. Green in late June. Provisions of the new law were simple. It required school board members in each county before December 1, 1945, to vote on making a school survey. If the vote was affirmative, a survey committee of nine was to be selected from those voting, five from rural school districts, and four from town districts. This committee would study the entire public school system, then file a tentative report with recommendations. Hearings then would be held, after which a final report would be filed. Then, if the final recommendation of the committee was in favor of reorganizing the districts into larger units, a referendum would be held, with urban and rural people voting separately. If both groups favored re-districting, it would be carried out. Every possible safeguard was provided to insure that whatever the result, it would be according to the wishes of the people themselves.

What followed was truly amazing. Before the deadline date of December 1, 1945, every county in Illinois had held a referendum. In 93 counties, people voted for reorganization by better than three to one, on the average. In nine counties the vote was adverse, by a small margin. These counties, with the exception of one, went for reorganization later. It was evident that the overwhelming majority of people favored larger districts and improved educational facilities.

The work of consolidation at first proceeded slowly. One difficulty was that the original emphasis applied mainly to grade schools. It became generally recognized that legislation was needed to allow consolidation embracing both grade and high schools in one district. It was then that Farm Bureau members became deeply interested in what is known as the "unit district," in which all grades, one through twelve, are under one school board, one administration, and one tax rate. The simplicity and economy of the plan appealed to farmers. There were at that time some hundred of such districts in Illinois, each with one high school and varying numbers of grade schools. John K. Cox of the IAA did a great deal, through platform and press, to explain the advantages of the plan.

The state legislature encouraged changing over to twelve-grade units by giving such districts a lower qualifying rate for state aid. This helped, but it was not until 1947, when the Community School District Unit Act was passed, that progress began in earnest. Under the provisions of this Act, the people of an entire area (an entire county, or parts of two or more counties) could adopt the unit plan for a 12-grade district, with one administration, and one tax rate. Within months of the passage of the Act, the people of Brown county voted for the unit plan by a vote of 873 to 54. Shortly afterward, Scott county people voted, three-to-one, for the unit system. Apparently, people had been waiting for just such an opportunity. They wanted to go all the way, rather than just reorganizing only the grade schools.

One factor that helped the movement along was that the state legislature had decreed that any school district had to be dissolved if its school remained closed for two years or longer. It had also decreed that a reorganized district must have a minimum of 2,000 population, and $6 million of assessed valuation. These provisions led to some bitter controversies. Local pride was strong in many communities. Where to locate the bigger school was a big problem. Some towns had great pride in their athletic teams; some felt that their towns would wither up if the school was closed and pupils carried by bus to other schools. To this day, some of these controversies have not been resolved. Some schools are still too small for efficient operation and high-grade instruction.

For the most part wholesale reorganization has been a huge success. By 1957, only twelve years after passage of the School Survey Act, the number of school districts in Illinois had been reduced from 11,955 to 1,849—a reduction of 85 per cent—and 72 per cent of the area of the state was in unit districts. The result was a vast upgrading of the quality of instruction. Money had no doubt been saved in many cases; but even if taxpayers were paying just as much as they would have paid under the old system, they were in fact getting a lot more for their money.

It should be noted that much of the early opposition to school consolidation had been based on the fact that poor roads in some areas made transportation of pupils a difficult matter. In Farm Bureau circles, this objection had been met by propounding the theory that once we got better schools, we would have much better arguments in favor of improved roads. Roads should be improved anyway. Then, in 1951, the IAA led the fight for increasing the state gasoline tax from three to five cents a gallon, and allocating 10 per cent of the funds to rural road improvement. That fight was won over bitter opposition, and it did much to ease the situation. In most communities, poor roads no longer constitute a valid reason against consolidation.

The state had followed the policy of withholding state aid funds from one-room districts with less than seven pupils, a minimum that was raised, in successive stages, to ten, twelve, and finally to fifteen. For high schools the minimum was fifteen pupils in each grade (daily attendance). These requirements led to charges of "forcing" consolidation, but in general, consolidation has become so popular that today one hears little objection to the rules. Very substantial increases in state aid funds during the 1950's have tended to reduce criticism.

The above discussion does not imply that Illinois has completely solved its rural school problems. It never will. Districts are still too small. The requirement of a population of 2,000 for a high school is too low, because that number of people will include only 80 to 90 pupils of high school age—far too few for efficient operation and effective instruction in the wide range of subjects needed to prepare young folks for life in the atomic age. Farm Bureau leaders fully realize that education will cost more in the future. It is also agreed that the tax base must be broadened in order to provide the money. The IAA has consistently favored the income tax as one measure that, sooner or later, must be adopted in Illinois. Property taxes have about reached the upper limit, and further increases in the sales tax are regarded as unlikely.

So, it could be fairly said that while the IAA work on school problems has not resulted in complete solutions to the many problems in public education, nevertheless any objective appraisal of its work must rate this job of school improvement as one of the big achievements of organized farmers.

Chapter 34

Adventures in
Local Government

From the earliest days of Farm Bureau, members sought help
from the IAA in working out local problems involving roads,
school tax rates, soil conservation, public health, and many other
public activities. Departments to deal with such problems had
been set up, with the head of each department reporting to various IAA officials. In order to streamline administrative procedures, President Charles B. Shuman in 1948 set up a division
of general services embracing property taxation, research, rural
school relations, veterinary medical relations, road improvement,
safety and public health, and soil conservation. Ivan E. Parett
was named director, and he reported on all these activities to
President Shuman. This arrangement continued until 1950, when
Parett was made head of a newly created department of public
relations, and John K. Cox, who had been handling rural school
relations, took over general services. A year later, two departments,
rural school relations and road improvement, were combined to
form a new department, that of local government, with Cullen B.
Sweet, who formerly headed the road improvement department,
as director.

Most of the first six months of 1951, Sweet spent at the legislature in Springfield as a member of the IAA legislative committee. (The late K. Taliaferro Smith, as chairman of the IAA public relations committee, headed the legislative committee.) Much time was devoted to carrying out the recommendations of the IAA road study committee of 1949. These recommendations were formally adopted by the voting delegates at the 1949 IAA convention, and another added, asking the state legislature to allot a percentage of the gasoline tax money to townships and road districts for improvement of local roads. The 1951 legislature complied with the latter request on the last day of the 1951 session, after a long and hard battle. Adlai Stevenson was Governor at the time. Thus it was that 24 years after the Illinois gasoline tax was first imposed, ten per cent of the funds were allotted to local road improvement.

Another IAA achievement at that session was the passage of a law which permitted counties to consolidate road districts into one county road district. (Laws passed in 1947 and amended in 1949 permitted two or more townships or township road districts to merge.) This law opened the way to huge savings in construction and maintenance, but as we shall see later, few counties have seen fit to take advantage of it.

Union county, acting under the 1947 law, had consolidated 13 road districts into four, with excellent results. In 1951, Randolph county created four consolidated districts out of eighteen, and a number of other counties began to investigate the possibility of getting more out of their road tax dollars. The next year, Pulaski, Williamson, and Massac counties voted in referendum to form county unit road districts. (It is interesting to note here that as far back as 1938 Hardin county people, without any law to authorize it, and without knowing whether it was legal or not, had in fact put all of their road districts in one county-wide district which still exists today.)

Many county Farm Bureaus set up road study committees, and it was confidently expected that great strides would be made quickly in road consolidation throughout the state. However, it

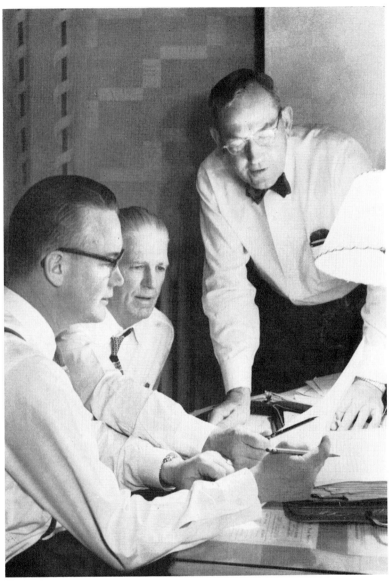

Early legislative team consisted of John K. Cox, K. T. Smith, and Cullen B. Sweet

has not worked out that way. The fact seems to be that the easy money that flowed in from the gasoline tax has taken the edge off the problem. Roads traveled by school buses and rural mail routes have been generally improved, and you find little concern among the people over the inefficiency of a system under which each township owns expensive road equipment that is used far below capacity. All surveys by independent agencies have proved that the township is too small a unit for efficient upkeep of highways. The situation is parallel to that faced by farmers since the war. Modern farm equipment is too costly to be used on small farms, hence the consolidation of farm lands into larger units. Farmers have met this situation in one way or another because they had to. But in the public business of construction and upkeep of highways, we permit the old system, with all of its inefficiency, to continue. It would seem that the easy money from the gasoline tax has actually retarded a movement toward consolidated road districts that could have saved a great deal of money.

In 1952, the IAA board of directors, remembering the outstanding work of the school and road study committees, set up the local government study committee to study and appraise the situation with respect to problems in this field, with special emphasis on taxes, and make recommendations.

The committee report, accepted by the IAA in 1952 and published in 1953, was quite revealing. To quote from the report:

"In Illinois it is possible for an individual family to live within the jurisdiction of as many as 15 different types of taxing districts or units. These taxing districts or units include county, township, incorporated cities, towns and villages, school, road, park, sanitary, mosquito abatement, forest preserve, public health, fire protection, river conservancy, tuberculosis sanitarium, and other municipal corporations or districts with power to levy taxes. . . ."

Some statements in the report were shocking to many people. For example: "Inability to collect taxes at the local level causes a demand for more federal and state aid. Such practice can eventually lead to the complete breakdown of local government and implant federal support and controls."

And further: "For the purpose of assessment, all property, both real and personal, must be listed at its full, fair, cash value. Even though this is the law, very little if any evidence exists which indicates that any property in the state is listed at full value." The uniform clause in property-tax laws was shown to be impracticable by noting that tax rates, applied to such property as stocks and bonds, would often exceed the earnings of the property. It was emphasized that inequities in assessment of property, as between townships and between counties, and between rural and urban property, were often flagrant. It was found that local assessors sometimes lacked any technical training for the jobs they held, and that many factors seem to prevent or hinder a board of review from doing the job for which it was created. To illustrate the lack of uniformity in assessments, it was pointed out that the State Revenue Department, which has the responsibility of equalizing local assessments between counties, used a multiplier of one (1) in only 42 counties. In others, it used multipliers ranging up to 7.6923 in two counties.

Attention was called to lack of proper budgeting expenditures, lack of proper accounting of expenditures, lack of intelligent planning in highway matters, to "uncoordinated and autocratic administrative control of local roads," and "expenditures of a large part of local tax money for the purchase of machinery which is idle much of the time."

The committee found that it faced frightfully complex problems, some of which it felt that it neither had the time nor the facilities to explore, and so indicated in its report. In its letter of transmittal to President Shuman, the committee, referring to the problems of local governments, said: "Before a complete solution is obtainable the Revenue Article of the State Constitution will have to be revised."

One tangible result of the work of the committee was the passage in 1953 of a law permitting the establishing of a county supervisor of assessments, either by the county board or by the people in referendum vote. (Such a law had been passed a few years earlier, but had been declared unconstitutional.) Many counties took action. Experience has been varied. In some counties, results have been remarkably good. In others, people have demanded a referendum and have voted the office out. In some cases, a campaign to abolish the office has been led by influential taxpayers who had had their taxes raised by the supervisor. In some cases, poorly trained men have been appointed to the office, and results have been what you could expect. Today, only about forty counties have a supervisor of assessments.

In 1953, Cullen B. Sweet moved over to the organization department, and Albert J. Cross was hired to succeed him. Cross had grown up in Kentucky, where his father and uncles had been deep in local politics for many years, and he was quite at home in a political atmosphere. He had a master's degree in agricultural economics, and was a graduate in law. He was jointly employed by the Bureau of Agricultural Economics of the USDA, and the Department of Agricultural Economics of the College of Agriculture at the University of Illinois before he came to the IAA.

Taking up where Sweet left off, Cross found many counties asking for counsel and assistance in determining whether they needed a supervisor of assessments. Before the end of 1954, eight counties had established the office, and several others were taking steps toward that end. Another phase of local government required attention as a result of a resolution adopted at the 1953 annual meeting. As a result of rapidly increasing industrialization and the movement of business and people into rural areas, owners of farms were facing new problems. Motels, trailer camps, taverns, and dance halls outside city limits were creating problems. In order to protect property values, as well as to protect health and safety, it was necessary for counties and municipalities to adopt sound policies in land use planning, hence the adoption of county zoning ordinances. The IAA resolution recommended that county Farm Bureaus in non-zoned counties study the problem, and that those in zoned counties try to determine the adequacy of existing ordinances in the light of changing conditions. Twelve Illinois counties already had such ordinances, and several others were considering enactment of them. Here was a new and important field which a county Farm Bureau cannot overlook as cities spread further and further into the countryside.

In 1957, the division of general services was abolished and the following divisions placed under General Counsel Paul E. Mathias: legal, transportation, property taxation, natural resources, local government, and legislation. (Transportation was moved over to FS Services, Inc., in 1962.)

Since problems in local government usually involve taxation, either directly or indirectly, Paul E. Mathias often asks Bert Vandervliet, who has been in charge of IAA's tax work since the retirement of the late John C. Watson, to help out on some problems. The sharp impact of such taxes on farmers is reflected in the fact that property taxes increased from $43 million in 1941 to $740 million in 1953, which accounted for the deep interest in the county office of supervisor of assessments during these years. (By 1957, taxes were to exceed $1 billion, and in 1962, rise to $1.4 billion.)

The subject of taxation is a "touchy" one always, and it is not surprising that the appointment of a county supervisor of assessments has not brought peace and harmony among the taxpayers involved. Tax experts are pretty well agreed that in assessing farm land, the poor land is usually assessed at a higher rate in relation to its true value than is good land. Consequently, if a supervisor of assessments undertakes to equalize assessments in accordance with the law, he is bound to arouse criticism from some farm owners who find their taxes increased. Bitter controversies have arisen over this issue, and will arise again. Some people question the value of having a supervisor of assessments at all.

In all cases where uniformity has been brought about by creation of the office, the man appointed has been technically well qualified for the work. Unqualified men have seldom achieved anything except further controversy. Time and experience will be needed to bring about anything resembling complete fairness in assessments. Oldtimers can remember when counties first began to appoint highway engineers. Many of the early appointees had more political assets than engineering skill, and results were unfortunate. After fifty years, however, the vast majority of county highway engineers are well qualified for their jobs. It may well be that we must go through a comparatively extended period of time before we achieve similar results in the field of taxation. One thing we can be certain of however, and that is that unless we do find some way of achieving the uniformity that the law specifies, we will continue to have confusion and chaos in this field.

In 1956 the IAA vigorously supported the campaign for amendment of the revenue article of the state constitution, to permit classification of property for purposes of taxation and to pave the way for a tax system that would provide the basis for a more equitable distribution of the tax load. But the proposal lost in the fall election.

Since the end of World War II, counties have been encouraged, through a system of grants-in-aid from the State, to establish county health departments (two or more counties may act jointly), and thirty counties have set up such establishments. In McDonough and Hancock counties, the county Farm Bureaus successfully opposed such a move some years ago, and in 1962 the Whiteside County Farm Bureau waged a battle against one. Reasons for opposition were principally that need for such action had not been proved, that it would result in waste and duplication of services, and that it would set up another governmental unit with taxing powers on top of other existing units, which might prove very costly. There must be a limit somewhere to the number of taxing units that property owners can support.

In 1962, the IAA also assisted the Morgan County Farm Bureau in defeating a proposal to create a park district that would have included all of the city of Jacksonville plus a considerable area of land around the city. To Farm Bureau members, it seemed that farm people would receive far less benefit from the park, relative to the taxes they would have to pay for its support, than would the townspeople, hence they made an all-out fight against it.

It should not be inferred that Farm Bureaus always oppose local projects involving additional taxation. They are often on the "pro" side in these matters, and the IAA personnel, upon request, helps them to set up a fire-protection district, a health department, or other improvement, the need of which has been proved.

410

Since so many local government matters are intimately involved with state legislation, Cross must spend a lot of time at Springfield during sessions of the state legislature, as a member of the legislative team whose other members are General Counsel Paul E. Mathias, John C. Cox, secretary of legislation, and one IAA board member, Clarence McCauley, chairman of the IAA legislative and public affairs committee. This team is accorded the highest respect by legislators and public officials, who invariably give proper consideration to any proposals advanced by Farm Bureau.

In 1962, nearly 12 years after its creation, the department of local government seems destined to be called on for more and more assistance by county Farm Bureaus. Rapidly changing conditions force more and more problems on communities and counties, more and more public services are demanded by the people. Cities sprawl out, new schools must be built, highways, pipelines, and power lines cut across farms, modern machinery must be bought to maintain highways, cost of government goes up. All of these factors must be faced by communities everywhere in the state, and the Farm Bureau is the organization best qualified to speak for farmers on issues raised. If Farm Bureau is to be worthy of the trust imposed in it, it must furnish sound counsel on how best to meet new problems. Thus, the responsibilities of the department of local government grow with the years.

Chapter 35

Better Seeds

The discovery of hybrid corn touched off in the Cornbelt a movement that was roughly comparable to the "gold rush" to California in 1849. By 1937, it was apparent to everybody that hybrid corn represented one of the greatest advances in agriculture ever recorded. As Jimmy Durante would say, "Everybody wanted to get into the act." It was a stampede.

In Ford county, Illinois, the late A. B. Schofield, a promotion-minded farmer, had sensed the unlimited possibilities that loomed ahead for hybrid seed corn, and he was convinced that farmers themselves ought to produce their own hybrids. He found sympathetic listeners among his fellow Farm Bureau members, and by 1937, he had support enough to take action. The Ford County Corn Growers was an organization which maintained several seed corn testing plants in the county. Farmers would put a barrel on a sled, hitch a horse to the sled and pull it through the corn field while they picked the best ears and tossed them into the barrel. They were selecting "utility-type" ears, the type that had been out-yielding all other types up to that time. The ears were taken to the testing stations, and the ears that survived the tests for germination and disease were taken home and used for seed the following year. Here, Schofield reasoned, was an organization that could easily be utilized to carry out his idea.

After many meetings and much discussion, sentiment was crystallized, and Ford county farmers bought stock, changed the name of the organization to Producers Crop Improvement Association, and went into business. Schofield was named president. The board of directors consisted of L. A. Barrow, Frank Anderson, George J. Arends, Floyd L. Hevener, Charles Dueringer, and Howard H. Stuckey. It soon became apparent that a manager was needed, so Schofield resigned as president to take over the management. L. A. Barrow succeeded him as president. Since the organization was set up as a cooperative, with preferred stock on a fixed-dividend basis, and profits distributed on a patronage basis, it was able to qualify for a loan from the St. Louis Bank for Cooperatives.

The reader might think, from the story so far, that this was a rash undertaking. Where were the hybrids to come from? There was an assured source. Louis Rust, a plant breeder for the Hiram Sibley estate, who had been working with hybrids since 1924, was giving his utmost in pushing the project. He made his best hybrids available. Others were contributed by the U.S. Department of Agriculture and the University of Illinois. The Sibley drying and storage facilities were utilized to process the first crop of some 10,000 bushels of hybrid seed grown in 1937. A little later, Albert E. Sandquist was hired as a full-time geneticist. He remained until 1945, after which Robert Copper succeeded him and remained until 1953, when he resigned to start farming in Mason county. His assistant, John D. Somers, took over then and is still in charge. He is the man who has eliminated the costly job of detasseling in Producer operations. This has been a technical development involving production of sterile female parents and pollen-restoring male parents. The process is too technical for discussion here, but it has been a very great advance in the business of producing hybrids.

The Sibley facilities were used for only one season, since a modern processing plant was built at Piper City in 1938. It was immediately apparent that the plant was too big for the needs of Ford county; therefore, Farm Bureaus in Livingston and Grundy counties were invited to join up, and they did, coming in on the same basis of stock ownership. Business increased so fast by 1940, and problems became so pressing, that Schofield and the directors agreed that they were somewhat beyond their depth, and that the best professional management should be found to take over. Accordingly, Lloyd R. Downs, who had been managing the Columbia Farmers Cooperative Grain Company in Monroe county, was hired as manager. New articles of incorporation and bylaws were adopted, and Howard R. Stuckey was elected president. He still holds that position in 1963.

Business increased steadily. By 1942, all outstanding indebtedness had been paid off, and patronage refunds were being paid. The hybrid seed was distributed through a number of county Farm Bureau service companies, and also through agents. As time went on, a number of service companies gave up the business, because it didn't fit too well into the business of distributing farm supplies, and soon the individual farmer agents were selling most of the corn.

In 1947, the Blackhawk Hybrid Seed Corn Association of Polo was taken over by an exchange of stock. A new and bigger warehouse had been built at Piper City, and a modern office building was under construction. An auxiliary drying and processing plant had been in operation at Fairbury since 1949. The organization was having "growing pains." Several problems were pressing. For one thing, it was felt that they needed a full line of seeds to sell. With gross business of more than $500,000, more capital and reliable business guidance were needed. The conclusion was reached that the organization should become a full-fledged affiliate of the IAA. This came about in April, 1949. The name was changed to Producers Seed Company, and an increase in capital stock was authorized. The IAA already held some "B" stock.

One of the first moves after reorganization was to expand sales of grass and legume seeds. Evart Vander Muelen, an experienced seed buyer, came in to manage that part of the business. He remained until 1952, when he was succeeded by Gould E. Metcalf, his assistant, who has carried on most capably ever since. A plant in Decatur was acquired to process field seeds and grass and legume seeds. Two years later, the facilities of the National Hybrid Corn Company at Normal were purchased.

In 1952, a fire completely destroyed the plant at Piper City, with the exception of the office building. A new plant, three times the size of the old one, was built immediately, which permitted abandonment of the Normal facility and the idling of the Fairbury plant on a standby basis.

During the past ten years, business has grown at a satisfactory rate. In 1960, sales exceeded $3 million. A good-sized research program is under way. Three nurseries are operated in Illinois, and one in Florida. The Florida investment pays off because it permits production of two generations in one year.

The field seed department has grown to the point that it contributes more to net operating income than sales of hybrid corn. Producers Seed Company now handles about a third of all grass and legume seeds sold in Illinois, which is certainly an impressive record. Lloyd Downs attributes this record to the fact that all field seeds sold since 1951 have carried an outright guarantee. Maintaining high quality standards has paid off.

An interesting sideline was established in 1962, when facilities for hog feeding were acquired at Forrest. Cull and "gradeout" corn is fed to hogs. Capacity is 800 hogs, and three lots can be fattened each year. This project is expected to yield a satisfactory profit.

It might be assumed that a cooperative owned by Farm Bureau members might easily have almost a monopoly on the business, provided it gives good service. This is far from the case. The cooperative must compete with other very fine producers of hybrid corn. Producers must compete with Iowa and Indiana and Ohio reputable marketers who sell in Illinois; but it cannot go to those states and compete with them on their own ground. Like any similar organization, Producers Seed Company feels the need to achieve greater efficiency through greater volume, but it is restricted to Illinois by its charter. Furthermore, many of the distributors, or agents, for other outstanding producers of hybrid corn are Farm Bureau members. The fact that Producers Seed Company is sponsored by Farm Bureau carries certain advantages; but just as certainly it carries obvious disadvantages. It can get ahead only through merit and meeting the competition. Producers has done this, and it has survived and prospered.

A few figures will indicate growth over the years. Stock investment of $40,000 has grown to around $600,000. Original cost of facilities now owned was about $1,185,500. Net worth is now in excess of $900,000. Patronage dividends of $1.5 million have been paid. The Producers Seed Company is now a well established business. Small though it is, compared to some of the giants in the industry, it must be accounted a successful cooperative enterprise that has stood the test of time.

Chapter 36

Natural Resources

The present department of natural resources of the IAA is the outgrowth of the old limestone-phosphate department which did so much in earlier days to make Illinois easily the leading state in the Union in use of raw rock phosphate and agricultural lime-stone. Up to 1932, an office had been maintained in Tennessee, where phosphate was bought and tested; but with the advent of the depression, volume fell so much that the office was closed, the director of the department was released, and its reduced activities were carried on by the IAA secretary. Volume dwindled until 1935, when nothing at all was done in an organized way to promote use of limestone and phosphate.

In 1937, the old limestone-phosphate department was reactivated as the soil improvement department, with John R. Spencer as director. By this time, it was apparent that many Illinois soils needed potash, as well as phosphate and limestone. Spencer worked with the University of Illinois in making plans for establishing experiment fields in the southern part of the state, to provide further information on potash needs. Farm prices were relatively high, due to the drouth of 1936, and Illinois farmers used about 50,000 tons of phosphate. Use of limestone took a big jump to a new all-time record of 1,250,000 tons. In 1938, the department was going well, and promoting the use of commercial mixed fertilizers as well as of limestone, phosphate, and potash. Estimated use of potash that year was 2,500 tons, and of commercial fertilizers, 2,000 tons. In 1940, use of limestone jumped to 2 million tons. Nearly all of it was now moving by truck, and many local deposits were opened up, close to the farms where it was used. Under the soil conservation program of the AAA, the Federal Government was paying part of the limestone and phosphate bill for cooperating farmers, thus boosting the use of these materials. In 1941, use of limestone amounted to 2,674,000 tons, and of phosphate, 68,290 tons.

With U.S. entry into World War II, all-out farm production was called for. In 1943, Illinois farmers used 3,773,000 tons of limestone, and 129,000 tons of rock phosphate. The all-time high was reached in 1945, with the use of 4,214,000 tons of limestone, and 218,986 tons of rock phosphate.

Federal subsidization of fertilizing materials, the exigencies of war, and OPA price regulation had brought sweeping changes in distribution. No longer was the bulk of limestone being distributed under a master contract through the IAA. With increasing use of mixed fertilizers, the Illinois Farm Supply Company entered the field, and also began distributing phosphatic materials and muriate of potash on a substantial scale. In 1945, Farm Supply sold 9,361 tons of mixed goods, 6,145 tons of superphosphate, 310 tons of triple superphosphate, and 4,047 tons of muriate of potash. There was no need for promotional activities, as demand was greater than supply. Spencer went on to other work, and nothing at all was done with the department for two years.

In 1948, the work was reactivated under a new title, the department of soil conservation activities. Since the use of commercial fertilizers had increased some ninefold since 1940, a lot of attention was given to this development. The use of high-analysis goods was pushed, because of lower cost per unit of plant food. Testing limestone and rock phosphate for quality and fineness of grind was carried on, but on a smaller scale. Roger E. Gish, director of the department, was available for counsel with farmers in proposed soil conservation districts, with farm advisers and farm program officials—in fact with anyone interested in promoting soil conservation. In 1950, Gish resigned to join Farm Supply in promoting sales of fertilizer and feeds.

The following year, the department was given a new name, the department of natural resources, and Ray Hunter became director. Hunter began working closely with the Association of Illinois Soil Conservation Districts, the 15 land use councils, and individual soil conservation districts. He conducted training schools for soil conservation district directors in order to promote sound principles of land use. He became deeply interested in a forestry program for Illinois. A year later, he organized and directed the first forestry camp for boys, where 44 boys from as many counties began to learn fundamental lessons in tree farming. Hunter helped to plan and stage the first farm forestry field day in Illinois. By 1954, new federal legislation extended financial assistance to improve small watersheds. This led to appointment of a state commission to study water problems and report to the 1957 General Assembly.

Ray Hunter resigned early in 1958 to do similar work for the California Farm Bureau Federation. William H. Brown, Jr., succeeded Hunter and continued the policy of close cooperation with all groups interested in conservation, development, management, and multiple use of all natural resources. The department now "cooperates in planning and conducting a state-wide informational program to develop the understanding of all Illinois citizens regarding the advantages of the watershed approach to flood prevention, surface water storage, and conservation of underground supplies," as stated in a resolution adopted by the IAA in 1956. Brown works particularly with the 98 soil and water conservation districts which serve all Illinois counties, and with their 16 land use and conservation councils and their state association. He works closely with federal, state, and local agencies which provide technical personnel to help landowners and farm operators plan and carry out land use programs geared to the capabilities of each acre and supported by conservation measures needed to hold the soil in place and at the same time conserve, develop, manage, and wisely use the water, forest, fish, game, and natural resources.

The IAA continues as the principal supporter of the annual boys' farm forestry camp. Natural resources groups are encouraged to adopt the conservation, management, development, and use philosophy, rather than the preservationist philosophy. The department assists Farm Bureau members in finding solutions to and abating problems of air contamination, stream pollution, saline water intrusion in wells, problems related to oil well flooding operations, open and mined area reclamation, watershed protection, and flood prevention. Brown edits a bi-monthly publication, "Insight," which carries natural resources information to leaders of all interested groups and agencies.

In recent years, a whole host of new problems have arisen as a result of federal laws initiating a massive effort by federal agencies to reach down to rural communities and guide developments in meeting new situations brought about by the trend to larger farms, loss of local industries in "disadvantaged" communities, and so on. Here, Brown's role is to keep IAA officials and staff informed, and to alert Farm Bureau members in the counties to the importance of their insisting that all undertakings be conceived, initiated, and carried out by local people, with such help as they may request from government agencies, as Congress intended.

Steps taken in this field could be grouped under the so-called Rural Areas Development Programs, starting with the Disadvantaged Areas Act of 1955. Under this Act, the Extension Service was assigned primary responsibility for carrying out local improvement programs, using federal funds over and above the usual Extension appropriations. The work was started in 1956 in 54 "pilot" programs in 24 states. By 1962, there were "RAD" committees at work in 23 Illinois counties. In March of 1961, Secretary of Agriculture Freeman announced that RAD programs would have top priority in USDA activities. A staff was assembled within the Department to give state and local assistance under the direction of the Director of the Agricultural Credit Services. In the Food and

Agriculture Act of 1962, Congress broadened the scope of RAD activities. Stated objectives of the enlarged program are to: create new economic opportunities through conservation development and multiple use of land, water and related resources; strengthen family farms; attract new industry; provide job training or retraining; develop more adequate community facilities; provide improved housing; and increase the income of rural farm and non-farm people.

In carrying out the purposes of the program, the responsibility of local leadership has been emphasized by the department of natural resources. The big aim is to provide new economic opportunities in rural America. County Resource Development Committees are expected to study the problems, needs, desires, and potentials of their areas in respect to the conservation, development and use of natural resources; analyze physical and economic resources, as well as industrial, agricultural, and business opportunities; labor supply and skills; housing and working conditions; and seek solutions, with technical and financial assistance from federal, state, and local governments. The program envisions long-term changes in diverting land now growing field crops to grass, trees, ponds for fish, wildlife, or other uses such as recreational development. Involved also are watershed improvements and water supplies for municipal and industrial uses. The broad program is to be integrated with various other programs, such as the Accelerated Public Works Program and the Manpower Development and Training Act.

One has only to study the scope of the changes contemplated to be struck by the plain fact that such a program, carried to its completion, would involve many billions, not millions, of dollars, and would most certainly change the face of rural America. Today, it is the activities of the many federal agencies involved that the IAA natural resources department must be concerned with because they portend a possible total eclipse of local initiative and control as the years go on.

And so, looking back forty years, we find that the IAA limestone-phosphate department which was set up to promote the use of plant foods, has now become a department faced with problems not even dreamed of in the early days, and with most of its original functions carried on by other agencies. FS Services, Inc., is selling plant foods to the tune of many millions annually, and will shortly be producing in its own plant a million tons of ammonia annually for fertilizer use, as well as producing potash and phosphates from its own deposits. There is no need now for testing limestone, since a government agency now renders that service. In the old days, sales of limestone were promoted by field tests which proved that it paid the farmer well to apply it on acid soils; now the Federal Government adds to the farmer's profit by paying part of the cost. Ditto for rock phosphate. The Extension Service now has the responsibility of carrying on the educational work for all federal agricultural programs.

One wonders if it is all for the best,—if it is a necessary part of progress. One wonders, too, what will be the final outcome. Are farm prices, as well as farm practices, to be dictated by a dozen federal agencies, each a part of a massive bureaucracy centered in Washington, costing as it does today, the equivalent of nearly half the net income of all farmers in the United States?

Chapter 37

Young People's Activities

From its beginning, Farm Bureau has encouraged organized activities for boys and girls. County Farm Bureaus sponsored 4-H club work and cooperated closely with teachers of vocational agriculture. As the years went on, demand arose for Farm Bureau to sponsor activities for young folks after they had left high school. Extension personnel gave valuable assistance in program planning and youth training activities. "Rural Youth" groups were active in many counties. In 1936, the IAA hired Frank Gingrich, a 4-H club adviser at the University of Illinois, to work full time in this field.

At that time, there were about 7,000 young men and women (aged 17 to 28 years) meeting regularly in 78 counties to discuss public issues, farm-home, and community problems. They were getting good training for future Farm Bureau careers. A number of them had shown such aptitude that they had been elected to membership on Farm Bureau boards of directors. It was the job of the new department to broaden the scope and enhance the effectiveness of county rural youth groups. A look at the 1937 program reveals a number of worthwhile activities. Nearly 400 young people from 49 counties put on radio broadcasts from seven downstate radio stations. One subject was: "How Does the Illinois Property Tax Affect the Future of Rural Youth?" Another was: "What Should Farmers Aim to Accomplish Through Organization?" Tours covering such subjects as livestock and produce marketing were conducted, as well as a tour to Chicago to see the IAA in operation. Many groups participated in farm and highway safety programs.

The work expanded fast. In 1938, there was activity in 86 counties, with more than 8,000 young people participating in such activities as summer camps, radio forums, marketing tours, tours of inspection of county Farm Bureaus, and so on. A project designed to train youngsters in public speaking attracted a big following. "Talk Fests" were staged in nine counties.

The work developed most satisfactorily in the ensuing years. The outbreak of World War II curtailed participation to some extent, for maybe 20 per cent of those active in 1941 were in the armed forces by 1942. Some of the county groups suspended activities. On the other hand, local activities were stepped up. Since the Sports Festival had to be discontinued for the duration of the war, young people in 11 counties arranged for county sports festivals which gave young people a lot of valuable experience. Young people had their own program as part of the IAA annual meeting each year. The activities were fully recognized as a valuable adjunct to Farm Bureau work. Frank Gingrich resigned in 1943, and in 1944 Ellsworth D. Lyon was appointed to succeed him. Training schools for young people, with heavy emphasis on public speaking and parliamentary procedure, were held in 1945, and proved popular and rewarding to participants.

By 1947, the work was going better than ever, with some 10,000 young people participating. Eleven district training schools were staged, with about 600 people in attendance. In 1948, the IAA board of directors made arrangements for the state rural youth committee to attend various official meetings, and for officers to attend district Farm Bureau meetings. The rural youth movement was coming of age.

During 1949, nearly 1,000 young people, or 10 per cent of those in the work, took part in the Talk Fests, and 2,500 participated in the skilled driver work sponsored by IAA. Three members officially represented Illinois young people at the convention of the American Farm Bureau Federation. Tours to study livestock marketing and soil conservation were held in 1950. Problems relating to farm ownership, health, and father-and-son partnerships were studied and discussed at many meetings. In 1951, Lyon resigned to go into insurance work. Roy Will carried on the work until February 1, 1952, when Edward W. Dalhaus was named director of young people's activities. He continued as director until he resigned in October, 1962, to take a job with the American Farm Bureau Federation.

Dalhaus set up a committee system under which responsibilities were widely distributed among five committees of ten members each, as follows: Rural Youth committee, camp committee, Farm and Home Week committee, IAA activities committee, and fall-conference committee. The state was divided into ten districts, with three meetings annually in each. An advisory committee of twelve members was set up, with representation from the IAA, Illinois Extension Service, Rural Youth, and the Illinois Home Bureau Federation. In 1954, the young people themselves, after much discussion, agreed on a statement of their responsibilities. They announced that their principal aim was, "to develop the individual's character, personality, sense of responsibility, and abilities for assuming roles of leadership; and to train young people to participate in a free farm organization of, by and for farmers themselves."

The new director had not been satisfied with the way things were going with the rural youth activities, but he didn't quite know just how the situation could be improved. Activities had centered on recreation and community-betterment. Folk dancing and square dancing were featured. The reasoning was that if a young man developed skill in calling square dancing or some other recreational activity, he would acquire confidence in himself, would come to feel at home before crowds, and would

427

learn to communicate effectively with his fellows—all of which might open the way to leadership in Farm Bureau as he grew older. Some years of experience were needed to convince Dalhaus that maybe the pattern could be improved. "You learn through your five senses," he said not long ago, "and you learn what your senses are exposed to. You learn by doing. We found out that if we expected young men and women to prepare themselves for Farm Bureau leadership, the best thing you could do for them would be to encourage their participation in Farm Bureau affairs—not in a play-acting sense, but in a real sense."

How to accomplish the above was something of a problem. One of the obvious ways to develop public speaking proficiency, of course, was to hold public-speaking contests. That was done, and the results were good. A number of young people did make substantial progress, and the competition was keen. In the fall of 1952, speaking on the subject of "Who Shall Speak for Farmers?" 51 young people from 37 counties competed in 10 district "talk meets." John Fisher of Mercer county, and Forrest Spangle of Jersey county took top honors; and Fisher went on to win second place in competition covering the entire Midwest, which permitted him to represent Illinois in the national contest staged by the American Farm Bureau Federation.

Early in 1953, the Illinois Rural Youth Committee went to Hagerstown, Maryland, for a week of intensive training in leadership skills. Later, several members went to Lincoln, Nebraska, to attend a conference of Farm Bureau leaders from the Midwest.

In addition to another Talk Meet, in 1954, a "Talent Find" was staged for the young people at the IAA convention. Purpose of this event was to uncover talent among the members in the fields of vocal and instrumental music, dancing, and novelty acts. Only 19 contestants appeared in district competition, of whom 10 were selected for the finals. This event proved quite popular.

The youth movement received a big boost at the 1954 IAA convention when delegates adopted a resolution, in part, as follows:

"The Illinois Agricultural Association recommends that County Farm Bureaus assist Rural Youth in developing and administering a statewide Rural Youth membership acquisition program.

"The Illinois Agricultural Association further recommends that representatives of Rural Youth and Farm Bureau attend and participate in each other's functions, not merely as a courtesy measure, but as the sole basis for a working relationship and mutual understanding."

Tremendously encouraged by this resolution, the young people went about their affairs with renewed enthusiasm. Over the years, they had demonstrated that they could do effective work in food promotion and accident prevention; now the organized study of citizenship, and economic and political issues was bringing them into marketing and policy development—in short, pretty well into the entire program of their county Farm Bureaus.

In recent years, the "discussion meet" has superseded the old public speaking contests. A discussion is spoken of as "the spoken exchange of ideas and information in an effort to understand or solve a problem." Winners are selected on the basis of their knowledge of the subject and the effectiveness of their presentation. County winners compete in six district meets at which three winners are named to compete in the state meet. Winner of the state meet competes with other state winners at the national meet held at the annual meeting of the American Farm Bureau Federation. These contests have provided the incentive needed to impel young people to make studies in depth of public issues, and to improve their technique in presenting their ideas. Dalhaus regarded this phase of the young people's activities as just about the best training a young person can get for leadership in Farm Bureau in later years.

After 1954, increased emphasis was put on training schools for young people. In Dalhaus' opinion, the young people's movement in Farm Bureau came of age in 1956, when 70 Illinois young men and women attended the training school sponsored by the

American Farm Bureau Federation, held at Carbondale. As he put it, these 70 young people, the leaders from many counties, indicated by their actions that they had definitely found a sense of direction that was impressive. As a group within the Farm Bureau group, they were full of enthusiasm, ready for hard work, and they seemed to know where they wanted to go.

The following year, the IAA Farm Bureau Young People (FBYP) became firmly established as a functioning unit of the organization. A study committee under the chairmanship of William J. Kuhfuss, who was then IAA vice president, was set up by the board of directors, of IAA, with instructions to make a report and recommendations with respect to the place that young people should fill in an organized way.

There were six IAA directors on the committee, along with two Farm Bureau women, and representatives of Extension and Vocational Agriculture. Young adults on the committee were: Duane Smith of Mt. Carmel, Wally Norris of Normal, Jeanne Breen of Tuscola, Frank Turnbull of Griggsville, Everett Smithson of Loogootee, Mr. and Mrs. Francis Bybee of Amboy, Mr. and Mrs. Russell Curtis of Carthage. After a few months of hard work, the study committee presented its report and recommendations, which the IAA board of directors accepted and adopted. The name, Farm Bureau Young People, was made official. County Farm Bureaus were asked to accept full responsibility for FBYP, which would include those between ages 18 and 30 (approximately). It was urged that county Farm Bureaus invite a FBYP representative to sit in at all board meetings in an advisory capacity. It was recommended that FBYP be permitted maximum freedom of action within the limits of Farm Bureau policy, and also that members be appointed to the regular Farm Bureau committees. It was suggested also that a state FBYP committee be set up, consisting of a member from each of the IAA director's districts. The IAA board invited FBYP to appoint a representative to sit in at all board meetings. In 1958, Eddie Bates of Kewanee became the first to serve in this capacity. In the same year, Duane Smith of Mt. Carmel, former chairman of the Illinois committee, was honored by being named chairman of the national committee sponsored by the American Farm Bureau Federation.

Now, in 1963, the FBYP has settled into a secure place in the Farm Bureau in Illinois. In 1960 the American Farm Bureau Federation awarded a trophy to Illinois for having the most outstanding Farm Bureau young people's program in the nation. In educational activities, the FBYP tends in recent years to give additional attention to the principles of successful business operation, including cooperatives, and to marketing. More members participated in marketing efforts in 1960 than in any other project.

In a number of counties, the FBYP helped to raise local funds for food promotion. The group seems to have finally hit on a formula for a balanced program that provides plenty of useful work that is rewarding to the individual as well as to promoting the well-being of the parent organization. Experience has proved that the county Farm Bureau that mobilizes its youth power truly enlarges the possibility for greater achievement.

One of the activities that has involved great numbers of people has been the "acquaintance" programs, conducted jointly by Farm Bureau and affiliates and the many chapters of the Future Farmers of America, which is made up of students of vocational agriculture in high schools. It is believed that giving these young boys a glimpse of Farm Bureau in action will certainly help to build better Farm Bureaus in the future.

After Dalhaus resigned, Kenneth Cheatham was named to succeed him in late 1962. Cheatham had had long experience in the Future Farmers of America. He was the first secretary of the local chapter in Bond county. In 1948, he was named Star Farmer of America, the first resident of Illinois to achieve that honor. From 1948 to 1954, Cheatham farmed for himself. After a serious back injury incapacitated him for heavy farm work, he went into sales work until 1956, when he was named secretary of organization in Douglas county. The next year he went to Vermilion county in a similar capacity and remained there until he joined the IAA staff.

After almost a year, Cheatham is having the satisfaction of

seeing the pioneering work of the past 10 years bearing real results. Firm in the belief that the major purpose of the young people's program is to develop qualities of leadership, he has worked with the county secretaries of organization, who are responsible administratively for the program in the counties, encouraging them to stress purposeful activities that will prepare youngsters for heavy responsibilities in their county Farm Bureaus.

Records for 1963 bear witness to the advances that have been made. There are now young people's committees in 81 counties, an increase of 15 in one year. Of the 598 members of these committees, 45 are directors of county Farm Bureaus. Of the 139 who attended the 1952 annual meeting of the IAA, 15 were voting delegates. Nearly 60 young people, in 29 counties, are on the membership committee of their county Farm Bureau. And 236 young people worked on Farm Bureau membership drives, signing up 203 new members. Young people have done effective work on meat promotion, marketing activities, citizenship programs, policy development, and policy execution. Young people registered their views on legislative issues with their state or national representatives in 2,500 instances. All the evidence indicates that the young people in Farm Bureau have made for themselves a permanent niche in the structure of Farm Bureau in Illinois. If the young people's movement in Farm Bureau seems to have reached a degree of maturity, one cause may rest in the fact that of the 598 young people on the county committees, no less than 451 are married. In no sense do they consider the young people's work a diversion, but a real opportunity to do something constructive to advance the cause of agriculture.

Chapter 38

To Market, To Market

The age-old complaint of farmers everywhere has been that they have little to say about the price at which they sell their products. Almost from the beginning, IAA encouraged commodity groups to form cooperative marketing organizations. I have recounted the results of Farm Bureau marketing projects in various chapters. The degree of success in marketing efforts has been extremely varied. Most tangible results have been recorded in livestock and dairy marketing, and probably the poorest have been in wool and egg marketing. The 40-year record of cooperative grain marketing efforts is extremely spotted. Rapidly-changing conditions in the dairy field resulted in the total reorganization of IAA affiliated processing and distributing cooperatives, which enjoyed outstanding success for a number of years. Some of the whole-milk cooperatives have stood the test of time, while others have fallen by the wayside.

Always under pressure to "do something" about marketing various products, IAA officials in 1952 decided to reactivate a division of marketing to develop new programs and methods in the field, to provide help and counsel to cooperatives in being or in the process of organizing, and to coordinate all marketing activities of the organization. To head it, they selected Walter B. Peterson, who had participated in the growth and development of Illinois Farm Supply during 18 years of service. In discharging the responsibilities assigned to it, this division has probably confronted some of the knottiest problems ever faced in the entire range of Farm Bureau activities. An example of the extremely grave problems faced is found in the annual report of the division for 1953, as follows:

"Since the end of World War II, dairy marketing has gone through a period of great turbulence. To determine the full effect of this, the cooperative marketing of dairy products was given thorough study. Karl Shoemaker of the University of Wisconsin was retained to make this study and he submitted his comprehensive report in January, 1953. His report covered over 200 typewritten pages. This report indicates that although over 50 per cent of the fluid milk products in Illinois comes under cooperative bargaining, yet the effectiveness of cooperative dairy marketing is not keeping abreast with the economic changes in the dairy industry. The report indicates further that many of our downstate bargaining associations are too small to cope with the changing markets and that there is need for joining bargaining associations with the operation of some Prairie Farms creameries. Failure to heed this could bring about increasing competitive pressures that will ultimately destroy some bargaining associations and cause some Prairie Farms creameries to close their doors. . . ."

This report proved prophetic to a painful degree, as has been indicated in chapters dealing with dairy marketing. The vast scale of cooperative business is indicated in the report of the division for 1954, as follows:

"Our problem today doesn't stem from a lack of numbers of cooperatives in Illinois. There are 264 cooperatives in grain that handle a combined volume of $317,500,000. Fifty cooperatives in Livestock handle a combined volume of $252,900,000. Seventy-two cooperatives in dairy handle a combined volume of $104,800,000.

"These cooperatives have functioned very well, squeezing margins at the local level, but in recent years the attractive profit margins have moved higher up on the marketing ladder to the so-called 'wholesale level.' Here we meet strong integrated competition. There is need, therefore, for the many local cooperatives to combine their volume, their strength and influence in forming stronger state-wide associations where their combined weight and influence can be focused on the larger marketing challenge. Certainly we cannot meet integrated competition on even terms with disintegration among cooperatives. . . ."

These statements indicate unmistakably that there is no place in this business for the amateur operator, and further that the cooperative manager must be able and in a position to move quickly to meet basic economic changes that occur in all business fields. All too often, cooperative business organizations have not rewarded management sufficiently to obtain and retain top-grade executives, and furthermore boards of directors have given them too little freedom of action to assure best results, and have been too slow to authorize drastic changes to meet new conditions.

In 1955, after several years of effort, the integration of the Illinois Grain Corporation and the Illinois Grain Terminals Company was accomplished, and new facilities leased in Chicago and built at Tampa, Florida, as reported in other chapters. In the livestock field, a movement which was to assume considerable significance in later years was inaugurated when the division arranged for an extensive meat promotion program in cooperation with the American Farm Bureau Federation, the National Grange, the National Council of Farmer Cooperatives, the National Association of Retail Grocers, and the National Association of Food Chains. Eugene V. Stadel, Peterson's assistant, had primary responsibility for this project, assisted by Arthur Seeds, who was to specialize in this field and later to continue the work on a nation-wide scale with the American Farm Bureau Federation.

Continuing efforts were being made to encourage each county Farm Bureau to set up a marketing committee, and then to work closely with the committee by supplying marketing information, providing exhibits for use at meetings, and by staging short courses in marketing wherever requested. In 1953-1954, for example, 66 short courses were held. The fact that sweeping changes were taking place at rates never before experienced made it necessary to keep persistently at the job of keeping local leadership informed of current developments.

It is worthy of note that in 1955 the Illinois Wool Marketing Association handled over a million pounds of wool in a state-wide pool. The IAA had concerned itself with wool marketing since 1920, and with more or less success, and it is interesting indeed to note that government efforts to control prices were probably the real cause of ending wool marketing activities. With the government practically fixing prices by use of incentive payments, it made little difference whether wool was sold through a producer pool or through independent marketing agencies. Since the passage of the Capper-Volstead Act in 1922 to foster cooperative marketing by farmers, the U.S. Department of Agriculture had spent millions to encourage cooperative marketing; but with the passage of the Agricultural Adjustment Act of 1933, government entered an era in which it was to spend *billions* annually to fix prices, thus lessening the need for cooperative enterprises. Without any question these developments had adverse effects on cooperative grain enterprises, but with varying impact on specific organizations. Thus, the really big grain enterprises with huge storage capacity could take advantage of the lush business of storing grain for the government, but others didn't share in this bonanza.

The story of the Illinois Cooperative Locker Service, first organized and incorporated in 1940 and reorganized in 1953 as the Illinois Locker Association, is an unhappy one. Although the first of the locker plants built (in Lee county) is still operating successfully, many others have gone by the wayside, with heavy losses to stockholders. It is not exaggerating to say that most of the locker companies were victims of undue enthusiasm during wartime meat shortages, and of promoters and sellers of locker-plant equipment at the beginning. Some were overbuilt, in the hope that the business would expand rapidly. During the war years, locker space was at a premium, and business boomed. It was misleading, to say the least, to assume that these conditions would continue; but in too many cases, plans were made on this assumption. Furthermore, soon after the war zero freezer compartments in household refrigerators became standard, and for many families this removed the need for a locker at the freezer plant. On top of all this, charges for locker space and services in most cases were not adequate to pay out. In 1953, for example, a survey and audit revealed that the average gross income per locker was $42.99, while operating expense per locker was $42.09. J. L. Pidcock, who came from Indiana in 1947 to manage the locker service, did everything possible to analyze the situation and give counsel to boards of directors of the local locker companies. He realized that many of them were in for trouble, and did his best to find the best way out for them. In 1948, Illinois Cooperative Locker Service had 40 local associations as members, which operated 104 locker plants and 25 slaughter plants, with a total investment of $4.5 million. In 1962, there were only 17 member companies, and only 11 of these were using the auditing service of the IAA. Of those audited, only three or four were doing well. It was obvious that the business had no future.

Activities of the marketing department took a decided turn in 1954, when county Farm Bureaus reactivated marketing committees. In 1955, a state-wide marketing committee, made up of one member from each of the 15 Farm Bureau districts (later increased to 18 districts), was created to coordinate the activities of all county committees. Promotion campaigns for meat and dairy products through 1955 and 1956 revealed the fact that farm people, particularly women, liked the promotion idea. More than 100 of them participated in a meat promotion project in Chicago, and 87 county committees staged some sort of activity in this field at home. In four counties, a special project for promoting meat sales through restaurants was carried out, with "Meat on the Menu" as a slogan. In 1956, the third annual dairy products promotion campaign was pushed with vigor, with 80 counties participating. Activities included taste-test demonstrations, distribution of promotion material, work with chain stores, and many special projects. Excellent cooperation was given by the American Dairy Association of Illinois, the Illinois Retail Grocers Association, the Illinois Dairy Products Association, and the Illinois Restaurant Association.

In the fall of 1956, a program of raising funds for promotion by farmers themselves was launched. Volunteers (farm men and women) solicited funds from their neighbors, and ended up with a kitty amounting to $61,291.53. An eye-catching exhibit, entitled "Food Is a Good Buy," was put together for the Chicagoland Trade Fair (1957) and also shown at the Illinois State Fair, the International Livestock Exposition, the International Dairy Show, and at many lesser shows. It was seen by more than a million people. This was the first of more than a dozen exhibits that have been shown since 1957, and all have been, in a sense, "smash hits" with the public. All of this has been made possible by contributions from farm people which have amounted to more than a quarter of a million dollars during the past five years. There have been "Better Breakfast" campaigns, "Food Comes First" campaigns, Lenten dairy promotions, all centering around the idea of better nutrition for better health and better living. Meat cutting and cooking schools have been conducted, poster contests for school children have aroused wide participation by public and parochial school students. These activities have been furthered enthusiastically by the entire commercial food industry.

On the business side, L. K. Wallace, who had an excellent background with dairy organizations in the eastern part of the United States, was employed as dairy marketing economist to conduct surveys and to counsel with dairy cooperatives on various problems created by changing conditions. Milk-marketing cooperatives often needed detailed economic information in considering the terms of proposed federal marketing orders, or in deciding whether or not an order is needed in their area. Since there were thirteen dairy marketing cooperatives affiliated with the IAA in 1959, there were problems galore to work on. Consolidation of the Prairie Farms member organizations entailed a great deal of study analysis and negotiation.

The department played a supporting role in launching the meat-type pig program of the Illinois Producers Livestock Association, which has proved so successful. By 1962, farmers (most of them in southern Illinois) were producing more than 100,000 pigs from some 11,000 approved sows, for placement by IPLA.

In 1959, the department was instrumental in getting through the legislature a bill appropriating $250,000 to be used in research in better marketing practices, new markets, new uses for farm commodities, etc. Many significant projects are now under way at the University of Illinois and Southern Illinois University because of these supplementary funds.

The department for several years has been promoting the idea of using meat for Christmas presents. The slogan, "Give Meat for Christmas—Always in Good Taste," seems to have caught on. When Eugene V. Stadel resigned to move to Iowa in 1960, Dwight Davis, who had twenty years of experience in the food business before he joined the IAA organization staff, took over food-promotion activities. A little later, Dwayne Martin became his assistant.

Marketing problems which have engaged the attention of the department in recent years seem to center on two major categories: 1. how to keep marketing practices up to date in line with swiftly changing conditions. 2. how to keep federal controls from dominating the food industry.

In the annual report of the department for 1962, category number 1 is referred to as follows: "Relatively small producer groups are finding it increasingly difficult to maintain their bargaining strength in the market place. Competition from large, efficient handlers, whose influence extends over wide areas, has become keen and intense. In order to meet the situation, some of the cooperatives have consolidated."

As to category number 2, witness the following from the same report: "Illinois Milk Producers' Association, after study and conferences with IAA staff members, has taken a firm position regarding the following important dairy marketing subjects.

"1. They recognize and support the basic fundamentals of milk marketing which are embodied in federal milk order programs. At the same time, they do not favor any regulatory programs which tend to insulate one market from another, restrict free movement of milk, or retard competition.

"2. Programs which set consumer prices or establish minimum markups for handlers are opposed because these regulations would establish margins wide enough to maintain existing inefficiencies and high costs in our processing and distribution systems. There is need for marketing efficiencies in order to be able to sell milk products to consumers at lower prices than currently exist. Demand for milk is elastic. Per capita consumption is declining. If we could regain the 1952 rate of per capita consumption, our market would be 140 to 145 billion pounds of milk annually, which is nearly 20 billion pounds more than the nation's total milk production in 1961."

In other words, it is easy to hurt the dairy industry by pricing dairy products out of the market. Producers are acutely aware that their incomes result from price times volume. The consumer is the final arbiter as to how much he is going to pay for any product. You can lead the consumer to the dairy products counter, but you can't make him buy.

Implicit also in the statement is recognition of the human tendency to relax behind a tariff or other kind of wall. Why make any attempt to produce and market more efficiently when government has fixed a price which will take care of inefficient producers? These are the facts of life that producers must face when government agencies undertake to control volume and price in the market place. It is obvious that only producers, through their own organizations, can bring effective pressure to bear on such problems. It is in this field, perhaps, that organized marketing groups can render their greatest service to farmers and also to the national welfare.

1962 was the year of final accomplishment—

a) Illinois Producers Livestock Association finally emerged as the consolidated organization after almost fifteen years of effort.

b) Prairie Farms Dairy, Inc., which was the result of consolidation of three large dairy operating organizations, proved to be more effective and profitable.

c) Illinois Grain Corporation hit a faster stride and greater profitability after a reshuffle in management and a revitalization of its merchandising program.

Over the years, IAA marketing people have carried responsibilities far beyond those involved in the mechanics of marketing. In the early years, they were pioneering in fields that had been discovered but poorly explored. They were the people who made the original studies, surveys, and analyses needed to enable the IAA board of directors to make a decision on whether or not they should enter a certain field of marketing. They were the ones who conducted the meetings of members to supply them with information about any new project, and then they helped to organize the campaigns to sell the stock in companies that were set up to operate in a given field. Furthermore, they had the responsibility of staffing the new cooperatives. Even after a new venture had been launched, it was the marketing men who counseled with the board of directors, as they wrestled with administrative problems and questions of policy. They were always available to boards, but it was essential that they appear only when invited. Board members themselves had to take the responsibility of making decisions. Marketing people regarded it their duty to help develop responsible leadership among farmers themselves, and the only way to do this was to give them responsibilities. They worked hand-in-hand with the board of directors of the Illinois Agricultural Service Company in this effort. Whenever a company got into trouble, marketing men were again heavily involved.

In the early days, particularly in livestock and grain marketing, the IAA called on its marketing men to do membership and field work for a new cooperative, but there were not enough of them to go around; and the result was that much of the field work was done by individuals who were too "evangelistic" in their approach. This led to difficulties, particularly in the case of U.S. Grain Growers, which were discussed in an earlier chapter. After a good deal of trial-and-error experiences, it became clear that any person doing field work for a marketing association should be employed by and held responsible to the management and board of directors of that association. That policy has been closely adhered to for many years.

Marketing affiliates have now fully matured, and most of them neither need nor ask for help in working out their management and personnel problems, long-range planning, research and marketing. However, counsel is always available, if needed. The marketing division today renders valuable service as a coordinating agency between the marketing associations and the county Farm Bureaus whenever a fundamental change is contemplated or a new program launched.

For the record, it should be stated here that farmers of Illinois, through the IAA, have spent more money (aid to Extension services excluded) in developing cooperative marketing services than has been spent in providing any other service to Farm Bureau members. During the decade of the twenties the emphasis on cooperative marketing was very great indeed, reflecting a conviction shared by many, many people (including Herbert Hoover) that herein lay the way of financial salvation of farmers. It was not until the decade of the thirties that the theory of salvation through price fixing by government became popular. I do not intend to imply that the two theories are mutually irreconcilable; but it seems apparent that if government fixes prices for farm products, then the role of the cooperatives has been greatly reduced to one in which it simply performs certain marketing services for which it collects fees. Certainly, the old conception of cooperation as a way of economic life has been drastically impaired, with its opportunities and its responsibilities proportionally reduced.

Be that as it may, the record plainly shows that Farm Bureau in Illinois has done more than any other organization or agency to develop cooperative marketing among farmers. As pointed out previously, there have been notable successes as well as discouraging failures. It is hard to define "success" in the area under discussion. For example, if we judge success on the basis of volume of grain handled, or even of livestock, it must be admitted that cooperatives have not drawn the allegiance of the majority of farmers. Independent old-line marketing agencies seem to do quite well. Maybe the proper role of cooperatives is primarily to provide more competition for such agencies. The evidence seems conclusive that cooperatives have provided such competition, and with wholesome effects.

Chapter 39

The Distaff Side

Farming in this country is pre-eminently a family enterprise with farmer, wife, and children as full partners as far as responsibility is concerned. All have their parts to play, and the success of the enterprise depends to some extent on teamwork among the members.

When counties first began organizing soil and crop improvement associations, there were no organized activities of a comparable nature for the women. But, as 4-H club work advanced, the work of the girls' clubs received increasing attention, creating a need for women leaders, and stimulated demand for a "Home Bureau" to promote home improvement much as the Farm Bureaus promoted soil and crop improvement. Under the terms of the Smith-Lever Act of 1914, home demonstration agents could be hired in counties, just as county agents could be hired, with federal financial help. When our country entered World War I in 1917, the Extension Service appropriation was sharply increased in order to promote increased production and conservation of food. Clearly, there was a big job to be done in encouraging women to preserve food by canning and drying, as well as in teaching women to use substitute foods when the usual foods were scarce. This led to the appointment of many more county home demonstration agents. Many additional Home Bureau units were organized to further the work.

In Illinois, home demonstration agents usually had their headquarters in the Farm Bureau office, along with the farm adviser. County Home Bureaus were organized, but there was only an informal tie-in with Farm Bureau. The Home Bureaus were simply organizations to carry Home Economics Extension work to homemakers, both rural and urban. For a long time, it had been assumed that the Home Bureaus were sufficient unto themselves, and for years practically nobody even suggested that Farm Bureau should concern itself with what went on on the distaff side. But there was an undercurrent of discontent among the wives of Farm Bureau members. Some complained that their husbands considered Farm Bureau as a sort of men's lodge from which they were unjustly excluded. They didn't particularly relish having their men away attending meetings while they sat at home. Even at the Illinois Agricultural Association annual meeting, the special one-day women's conference was planned by the Illinois Home Bureau Federation and was a combination of entertainment and matters of homemaking interest for women attending the convention. Illinois women did not feel included in the regular business of the convention.

Many women, actively concerned and helping in farming business, were also interested in the farm organization to which their husbands belonged. Certain spokesmen for them presented their interest to the IAA leadership without result for many years. Finally their pleas for recognition had to be met. When Charles B. Shuman became IAA president, he was sympathetic to the women, but it was not until 1952 that definite action was taken by the IAA board of directors by approving the creation of a department of family activities. The objective of the department was "to promote, to assist in planning, and to coordinate farm-home and family activities in conjunction with the general Farm Bureau program of the county and of this association." Miss Jean Kinzler, a home economist who had been doing demonstration work with the National Livestock and Meat Board, was appointed as director, and the work got under way early in 1953.

With her background in food-promotion, Miss Kinzler proved a valuable asset as IAA concern increased in this field. It was soon apparent that Farm Bureau women could do excellent work in the field of public relations, and were more than willing to take on this task. In one year, 943 Farm Bureau women participated in a state-wide dairy promotion program. It was not long until the women were working on various projects with the Illinois Chain Store Council, the Illinois Nutrition Committee, the National Safety Council, and others. Close cooperation was given at all times to the Illinois Home Bureau Federation.

By 1955, it was apparent that the women could make a valuable contribution to Farm Bureau in many fields, notably in school affairs, public relations, food promotion, and legislative matters. In December, 1954, at the annual meeting of the American Farm Bureau Federation, a pattern for direct participation of women in Farm Bureau affairs was set by the dissolution of the separate organization, the Associated Women of the American Farm Bureau Federation, and the creation of an American Farm Bureau Women's Committee as an integral part of the national organization. By action of the IAA board in January, 1955, the first IAA women's committee was set up, having one member from each of the then existent fifteen IAA districts. At its second meeting early in May, 1955, the committee organized itself, selecting Mrs. Loren E. Johnson as chairman and Mrs. William Sauer as vice chairman. Miss Kinzler resigned to get married, and Mrs. Florence Thomas, who had worked with the state department of vocational education, was employed to succeed her. (Mrs. Thomas worked most effectively until she resigned in 1962 to work with the American Farm Bureau Federation.)

The objective of the women's committee has been, and is now, to assist in every possible way in carrying out the entire Farm Bureau program. Beginning in 1956, the IAA women's committee, each year, formulated a program of work covering areas of organization-membership, policy development, policy activation, marketing, and public relations. This program, after approval by the IAA board, has been sent to the counties as a guide for women's participation in the work of Farm Bureaus. For women to render effective service to organization, it is necessary for those participating to be fully informed on all issues, and to be able to discuss them intelligently. The women responded enthusiastically to the opportunity to help. By the close of 1956 some 90 county Farm Bureaus had set up women's committees, and many women had been appointed to serve on several Farm Bureau committees in such matters as marketing, legislation, education, and local government.

From the beginning, special care was taken to avoid duplicating the work of other organizations, notably the Home Bureaus and Extension Councils. Many of the women who are most active now in Farm Bureau are women who have been leaders in the Home Bureau. Some apprehension that Farm Bureau women's work would interfere with, duplicate, or lessen the effectiveness of the Home Bureau-Home Economics Extension program was dispelled when it early became clear that Farm Bureau women's activities were distinct and separate from the activities of Home Bureau and Home Economics Extension. Farm Bureau activities were pertinent to the organization concerned with the business of farming, as distinguished from the organization concerned with homemaking. Furthermore, homemakers in Home Bureau are both urban and rural, as the Home Economics Extension was established to serve all homemakers.

The effectiveness of the new program of sharing the work with women has been demonstrated in a few cases in which husband-and-wife teams went out on membership drives. As early as 1957, when womens' work was just getting under way, women helped on Farm Bureau membership drives or at the kick-off meetings in 20 Illinois counties.

In 1960, in 33 counties women actually helped sign new members. Also, in 1960, in at least two counties (Jefferson and Effingham reporting) women competed against the men in signing new members. In each case, the women won.

In 1961, women helped sign members in at least 27 counties. They attended board meetings in 66 counties, served on county Farm Bureau committees in 41 counties. In terms of the IAA organization, county women have been included in IAA district meetings and the six organization district meetings.

The women are justly proud of the work they have done in getting out attendance at policy-development and policy-execution meetings, and in impressing legislators in Congress and the state legislature with prevailing farmer attitude on pending legislation. In 1961, for example, more than 6,500 letters were written by farm women in Illinois to their congressional representatives on two issues, farm program and federal aid to education. This has proved to be an area in which women can be particularly helpful. It's quite a chore for a farmer to take time out during busy seasons to write to his senator or congressman. Experience has demonstrated time after time that farm women, working on an organized project of this kind, will somehow find the time to do it. They have been a tower of strength for the Farm Bureau in recent years in this field, and their work has been recognized and applauded by IAA officers and board of directors. They have become a truly potent force in Farm Bureau affairs.

In addition to helping in regular Farm Bureau activities, women have carried full responsibility for a few special projects, such as nurse recruitment and rural safety. In 1957, at least eight county women's groups, in cooperation with local high schools, arranged to take groups of girls on hospital tours, hoping to interest some of them in nursing careers. This activity was quite timely, since at that time many nursing scholarships were available but unused.

In 1958, a state-wide campaign was launched to reduce driving hazards in rural areas, where some 20 per cent of accidents occur as a result of vision-obstructed corners. In every county in which Farm Bureau approved of the campaign, women made a survey, marked the dangerous spot, then sought permission of the landowners to cut the brush and weeds or top the cornstalks that were obstructing vision. In the vast majority of cases, such projects proved highly successful. In many places, improperly placed highway signs were moved, or other steps taken to make the corner safer. Campaigns were completed in more than half of the counties. The campaign was continued with even more vigor in 1959. Some 1,800 women surveyed 2,909 corners, found 899 unsafe, and carried out improvements in 777 of them. Radio and TV stations and newspapers throughout the state cooperated by calling public attention to the campaign. The Illinois Farm Supply Company (now FS Services, Inc.) cooperated by having safety posters made for the women to distribute to places of business and public places. The IAA insurance companies helped the campaign in many ways. Public response to this effort was most gratifying, so much so that some of the women who took the lead reported that this project was the most rewarding project they had ever undertaken. They felt that they had made a lasting contribution to public safety.

The smashing success of the 1958 "clear corners" campaign led the women to extend it to other counties in 1959, and also to sponsor a movement to induce farmers to carry auxiliary lamps on all tractors, not just those lacking headlamps, which could be plugged in and used when moving the machine on highways at night. (Headlamps and rear lamps sometimes fail.) Farm machinery dealers were invited to cooperate and many of them helped out. A new state law requiring all slow-moving vehicles to carry a flag or flashing light helped to add momentum to this campaign. The 1959 campaign was so successful that it won second place in Carol Lane awards for safety given by the National Safety Council.

The family activities department in 1958 made notable contributions to the food-comes-first and better-breakfast drives, as well as to the better citizenship activities. The work accomplished was so impressive that the voting delegates at convention time strongly recommended that women be appointed to standing committees of county Farm Bureaus, and invited to participate in board meetings. (This had already been done in some counties, 26 in 1957, and by 1959 the IAA had already arranged for the chairmen of the women's committee to sit in at all board meetings as an advisory member.)

In 1957, Farm Bureau women were largely responsible for the IAA winning an American Farm Bureau Federation award for outstanding work in dairy promotion. More than 4,500 men and women had participated by visiting stores, dairy bars, and other distribution centers, passing out samples for "taste tests" on sour cream, cottage cheese, and other dairy products. The work was done in 86 counties, with spectacular results in some. Some stores reported increased sales of up to 40 per cent on some products during the campaign.

Comparable results were recorded in many meat-promotion campaigns. Some two thousand Farm Bureau women in forty counties spent two days in two hundred stores in October, 1962, passing out promotion material and samples of smoked pork butts. In some stores, results were spectacular. Store managers were enthusiastic. In most cases, managers had stocked up on pork butts, and in some cases the entire stock was sold before noon on the first day. It is a well-known fact that the cheaper cuts of meat often go begging, largely because ways of preparing them so as to make them highly palatable are not well known. Pork butts were selected for emphasis in this campaign because of the declining popularity of pork in most households. (It should be remembered that the Illinois Producers Livestock Association is working on another angle of the pork problem by encouraging the production of meat-type hogs. Carcasses of meat-type hogs carry a lower per cent of fat than lard-type hogs, hence all cuts from these carcasses are more palatable.) If a demand can be built up for the lesser known cuts of pork, better returns for the entire carcass can be realized.

In many cases, store managers cooperated by posting special prices for other cuts of meat, such as smoked hams, slab bacon, and beef liver. The event was so popular with store owners and managers, that in some counties there were not enough farm women to go around. Some had to postpone the event for this reason.

Another project which aroused considerable interest was called "freedom bookshelf." The women undertook to see to it that books dealing with the principles underlying our form of government were placed in public libraries, school libraries, and Farm Bureau offices. More than 2,000 records of "The Star Spangled Banner" were distributed to schools. Informal meetings, called "kitchen konferences" were held in hundreds of farm homes to get neighbors together for discussion of public issues.

Mrs. Loren Johnston of Knox county retired as chairman at the end of 1961, to be succeeded by Mrs. R. W. Chambers of Ford county. Mrs. W. F. Neuman of Rock Island county was chosen vice chairman. Mrs. Florence Thomas resigned as director early in 1962, and Miss Coena Blair, a former 4-H club member in Champaign county, and a 1960 graduate of the University of Illinois, was appointed to take her place. After ten years of existence, the department of family activities seemed to have become firmly established as an increasingly important factor in Farm Bureau work throughout the state. Farm Bureau men, observing the activities of the women, quickly recognized the plain fact that they took naturally and enthusiastically to such projects as food promotion, school affairs, community problems, public relations, policy development, and legislation. It is generally agreed that the future holds a bigger place, and a most important one, for women in Farm Bureau.

Chapter 40

Reflections

In the preceding pages we have described the remarkable, and, perhaps startling developments, that have transpired in the half-century since the inception of the idea of having a farm adviser in each county to help farmers with their problems. It will be recalled that the services of a "soil expert," as the farm adviser was usually called in those days, were available only if farmers formed an organization and raised some money to support the project. Four of the first ten county organizations carried the name, "soil and crop improvement association"; two, "soil improvement association"; two, "agricultural improvement association"; and two, "Farm Bureau." It was quite obvious that the improvement of agriculture was the sole aim of the new associations.

The "improvement of agriculture" covered a multitude of activities. In fact, some farm advisers had been on the job only a few months before they started advising farmers in their purchases of such items as fertilizer, limestone, and seeds. Farm advisers helped farmers to organize cooperative ventures of many kinds. They were, in fact, considered "hired men" who were glad to help farmers with almost any problem that presented itself. We must remember that the farm advisers were operating under a state law which designated the county Farm Bureau as the official agency through which agricultural extension work was conducted. The farm advisers generally felt that the effectiveness of their work was doubled or tripled by having a strong and unified organization backing them up. Under this system, they made giant strides in improving agricultural practices, which after all, was the grand objective of the entire movement. They were "farm leaders" in the truest sense, and many of them worked for farm legislation such as the McNary-Haugen legislation of the early days.

Today, the situation is quite different. The time came when the Extension Service was to be "divorced" from Farm Bureau. By this time, Farm Bureau was sponsoring in every county a large number of business services, and it was necessary to have someone in the office to direct the activities. With IAA cooperation, county Farm Bureaus began years ago to train for and appoint full-time men to such jobs. The job was entitled "Secretary of Organization" but in addition to responsibility for membership, he had the responsibility of managing the county Farm Bureau for the board of directors.

Anyone unfamiliar with the old system can't possibly appreciate the extent of the change that came about when Farm Bureau was separated from Extension. It is quite true that in many counties Farm Bureau leaders are appointed to membership on the county Agricultural Extension Council which now develops the Extension program, but the old happy and informal, and incidentally, quite efficient arrangements are gone. The farm adviser's hands are tied, as far as Farm Bureau promotion, legislative, or business matters are concerned; and the secretary of organization has no voice in the county Extension program. Therefore, the paths of Farm Bureau and Extension are separate and distinct. Extension is busy with educational and demonstrational activities, and county Farm Bureaus concentrate pretty largely on legislative and commercial problems. There is evidence that the trend of

454

the times is toward centralizing more and more authority in Washington, and a corresponding lessening of state and local responsibility. There are many who dislike this trend, but you see it in labor relations, in matters of health and welfare, in public education, in farm price fixing, and in practically all matters in which federal relationships with state and local governments are involved.

Perhaps the most sinister aspect of government control of agriculture is the plain fact that it gives the Secretary of Agriculture direct control of an army of employees, which can, have been, and are being used for partisan political purposes—in spite of all protestations to the contrary. Traditionally, the Extension Service, which is the educational and demonstrational arm of the U.S. Department of Agriculture, was considered to be, and in fact has been singularly free of the taint of partisan politics. But with the advent of the New Deal, "action agencies" such as the Agricultural Adjustment Administration, the Soil Conservation Service, the Farm Security Administration, and many others—all of which were created to meet problems incident to the great depression and most of which were regarded as temporary expedients to overcome an economic emergency—the old idea that agricultural agencies were above politics simply went out the window. With an effective field force at his command, deployed into the remotest sections of the entire country, the administrator of every agency was subject to almost irresistible temptation. Most of them succumbed to temptation and began to entrench themselves and their agencies. The fact that there was a worthy purpose back of each agency made it all the easier for those at the top. Who can be against rural electrification or soil conservation? And if farmers and rural industries get electric power at subsidized rates, are they going to complain—even if the whole REA apparatus is utilized in a nation-wide campaign for expansion of government's role in production of electricity?

The tendency of a federal bureaucracy is always to expand. The lust for power is insatiable. The long arm of the superstate reached out in the late thirties for control of the farm credit agencies. This effort was repulsed by a grassroots counter-offensive, but it came near succeeding. It should serve as a warning to those who seem to believe that life in McLean county, Illinois, for example, can be made rich and rewarding only if the Great White Father in Washington reaches out here in his benevolence to fix our prices, pave our roads, educate our children, keep us in health, provide us with comforts and luxuries at subsidized rates, pay us for better farm practices—in short, to make life easier for us.

As to the Farm Bureau itself in Illinois, it would be fair to say that it has succeeded beyond the dreams of the founders. There is little question as to what has been the greatest disappointment over the years. It is the failure to bring about effective stabilization of farm prices through legislation. The various laws that have been enacted to stabilize farm prices have cost the nation billions of dollars in taxes. They have saddled the Federal Government with the ownership of a vast accumulation of farm surpluses that have been paid for but not used, they have resulted in a vast horde of federal employees needed for administration; but the basic problem looms as big as it did in 1933. There have been years since World War II in which the Federal Governnment has spent in the name of agriculture, to keep farmers in business and to stabilize their prices, the equivalent of more than half of the national net farm income. It is true that a lot of the spending has been for school lunches, for regulatory services that are for the welfare of all the people, and should not be charged to agriculture; but the fact remains that the bulk of the money has been spent in fruitless attempts to control production and surpluses. When one considers the fact that the U.S. Department of Agriculture is second in size only to the Pentagon, and the further fact that the agricultural appropriation is equal to that of the Health, Education and Welfare Department, is equal to that for taking care of the veterans of all U.S. wars, and the further fact that these expenditures are made on behalf of a group that now numbers only ten per cent of the population—when you consider these things, you are bound to wonder if things have not gotten out of line. Many have concluded that the government has made a mess of trying to run agriculture, and it's time to turn the job back to the farmers.

Delegates to the IAA conventions can be quite plainspoken when occasion demands. For example, here are excerpts from the resolutions adopted at the 1951 convention:

"The long-range national farm program incorporated in the legislation now in force was largely developed by the American Farm Bureau Federation after years of experience and study. This legislation does include many sound, basic principles. The price support and production adjustment provisions of the law are for use, when necessary, to prevent the collapse of agricultural prices. It was not intended that these devices should be used year after year regardless of farm price levels. In fact, their effectiveness in time of stress will be seriously impaired by the present policy of continued government regulation and manipulation during periods when farm prices approach or exceed parity. We do not believe that there is need for drastic change in the farm program legislation. However, we insist that all subsidies, and acreage adjustments be suspended, as originally intended, and be reactivated only when necessary.

"Soil conservation and soil fertility maintenance costs are legitimate production expenses. Agricultural prices now average approximately 100 per cent of parity. We, therefore, insist that the Agricultural Conservation payments subsidy program be discontinued."

That is language that anybody can understand. Observe that the delegates approved the idea of government aid when farmers faced an emergency, but criticized its continuance after all actual need had passed.

If organized farmers are unhappy over the dismal results of their efforts to secure effective national farm legislation, those in Illinois can be quite happy over the results they have attained in the cooperative business enterprises they have founded. As I have reported in previous chapters, a number of cooperative marketing ventures have fallen by the wayside. But in the fields of insurance and the distribution of farm supplies, Farm Bureau members can

457

and do take enormous pride in the fact that most of their ventures have been smashing successes. Just why cooperative buying has been universally supported and more consistently successful than cooperative selling is somewhat of a puzzle.

Viewed as a whole, IAA cooperative efforts in the commercial field have proved most rewarding. It is not unusual for the county farm supply companies which distribute petroleum supplies, feeds, fertilizer, fencing, and steel products to earn as much as 20 per cent on their investment, after taxes, as an average for the state. Can any member be unhappy over such success? Yet there are those who complain that in Illinois the Farm Bureau has gone "too commercial." Some say "I'll bet the IAA wouldn't have half the membership it has if it weren't for the commercial services." The answer seems to be that the IAA set up business services in response to all but unanimous demand on the part of members; and generally these services have been so satisfactory that members wouldn't think of abandoning them. If an organization pleases its members with the service it renders, why should anyone complain about that? One thing is certain, and that is that Farm Bureau members have derived vastly more satisfaction from the money they have invested in businesses that they own and control, than they have derived from the money they have invested in trying to secure national legislation to raise farm prices.

No reasonable man can doubt that the officers and directors of the IAA have guided the institution along the lines that the vast majority of members wanted it to go. Since the IAA president is elected for only one year at a time, and directors for two years, with one-half elected each year, it is an easy matter for delegates to change leadership very quickly if they desire to do so. And farmers are not at all backward about expressing their disapproval in case their leaders do not perform as they should. The organization is organically and functionally sound today, primarily because it has moved into new fields only after long deliberation and only when assured of the solid support of the membership. That is one of the secrets of its impressive achievements.

In 1958, when President Otto Steffey died suddenly, Vice

President William J. Kuhfuss was named his successor. The new president was (and is) a highly successful breeder of Angus cattle, in partnership with his brother Alvin, on an 880-acre farm, as previously indicated. He had to make drastic adjustments at home in order to devote full time to Farm Bureau.

The problem of leadership in a farm organization of the size of the IAA and its business affiliates is a big one. The man who leads the IAA and its affiliates carries enormous responsibilities. It is essential that he be a man of mature judgment, yet he must be young enough to be receptive to new ideas, and physically strong enough to withstand the rigors of the job, which are considerable. He must have a good understanding of business principles and practices. He must be a successful farmer, and he must retain his farm business if he is to remain in office. He must have his personal affairs in such order that he can be away from home most of the time. It is highly important that he be a good administrator. Farmers who can meet such requirements and make such adjustments are few and far between, but whenever a new leader is needed, a fully-qualified man seems to appear. It should be pointed out that few qualified men would take the job for the money it pays or for the security it offers. The job carries neither pension rights nor job security. Considering all these factors, you can see at once that the number of capable men who could consider accepting the job is very small indeed.

Some people deplore the fact that gifted and capable men are unable to accept a call to leadership because they simply cannot afford to leave the management of their farms to someone else. But here is another side to this question, and it may well be that it works out to the ultimate benefit of the organization. The fact that the position carries with it no financial inducement means that anyone who accepts it must do so for other reasons than desire for personal gain. It follows that only those truly dedicated to Farm Bureau will make the necessary sacrifices that go with leadership. And dedicated leadership is one of the basic essentials to the welfare of the organization.

Almost any observer will agree that the IAA has indeed been

fortunate in the leadership that has risen to the top, and that the absence of substantial material reward as one of the attractions of the office of president has been a wholesome thing.

The Illinois Agricultural Association is today, as it has been practically from the date of its reorganization in 1919, the largest and best-financed state Farm Bureau in the country. With just over 195,000 members, its influence extends to every county and every township in the state. Through it, the farmers of Illinois own business enterprises with a total net worth of $85 million. Since the overwhelming majority of the real farmers in Illinois are members, and since its policies have so invariably been conservative, yet constructive, it commands a wholesome respect on the part of citizens in other walks of life. Its voice carries considerable weight in the state legislature. Appropriately enough, the center of its far-flung operations is not too far from the center of the state, just outside the city of Bloomington, in McLean county, which is often referred to as the leading agricultural county in Illinois. Its home is structurally beautiful, of enduring materials, and of imposing dignity which reflects the importance of agriculture in the economy of Illinois. The organization has indeed reached maturity. It is solidly entrenched as a major force in the agricultural world, and it gives every indication that it will hold its high position for generations to come.

THE PIONEERS

Original Name	First President	First Farm Adviser	Adviser Began Work
De Kalb County Soil Improvement Association	D. S. Brown	William G. Eckhardt	6– 1–12
Kankakee County Soil & Crop Improvement Association	C. E. Robinson	John S. Collier	6– 1–12
McHenry County Soil Improvement Association	H. E. Whipple	Delos L. James	2– 1–13
Livingston County Soil & Crop Improvement Association	W. H. Bentley	Roy C. Bishop	2–10–13
Will County Soil & Crop Improvement Association	E. L. Wilson	Frank C. Grannis	4– 1–13
Du Page County Agricultural Improvement Association	Herman Bandemer	Edward B. Heaton	5– 1–13
Kane County Farm Improvement Association	J. P. Mason	Jerome E. Readhimer	6– 1–13
Tazewell County Farm Bureau	H. W. Danforth	E. T. Robbins	6– 1–13
Peoria County Farm Bureau	Charles Gordon	Henry Truitt	6–16–13
Champaign County Agricultural Improvement Association	C. L. Van Doren	Charles H. Oathout	9– 1–13
Winnebago County Farm Improvement Association	E. F. Derwent	Albert M. TenEyck	1– 1–14
Iroquois County Crop & Soil Improvement Association	Merton Parker	Lewis W. Wise	4– 1–14
Bureau County Agricultural Improvement Association	W. E. Sapp	Charles J. Mann	6– 1–14
La Salle County Better Farming Association	T. W. Esmond	Ira S. Brooks	9– 1–14
Farmers' Soil & Crop Improvement Association of Grundy County	Fred Harford	Frank H. Demaree	11– 1–14
Adams County Farm Improvement Association	H. F. Chittenden	Earl W. Rusk	4– 1–15
Hancock County Soil Improvement Association	Robert Baird	A. M. Wilson	4– 1–15
McLean County Better Farming Association	Lyle Johnstone	D. O. Thompson	4– 1–15
Mason County Farm Bureau	Charles Borgelt	Frank D. Baldwin	7– 1–15
Woodford County Farm Bureau	Howard Leonard	M. L. Mosher	1– 1–16
Lee County Soil Improvement Association	S. L. Shaw	Leland S. Griffith	3– 6–16
Mercer County Crop Improvement Association	G. H. Campbell	I. F. Gillmor	4– 1–16
Rock Island County Agricultural League	S. L. Woodburn	Palmer R. Edgerton	12– 1–16
Fulton County Agricultural Association	C. L. Whitnah	Aaron W. Miner	3– 1–17
Lake County Farm Improvement Association	R. F. Rouse	Warren E. Watkins	3– 1–17
Randolph County Soil & Farm Improvement Association	F. H. McKelvey	John J. Doerschuk	7– 1–17
Ogle County Farm Bureau	James Carmicheal	George T. Snyder	10– 1–17
Henry County Farm Bureau	J. W. Morgan	John T. Montgomery	11– 1–17
Saline County Farm Bureau	C. H. Baker	Earl A. Price	1– 1–18
Effingham County Farm Bureau	F. G. Burrow	Herbert J. Rucker	2– 1–18

Original Name	First President	First Farm Adviser	Adviser Began Work
Logan County Farm Bureau	W. E. Birks	Elmer T. Ebersol	2- 1-18
Macoupin County Farm Bureau	H. W. Rice	William P. Miller	2- 1-18
Moultrie County Farm Bureau	W. A. Steele	Allen L. Higgins	2- 2-18
Clinton County Farm Bureau	Gerhard Holtgrave	Charles H. Rehling	3- 1-18
Macon County Farm Bureau	A. A. Hill	Sidney B. Smith	3- 1-18
Morgan County Farmers' Club	C. S. Black	George B. Kendall	3- 1-18
Vermilion County Farm Bureau	C. R. Finley	Arthur Lumbrick	3- 1-18
Sangamon County Farmers' Association	P. J. Telfer	Irwin A. Madden	3-11-18
Coles County Agricultural Development Association	Roscoe Farrar	Melvin Thomas	3-16-18
Stephenson County Farm Improvement Association	L. M. Swanzig	George F. Baumeister	3-16-18
Christian County Farm Bureau	W. McCluskey	Clair E. Hay	4- 1-18
Edgar County Agricultural Improvement Association	O. J. Linebarger	Walter B. Gernet	4- 1-18
Henderson County Farm Bureau	R. N. Clarke	James H. Miner	4- 1-18
Madison County Farm Bureau	Frank Troeckler	Julian B. Haberkorn	4- 1-18
Monroe County Farm Bureau	J. C. Gummersheimer	James A. Tate	4- 1-18
Montgomery County Farm Bureau	H. A. Cress	Alden E. Snyder	4- 1-18
Union County Farm Improvement Association	C. W. Ware	Charles E. Durst	4- 1-18
Jersey County Farm Bureau	J. R. Fulkerson	Clifford E. Wheelock	4- 4-18
De Witt County Farm Bureau	S. H. Wisegarver	Floyd L. Johnson	4-15-18
Richland County Farm Bureau	John S. Howe	Harry B. Piper	4-15-18
Crawford County Farm Bureau	Carleton Trimble	Clarence C. Logan	4-20-18
Greene County Farm Bureau	Louis Lowenstein	Eugene M. Phillips	4-26-18
Whiteside County Farm Bureau	C. L. Passmore	Stephen J. Craig	5- 1-18
Shelby County Farm Bureau	J. K. Hoagland	Charles H. Belting	6- 1-18
Williamson County Farm Bureau	George Harrison	William E. Hart	6- 1-18
Warren County Farm Bureau	E. V. Bruington	Ralph R. Wells	7- 1-18
Jackson County Farm Bureau (1)	William Ziegler	Clair J. Thomas	8-16-18
Clark County Farm Bureau	J. A. Kettring	Edward H. Walworth	9- 1-18
Knox County Farm Bureau	C. M. Hunter	Emil M. D. Bracker	9- 1-18
Marion County Farm Bureau	Joseph Schwartz	F. J. Blackburn	9-26-18
Cass County Farm Bureau	W. A. McNeill	Robert W. Dickenson	2- 1-19
Johnson County Farm Bureau	J. C. B. Heaton	Ora M. McGhee	3- 1-19
Menard County Farm Bureau	E. G. King	Garfield J. Wilder	3- 6-19
McDonough County Farm Bureau	H. P. Hunter	R. C. Doneghue	3-15-19
Piatt County Farm Bureau	M. E. Wise	Arthur E. Burwash	4- 1-19
St. Clair County Farm Bureau	Alvin O. Eckert	B. W. Tillman	6- 1-19
Ford County Farm Bureau	C. W. Knapp	Francis C. Hersman	7-26-19
Edwards County Farm Bureau	Walter Tribe	Harry R. Pollock	8- 1-19
Franklin County Farm Bureau (2)	J. R. Midyette	Henry A. deWerff	9- 1-19
Pike County Farm Bureau	Jesse Thompson	Otis Kercher	11- 1-19
Stark County Farm Bureau	W. W. Wright	Evlan E. Brown	1- 1-20
Carroll County Farm Bureau	George C. Lamp	George R. Bliss	2- 1-20
Marshall-Putnam Farm Bureau	W. G. Griffith	Frank E. Fuller	2-20-20
Brown County Farm Bureau	Robert Shields	Aubrey E. Davidson	4- 1-20
Bond County Farm Bureau	Fred Baumberger	Charles Tarble	4-17-20
Jo Daviess County Farm Bureau	John E. Bonnet	Clifford C. Burns	5- 1-20
Lawrence County Farm Bureau	W. F. Crews	Henry C. Wheeler	5- 1-20
Douglas County Farm Bureau	John McCarty	Frank W. Garrett	6- 1-20
Kendall County Farm Fureau	I. V. Cryder	Earl A. Price	6- 1-20

462

Original Name	First President	First Farm Adviser	Adviser Began Work
Schuyler County Farm Bureau	W. H. Young	George E. Gentle	6- 1-20
Boone County Farm Bureau	Robert Cummings	James C. Kline	6-15-20
Wabash County Farm Bureau	Robert Schrodt	Forrest A. Fisher	6-16-20
Cook County Farm Bureau	H. A. Dooley	Charles E. Durst	7- 1-20
Pulaski County Farm Bureau (3)	R. B. Endicott	William R. Eastman	9-10-20
Scott County Farm Bureau	C. J. North	Guy H. Husted	11-22-20
Calhoun County Farm Bureau	Albert Franke	John H. Allison	2- 8-21
Jefferson County Farm Bureau	W. T. Wooden	Bertram Abney	3-15-21
Massac County Farm Bureau	George Arensman	Ora M. McGhee	5- 1-21
Clay County Farm Bureau	Clint Logan	William E. Hart	6- 1-21
White County Farm Bureau	Will Land	Edward W. Creighton	6-19-21
Cumberland County Farm Bureau	G. C. Holsapple	Charles B. Price	7- 1-21
Gallatin County Farm Bureau	G. E. Scherrer	Cecil W. Simpson	9- 1-21
Pope County Farm Bureau (4)	A. H. Floyd	Levett Kimmel	9- 1-21
Wayne County Farm Bureau	C. L. Wood	Charles T. Hufford	10- 1-21
Washington County Farm Bureau	J. R. Hood	George E. Smith	9- 1-26
Fayette County Farm Bureau	Roy H. Thoman	Jonathan B. Turner	3- 1-35
Jasper County Farm Bureau	Clay Trimble	Russell E. Apple	10- 1-36

(1) Perry county joined to Jackson county 6-5-37.
(2) Hamilton county joined to Franklin county 2-1-37.
(3) Alexander county joined to Pulaski county 2-3-30.
(4) Hardin county joined to Pope county 11-18-31.

The 1963 board of directors. Front row, left to right: William J. Kubfuss, H. E. Hartley, Eric E. Anderson, R. E. Lamoreux, William C. Steinert, John K. Freebairn. Second row: Clair J. Hempbill, Guy K. Gee, Lowell Risser, Roger Carr, Vernal C. Brown, Boyce Moore, Carl Heerdt, Merle Jeffers. Back row: Leath Postlewaite, Kenneth W. Klarman, Wilbert Engelke, Carl E. Guebert, Clarence McCauley, William Sauer, Mrs. R. W. Chambers, Sr., Mike Englum.